P9-ECU-179

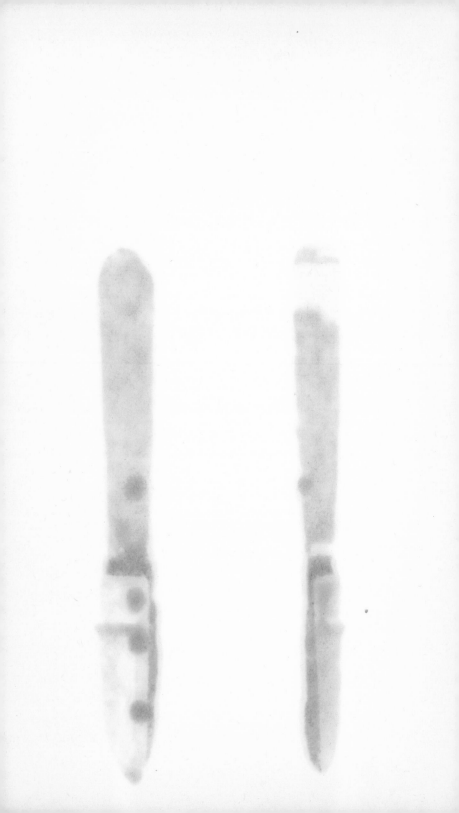

THE RECOVERY OF GERMANY

THE RECOVERY OF GERMANY

BY

JAMES W. ANGELL

PROFESSOR OF ECONOMICS IN
COLUMBIA UNIVERSITY

ENLARGED AND REVISED EDITION

GREENWOOD PRESS, PUBLISHERS
WESTPORT, CONNECTICUT

The Library of Congress has catalogued this publication as follows:

Library of Congress Cataloging in Publication Data

Angell, James Waterhouse, 1898-
    The recovery of Germany.

    Original ed. issued in series: Publications of the
Council on Foreign Relations.
    Includes bibliographical references.
    1. Reconstruction (1914-1939)--Germany. 2. Germany--
Economic conditions--1918-1945. I. Title.
D659.G3A7 1972   330.943'08   75-138197
ISBN 0-8371-5550-9

Originally published in 1929
by Yale University Press

Reprinted in 1972 in an unaltered and unabridged edition
with permission

First Greenwood Reprinting 1972

Library of Congress Catalogue Card Number 75-138197

ISBN 0-8371-5550-9

Printed in the United States of America

COUNCIL ON FOREIGN RELATIONS

The purpose of the Council on Foreign Relations is to study the international aspects of America's political, economic, and financial problems.

In addition to holding general and group meetings, the Council publishes *Foreign Affairs*, a quarterly review; the annual *Survey of American Foreign Relations*; the *Political Handbook of the World*, issued annually; and individual volumes on special international questions.

INTRODUCTION

THIS study of the economic recovery of Germany since the war was made under the joint auspices of the Council on Foreign Relations and the Columbia University Council for Research in the Social Sciences. It had its origin in the study-groups of the Council on Foreign Relations itself. For several years one of these groups has been following with deep interest the vicissitudes of Germany's economic situation, and eventually came to the conclusion that fuller information was required on the character and degree of the country's recent economic progress, especially the industrial and commercial rehabilitation which has taken place since 1924. The group therefore proposed to send to Germany one of its own members, Professor Angell of Columbia University, to make further investigation and to report his first-hand observations. The Council on Foreign Relations has undertaken the publication of the resulting work as part of its plan to issue individual volumes on special international questions. This volume follows H. Foster Bain's study of *Ores and Industry in the Far East*.

It is unnecessary to emphasize the importance of obtaining as impartial and accurate a picture as possible of Germany's economic situation and prospects. The American investing public has absorbed a long series of loans to German governments and industries. It has thereby recognized, under the leadership of its industrial and financial interests, the need of restoring Germany's economic position, and has shown its confidence in German recovery. It is also well known that for some time to come Germany must continue to borrow abroad, and a large part of these new securities will undoubtedly be offered in the American market. On both counts, the economic welfare of Germany is of great and direct concern.

There is a further material reason for American interest in Germany's recovery. As Professor Angell points out, "the United States, as the only large net creditor in the Inter-Ally debt account, is also much the largest ultimate recipient of the money which will originally be paid under the head of Reparations." Germany's capacity to pay these Reparations obligations is closely related to her ability to meet the service charges on her mounting indebtedness to private investors abroad; and the bulk of the Reparations transfers will join the large flow of her interest and profits payments to the United States. Both directly and indirectly, Germany as debtor thus faces the United States as creditor. The political aspects of this relationship are not here under consideration, but it is a part of Professor Angell's task to examine the economic problems at issue, problems which must eventually be solved in terms of national productivity and international trade.

The importance of the theme of this book is not limited, however, to its bearing on the American creditor position. Before the war Germany had risen to a high place among the world's greatest industrial and commercial nations. Shorn of possessions by the Treaty of Peace, and shattered by an unexampled monetary disaster, where does the country now stand among the great competitors? Germany today, as Professor Angell points out, still has the largest coal reserves of all the countries of the European continent, as well as considerable supplies of other industrial raw materials;

she retains a high position, and in many branches an undisputed leadership, in science and the industrial applications of science; her laboring population has a will to work and an adaptability to industrial pursuits which are unsurpassed in Europe; her business men are carrying out a deliberately planned and increasingly effective reorganization of industry and commerce in a program of "rationalization"; and the German nation has shown its inherent moral strength in regaining, after a devastating experience, a large degree of political and social stability. The accomplishment has already been great. What of the future? What reckoning is to be made of German activity and power in the intensified international competition the world is now facing?

There is evidently room here both for fact and for forecasting. Professor Angell presents a carefully analyzed array of facts; he is cautious in his forecasting; he points out weaknesses and dangers. But he believes that, in the net, all indications lead to a hopeful conclusion. Germany will slowly but steadily grow in economic strength and prosperity, and will consolidate her position among the leading industrial and commercial nations of the world.

CHARLES P. HOWLAND

AUTHOR'S PREFACE

THIS book is the outcome of study and travel in Germany during the year 1928–29. It is based on three principal types of information: conversations with many people in public and private life, personal observations made in the course of visits to over fifty factories and mines during November and December, 1928, and official and other compilations of material, chiefly statistical, bearing on industrial and financial conditions since the war. The enterprise originated in the discussions conducted in one of the study groups of the Council on Foreign Relations, and my first great obligation is to acknowledge with deep gratitude the encouragement and support the members of this group have given. I also desire to express the sincerest appreciation for the unfailing courtesy and generous help which was extended to me wherever I went in Germany.

I am especially indebted to Mr. Paul M. Warburg and Mr. James Speyer, of New York, and Mr. Edward W. Grew, of Boston; to Professor M. J. Bonn and Professor Melchior Palyi, of the Handelshochschule, Berlin; to Director Otto Fischer of the Reichs-Kredit-Gesellschaft, Director Arthur Salomonsohn of the Disconto-Gesellschaft, Director Oscar Wassermann of the Deutsche Bank, and Director Jakob Goldschmidt of the Darmstädter- und Nationalbank; to Professor Georg Schlesinger, of the Technische Hochschule, Berlin; to Professor Josef Schumpeter, of the University of Bonn; to Dr. Nordhoff, Director of the Statistical Division of the Reichsbank; to Dr. Rudolf Roessler, of Berlin; to Dr. Julius S. Klein, Assistant Secretary

of Commerce, Washington, Mr. F. W. Allport, American Commercial Attaché in Berlin, and Mr. W. T.
Daugherty, American Trade Commissioner in Berlin;
and to many others whom lack of space rather than
lack of appreciation prevents my thanking by name.

I am also indebted to the Reichsverband der
Deutschen Industrie, particularly to Director Ludwig
Kastl, and to Mr. Hartmann and Dr. Max Metzner, of
its staff; to the Verein Deutschen Maschinenbau-An-
stalten, particularly to Mr. Schulz-Merin; to various
members of the staff of the Office for Reparation Payments, Berlin; and to the Federal Statistical Office, Berlin, especially to Director Ernest Wagemann and to Dr.
Nathan. The Statistical Office placed every facility at
my disposal, and its staff gave unselfish help in the frequently difficult task of interpreting correctly the raw
material of statistics. I am likewise under great obligation to the managements of the companies, too numerous
to list here, whose plants I was permitted to visit. Their
courtesy and frankness in discussing their problems
gave me an insight into various important aspects of the
industrial situation which could not have been obtained
in any other way.

I was fortunate in being accompanied on these industrial trips by Dr. Otto Bredt, of Berlin, to whose wide
knowledge and sound judgment much of whatever merit
this book possesses is due, though it is only fair to
exempt him from responsibility for the views it presents.
I also owe the sincerest thanks to Dr. Issai Hosiosky,
who was my research assistant in Berlin, for his diligence
and skill in assembling materials and for the many
profitable suggestions he made.

The book was read in manuscript by Professor E. F.
Gay, Professor W. C. Mitchell, and Mr. Charles P.

Howland, and the concluding chapter by Mr. John Foster Dulles. These gentlemen are in no way committed by the conclusions reached here, but I am much indebted to them for their comments. My wife has worked through the book with me in all its stages, and has criticized it with generous care. The index was prepared by Mrs. Laura Hadley Moseley.

I should also like to express my appreciation of the accuracy and speed with which the Yale University Press has put through the work of publication.

J. W. A.

West Chop, Massachusetts
  August 16, 1929.

PREFACE TO REVISED EDITION

IN this second revised edition, a number of minor corrections have been made, and a short supplementary chapter has been added to take account of the general course of events from 1929 to the beginning of 1932. No attempt has been made to bring the main body of the material up to date, however, since to do so would entail reworking the whole book.

The world depression began to unfold just as the first edition of this book went to press. In consequence, a number of the observations and estimates presented in the last half of Chapter XI now seem, if not flatly wrong, at least seriously overoptimistic. I have thought it better, however, not to delete the sections involved, partly for the sake of intellectual honesty and partly because I believe that, with allowance for certain changes which have taken place since 1929 and which may well prove permanent, the content of those sections is still substantially correct. The drastic fall in world prices will almost certainly compel revision or even complete abolition of the Reparations charges on Germany. But that fall in world prices has not in itself permanently impaired Germany's own general economic strength. Every leading country has suffered severely from the depression, and if Germany has suffered more than the others, at least she was not alone. When the world depression begins to lift, and especially when a reasonable adjustment of the Reparations obligation has been effected, I believe that Germany will once more emerge as the leading industrial nation of the European continent, and that she will go steadily forward in strength and prosperity.

J. W. A.

New York City
   February 7, 1932.

CONTENTS

THE RECOVERY OF GERMANY

CHAPTER I

FROM REVOLUTION TO VERSAILLES

I. INTRODUCTION: 1914–1924

AT the outbreak of the World War, Germany was in the full tide of industrial and commercial power. Fifty years before, she had been a mere congeries of semi-independent and mutually antagonistic States, most of them small in size and having little economic importance. By 1914 she was one of the three great industrial nations of the world, strong, united, and prosperous. She had left France hopelessly far behind, and was already passing England in the unceasing race for European economic leadership. Of the half dozen principal branches of modern industrial production, she had achieved double or more than double the output of England in iron and steel, machinery, electro-technical products, and chemicals. She lagged behind only in coal and in textile production. Her merchant fleet was rapidly expanding, the volume of her foreign trade was exceeded only by England's, and her investments covered every quarter of the globe. The United States alone was clearly ahead of her in the world industrial field, and had there been no war even the American supremacy might soon have been challenged.

Less than ten years later, in 1923, Germany was apparently a broken wreck. She had lost the war; under the terms of the Treaty of Versailles she had ceded an eighth of her territory and population and all her colonies; she was legally bound to meet a Reparations charge which eventually proved impossible; she was in the throes of a cataclysmic currency depreciation; and her economic life was almost at a standstill. The return of Alsace and Lorraine to France had shattered the highly organized and sensitive structure of her iron and steel industries, most of her merchant marine and her foreign investments had been seized or surrendered, and her credit in the world's capital markets was gone. On any reasonable basis of judgment, the days of her industrial leadership seemed over. The majority of competent observers agreed that it would take many years, perhaps decades, to restore the German economic machine even to the state in which it had been before the war; and meanwhile the other principal nations would have gained a superiority which would be beyond hope of successful rivalry. The future apparently promised the country little but desperate struggle and suffering, and that in return for a small and uncertain reward.

Yet now, only six years after her utter collapse, Germany is once more one of the great industrial nations. Her production of iron and steel, though somewhat below the pre-war level, is still far ahead of England's, her output of electro-technical products and of chemicals is much greater than that of any other European country, and her output of machinery is equaled in Europe only by England. Her textile production as a whole is at about the 1913 volume, her production of coal, and the volume of her foreign trade, are not far behind, and her merchant fleet is being steadily built up again. Germany's industrial supremacy on the Continent is once more established beyond challenge, and she is rapidly increasing her power. Despite the enormous losses of the war and the inflation period, despite the steady payment of unprecedented sums to other countries on Reparations account, and despite one of the heaviest tax burdens in the world, Germany's real income and the standard of living of the great majority of her people are at least as high as they were in 1913. The general condition of her working class is probably somewhat better than it was then; and although she has as yet had no period of genuine and widespread prosperity, the foundations of her industrial life are once more strong and sound. In less than six years, she has climbed up from the pit of prostration and despair to an assured position of world leadership. It is one of the most spectacular recoveries in the world's entire economic history.

But while the rapidity and the scope of German economic reconstruction have been little short of phenomenal, in many directions there is still much to be done, and numerous weak spots remain. Many foreigners, and Americans especially, have formed a quite exaggerated idea of Germany's present prosperity and economic power, and of the threat she offers to other industrial nations in the world's markets. Of the future no one can be sure, but the Germany of today is very far from being the industrial and commercial Juggernaut which her competitors have feared. It is the purpose of this book to show, as far as the available information permits, just what progress Germany actually has achieved during the past ten years in the principal branches of her industry, and then to make an appraisal of her present strength and probable future in the world's industry and commerce.

II. REVOLUTION AND CONSTITUTION

THE history of Germany in the first years after the war is very largely the history of two quite different yet interrelated struggles. The first, which dominated the stage from 1918 to 1920, centered around the overthrow of the old imperial and aristocratic *régime*, and the eventually successful attempt to establish a democratic Republic in its place. The second was the struggle of the

Allies, in the face of inevitable German opposition and despite the self-contradictory and impossible character of many of their own demands, to enforce the terms of the Treaty of Versailles, especially the Reparations clauses. This latter struggle shaped the whole tragic course of events in Germany from 1921 to 1924. Both movements were primarily political in their origins, but each had far-reaching economic consequences.

The German Revolution of 1918 is a curious chapter in the world's history. It was extraordinarily sudden; as far as the great bulk of the German people were concerned it was quite unpremeditated; and it was extraordinarily easy. It gave rise to almost no bloodshed at the time, for there was almost no opposition to overcome. It was more like an instantaneous change in the physical constitution of the entire German universe. In September of 1918 Germany was an Empire embattled. The Kaiser was still the Supreme War Lord, pursuing his divinely destined occupation, the military aristocracy was still dominant in the councils of the nation, and although the informed observer could already detect ominous cracks in the glittering imperial structure, the great mass of the German people, kept in ignorance of most of what was really happening on the Western Front, were still serenely confident of ultimate victory. Then at the end of October a revolt broke out among the sailors at Kiel, spread rapidly, and was soon joined by the army; on November 8 the crushing terms of the Armistice were transmitted by the Allies, and for the first time revealed to the people at large the extent of the military defeat; on November 9 the Kaiser abdicated, and the Socialists took over the government; and on November 11 the Armistice was signed. In fifteen short days expected victory had turned into national catastrophe, and military imperialism had fled before a socialist dictatorship.

The Revolution was really not so much a revolution as a collapse, an automatic reaction against a state of affairs which had become unbearable. With the sudden public realization of military failure, and the bitter knowledge that all the suffering and sacrifice of the previous four years had been in vain, a violent revulsion of feeling ensued against the whole order that had brought about the existing situation. The change was carried through by the Socialists, while the bourgeoisie looked on, too stunned either to hinder or to help, and the old military aristocracy fled.

At first the new Government was almost purely socialist in character, and it seemed probable that far-reaching changes in the form and organization of Germany's entire economic life would result. But the Socialists encountered trouble almost at once, and were never firmly in the saddle. Partly because of a fundamental desire for peaceful and democratic methods, partly because of dissensions within their own ranks, they were unable to establish a strong and dominant *régime*. When the elections for the National Constitutional Assembly were held in January, 1919, only two months after the Revolution, the Socialists polled fewer votes than did the combined bourgeois parties, and the real control of the new Republic soon passed from their hands. The Weimar Constitution of August, 1919, which established the forms of government under which Germany has lived ever since, created no socialist utopia; instead, it set up a democratic republic pure and simple. Beyond a few clauses which for the most part have remained only empty phrases, it is impossible to find any trace of real socialism in its provisions. Indeed, since the first 1919 election the Socialists have never been supreme in the country as a whole. They have governed, so far as they have governed at all, by means of coalitions, and only in virtue of their position as the largest minority party.

As time went on, it became clear that the Revolution of 1918 had fundamentally changed the political and social constitution of Germany. It had destroyed the old imperial rule and the military aristocracy, and had set up a democracy in their place. But it also became clear that the Revolution had had extraordinarily little effect on the form and working of the country's economic life. Although it was carried through by the Socialist parties themselves, it did nothing of an enduring character to alter the existing organization of production, distribution, and exchange. The so-called "socialization" of the coal, potash, and electrical industries has in point of fact been little different from that familiar process, of combination and central control, at which intelligently directed and unhampered private capitalism would itself aim in similar circumstances. The reaction after the Revolution blocked any real nationalization in these industries, and any extension to other groups, and even in the "socialized" industries government regulation has not altered the fundamental fact of private ownership. In addition, the machinery which the Constitution set up to insure the representation and the partial control of labor in industry has thus far had little or no effect on the actual course and conduct of business, and remains a political gesture. The principal tangible gains which the Socialists can claim to have secured in the economic field are the nominal establishment of the 8-hour day (which is subject to many legalized exceptions), improvement of the elaborate system of social insurance, effective recognition of the trade unions, and the establishment of legal wage agreements throughout the country. Yet these are all measures of types which other enlightened countries, of however capitalistic a complexion, have also established or tried. Thorough-going socialization in Germany, if indeed it will ever be realized at all, is still an achievement for the future.

III. ARMISTICE AND TREATY

BUT the great immediate problem in Germany soon ceased to be the establishment and consolidation of the new political and economic *régime*. From 1920 to 1924 the controlling issue, the pivot on which Germany's whole economic life turned, was the efforts of the Allies to enforce the terms of the Treaty of Versailles, especially the Reparations clauses. The Weimar Constitution had set up a wholly untried Republic on the ashes of military imperialism and socialist dictatorship, and the mere attempt to get the new State going as an instrument of government gave rise to the gravest difficulties. Yet even before the Republic had been officially proclaimed, its very existence was vitally threatened by the conclusion of the Treaty of Peace. The Treaty deprived Germany outright of great sections of her existing economic wealth and strength, and then in addition made further enormous demands for future payments which experience eventually showed to be of an impossible magnitude. For the next five years it was uncertain whether Germany would be able to survive at all. The history of the period is the somber record of a desperate national struggle, in the face of overwhelming odds, merely to keep alive. Before it was over she had been swept to the extreme verge of disintegration, a large part of her people had been reduced to penury and even starvation, and the foundations of her economic life had been shattered. From 1920 to 1924 the trend of events was continuously and increasingly downward, and the end was reached only at utter collapse.

To understand the development of the situation, it is necessary to examine the principal terms of the Armistice and the Treaty, and to realize the extent to which the cessions demanded of Germany and the losses imposed on her weakened the constitution of her whole economic life.

The military terms of the Armistice, submitted to the Germans on November 8, 1918, and accepted November 11, required the immediate evacuation of all conquered territories; withdrawal of all German troops beyond the Rhine; Allied occupation of the left bank of the Rhine, and of 30-kilometer bridgeheads on the right bank at Cologne, Coblenz, and Mainz; creation of a neutral zone 10 kilometers wide on the right bank; the delivery of guns, airplanes, and other war material; and finally the surrender of the fleet. The more strictly economic terms stipulated the delivery of 5,000 railway engines and 150,000 cars, the whole of the railway of Alsace-Lorraine and its equipment, 5,000 motor trucks, and the return of the gold taken from the banks in the conquered territories. In addition, the strangling Allied blockade on the movement of goods into and out of Germany was to continue until the final peace treaty should be signed; and Germany's obligation to make reparation for the damage done in Allied territory was declared, but was left undefined. The terms were severe, and contained an ominous threat of what might be expected later, but there was no option. In the face of military defeat in the west, and of political and social revolution at home, the German delegates could only accept.

Six months later the Peace Treaty was at last drawn up and presented to the Germans, and after fevered negotiations and arguments, was signed on June 28, 1919. Apart from the clauses designed to enforce the virtually complete demilitarization of Germany, the Treaty contained far-reaching territorial and economic provisions. The Allied occupation of the left bank of the Rhine and of the bridgeheads was to continue in full vigor for five years, and would not be entirely terminated until 1935.[1] In addition, large cessions of territory were required. In the west, Alsace and Lorraine were ceded to France, as were the Saar coal mines. The Saar territory itself was to be administered by the League of Nations for 15 years, after which a plebiscite should determine whether France or Germany was to have it.[2] One small district on the Belgian frontier was given to Belgium, and two others were ceded subject to plebiscites, which were later decided, despite charges of coercion and maladministration, in Belgium's favor. The Duchy of Luxemburg was also removed from the German customs union. In the north, the upper part of Schleswig was given to Denmark after a plebiscite. In the east great slices were cut off. A considerable part of Posen, West Prussia and Upper Silesia was ceded to Poland; the Danzig district was made a Free City under the League; Memel was internationalized; and East Prussia was separated from the rest of Germany by a

[1] The occupied territory was divided into three districts which were to be evacuated in 1925, 1930, and 1935, conditional on Germany's fulfilment of the other provisions of the Treaty. Meanwhile Germany was to pay all costs of the armies of occupation, the missions of control, etc. The evacuation of the first district, scheduled for January, 1925, was not actually completed until June of that year.

The occupation has not materially hampered normal economic life in the regions affected, but there have been a good many unfortunate incidents, especially in the earlier years, and many charges of industrial espionage.

[2] If returned to Germany, she is to compensate France for the value of the coal mines.

wide corridor giving Poland access to the Baltic. The
fate of the rich industrial district of Upper Silesia was
left to a plebiscite, which was eventually held in 1921.
Although the vote of the district as a whole in this plebiscite was then in favor of Germany, the Treaty had
contemplated partition, and the industrial basin, made
up of closely knit coal mines and steel mills, was split in
two, with the larger part going to Poland—again in the
face of bitter protests from the Germans. Finally, outside of Europe the Treaty made a complete sweep of the
German colonial empire, and under the device of manda-
tories divided it up among the principal Allies.

These territorial provisions carried with them economic losses to Germany which in most cases were far
larger than in proportion to the mere size of the area
ceded. Lorraine contained the greatest part of Germany's supply of iron ore, and an important section of
her steel industry; Alsace had both potash deposits and
a strong textile industry, which were later to become
serious international competitors of Germany; Upper
Silesia had rich coal seams, and another important division of the steel industry; and the other territory ceded
in the east was nearly all good agricultural land. But
the economic provisions of the Treaty did not stop with
this. In addition, Germany was required to deliver an
average of nearly 38 million tons of coal a year to
France for 10 years, as compensation for the French
mines which had been ruined; large quantities of benzol,
coal tar, ammonium sulphate, and other chemicals and
dyes; literally millions of head of livestock of all kinds;
and the largest part of the merchant fleet, including all
vessels of over 1,600 tons burden. She was to bear the
costs of the Allied armies of occupation and the various
commissions; consent to the sale of all German private
property in the Allied countries for the benefit of the

Allies;[1] and in her foreign trade was to grant the Allies most-favored-nation treatment for five years, and other politico-commercial concessions, without receiving similar privileges in return.

Yet even this was not the end; had it been so the burden, heavy though it was, could still have been borne. In addition, Germany was to make good, as seemed only just, all the damage caused by her armies to the peoples of the Allied powers. The amount at which this damage was to be valued was not set in the Treaty itself, but was to be determined by an Allied commission by May 1, 1921. Meanwhile she was to pay by the latter date the sum of 20 milliard gold marks (5 milliard dollars);[2] and was to give bonds or the promise to issue bonds for a further 80 milliard marks (20 milliard dollars).

These last were the Reparations clauses of the Treaty of Versailles, the principal focus around which was centered all the struggle and misery of the next five years. In submitting to them Germany signed, however unwillingly, a vast blank check. She agreed to pay an unspecified but vast sum, the size of which was left to her late enemies to determine. Even so the arrangement, perhaps subsequently modified in the light of experience, might have proved workable had the Allies held to their original definition of "war damages." But they did not. Under the pressure of domestic politics, and under the necessity of keeping at least some of the promises made to their voters after the Armistice, the Allied leaders ex-

---

[1] Some of this property or its equivalent, however, was subsequently restored. The United States, for example, undertook in February, 1929, to make returns valued at $250 millions. See *Wirtschaft und Statistik*, March 2, 1929.

[2] Throughout this book the more convenient European practice will be followed of calling 1,000,000,000 a *milliard*, not (as in the common American practice) a *billion*. The European billion is 1,000,000,-000,000.

tended the term to include not only physical damages, but also all pensions and other compensations to the Allied soldiers and sailors and their beneficiaries.

Whatever the ethics of the new definition from the Allied point of view, the result was that the Reparations charge finally placed on Germany was more than doubled. On May 1, 1921, the Reparations Commission announced that this charge had been set at 132 milliard gold marks (31.5 milliard dollars). Relative to Germany's general economic condition at the time, and relative to any payments she might conceivably be capable of making in the next few years, the figure was simply illusory. Even at the height of Germany's pre-war prosperity it would have entailed a burden far beyond her power. When applied to the Germany of 1921, weakened as she was by her own war losses and crippled by the territorial cessions stipulated in the Treaty, it was purely absurd. Regardless of the political and moral justification for the Allies' action—and it was great— the subsequent course of events showed that Germany was physically incapable, whether her intentions were good or bad, of meeting the Reparations demands in full. Germany had signed the blank check, and the Allies had filled in the figures, but until 1924 it seemed extremely probable that the check would be worth rather less than nothing. The forceful and often ill-advised efforts of the Allies themselves to begin the process of cashing it produced, not receipts for their treasuries, but the gradual disintegration and collapse of the German economic machine itself.

IV. SUMMARY OF LOSSES AND CESSIONS

SUCH were the principal terms of the Armistice and the Treaty of Peace. At the time, many Germans declared that their devastating severity had been exceeded in all the world's history only by that utter destruction of Carthage which was enforced by Rome. The implications of the statement are hardly correct, but that the Treaty provisions have had a crippling effect on German economic life is beyond dispute.

A rough idea of the extent to which the country's economic strength and productivity were weakened by the war and by the Treaty cessions can be formed from the following figures.[1] At the outbreak of the war Germany's population was about 67,000,000, roughly two-thirds of the population of the United States at the time. In the war itself, 1,885,000 men were killed, and those who were wounded suffered losses in earning capacity equivalent to another third of a million. The cessions of territory under the Treaty involved a further loss of six and a half million. The total loss from the war and the Treaty together was thus 8,700,000 in round numbers, or 13 per cent of the pre-war population. But the real effect on the German man power was even greater than the figures indicate. A much diminished birth rate, and the malnutrition and even outright starvation of both children and adults in consequence of the war-time food shortage, have seriously impaired both the numbers and the quality of the population itself. During the war Germany suffered less than the Allies in terms of the destruction of physical wealth, but she suffered much more in terms of the health and strength of her people.

The European territory ceded amounted to 13 per cent of the pre-war area. In addition Germany lost all her colonies, with an area of about 5½ times that of European Germany in 1913. The colonial population was somewhat more than 12 million, but less than 30,000 were white.

[1] For full data see Appendix I.

The direct reduction in German productive capacity was of course very different in the different branches of economic life. Apart from losses during the war itself, the cessions of territory under the Treaty entailed large surrenders of industrial raw material supply and of industrial plant. A few examples are illuminating. In coal mining, the area ceded had produced 15.7 per cent of the value of the 1913 output; in iron ore, 48.2 per cent; in the iron and steel industry an average of about 19 per cent; in zinc ore and smelting, 59 per cent; in lead ore and smelting, 24 per cent; in sulphur, 12 per cent; and so on.[1] In addition, 15.5 per cent of the arable land area was ceded, and about 12 per cent of all the livestock. Taking German industrial and agricultural production as a whole in all its branches, the average loss in property, plant, and equipment was thus about 15 per cent of the pre-war holdings.

But here again the real effect on Germany's productive capacity was greater than the average figure alone would indicate. The losses in the fundamentally important coal, iron, and steel industries were much higher than this; and the Treaty cessions completely disrupted that highly organized interdependence of Ruhr coal and Lorraine iron on which Germany's pre-war industry had been based. It was years before the German steel industry regained its pre-war capacity. In many other directions, too, the Treaty cessions broke down the pre-war organization of industry and commerce, so that for a long time even the industrial plant which Germany retained was incapable of working at its former level of efficiency. The only offset to this was that in later years,

[1] Of the principal known German reserves of minerals, 36 per cent of the coal was ceded as measured by *tonnage* (much, however, of inferior quality); 72 per cent of the iron ore; 63 per cent of the zinc ore; and 2 per cent of the potash.

when the plant and equipment surrendered under the Treaty had finally been replaced, the average age of the German industrial installations was necessarily less than the average age in the other European countries, and their average technical efficiency was hence usually greater. Finally, the figures thus far given take no account of the almost complete loss, during and after the war, of Germany's investments and other holdings abroad. These holdings amounted in 1913 to nearly 28 milliard marks (6½ to 7 milliards dollars) and constituted nearly 10 per cent of the country's estimated national wealth in 1913.[1]

The Germany of 1920 was thus very different from the Germany of 1913. She had lost or ceded 13 per cent of her 1913 population, 13 per cent of her European territory, all her colonies, and about 15 per cent of her total productive capacity. The whole structure of her industry and commerce had been forced into new channels by the war, and had then been completely disorganized by the cessions under the Treaty. She had been through a political revolution, and had of necessity signed the Reparations blank check. She was far weaker economically and politically than she had been in 1913.

[1] The Institute of Economics estimates the loss in German national wealth from 1914 to the end of 1921 at about 135 milliard marks. This figure includes not only the items given above, but also depreciation of plant and equipment, non-replacement of stocks, etc. Helfferich's estimate of the German national wealth in 1913 (which may well have been too low) was 300 milliard marks; and this would indicate that the loss from 1914 to 1921 amounted to about 45 per cent of the pre-war wealth. Except on a rather narrow definition of national wealth, however, this percentage is probably too high. Germany's history after 1921, though black enough during the inflation period, does not suggest a loss of this magnitude. See H. G. Moulton and C. E. McGuire, *Germany's Capacity to Pay* (New York, 1923), p. 192.

On the loss of foreign holdings, see the end of the next Chapter, and Appendix III.

but she was being compelled to take on burdens which in 1913 would have seemed impossible. What would happen? The Allies insisted, however much against the judgment of their own wiser statesmen, that Germany could and should pay the full charge placed upon her, but bitter experience swiftly showed that there could be only one outcome. The cycle of inflation, disintegration and catastrophe was soon under way.

CHAPTER II

REPARATIONS, INFLATION, AND COLLAPSE

TO form any clear picture of Germany during the period from the close of the war to the end of 1923 is not easy. Event followed event, and political misfortune precipitated economic disaster, with a speed which in retrospect is bewildering. Scenes and personalities and forces were in a state of ceaseless flux, and no man knew what the next day might bring. After 1920 the dominant motive in the whole drama was the Reparations question, and the supreme economic fact was currency depreciation, but there were many other forces at work, and many other major changes occurred.

It is not proposed to undertake a detailed history of the period. Some idea of the course of events is necessary, however, in order to understand the nature of the permanent effects which were produced by inflation and by the Reparations struggle on the foundations and organization of German economic life. The best measure of what was happening is the movements of the foreign-exchange rates. These rates were a sensitive financial barometer which revealed the shifting pressures on Germany's economic life. By following their fluctuations, we can get a fairly accurate impression of the significance for Germany as a whole of the successive political and financial developments in these years, and of the increasingly critical state to which the country was brought.

At the close of the war Germany's financial situation was bad, but still far from desperate. She had paid for the war very largely by loans rather than by taxation, it is true, and her public debt was some thirty times greater than in 1913, but even so it was little larger than the French or the English debts, and a number of the Allied countries were confronted with financial problems of quite the same order of severity. When regular foreign-exchange transactions were first resumed between Germany and the United States, at the end of 1918, the mark was still quoted at more than half its pre-war par value,[1] a rate which contrasts favorably with the levels reached some years later by the French, the Italian, and the Belgian exchanges.

But the political and financial situation was essentially unstable. The new and inexperienced socialist dictatorship was fighting for its life, and was at first in no position to begin the vitally necessary reorganization of the national finances; no one knew what ominous dictates would come from the Peace Conference, already sitting in Paris; and the foreign exchanges soon began to depreciate still farther. The rate on New York, which had averaged 8.50 marks to the dollar in January, 1919 (par was 4.20), went above 10 in March, and by May was above 13. The announcement of the crushing terms of the Peace Treaty early in May caused a new depreciation, and by the end of July the first great collapse of the mark was under way. It was checked only in March, 1920, when a rate of 100 had been reached; that is, 4 per cent of par. Then followed a period of recovery, and by June of 1920 the rate was again below 40. Foreign sympathizers and speculators had bought large quantities of German currency, thus helping the exchanges, Erzberger's drastic revenue measures had begun to bear

[1] See Chart I, below, and Appendix III. The rates quoted here are the official rates, which were controlled. They are hence to some extent artificial, and more favorable to Germany than they would have been in a perfectly free market.

ıruit, the Government had slashed its expenditures and thus reduced its current deficit, and it looked as though the mark might at least be stabilized, if not restored to parity. Indeed, the very rapidity of the exchange recovery was itself a source of difficulty, for it produced a severe crisis. Mark prices fell, current rates of interest and of wages became exorbitant, and for a time industry was at a standstill. During the next twelve months, although the exchanges fluctuated widely, no severe new depreciation took place, and in April, 1921, the dollar rate was still around 60.

In the middle of 1921, however, two things happened which definitely sealed the fate of the old mark currency. One was the fixing of the Reparations charge, and the announcement by the Allies of drastic terms of payment. The other was the Upper Silesian decision. On May 1, 1921, as already pointed out, the Reparations Commission announced that the total figure for the damage to be made good by Germany under the head of Reparations was 132 milliard marks (31.5 milliard dollars). At the same time it asserted, in the face of German protests, that less than half the payments Germany had agreed to make prior to May 1 had actually been received. A few days later, on May 5, the Allies gave concrete expression to these findings, and issued the so-called London Ultimatum. Germany was required to deliver three sets of bonds, for 12, 38, and 82 milliards of gold marks, respectively; was to pay 1 milliard marks through the summer, and thereafter 2 milliards a year; and in addition was to pay over the proceeds of a 26 per cent tax on her exports to the Allies, up to a total sum on all accounts of 3 milliards a year. She was given six days in which to accept these terms. In the event of refusal, the Allies would occupy the Ruhr. The contemporary German Government would not consent to conditions which they thought they could not fulfil, but a new cabinet under Doctor Wirth agreed to attempt the impossible task, and began the payment of the first milliard.

The new arrangement was kept going for several months, and although the quotation on the dollar began to climb again, for a time nothing very spectacular happened. Then came the Upper Silesian decision. In March, 1921, a plebiscite had been held to determine whether the contested region should go to Germany or to Poland, and had resulted in a 7 to 5 vote in favor of Germany. But the terms of the Treaty of Versailles had indicated partition of the district, not outright assignment to one claimant or the other, and the Allies accordingly attempted to draw the new boundary according to the vote by communes. Unable to agree among themselves, however, they referred the question to the League of Nations in August. The award was announced October 12, 1921. It drew a line straight through the industrial basin, and split the tightly knit coal and steel industry in two. The decision was a serious economic loss to Germany, and an even more severe blow to what was left of her political and financial prestige. The immediate result of these two developments was a further severe depreciation of the mark. Under the pressure of meeting the payment of the first milliard stipulated in the London Ultimatum, the dollar rate rose from an average of 62 marks in May of 1921 to 84 in August, and to 105 in September. In the week after the Upper Silesian award, in October, it jumped to 156. By the end of November it was at 270, or only 1.5 per cent of par. There it stopped for a time, however, and even recovered a little. Until the late spring of 1922 no further important depreciation occurred.

But then began what proved to be the last chapter in the history of the mark. In June, 1922, the exchanges started to depreciate again. The principal reason for the new collapse was the combined effect of large cash payments to the Allies and foreign-exchange speculation, but great weight must also be attached to the adverse effects of the murder in that month of Walter Rathenau. He had been the apostle of the fulfilment of the Treaty terms, and his death cut away one of the strongest pillars of the new Germany.

In July the Government asked for a two-year moratorium. Failing that, a financial crash was declared to be inevitable. The Allies met in London in August to discuss the request, and the steadily growing cleavage between France and Great Britain on the Reparations question now became manifest for the first time. Great Britain supported the German position, as did Italy and Belgium, but France violently disagreed. Poincaré, instead of granting the moratorium, proposed to seize such "productive guarantees" as the State coal mines and forests, in order to assure the Reparations deliveries which he declared Germany was stubbornly refusing to yield. The conference broke up in open discord, but the ominous course of future events was written plainly for all to see. The mark, which had been at an average of 493 to the dollar in July, shot up to 1,200 at the end of August, and to over 8,000 in the middle of November, nearly a twenty-fold depreciation in 4 months. It was also at this time that the internal "flight from the mark" first became a major factor in current life. Everyone who was unfortunate enough to possess mark currency was in danger of having it lose half its value in his pocket overnight, and the moment people received payments in marks they dashed off with the money to buy food, clothes, houses, scrap iron, or anything else which had an inherent worth, and which would not waste away. In addition, the more fortunate ones bought foreign exchange, and thus got their funds out of the country. Indeed, later on the depreciation became so rapid that prices in many shops were adjusted to the exchange rates every hour or two, and eventually were fixed outright in foreign currencies.

France did not long postpone the threatened seizure of guaranties. On January 10, 1923, the French and Belgian governments announced that because of defaults in the German Reparations deliveries, a Mission of Control[1] would be sent into the Ruhr, the heart of the German coal and steel industries, and that the Mission would be accompanied by adequate troops. The next day the Mission settled at Essen, and a state of siege was proclaimed. It was a declaration of war in all but name. Sabotage and disorder inevitably followed at once, and what had been politely described as economic supervision soon gave way to the bitter realities of military occupation. The costly, vindictive, and short-sighted Ruhr invasion had begun. The mark, which had recovered somewhat at the end of 1922, responded instantly, and soared to over 40,000 by the end of the month, a loss of five-sixths of its remaining value in three weeks. But there it stopped again, and even recovered a part of the loss. Not until May did it begin the last terrific depreciation, which ended only with its complete disappearance.

The final collapse of the mark was due in part to the direct economic effects of the Ruhr invasion itself, in part to the measures with which Germany sought to retaliate. French and Belgian troops were poured into the occupied district. Coercion led to resistance, and that to new coercion. Officials were expelled, industrial leaders

[1] The Mission Inter-Alliée de Contrôle des Usines et des Mines, commonly referred to as the MICUM. The French dominated the Ruhr invasion throughout. Great Britain and Italy took no part in it.

fined and imprisoned, the press was muzzled, courts-martial flourished, and blood was shed. Coal mines and steel mills and machine shops were seized, and a strangling cordon was established which effectively cut off the industrial heart of Germany from the rest of the country. Against these measures a stubborn campaign of passive resistance was set up. The industrial leaders who alone could run the complicated Ruhr machine slipped away, a large part of the laborers refused to work until compelled by imminent starvation, all Reparations deliveries to France and Belgium were stopped, and the railway, postal, and telegraph services relapsed into chaos. Meanwhile the civilian fighting line was aggressively supported from the political and financial base in Berlin. German citizens were forbidden to execute foreign orders under heavy penalties, and the government undertook to maintain all those who lost their livelihood or were expelled from their homes in the struggle. At the same time the Reichsbank extended enormous credits to the industrial and commercial enterprises of the Ruhr, to enable them to carry on the contest.

For a time it was a deadlock. France received only such coal deliveries, ostensibly the chief purpose of the invasion, as she could transport with her own staff, and at first Germany did not yield. But without the coal and steel of the Ruhr she could not long exist, and the strain of financing the campaign soon began to tell. By May, 1923, the exchange rate on the dollar had climbed above 40,000 again, and from there it shot up to stellar magnitudes. On September 27, 1923, after more than 8 months of desperate struggle, the German Government at last surrendered unconditionally. The orders for passive resistance were withdrawn, and the embargoes on Reparations deliveries were raised. But Poincaré, instead of giving immediate relief, allowed the character of the occupation to remain unchanged throughout the autumn, and even encouraged a renewal of the separatist activities in the Rhineland. The withdrawal of the French troops did not begin for another full year, and Germany's industrial life revived only slowly and painfully. Meantime the mark, already almost abandoned, reached the incredible figure of 4,200,000,000,-000 to the dollar in the middle of November, 1923. At that point it was replaced by a new currency, and from then on conditions gradually improved, though at first almost imperceptibly. The chapter of catastrophe was ended.

The actual termination of the currency inflation was really the result of a dramatic though legitimate confidence trick. Beginning with August of 1923, the government and the banks had made a series of desperate efforts to check the collapse of the old mark, or, failing that, to set up some stable unit of value in the whirling morass of inflated paper. So-called gold loans were floated in small denominations, based on the dollar and designed to serve as emergency currency; private holdings of foreign bills and foreign securities were seized and used to bolster up the exchanges; a money based on the relatively stable value of rye was proposed, as were other stop-gap currencies; and numerous other devices were tried.[1] But it was all in vain. The old mark continued to depreciate with cyclonic speed, and interest rates, as a partial offset, went as high as 20 per cent *per day*—equivalent to 7,300 per cent a year! Then on Oc-

[1] A concise and dramatic picture of the height of the inflation period is given by the chronology of events compiled in the *Frankfurter Zeitung's* Quarterly, *Die Wirtschaftskurve*, 1924, I, 8–12. As far back as the end of 1922 the practice had been introduced of making long-time loans in terms of pounds of rye, and in 1923 loans were also based on units of coal, potash, coke, and even electric kilowatts. Be-

tober 13, 1923, a decree was passed for the establishment of a new Rentenbank, which was to set up a Rentenmark currency; and a month later, on November 15,
the issue began. The new currency was at first put out
without compulsory circulation, but it rapidly gained
in favor, and in the middle of December it was coupled
to the old money at the rate of 1,000,000,000,000 old
marks for 1 new Rentenmark. From that time on the
German currency ceased to depreciate. The old notes
gradually disappeared from circulation, and by the
spring of 1924 had completely gone.

Yet the new money really rested on a very uncertain
foundation. The original Rentenmarks were denomi-
nated in gold, but they had no gold basis, and were of
course not convertible. They were nominally issued
against a mortgage on all the land and houses in Germany, but that sort of security, when subjected to real
pressure, is almost worthless as the basis of a stable currency. As a matter of practice, the holder of a Rentenmark who desired to convert his money into something
having "real" value could not have demanded in exchange his proportionate share of a specific piece of
land. Even had he been able to enforce the claim, what
he received would have been of little or no use to him.
The history of the *assignats* during the French Revolution shows how easily and how swiftly a currency based
on land, and therefore of necessity not readily convertible
into something having a stable and generally accepted
value, can itself collapse. Instead, the main foundation

cause their value was unaffected by the fluctuations of the mark, these
loans enjoyed great popularity.

For a circumstantial account of this period, given by the man
whose perseverance and skill contributed most to the final accomplishment of stabilization, see Dr. Hjalmar Schacht, *The Stabilization of
the Mark* (New York, 1927).

on which the original Rentenmark rested was really
nothing other than public confidence. There was tacit
general agreement, after five catastrophic years of inflation, to pretend that the new currency was really
something having an inherent and fixed value. But for
many months its existence was precarious, and at times
it went to a discount of as much as 10 per cent or more
against gold. Had the Government not managed, by
heroic measures, to get its budget balanced, the new currency could not have lasted; and had the adoption of
the Dawes Plan late in 1924 not made possible the final
erection of what is for all practical purposes a gold
standard monetary system, Germany would almost certainly have gone through a new tidal wave of inflation.

II. THE RESPONSIBILITY FOR INFLATION

SUCH is the record, in briefest outline, of the successive
phases of the German inflation. We have for convenience
traced its development chiefly in terms of the fluctuations of the foreign-exchange rates, but the movements
of any other index of general economic conditions—
prices, wages, currency circulation, the volume of
Reichsbank credit, the public debt of the Reich itself—
tell a substantially similar story.[1]

It is no part of the province of this book to examine
the causes of the inflation and collapse at length, but a
little must be added to what has already been said. At
the time of the inflation, and afterward, many foreigners asserted that the German Government was deliberately depreciating the currency in order to bring
about a crash, and thus to checkmate the Allied efforts
to extract Reparations payments. That particular
charge, which rests on a survival of war psychology, is

[1] For the principal statistics bearing on the inflation period, see
Appendix III, below.

I. FOREIGN EXCHANGE, PRICES AND CURRENCY, 1919–1923

A Foreign exchange: Par = 100.
B Wholesale price index: 1913 = 100.
C Currency circulation: 1913 = 100.

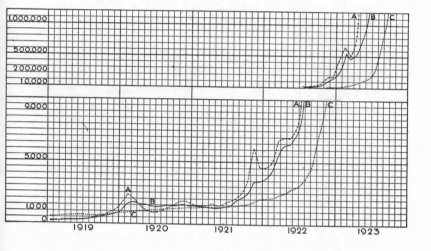

II. FEDERAL FINANCE, 1920–1923

A Expenditures.   B Receipts.

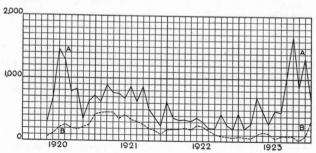

unproved and untrue, but in other respects the German Government was not free from blame. An examination of the order of events in the three principal periods when the depreciation was increasing rapidly—in the latter part of each of the years 1920, 1922, and 1923—casts a good deal of light on the situation (see the accompanying Chart I).[1]

In every case the first thing that happened was a renewed depreciation of the foreign exchanges, followed closely by an almost equivalent rise in internal prices, and more slowly by wages. As the depreciation progressed, wage rates were set more and more in accordance with the movements of the cost of living index, or even of the exchanges, and were revised frequently—at the end of the period every day or two, in many cases.[2] The increase in the currency circulation and in the floating debt of the Reich followed only more gradually, and was primarily a result rather than a cause. In no case did the increase in the volume of the currency *precede* the rise in price and the exchanges; and to that extent the German Government must be exonerated. The successive waves of exchange depreciation in turn, as we have already seen, were due in the first instance to ad-

[1] In order to take in the extremely wide fluctuations involved, the chart is constructed with two different scales. Even so it cannot include the movements in the latter part of 1923,—when the mark had depreciated so far, however, that its gyrations had lost most of their significance. This type of chart is preferred here to the scientifically more defensible logarithmic chart because the latter, on any practicable size of paper, damps down the smaller fluctuations. To the unaccustomed eye it also conceals the almost continuous *acceleration* in the progress of the depreciation. The device of a double scale is also used for Chart III, below.

No account is taken of local currency issues, for lack of comprehensive data on them.

[2] The general disorganization then prevailing makes it impossible, however, to construct a satisfactory wages index.

verse political events: the announcement of the terms
of the Peace Treaty, the setting of the Reparations
charges, the London Ultimatum and the Upper Silesian
decision, the inception of the Ruhr invasion, and finally
the eventual collapse of German resistance. In the last
analysis, however, these events taken together were
themselves the product of the fundamental contradic-
tion between the two great aims of the Allies, security
and Reparations. Complete security entailed crushing
Germany's military and economic power, but a crushed
Germany could not and did not pay Reparations. The
German foreign exchanges were jammed between these
two millstones, and the value of the mark was ground to
dust.

But if the action of the Allies led to exchange depreciation, and if exchange depreciation inevitably produced currency inflation and soaring prices, must not
the German Government be freed of all responsibility?
Not entirely. Although partly because of domestic circumstances which it could not control, after the first
year or two it did little that was effective in improving
the situation, and toward the end did much that made it
worse. The fundamental difficulty was the state of the
Reich finances. In the five years from 1919 to 1923 the
Government's receipts, measured in gold values, never
came anywhere near to equaling its expenditures, and
for the period as a whole averaged only about 25 per
cent of them (see Chart II, above). Proximately, this
state of chronic deficit was again due to the waves of
exchange depreciation and the consequent further increases in prices. However adequate a given tax measure
might have seemed at the time it was passed, weeks or
months necessarily elapsed before the receipts began to
come in; and in the meantime a further depreciation of
the exchanges had usually pushed prices and wages still

higher, and with them most of the Government's current expenditures. A deficit of course resulted. To meet it, the Government had to resort to further borrowing, which led to the printing of more notes, and the vicious circle of inflation was thus renewed. Moreover, despite the unceasing growth in the note issue, the rise in prices was even more rapid, and the gold value of the total currency circulation fell to absurdly low figures—at one time to less than 1 per cent of the pre-war level. An acute currency shortage resulted, and to keep the country's economic life going at all still more notes had to be printed. It should be observed, however, that the Government did not itself print notes, except for the negligible volume of Reichskassenscheine. After the end of the war the deficits in the budget were met chiefly by floating short-term treasury loans of various sorts. Of these an increasingly large proportion were discounted at the Reichsbank in exchange for Reichsbank notes, and this produced the principal increases in the currency circulation.[1]

But this is not the whole story. There were at least three periods of several months each (in early 1920, and at the turn of 1920–21 and of 1921–22) when the exchanges were relatively stable and even improving. If the Government was able to stabilize the currency in 1923, in the midst of the Ruhr invasion, the task should apparently have been far easier at some earlier date. The truth of the matter is that the Government, never very strongly in the saddle, could not or would not enforce severe taxation, the only way of breaking out of the deficit-inflation circle. In 1919 Erzberger had set up a stringent system of direct taxes, covering income,

[1] The volume of Darlehnskassenscheine, emergency paper and gold note issues, issues of the private banks, and so forth, was relatively small.

property, war profits, and inheritance, and also including a severe capital levy, but the methods of administration in force made the results wholly inadequate. Collections were not effected until many months after the corresponding assessment, and the progressive depreciation therefore rendered the yields small, while the capital levy was paid in almost worthless war bonds that brought in no new funds to the treasury. After the first year of them (1920–21) the Erzberger direct taxes were in effect abandoned, and chief reliance was placed on indirect taxation. The net result was that the Government's revenues continued to fall far below its current expenditures, and the resulting deficits led inevitably to renewed inflation.[1]

Moreover, the resort to indirect taxation meant that the largest part of the burden fell on those least able to bear it, the workers and the small rentiers. The propertied classes managed to evade most of the measures aimed at them, and refused to permit stricter control, while the intangible forms of capital, always elusive, escaped almost untouched. A considerable part of the blame for Germany's failure to stop the inflation before it got beyond all bounds must therefore be placed on the industrial and commercial capitalists of the day, rather than on the Government alone. The large industrialists, as will be shown presently, were also the principal beneficiaries from the progressive inflation, and it was to their immediate if not to their ultimate interest that the inflation should continue. Their allegiance to the new State was weak, as might be expected, but in pursuing their own profit at its expense, they did much to destroy the currency.

[1] The budget of 1922–23 also provided for a compulsory stabilization loan, but the yield was only about 12 million gold marks, and this attempt to stabilize collapsed.

Finally, during the Ruhr invasion itself the Government and the Reichsbank poured out currency and credit with reckless abandon to finance the campaign of passive resistance, especially after May, 1923. However great the political justification, from the financial point of view the policy was suicidal. The closing chapter in the collapse and extinction of the mark itself was at least as much the work of the German leaders themselves as of the Allies.

The account of the Allied action which has been presented here of course deals only with its unhappy effects on Germany. There was, however, a good deal of justification from the Allies' side for the steadily increasing pressure which they exerted. Apart from the inherent justice of the demand for physical reparation of wanton damage, and the natural fundamental desire for military security, all of them were faced with severe budget deficits, due in considerable part to reconstruction work already undertaken, which it seemed only fair to expect conquered Germany to make good. The Continental Allies were also suffering from an acute shortage of coal, coke, wood, and other materials, which they thought Germany could provide.[1] These conditions were especially acute in the case of France, and they go far to explain, if not entirely to excuse, the successive coercive measures taken by the French statesmen. With respect to the Ruhr invasion, however, it must be pointed out that the receipts on Reparations account which it produced were of merely negligible size. The operation was very costly in terms of money, and its principal yield was a large additional crop of German distrust and hate, much of it well founded. The use of colored

[1] On the fuel question and its relation to Reparations, see Guy Greer, *The Ruhr-Lorraine Industrial Problem* (New York, 1925), Chaps. 4–7.

troops in the invaded districts proved especially obnoxious.

So far as concerns the period from 1919 to 1923 as a whole, no generally accepted figures exist to show the amount actually paid by Germany as Reparations. To the end of 1922 the official estimate of the Reparations Commission, an estimate certainly involving undervaluation, was roughly 8 milliard gold marks. Professor Gide estimates 14 milliards, Moulton and McGuire 26, and German claims run up to 42 or 43 milliards.[1]

III. THE DISTRIBUTION OF WEALTH AND INCOME

THE outstanding economic result of the currency depreciation in Germany was the catastrophic changes it produced in the distribution of wealth and income. Although some groups, chiefly the industrialists and agriculturists, were able to turn the inflation to their advantage, their gains were made almost entirely at the expense of other people's loss, and the great bulk of the population suffered severely. By the end of 1923 the real income of the country as a whole was hardly half of what it had been before the war. Yet even this decline, great though it was, had a less permanently crippling effect upon German economic life than did the changes in the division of the income itself, and in the distribution of wealth.

The basic facts were very simple. As the currency depreciation progressed and prices rose, the "real" value of the mark of course steadily fell; it would buy only a smaller and smaller quantity of goods and services than before. In consequence, the real value of all incomes which were paid in the form of a fixed number of marks also fell. Interest, rents, wages, salaries, pensions, and

[1] For a summary of these and other estimates, see L. Brentano, *Was Deutschland Gezahlt Hat* (Berlin, 1923).

so on, and the tax revenues of the Government, were incomes of this sort. Except insofar as they were later adjusted to the rise in prices by an increase in the number of marks paid, the purchasing power or the "real" value of all these incomes declined almost continuously, and the recipients suffered. On the other hand, everyone who paid out such incomes—public and private borrowers, employers of labor, those who had rented land or houses, and so on—found that the real value of what they had to pay was also declining, and to that extent they profited. A similar situation developed with respect to wealth itself. The people who owned bonds, mortgages, currency, and all other evidences of indebtedness which were expressed in terms of a fixed amount of money found that the real value of their wealth was falling, while at the same time, and in proportion as the creditors lost, the debtors of course gained. The currency depreciation thus automatically altered the distribution of both wealth and income, and while a part of the population benefited, the great majority suffered severely.

The class which lost least and profited most from the inflation was the industrialists. The principal reason was that the money incomes of the industrial firms, their receipts from the sale of their products, usually increased much more rapidly than their money expenses, and left them with correspondingly larger profits. After each new rise of the foreign exchanges, the first thing that usually happened was a new advance in the principal wholesale prices. Wages, salaries, rents, interest rates, and taxes rose only later and much more slowly, and in the interval the increased spread between them and prices was clearly pure gain for the industrialist. Moreover, the common lag of both wholesale prices and costs of production behind the movements of the foreign-exchange rates gave the German manufacturer a great advantage over his foreign competitors. He was able to undersell them abroad, and still make unusual profits, while at the same time he enjoyed a virtual monopoly of his home market. Finally, the manufacturer also profited enormously insofar as he was able to operate on borrowed money. When the time came for repaying the loan, he nearly always found that he was giving back a much smaller real value than he had received. The number of marks was the same, but their purchasing power, except in a few short periods, was less, and he therefore really got a part of his materials or his new plant cost free. However high the rate of interest was pushed, it was almost never high enough to offset this progressive depreciation of the currency. In most cases the depreciation not only served to pay the interest on the loan, but left the debtor with a large net profit as well![1] The royal road to fortune in those days lay not through lending but through borrowing, and many followed it. The industrialists gained most because their credit was better and they could borrow the largest sums, but many others, financial leaders and pure speculators and almost all others who could induce the banks to lend them money, soon learned the trick and became rich.

If the currency depreciation put enormous and largely unearned profits in the pockets of the industrialists, the speculators, and borrowers in general, it

[1] That is, the "real" value of the quantity of currency originally borrowed was usually greater than the real value which this same quantity of currency had at the date of repayment later, *plus* the real value of the interest payments. Even the rise of interest rates, at one point in 1923 to 20 per cent per day—7,300 per cent a year—did not suffice to offset a currency depreciation which sometimes halved the value of the mark overnight.

was hardly less kind to the agriculturists. Mortgages were paid off in depreciated currency at a fraction of their original real value, current debts were wiped out, and soaring prices enabled Junker proprietor and peasant alike to make extensive improvements. Limitation of the area of cultivation, and the deliberate feeding of cereals and milk to livestock, forced prices still higher, while the rise in the exchange rates shut out foreign competition. The socialist government, which the large aristocratic landowners naturally detested, tried to protect the town dwellers, but to no avail. When it imposed a flat levy of one-tenth of the harvest, after the termination of food control in 1921, the agriculturists blandly raised the prices of the remaining nine-tenths to a point which, despite the high exchange rates, was actually above world levels. The only result was to hurt the consumer, and the levy was soon dropped. Until the stabilization restored the dominance of world prices, and permitted imports to be made from abroad, the food growers were masters of all they surveyed. The rest of the population might suffer, but that was merely regrettable. Meanwhile, there were profits to be made.

While the industrialists and the agriculturists prospered, the working classes suffered. Throughout the inflation period, wages always lagged far behind the rise in general prices and in the cost of living. Continuous attempts were made to increase wages in proportion to the rise in prices, but until the autumn of 1923 they were paid on the basis of an index of the prices which had prevailed one month before. This interval was large enough to rob the workers of much of the real value of their wages. The numerous strikes of the inflation period —many of which were undertaken, however, for political rather than for purely economic reasons—also had little lasting effect in improving wage levels. Before a given agreement could be put into force, a new depreciation usually robbed the workers of most of their gains. After the autumn of 1923, however, and until the end of the inflation, wages were paid on the basis of the dollar exchange rates of the previous week. It is also interesting to observe that there was a strong tendency for the money wages of the unskilled grades of labor, and of women, to rise more rapidly than those of the skilled grades. Or, put the other way around, the real wages of the last group fell further and more rapidly relative to the pre-war position. It is true that there were certain offsets to this wage situation. The artificial prosperity of industry, which kept the mines and factories going full blast, meant that there was work for almost everybody. Unemployment dropped to very low figures, and the legal 8-hour day made working conditions reasonably good. Until the end of 1921 there was also a bread subsidy, while rents were kept low by government action. But under the tax system then prevailing the bread subsidies were in effect paid chiefly by the consuming public, including the workers themselves; and the workers also had to pay a flat weekly tax of 10 per cent on their wages.

The paradoxical result of these conditions was that the working class, in the face of full and steady employment, was chronically underpaid and half starved. The money wages of the workers were never high, but their "real" wages, what they actually received in terms of commodities, were pitifully low. At times they dropped to less than half the bare minimum of subsistence, and literal slow starvation was the fate of many. The full effects, which became apparent only in later years, were almost as bad as those of the war itself: great gaps in the child population because of high infant mortality and a low birth rate; many of the remaining children undernourished, rickety, or tubercular; a disproportionately high death rate among adults; and a protracted weakening of the health and strength of the country's labor power.[1]

The group which suffered most from the inflation, however, was the group which was also least able to defend itself: the middle classes among the town dwellers. The industrialists and agriculturists had on the whole little to complain of, and labor had always the last resort of the strike, but the middle classes had nothing. Composed largely of people with small fixed incomes, such as salaried officials and clerks, recipients of pensions, and little investors living on interest and rent—of whom the latter group were hit especially hard by the government control of city rentals—they were precisely the group most exposed to the evil consequences of currency depreciation, while they lacked both the knowledge and the opportunity to combat it. Their savings disappeared, their pensions and annuities melted away, and the sons who might have supported them had all too commonly been killed in the war. Hundreds of thousands of educated men and women, too old or feeble or untrained to earn their own living, were abruptly faced with starvation. Many died. The others, passing from day to day without hope, survived only by the sacrifice of treasured books, furniture, jewelry, and all their salable possessions, and at the end by domestic and

[1] For a more detailed picture of the effects of the war and the inflation period on the population see Chap. VIII, especially Chart X, below. Some interesting though largely discontinuous statistics on the position of labor during the inflation are given in M. P. Price, *Germany in Transition* (London, 1923), pp. 161–179. Also see contemporary issues of *Die Wirtschaftskurve, Finanzpolitsche Korrespondenz* (edited by R. R. Kuczynski), and the other economic periodicals.

foreign charity. Their history is one of the most genu-
inely pitiful chapters in all the war and post-war
tragedy.

Such were the principal changes in the distribution of
wealth and income which the inflation brought about.
The net effect was to increase enormously the share of
the industrialists and agriculturists, at the expense of
the workers and the middle classes. The gain arose
chiefly from the wiping out of the old industrial mortgages and debentures, which had been extensively held
by the small investors; and from the forced sale, in return for worthless currency, of a great deal of other securities, land and property, which were directly or indirectly bought by the people who hold financial power
today. In addition, the wiping out of most of the old
debt of the Reich and the other governments, likewise
held primarily by small investors, has made the burden
of taxation which industry and finance must bear distinctly smaller than it would otherwise have been; and
has thus in effect operated to transfer a further quantity of wealth and income from the middle classes to the
financial and industrial leaders. It is true that the
stabilization and the post-stabilization crisis to some extent reversed this situation. The farmers plunged from
prosperity into bankruptcy, while labor eventually more
than regained its position. But the industrial and financial leaders now have a larger share of the national
wealth and income than they had before the war; and
the prosperity of the middle classes, which had been a
vital element in Germany's pre-war economic power,
has been severely impaired. The inflation period forced
the apportionment of the country's wealth and income
into new patterns and channels, and it will be many
years before anything like the old distribution is re-
established.

IV. THE FINANCIAL POSITION OF INDUSTRY

THE effects of the inflation period on the structure and organization of industry itself were no less pronounced. To the end of 1922 the inflation produced feverish industrial activity, prosperity, and expansion, even though the total volume of production itself was far below normal. But when the currency stabilization at the end of 1923 at last compelled an appraisal of the true facts of the situation, the high activity was found to have been almost wholly artificial, and the prosperity ephemeral. The more permanent gains were largely financial alone, and even so were usually not great, while in many directions the competitive power and general strength of German industry had been seriously weakened.

From the point of view of the individual industrial firms themselves, the most favorable side of the inflation was the financial one. Some firms, through failure to gauge the situation correctly or through internal mismanagement, or for other reasons, went bankrupt and disappeared, but for the great majority the inflation as such was an almost unmixed financial benefit. Of this something has already been said. In the first place, nearly all the long-term debts incurred before 1918 and in the early stages of inflation were wiped out by the depreciation, and the borrowers received the land, plant, and machinery which had been bought with the loans almost cost free. This reduction in capital charges, often very large, was a pure gain for the companies. Of course Germany as a whole did not benefit, except to the limited extent that the loans involved had been held abroad: what the companies gained other people lost. The benefit to the companies themselves, however, was real enough. Second, wages, salaries, and taxes lagged far behind the rise in wholesale prices, and thus increased the margin of profits. In many cases the prices of those industrial raw materials and half-finished goods which were produced within Germany, and which had only a limited market, also lagged behind the prices of finished goods, and thus gave the manufacturers involved a further advantage; though for industry as a whole this too was of course only one man's gain at the expense of another's loss. Similarly any contract for future delivery at a fixed price and any of the ordinary commercial arrangements for deferring payments usually entailed a loss for the seller, and a corresponding gain for the buyer. In consequence, there was a continuous pressure on the part of the sellers for full payment with the order, or for contracts in gold, while the buyers of course preferred to make payments in paper and if possible to defer them. On the other side of the account, however, must be set the enormous rise in terms of *mark* prices of those raw materials which had to be imported from abroad.

Third, in almost all lines trade was extremely active to the end of 1922, and this allowed the manufacturer to take full advantage of the two sets of conditions just described. The activity was due to various causes. It came in part from the return of industry and commerce to more normal channels after 1918, and the consequent reappearance of demands which had been limited or shut off during the war itself; partly from the urgent necessity of making good the four war years, during which most plants had necessarily been allowed to depreciate and stocks of goods to run down; and partly from the large export market temporarily created by foreign-exchange depreciation. In the closing years of the inflation period the latter was the most important

factor. The bounty on exportation not only increased
the volume of production, but also allowed the exporting
firms to make very large profits.[1]

Finally, the manufacturers soon learned the inflation-period trick already described, of getting rich by
borrowing. Until the end of 1922 the quoted rates for
money did not average above 10 per cent a year, and
although the figure actually paid by the borrower was
usually somewhat higher, it never by any remote possibility offset more than temporarily a currency depreciation which, except for 1920, ran in terms of hundreds
and thousands of per cents a year. The difference between the rate of interest paid and the annual rate of
depreciation was a net profit for the borrower. Of course
not every firm was able to benefit by this situation.
Many were too small, or had too poor a credit standing,
to induce the banks to make any important volume of
loans to them. But most of the larger firms, especially
the great "mixed" coal, steel, and manufacturing enter-

[1] This export dumping was the principal reason which led the Allies, who were hard hit by it, to impose a 26 per cent tax on German
exports in 1921, nominally as a means of increasing Reparations receipts. This once more brought out the familiar paradox: the creditors
wanted their money, but also wanted the debtor to sell his goods not
to them, but to a third party; and no one wanted to be the third
party.

Despite the export premium, German exports averaged less than
half the pre-war volume, as shown by these official estimates (see Appendix III):

Year	Value: million marks	Weight: million tons
1913	10,198	73.7
1920	3,724	19.8
1921	3,003	13.8
1922	6,199	21.6
1923	5,352	12.7

The breakdown of the customs frontiers during the Ruhr invasion,
however, makes the figures for 1923 almost pure guesswork.

prises of the Ruhr, gained enormously. They were able to rebuild and improve their plants at trifling cost, and some of them, by buying up other companies, swelled into gigantic concerns that for a time threatened to strangle the country. Indeed, it is not far from correct to say that the big borrowers virtually stole the banks.

The nature of what happened in general with respect to bank loans is graphically illustrated by the movements of the total credits granted to industry and commerce by the Reichsbank (see Chart III). Although the volume of these credits increased enormously in terms of paper marks, their real gold value, except for a few months in 1920, dropped steadily. It fell from a monthly average of roughly 8,500 million marks at the beginning of 1919 to barely 70 millions at the stabilization—under

III. TOTAL COMMERCIAL CREDITS GRANTED BY THE REICHSBANK, 1919–1923

I. IN PAPER MARKS

MILLIARD MARKS

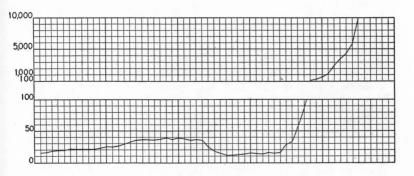

II. IN GOLD MARK EQUIVALENTS

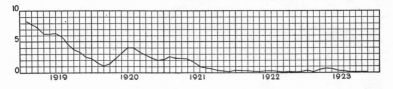

17 million dollars! The largest part of this decline represents the loss of funds which were in effect, though not in law, given cost free to the bank's debtors. Until the middle of 1922 the Reichsbank discount rate was kept persistently at 5 per cent, and although it was raised as high as 90 per cent by October, 1923, this rate was trivial in comparison to the prevailing rate of currency depreciation. It is hard to find any justification for the Reichsbank's policy up to the beginning of 1923, when it sacrificed everything else in order to finance the campaign of passive resistance against the Ruhr invasion. The position of the private banks was not very different. Whatever the explanation for their action—political motives, the necessity of keeping industry and commerce going, or failure to gauge the general situation correctly—the net result was that they simply presented a considerable part of their assets to their larger debtors. These debtors were chiefly the big industrialists. They undoubtedly exerted a great deal of pressure on the banks, especially on the Reichsbank itself, to continue that policy of lending and credit inflation which they themselves found so profitable. Insofar as Germany's own actions were responsible for the inflation, a good deal of the blame must therefore be laid on their shoulders. The man now most universally condemned in this respect is Hugo Stinnes, who died in 1924, but there were many others.

The financial position of industry as a whole was thus good during most of the inflation. If conditions were unstable, still profits were high, and they often amounted to several times the "real" value of the companies' total assets each year. Moreover, through their foreign connections, many firms were able to place a considerable part of their profits abroad, where further depreciation and confiscatory taxation could not touch them. This general state of affairs continued until the Ruhr invasion at the beginning of 1923. Even then a good many firms continued to make money until the stabilization at the end of the year brought a terrific reversal, and showed how artificial and unsound most of the inflation-period prosperity had been.

V. INDUSTRIAL PRODUCTION AND TECHNIQUE

In other respects the effects of the inflation on industry were less favorable, and conditions developed which in the long run proved to be a severe handicap. In the first place, the physical volume of production, despite high profits and even after allowing for the cessions under the Peace Treaty, remained almost continuously below the 1913 level. To some extent this decline was due to the disruption of extant commercial and industrial organizations produced by the terms of the Peace Treaty itself, but in largest part it came from the failure of the money incomes of the great majority of the population to keep pace with the rise in prices. The consequence was that the market for consumers' goods in Germany was severely restricted by sheer lack of domestic purchasing power. The principal activity of industry as a whole lay not in manufacturing for domestic consumption but in manufacturing for export, and in making producers' goods, plant and equipment, for itself.[1] When the stabilization later cut off a good deal of the export market many enterprises found themselves in

[1] The following table gives some idea of the volume of production during the inflation. The general production index is that compiled by Hugh Quigley in the *Deutsche Volkswirt* for Feb. 22, 1929. Although its base is narrow, it is the best available for the period. It should be borne in mind that the cessions under the Treaty deprived Germany of 19 per cent, by tons, of her 1913 coal production, of about 19 per cent of the steel production, and for industry as a whole an average of

desperate straits, for the buying power of the German public, crippled during the inflation, revived only very slowly.

In the second place, the general state of industrial technique deteriorated, both relative to the position of other countries and even in absolute terms. The war itself, and then the foreign-exchange depreciation, kept out almost all manufactured imports for nearly ten years, and the German industrialists were protected throughout the whole period from foreign competition in their own home markets. Inevitably, therefore, with a few exceptions they entirely failed to keep pace with technical progress in other countries. At the same time the very low rates of wages, measured relative to prevailing prices, removed all incentive to increase the mechanization of the industrial plants. There were few of the simpler processes which could not be performed more cheaply by hand than by additional machinery, and in many cases it even paid to shut down existing machinery and to use hand labor instead. This was especially true of light transportation within the plants, mechanical conveyor and assembly systems, and some of the simpler machine-tool operations. The same type of

about 15 per cent. For more complete data and sources see Appendices I, IV, V, and X, below.

Year	Coal Million Tons	Per Cent of 1913	Raw Steel Million Tons	Per Cent of 1913	General production index: 1913 = 100
1913	209.5*	100*	17.1*	100*	100
1919	137.5	66	6.9	40	53
1920	156.2	75	8.4	49	62
1921	163.6	78	9.9	58	78
1922	160.5	77	11.2	65	89
1923	88.7	42	6.2	36	56

* Pre-war boundaries, excluding Luxemburg.

situation prevailed in commercial life generally, in office management, and so on. Labor became a very small part of total costs. In addition, much of the new plant erected during the inflation later proved to be badly designed or badly laid out, and was incapable of production at modern standards of efficiency. The paradoxical result of these various conditions was that although business was active and employment good during most of the inflation period the total *output* was small, for industry was relatively inefficient. These same technical factors, together with the general social and political disorganization of the time and the literal underfeeding of the workers, also caused output per man to drop to levels far below normal. When the stabilization once more exposed Germany to world competition, she found that her industrial technique was years behind, and had to undertake a painful and costly reorganization.

The new buildings and machinery installed from 1919 to 1923, just referred to, gave rise to another problem. They were erected in desperation, as the only available way of investing profits safely and preventing them from melting away on the first new wave of inflation, and were literally life-savers at the time. But a considerable part of them, coming on top of earlier expansions undertaken to meet the terrific pressure of war demands, constituted an addition to the country's plant and productive capacity which sad experience subsequently showed to be wholly unneeded. They were built at a cost which in gold values was trivial, and despite their common technical inefficiency could therefore often compete successfully with much newer and better designed installations. Especially in certain divisions of the machinery and textile trades, the result has been a chronic state of overproduction, excess capacity,

and general inability to make money; a state which is
being overcome only gradually.

There appears to be no good estimate of the extent of
the new industrial construction during the inflation
period, and any attempt to compute it in terms of the
money values of the time is of course futile. The writer's
personal observation, however, indicates that between
20 and 25 per cent of the now existing equipment of
German industry was built or bought in the inflation
period. Even when this equipment was badly designed,
or was made out of date by later technical advances, it
usually entailed no loss to the companies themselves. In
many if not most cases its cost, translated into present
values, was actually less than its value today as sludge
and scrap iron! Moreover, the capital charges on all the
plant built before 1924 are far lower than they would be
had there been no inflation. Virtually all the loans made
before 1924 have been wiped out, and even that part
of the inflation-period extensions which was built out of
profits cost very much less in gold values than it otherwise would have. This operated to increase Germany's
competitive power in the world markets very materially
for a time. The extensive reconstruction and reorganization of the last three or four years has sent capital
charges up again, however, and it may be doubted if
she now enjoys any advantage over other countries in
this respect.

VI. INDUSTRIAL ORGANIZATION. THE COMBINES

THE inflation period thus had a great and enduring effect upon the financial and technical aspects of industry, and upon the volume of production. It also had a
pronounced effect, and in certain branches a spectacular one, upon the forms of industrial and commercial organization. It led to a mushroom-like growth of new

enterprises; to the recrudescence of an aggressive and even virulent cartel movement; and to the development of enormous combines and trusts.

Various factors contributed to the rapid formation of new enterprises. The disorganization produced by the war and the Treaty of Peace broke down many of the pre-war commercial relationships; and both this and the collapse of some of the older firms left gaps into which new enterprises could step. The chaotic and fluctuating state of prices also gave the shrewd trader innumerable opportunities to make a profit, while the low levels of wages, taxes, and capital charges provided a strong inducement to enter the manufacturing field, and anyone who could get the banks to lend him enough money was assured of prosperity. But the chief explanation was doubtless the fact that large numbers of clerks, officials, and others with more or less fixed incomes saw the value of what they received steadily declining as the depreciation progressed, and concluded that the only way to survive was to set up in business for themselves, where they might benefit instead of suffer from rising prices. Whatever the cause, however, the number of separate enterprises increased to four or five times what it had been before the war. The new concerns were mostly small and weak, and many were shaken out in the post-stabilization crisis, but even today the number is more than twice what it was in 1913.[1] This permanent increase, which is much larger than the increase in the volume of business to be done, must be regarded as an impairment of the general strength of German industry.

The inflation also had a stimulating effect on the cartel movement, though for rather different reasons.

[1] See Chap. VII, below.

In the United States the antitrust laws have made any formal cartel organization impossible, but in Germany the cartels have played an important part in the whole development of industry since the 1870's. They may be loosely defined as any association of independent enterprises formed to regulate for the common benefit either prices, production, markets, or the conditions of purchase or sale, or for two or more of these purposes. During the war the virtual elimination of competition for domestic markets, in consequence of the enormous volume of government orders, had relegated the cartels to the background, but in the inflation period they sprang to life again with a great increase in both numbers and strength, and enabled their members to exploit the situation. The abuses of which the cartels were accused, however, and which precipitated a storm of public protest, did not arise from any attempt to control prices as such, or even to limit production. They came from the cartels' violent efforts to pass all the risks of currency fluctuation on to the purchasers of their products by rigidly controlling the conditions of purchase and sale, a measure which in most cases indirectly but very effectively raised real prices as well. The continued public criticisms culminated at last in the passage of the Cartel Law of October 13, 1923, which provided for control and publicity,[1] but by that time the active influence of the cartels had already begun to wane. It is almost impossible to set up any accurate measure of the power of the cartels at different periods, and the wide differences in their scope and strength make mere numbers no guide. Using a rather strict definition of the word cartel, an official inquiry placed

[1] The empowering law was passed Oct. 13, 1923; the executive decrees were issued Nov. 2, 1923.

their number in 1905 at 385, while a semiprivate investigation placed it at over 1,500 in 1923, at the height of the inflation.[1] The increase in power of the cartels as a whole, however, was far less than this increase in numbers would suggest. It is doubtful if their effect on German economic life as a whole was really very much greater in 1923 than before the war, outside of the coal, iron, and potash industries. On the other hand, in these particular industries cartels were established under Federal law which in many respects were compulsory monopolies.

The dominant factor in German industrial organization during the inflation period, however, was not the cartels but the large combines and trusts. The cartels, although a device adequate for dealing with most of the problems of pre-war industry, were swept entirely out of their depth by the intricate, critical, and rapidly changing conditions of the post-war period. They lacked both the flexibility and the power requisite to meet the new situation. A compact and unified type of organization, under strong and even ruthless leadership, was the only possible solution, and the result was the swift development of numerous big combines of one form or another.[2] This development was the direct outgrowth of two conditions, produced both by the territorial cessions under the Treaty of Peace and by the inflation itself. One was the extreme uncertainty of the supply of raw materials, the other the disruption of the previously existing physical organization of production.

---

[1] See M. Metzner, *Kartelle und Kartellpolitik* (Berlin, 1926), p. 11.

[2] Two principal types should be distinguished: the *Konzern,* in which the constituent firms retain their individual legal identities, as in the old American trust; and the *Fusion,* or complete merger. For brevity, though at the expense of strict accuracy, the two will be lumped together here under the loose term "combine."

The territorial cessions had an especially crippling effect on the coal and steel industries. Germany was deprived not only of roughly half her iron ore and much of her coal, but also of nearly a fifth of her iron and steel manufacturing plants. Most of these plants, especially those in Lorraine, had been built as an integral part of the Ruhr industrial complex, and in surrendering them many of the Ruhr firms lost the equipment for carrying on one or more of the major operations in their own production sequence. One firm retained its coal mines and rolling mills, for example, but lost its blast furnaces; another retained those sections of its mills making finished products, but lost the antecedent sections; and so on. The remaining plants were compelled to combine extensively, both horizontally and vertically, in order to supplement one another's losses and even to keep going at all. In other branches of industry this situation was less acute, but a good deal of disorganization and consequent combination nevertheless occurred. The inflation itself, on the other hand, made the supply of raw materials extraordinarily uncertain. In consequence of the rapid fluctuations in the value of the currency, the purchase of raw materials and half-finished products in the open market became a pure gamble, while at the same time the general restriction and disorganization of production often led to a literal physical shortage. The larger enterprises, in order to live, found it essential to provide for a regular supply of materials by the control or outright purchase of the sources of supply themselves, and this led them to vertical expansion. The markets for finished products were often uncertain as well, and this led to expansion in the other direction. Finally, the peculiar credit conditions prevailing during most of the period from 1919 to the

end of 1923 made it easy for a combine, once successfully started, to borrow money for further expansion,
and thus to continue the process of growth in an ever
widening circle.

The movement was most pronounced in the coal-iron-
steel complex. The losses and disorganization produced
by the Treaty cessions, already commented on, provided
a powerful motive for combinations among the remaining firms in order to secure a continuous flow of production.[1] At the same time, the urgent need for assured
supplies of materials and for assured markets compelled
them to push still farther that process of vertical inte-
gration, which had already been well advanced before
the war. The more successful enterprises soon began to
expand horizontally as well. By the end of 1923 ten big
combines controlled between them half or more of the
total Ruhr production of coal, raw iron, and steel.
Of these the most spectacular was the Stinnes concern
(the Siemens-Rhein-Elbe-Schuckert-Union). Beginning with shipping, coal, and steel, during the inflation
Stinnes amalgamated with Siemens-Schuckert, one of
the largest electro-technical firms in the world; acquired
machine shops, paper mills, forests, banks, newspapers,
hotels, and a host of other enterprises; and developed
connections all over the world. This gigantic but amor-
phous structure had been built very largely, however,
on borrowed money and confidence. Taken as a whole,
it had no *raison d'être* as a production unit and little
real strength, and at the critical test of stabilization it
collapsed. The coal, iron, and steel units in the Stinnes
group, however, comprised by themselves alone a fairly

[1] The funds received from the Reich as compensation for the losses
under the Treaty, however, eventually enabled them to build new and
better plants in Rhenish Westphalia, and to that extent diminished
the organic necessity for combination.

well-balanced group, and with certain additions later became the nucleus of the great steel trust, the Vereinigte
Stahlwerke A.-G. Of similar character, though smaller,
was the combine between the Allgemeine Elektrizitäts
Gesellschaft, Krupp, and Otto Wolff. It too broke down
into its original units at the stabilization. The other consolidations in the coal and steel industry were smaller
and less ambitious, and despite heavy post-stabilization
losses most of them managed to survive.

Large combines were also effected in potash, copper,
lead, zinc, petroleum, and other basic materials. In the
finished-goods industries, on the other hand, the combines usually consisted only of smaller groups, which
aimed at specialization and horizontal expansion. Such
combinations appeared in machinery, hardware, textiles, paper, ceramics, foodstuffs, and so on. The chief
exception was in the chemical industry, where the
Badische Anilin was already laying the foundation for
the great Dye Trust, and where several other large
groups were formed.[1]

Such were the principal changes in industrial organization which the inflation period witnessed: a great
increase in the number of separate enterprises, a revival of the cartel movement, and an extraordinary development of large combines and trusts. These changes
were due in some measure to the territorial cessions under the Treaty, but chiefly to the wholly abnormal conditions produced by the inflation itself. When stabilization at last put an end to inflation, at the close of 1923,
a movement in the opposite direction developed. But the
number of enterprises is far greater even today than it
was before the war; the nature of the control to which

[1] On the whole combination movement in this period, see the publication of the Statistisches Reichsamt, *Konzerne . . . Ende* 1926 (Berlin,
1927), pp. 3 ff.

the cartel movement is subjected, if not the general
character of the movement itself, has been distinctly
altered; and the growth of the combines, though
checked for a time, still continues. The inflation period
thus left an enduring mark on the pattern of German
industrial organization.

VII. THE LOSS OF FOREIGN INVESTMENTS

THE war and the inflation had two other important consequences, one of which had the gravest effect on Germany's financial and industrial life. The first and more
serious was the loss of nearly all the pre-war investments
and other holdings abroad, the other was the so-called
"flight from the mark" during the inflation period. No
really accurate estimates have been or can be made of
these movements, but a glance at some of the commonly
accepted figures will indicate the general magnitudes
involved.

The total assets of Germany in foreign countries before the war are usually placed at nearly 28 milliard
marks (6.5 milliard dollars), of which 18 milliards were
in the form of securities. Of these assets, a considerable
part was in the Allied countries and the United States,
and was seized and liquidated at the outbreak of war.
Another part was in Austria-Hungary and Turkey,
and was wiped out by the collapse of those countries. A
third large portion, in the form of securities, was exported privately by German citizens during and after
the war to protect their funds from currency depreciation, taxation, and war risks, and to buy food and industrial raw materials; and most of this too was eventually lost in various ways. Of the original 28 milliards,
not more than 1 or 2 milliards at the most were left by
the end of 1923; and it is more probable that almost the
whole investment was wiped out. This enormous capital

loss, equivalent to nearly 10 per cent of Germany's entire estimated wealth in 1913, also had a disastrous effect on her international economic position. Before the war she had paid for the continuous deficit in her balance of trade largely with the income from her foreign holdings, and in part with the income from her merchant fleet, most of which was likewise now lost.[1] After 1923 the trade deficit continued to exist, but the means to meet it did not. She was compelled to borrow steadily, and the interest payments on the loans increased her annual international deficit still further.

The flight from the mark during the inflation period was even more spectacular, if less serious in its long-run consequences. As the currency depreciation proceeded everyone who was in a position to do so tried, despite stringent government regulations, to convert his wealth into foreign currencies, in order to protect it from further depreciation and from confiscatory taxation. At the same time thousands of foreign speculators, more optimistic than the Germans themselves, bought almost unlimited quantities of mark notes, bank deposits, securities, real estate, and other property. The net result was a very large transfer of assets from German to foreign hands. For a time it looked as though the currency depreciation were allowing the foreigners to gut the country of everything salable, but the stabilization produced a violent reversal. The mark notes, bank deposits, and securities became practically worthless, and most of the foreign speculators found that in place of profits they had a pure loss. American speculators seem to have been especially hard hit, and lost millions of dollars. Those who bought real estate, how-

[1] For data and sources on the loss of foreign investments see Appendix III, below; on the pre-war balance of payments, Appendix XIV.

ever, did not fare so badly. There were apparently times when a large modern house could be bought for the equivalent, in depreciated marks, of a ten dollar bill.

Germany, on the other hand, benefited in proportion as the foreigners suffered: one of the few gains the inflation conferred upon her. She used the proceeds of foreign speculation from 1919 to 1923 to meet the current deficit in her balance of trade, to make Reparations transfers, and to build up again a small volume of foreign holdings. At a rough estimate, from a half to two-thirds of these operations eventually cost her literally nothing. They were a free gift, of perhaps 10,000 to 12,000 million marks ($2,500 millions or more), from the involuntary philanthropists in other countries.[1]

VIII. SUMMARY

SUCH was the history of the inflation period, and such were the principal economic changes which followed in its train. For the largest part of the German population, it was a period of terrible suffering and despair. Through five long years they lived on the extreme verge of starvation, while their savings wasted away and their salable possessions went piecemeal to help to buy the next day's pittance of food. The prosperity of a small minority of industrial and financial leaders and speculators, and of the agriculturists, was no offset to the general distress and poverty. The health and strength of the present generation were permanently impaired, and its growth in numbers was retarded. The psychological consequences were also necessarily bad, and the morale of the people was lowest at precisely the time when the severest demands were placed upon it.

The inflation seriously weakened the economic

---

[1] For more detailed figures, see Appendix III, below.

strength of the country in other enduring ways. The distribution of wealth and income was violently altered, and in a way which greatly reduced the general buying power of the German people; vast amounts of money were spent in building plant and machinery, much of which had to be scrapped later; and the general state of industrial technique remained stagnant. Many of the new enterprises and giant combines which sprang up during the inflation were also inherently unsound, and at the stabilization collapsed into mere wreckage. Even after all allowance for the direct effects of the Treaty cessions, industrial Germany was far weaker at the close of 1923 than she had been at the beginning of 1919.

During and after the inflation period, it was not infrequently contended in foreign countries that the inflation itself had been a source of large gain to Germany. It is true that she benefited in so far as foreigners held marks or mark securities which subsequently became worthless, but this was only a trifling offset against the general aggregate of losses. With respect to the relations between one German and another, the apparent gains were purely bookkeeping entries. What one person or group gained another lost. If individual companies profited from the wiping out of their debts, the investors and other creditors who had held these debts obviously lost exactly what the companies gained. It is also true that the disappearance of these capital charges gave the German exporting firms an advantage in the foreign markets, but this advantage was in most cases only temporary. It was later offset, or more than offset, by the charges for the far-reaching technical reorganization and reconstruction which the great majority of firms were compelled to undertake after the stabilization. Against these gains, such as they were, must be placed the fact that for the country as a whole the general disorganization and instability which accompanied the currency depreciation produced a severe decline in the total volume of the national production, and therefore in the total real income of the people. Although business was active during most of the period, in the sense that the plants were working full time, and although profits were high, technical inefficiency and low output per man resulted in a *total* output which was far below normal. Despite the excessive prosperity of certain numerically small groups, the real income of the average German in these years was hardly two-thirds of what it had been before the war. To the poorer classes this decline meant desperate poverty and even starvation. By no stretch of the imagination can these changes be regarded as anything but a crippling blow to the country at large.

A good share of responsibility for the enormous individual suffering and national loss which the inflation produced must be laid at the doors of the contemporary German Government. The charge that it depreciated the currency deliberately is unfounded, but the measures it took to combat the inflation were weak and ineffective, and at the end both the Government and the Reichsbank cast all financial sanity to the winds in a desperate effort to combat the Ruhr invasion. It was a dramatic coincidence that the three men who were probably most responsible for the inflation catastrophe from the German side—Helfferich, the Finance Minister, Havenstein, Director of the Reichsbank, and the industrial capitalist Stinnes—all died within a few months of one another, in 1923 and 1924. The principal ultimate cause of the whole inflation catastrophe, however, was the terrific pressure exerted by the Allies to enforce impossibly large Reparations payments. Weakened by the war, and still more by the Treaty cessions, Germany was not physically capable of satisfying the Allied demands. The foreign exchanges collapsed, prices shot up, and the Government, in the endeavor to keep itself alive and to meet the Reparations payments, resorted to borrowing and to the printing press. In effect, through the combination of internal weakness and external pressure, it committed financial suicide.

CHAPTER III

THE DAWES PLAN AND RECOVERY

I. THE SECOND PHASE OF REPARATIONS

AT the end of 1923 Germany was still in desperate straits. The currency had been more or less stabilized for the moment by the virtual scrapping of the old money and the adoption of the Rentenmark, but the stabilization itself had produced a violent economic crisis. All the conditions and movements of the preceding period were abruptly reversed. Prices stopped rising and began to fall, an acute capital shortage developed, business came to a standstill, and unemployment shot up to nearly 30 per cent of the trade union membership. Most important of all, and despite the Ruhr invasion, the Reparations question was still completely unsolved. Germany had surrendered unconditionally, but not a French soldier had been withdrawn from the Ruhr itself, and there was nothing to prevent the Allies from taking additional and even more drastic steps to enforce Reparations payments. Had they actually attempted further coercion at that time, Germany would have been swept inexorably back into the pit of inflation.

But negotiations looking toward a solution of the Reparations problem were already under way, and soon led to the setting up of arrangements which both took Reparations out of the field of international politics for a number of years and gave Germany time to get back on her feet. During the period of passive resistance the German Government had begged for an international expert inquiry into the country's capacity to pay. The French and Belgians at first refused, but later reluctantly consented to the setting up of a committee with this general field of reference. On November 30, 1923, the Reparations Commission announced that two committees of investigation would be appointed. The committees were soon set up, and were both at work by the end of January, 1924.

The First Committee, under the chairmanship of General Dawes, was charged with an inquiry into the means of balancing the German budget and the measures to be taken to insure the stability of the currency. Its conclusions and recommendations, submitted on April 9, 1924, constituted the so-called Dawes Plan. After some delay, the Allies met in London in July to discuss the new proposals; the Germans were called in; and on August 16 the plan was approved. The documents were formally signed at the end of the month, and the Plan went into effect September 1, 1924. No attempt was then made to determine the total sum to be paid as Reparations, nor the duration of the payments, and the figure of 132 milliard marks (31.5 milliard dollars) which had been set at London in 1921 still remained the nominal claim of the Allies. But a workable schedule of annuities was established, beginning at a low level and rising for the first five years, and Germany was thus assured of an ample period for recovery. The signing of the London agreement was also followed by a partial evacuation of the Ruhr, the return of the political and industrial leaders who had been exiled, and the restoration of the Rhineland railways to German hands.

The Second Committee, under the chairmanship of the British financial leader, McKenna, was given what turned out to be a simpler and less important task. It was charged with estimating the value of the capital which had fled from Germany, and of considering means for bringing about its return. The report of the Committee, submitted at the same time as the Dawes report, called for no executive action. It estimated the amount of German capital then abroad at from 6,000 to 8,000 million marks (1,400 to 1,900 million dollars), and declared—quite correctly as it proved—that the restoration of financial and political stability would lead to its return. The return depended, in other words, on the success of the Dawes Plan.

II. THE DAWES PLAN

UNDER the terms of reference established by the Reparations Commission, as just pointed out, the Dawes Committee was nominally restricted to the questions of budget equilibrium and currency stabilization. It proved impossible, however, to divorce these questions from the problem of Reparations or from the existing difficulties of German industry and commerce, and before its labors were finished the Committee had of necessity dealt with almost every important aspect of German economic life.

The Plan which was the product of the Committee's investigation brought about four great changes in the position of Germany, changes which vitally affected both her internal situation and her relations with the rest of the world. Before describing the main features of the Plan itself, it will be helpful to point out the nature of these changes, since they place the Plan in its most significant light. First, and at bottom most important, a limited and reasonable schedule of Reparations payments was established, beginning at a small volume and reaching full size only after five years. As long as the Plan remains in force, the payments thus scheduled constitute the *total* charge which the Allies can impose.

They include not only Reparations proper, but costs of the armies of occupation and the various agencies of control and administration and the awards of arbitral commissions. Germany was thus protected from the drastic and excessive demands which had been the principal reason for her previous collapse. Moreover, her obligations were declared to be fulfilled when she had made payments to the proper authority *in Germany, and in German marks*. She was no longer required to pay in the currencies of the creditor Powers, and in this way was also protected from depreciating the foreign exchanges anew in the effort to make transfers abroad herself.

Second, with whole-hearted German coöperation, the Plan set up a workable system of internal taxes and other levies to provide funds for the scheduled payments. The German Government as such was thus relieved of current responsibility for meeting the charges as long as the Dawes Plan revenues should prove adequate. If their yield became insufficient to meet the payments, however, the whole budget of the Government itself was liable; and of course in the last analysis Reparations are a first charge on the total assets of Germany as long as the original provisions of the Treaty of Versailles remain in force.

Third, the limitation on the size of the current Reparations payments and the establishment of an autonomous revenue system to defray them left the Government free to finish the reorganization of its own finances, and to consolidate the momentary equilibrium of its budget. The stability of the budget was soon assured, and thereby provided the prime requisite for internal stability of the currency. With the national finances and the currency stabilized, the return of the general eco-

nomic life of the country to normal channels was then at
last made possible. In effect, the Dawes Plan thus did
for Germany what the pressure of the Allies and the
weakness and mismanagement of her own Government
had hitherto prevented her from doing for herself.

Finally, the establishment of the Plan and its obviously successful operation themselves constituted a
guaranty, non-formal and non-legal but completely
effective, of the soundness of Germany's currency and
credit. The psychological effect on the Germans themselves, after five years of constantly fluctuating money
and prices, was very great, but even more important was
the effect on foreign countries. Confidence in Germany
abroad, badly shattered during the inflation period,
soon revived. This in turn made possible the enormous
inflow of foreign funds which, especially in the earlier
stages, has played so vital a part in Germany's economic
recovery.

III. MAIN PROVISIONS OF THE PLAN

THE recent successful conclusion of the long-drawn-out
Paris Conference means that in all probability still another and more definitive arrangement will soon be set
up for the regulation of Germany's Reparations payments.[1] The Dawes Plan, however, constituted the
framework within which most of Germany's economic
life was conducted during the five critical years of recovery, and was the stepping stone without which the
recovery itself would have been almost impossible. Some
knowledge of its provisions is therefore essential.

The detailed machinery of the Dawes Plan itself has
often been described elsewhere,[2] and a brief outline is

[1] The recommendations of the Paris Conference are described in
Chap. XI, below.
[2] See especially H. G. Moulton, *The Reparations Plan* (New York,

enough here. The greatest part of the Plan, though under various disguises, was simply a system of taxation
under foreign supervision, and in part under foreign
control. The principal beneficiaries were of course the
creditor Powers, but the German Government itself also
participated extensively in the yields of certain of the
taxes prescribed. The payments were made directly or
indirectly to the representative in Germany of the creditors, the Agent General for Reparations Payments, and
were then distributed by him in the prescribed ways and
amounts. The payments themselves came from four
sources: the budget of the Reich, a transport tax, interest and amortization on industrial debentures, and
interest and amortization on railway bonds. The
budget charge was secured from certain sources of ordinary revenue which were placed under control, and
which were paid directly to the Commissioner of Controlled Revenues created under the Plan. These controlled revenues, all long familiar, were the customs receipts, the beer, tobacco, and sugar taxes, and the alcohol monopoly. They provided half of the normal or
standard annuity under the Plan, and have been so
productive that large and continuous repayments have
been made to the German Treasury.[1] The transport tax,

1924); and, for more critical if also less conventional treatment, R. C.
Long, *The Mythology of Reparations* (London, 1928). Detailed reference need not be made to the reports of the Agent General and of the
various commissioners and trustees set up under the Plan.

The Dawes Plan will be described here in the past tense, although it
is not anticipated that the recommendations of the Paris conference
will come into effect even retroactively before Sept. 1, 1929, at the
earliest.

[1] For the year 1928–29, the estimated total yield of the controlled
revenues was 2,760 million marks (*Report* of the Agent General, Dec.
22, 1928, p. 57). Of this, 1,250 million marks—only 47 per cent—was
required to meet the Reparations charge on the budget. The balance
reverted to the Federal Government.

which will probably now be incorporated in the ordinary Federal budget, was also in use long before the war. It is a tax on the gross revenues of the railway systems. It varies between 11 and 16 per cent for most passenger traffic, 7 per cent for freight traffic other than coal, and in the aggregate averages about 6 per cent of the total gross receipts. From 1924 to 1926 it was paid directly to the Agent General for Reparations Payments, and was hence in a sense also a "controlled" source of revenue, but since 1926 it has been paid direct to the Finance Ministry, which in turn paid the Agent General. It provided 11.6 per cent of the standard annuity under the Plan.

In addition to these explicit tax measures, revenue was secured from two sets of capital charges, one placed on German industry and the other on the railways. The charge on industry was formally justified by the fact that the pre-war indebtedness of the industrial enterprises had been virtually wiped out by the inflation, while many firms had also benefited in other ways. The total charge was set at 5,000 million gold marks (1,200 million dollars), to be represented by first mortgage bonds bearing 5 per cent interest and 1 per cent amortization yearly.[1] These payments formed 12 per cent of

[1] As the arrangement worked out, about three-quarters of the payments under the Industrial Debentures came from firms which themselves issued their own mortgage certificates, to the prescribed total of 5,000 million marks (representing 15.73 per cent of the assessed value of their business capital—land, buildings, machinery, etc.). The remaining quarter came from firms which did not issue certificates, but which were nevertheless obligated to pay. The individual mortgages were turned over to the Bank for Industrial Obligations, which administered them and which issued its own negotiable bearer bonds, plus a government guaranty, against them. The latter bonds were turned over to the Trustee for the German Industrial Debentures, who may sell them, though to date no sales have been made. See the report of the Trustee for Sept. 30, 1925, as well as later ones; and the reports of the Bank itself.

the standard annuity. The wiping out of the pre-war debts also justified the placing of a large capital charge on the German railway system. The charge was set at 11,000 million gold marks (2,600 million dollars), also carrying 5 per cent interest and 1 per cent sinking fund yearly.[1] These payments formed 26.4 per cent of the standard annuity. Altogether, including the transport tax, the railways thus bore 38 per cent of the Reparations payments in the standard year.

The railways themselves, formerly under government ownership, were converted into a joint-stock company under German management. 13,000 million marks of common shares were issued and turned over to the Government, as were to be the proceeds of the sale of 500 millions of preference shares, though these last have not yet been brought out. Another 1,500 millions of preference shares were set aside in the treasury of the company for subsequent sale, to provide funds for meeting debts, expansion, and so on.[2] The total capital of the company, including the mortgage, is thus 26,000 million marks (6,200 million dollars). A Trustee for the German Railways Bonds was created, and also a Commissioner for the German Railways. The railways thus remained government owned, but under private German management and semiofficial foreign supervision.

Such were the sources of revenue set up under the Dawes Plan. It was clear that Germany could not at once begin paying these sums in full, however, and the annual payments were therefore graduated from a total of only 1,000 million marks in the first year, 1924–25,

[1] The pre-war debt of the government railways was nearly 11,800 million marks. At present values, this is equal to 16,500 million marks. The new debt was therefore only two-thirds of the old one. See the Reichsverkehrsministerium publication, *Die deutschen Eisenbahnen 1910–1920* (Berlin, 1923).

[2] Nearly half of the preference shares are still unsold.

to the standard annuity of 2,500 millions (600 million dollars) in the year 1928–29. Moreover, in the first year a virtual moratorium was granted. The bulk of the payments for that year was derived from the proceeds of a foreign loan of 800 million marks (190 million dollars), floated by the German Government in November, 1924, with Allied and American coöperation.[1] On the other hand, in the expectation that eventually Germany would more than regain her former strength provision was made for an index of prosperity and of the value of gold, according to which the contributions from the budget might be adjusted after the year 1928–29.[2]

In addition, as the final safeguard for the structure, the Reichsbank was reorganized. It was given the virtually exclusive privilege of issuing notes,[3] and was to keep them on a stable basis in relation to gold. A gold coinage has not yet been created, but the Bank actually pays bar gold against its notes on demand, although not legally required to do so. It also serves, like any cen-

[1] The German External Loan 1924, bearing 7 per cent interest. It matures in 1949, unless previously redeemed, and is a first charge both on the payments under the Dawes Plan, and on all other assets of Germany included under the general charge set up by the Treaty of Versailles.

[2] The sources of the annuities have been as follows, in million marks:

	1924–25	1925–26	1926–27	1927–28	1928–29
German External Loan 1924	800	—	—	—	—
Budget of the Reich	200	250	410	500	1,250
Transport tax	—	250	290	290	290
German Industrial Debentures	—	125	250	300	300
German Railway Bonds	—	595	550	660	660
Total	1,000	1,220	1,500	1,750	2,500

[3] The Rentenbank notes are being steadily retired in favor of the Reichsbank issues, and at the end of 1928 amounted to only 8 per cent of the total circulation. Four private note banks also issue notes up to

tral institution, as the fiscal agent of the Government and as a banker's bank, establishing the official rate of discount. In addition, it acts as the depository for the Reparations payments. On the other hand, it was freed from all government control, and its advances to the Government, by which in the mechanical sense most of the earlier currency inflation had been brought about, were limited to a maximum amount of 100 million marks and to a maximum term of 3 months. All indebtedness of the Government to the Bank must be paid off by the end of each business year. Finally, its active management was left in private German hands, but under the supervision of a Board of which half the members, including a Commissioner, are foreign.

The framework of the Dawes Plan was thus an elaborate system for revenue collection, and for supervision and control. It was a system, however, which treated Germany's obligations as fulfilled when she had paid the specified sums to the Agent General *in Germany*, and in German currency. The problem of getting the proceeds into the hands of the creditor Powers still remained. Since the inception of Reparations payments under the Treaty, these payments had always taken two forms: deliveries in kind, and transfers in cash—that is, in foreign bills of exchange, foreign currencies, and gold. This double arrangement was continued, but with certain essential modifications. All contracts between producers in Germany and buyers in the Allied countries, which it was desired to handle as deliveries in kind, were

a fixed maximum total of 194 million marks, or 2.9 per cent of the present circulation. Coins form about 15 per cent. The balance, or about 79 per cent, is notes issued by the Reichsbank alone.

It should be observed that the legal name of the present currency unit is the *Reichsmark,* with the same value as the old mark ($0.2382). Except where necessary to distinguish, however, the shorter term *mark* will be used here.

now effectively if not formally brought under the control of the Transfer Committee. The contracts having passed through the appropriate machinery, the Agent General then paid the German exporter in marks pursuant to the terms of the particular contract, and out of the balance of the creditor Power involved, say France; and the French Treasury in turn received payment from the French importer in French currency. The whole transaction was thus conducted without the use of bills of exchange to make payment, and of course had no direct effect on the exchange rates.[1]

The sums paid the creditor Powers through deliveries in kind and other Reichsmark payments, however, have never equaled the total of the scheduled annual obligations, and since 1927 have amounted to less than half of them. The balance has had to be transferred in foreign currencies bought with German marks.[2] This situation obviously gave rise to the danger that, under adverse conditions, the effort to make such transfers would force up the price of the foreign currencies themselves, in terms of marks; in other words, that the transfers would depreciate the foreign exchanges, imperil the stability of the currency, and thus threaten a new inflation. To

[1] The Transfer Committee, discussed below, could also approve contracts which to some extent anticipated the current crediting of funds to the account of the creditor Power. The principal commodities making up the deliveries in kind have been coal, coke, dyestuffs, fertilizers, wood and wood pulp, construction materials, and machinery, but the range is wide. (Certain commodities are excluded; see the *Report* of the Agent General for Dec. 22, 1928, p. 24.) These contracts for deliveries in kind were viewed very favorably by both buyer and seller, despite the additional formalities necessary, since the credit conditions were excellent and prices usually satisfactory. The Allied governments have also been at pains to encourage the making of such arrangements. The effect on German industry has been to give it an export market of considerable size, in part non-competitive, much of which it would otherwise not have had.

[2] The sums actually paid to the Allies in the first four annuity years

guard against the danger, the Dawes Plan created a Transfer Committee operating under the chairmanship of the Agent General. The Committee was charged with the duty of regulating both deliveries in kind and transfers in foreign currencies, in such fashion as to protect the German exchanges and to assure the stability of the German currency itself. If it believed the exchanges to be in danger, it could at any time stop the flow of transfers and even of deliveries in kind, and could thus allow the Reparations payments received from the German

were transferred in the following forms, in million marks (see the *Report* of the Agent General for Dec. 22, 1928, p. 23):

	1924–25	1925–26	1926–27	1927–28
Deliveries in kind	414	658	617	725
Armies of Occupation and miscellaneous	208	102	82	71
Total transfers by Reichsmark payments	622	760	699	796
Cash transfers	—	71	259	468
Reparation Recovery Acts	180	243	290	351
Service of German External Loan 1924	78	97	91	90
Miscellaneous	13	5	43	34
Total transfers in foreign currencies	271	416	683	943
Total transfers effected	893	1,176	1,382	1,739

The total transfers actually effected were slightly less than the annuities received, the difference representing balances held by the Agent General. The proportion of deliveries in kind in the total has fallen steadily, from 70 to 46 per cent. Pure cash transfers, arising from exchange purchases in the open market, still form only 28 per cent of the total. As administered in recent years, the British and French Reparation Recovery Acts entailed a voluntary surrender by the German exporter (or more usually by a loose association of exporters) of the requisite amount of foreign exchange to the Agent General, who then effected payment to the corresponding creditor governments. This system permitted precise control over the *total* transfers to the creditors.

authorities—which were made only in German currency
—to accumulate. The necessity for this latter step has
not arisen on any important scale. If it had, under the
Dawes Plan provisions, the Reparations funds could be
accumulated to a total of 5 milliard marks, either kept
on deposit with the Reichsbank or invested in German
securities, or both. When that total was reached, further
payments by Germany were to be reduced to prevent
additional accumulation, and might even cease until
transfers to the creditor Powers could be begun again.
Finally, the German Government and the Reichsbank
were required to facilitate in every way the work of the
Committee in transferring funds and protecting the exchanges; and the Reichsbank could be requested to adjust its discount rate to promote these ends. The German authorities have given whole-hearted coöperation,
however, and until the spring of 1929 no major transfer
difficulties developed.

It may be remarked in passing that as long as the
Dawes Plan continues in operation, the much agitated
question of the possible priority of Reparations transfers over the service of private loans and other advances
to Germany is simply beside the point. The German
companies and governments which are indebted to private creditors abroad can bid up the exchange rates as
high as necessary in order to obtain foreign funds,
whereas the Transfer Committee is expressly restrained
from doing so. If the exchanges go materially beyond
the gold-export point, or even, in the judgment of the
Committee, reach merely a threatening level, Reparations transfers under the Dawes Plan automatically
stop: they have no priority. But this essentially temporary arrangement does not vitiate the ultimate claim
of the Allies, under the Treaty of Versailles, on all the

revenues and assets of the Federal and State governments. Reparations payments undoubtedly have an underlying legal priority over all private claims, a priority which might again become actively effective in the event of the termination of the Dawes Plan agreements unless some other similar arrangement were set up. How this difficult problem will be taken care of under the new agreements remains to be seen. At the date of present writing, it appears probable that the Treaty priority will be surrendered.[1]

The distribution of the receipts from Germany was effected under a rather complex arrangement. The first charge on all receipts was made the service of the German External Loan 1924. Then came certain other priorities, chiefly costs of administration of the various Inter-Allied Commissions, and then the shares of the creditor Powers themselves. These shares followed roughly the percentages agreed upon at the Spa conference of 1920: France 52 per cent, Great Britain 22, Italy 10, Belgium 8, others 8. They differed slightly in that they included allowances for and costs of the armies of occupation, for restitution, and so on. The United States was assigned 2¼ per cent of the Reparations receipts against awards and claims, but not to exceed 45 million marks a year (the sum actually received in 1928–29) ; and in addition got 55 million marks annually against army costs in arrears. The total American share was thus 100 million marks ($23,820,000) a year.

These were the major provisions of the Dawes Plan. Regarded as a working mechanism, the Plan was in essence little more than a system of taxation and tax administration, but it was a system equipped with elabo-

---

[1] See Chap. XI, below, on the transfer provisions of the new plan.

rate safeguards to assure its own successful operation.
Of the resulting revenues over one-third came directly
from the railways, one-ninth directly from industry, and
only a half from the remaining ordinary forms of taxation. Should the other prescribed sources of revenue
prove inadequate, the ultimate burden of meeting the
scheduled Reparations payments was placed directly on
the German budget; and should that in turn fail the
creditor Powers had, as their final security, the underlying charge on all the assets and revenues of the Federal and State governments established by the Treaty
of Versailles.

But the revenues have thus far proved more than adequate to meet the prescribed payments. The Dawes Plan
was so broadly conceived, and so well adapted to the conditions of German economic life, that no significant disturbance has resulted from its inception and operation.
The formal taxes it utilized had long been familiar, and
the yields demanded from them were moderate, while the
charges placed on industry and the railways were much
less than those which would now exist had the inflation
not wiped out a large proportion of their pre-war capital debt. Nor has the total burden placed on the German
economy proved excessive. As will be shown in a later
chapter, even the standard Dawes Plan annuity of
2,500 million marks, which is nearly 500 million marks
larger than the average annual payment contemplated
by the recent Paris Conference, amounts to less than
15 per cent of the present total cost of government in
Germany, and to less than 4 per cent of the present German national income. Whether even the smaller average
sum agreed on at Paris, *relatively* not very great but of
large absolute magnitude, can be continuously transferred abroad without impairing the productive ca-

pacity of the country is another question, and one which must be deferred. Up to the present time, however, and despite the bitter criticisms of certain German writers and politicians, the principal injuries which the Dawes Plan has actually inflicted—and they have not been great—have been psychological rather than economic. They have arisen from the natural general humiliation at being submitted to any system, however friendly in its execution, of protracted supervision and control by foreigners.

IV. THE CAUSES OF RECOVERY

THE supreme test and defense of the Dawes Plan lies in the history of Germany during the five years of its operation. Germany has recovered. Taking the country as a whole, she has more than made good the losses inflicted by the war and the inflation period, and in most branches of her economic life is at least as strong now as she was in 1913. The stabilization of the currency at the end of 1923 was followed by a severe crisis, but some months after the coming into operation of the Dawes Plan business began to revive, and in 1925 the general volume of industrial production for the first time drew near the pre-war level. The pace proved to be too fast, and a recession developed in 1926, but 1927 and the first part of 1928 witnessed a second rapid and much sounder expansion. Since the middle of 1928, partly because of uncertainty over the outcome of the recent Paris Conference, business has marked time and has even declined somewhat, but the average degree of activity is still high. The volume of industrial production is well above the 1913 level; most industrial firms, if not conspicuously prosperous, are nevertheless making money; and on the average the German population is at least as well off now as it was before the war, despite the continued suffering of large groups of the old aristocracy and the middle classes. The Government's budget has remained in balance, and the Reichsbank is once more one of the world's soundest institutions. Germany's general industrial strength is now greater than that of any other Continental country, and in a number of important lines she has even passed Great Britain, while her foreign trade is slowly but surely regaining its pre-war size. Finally, the scheduled Reparations annuities have been paid promptly and without difficulty.

The speed and comprehensiveness of this recovery are indeed phenomenal, especially when one recalls, what the Germans themselves are prone to neglect in discussing the present situation, the utter prostration and despair into which the country was plunged at the turn of 1923–24, less than six years ago. There are inevitably weak and even dangerous factors in the position today, and certain branches of economic life are still in serious difficulties, especially agriculture, but the structure as a whole is fundamentally sound. It is no literary exaggeration to describe Germany as the modern Phoenix. The question of how the recovery was brought about, how far it has gone, and what the present position really is, so far as concerns the principal branches of German industry, is the field of the subsequent chapters in this book. The substance of what has happened, however, can be described in a few words.

The setting up of the Dawes Plan alone naturally did not bring about economic recovery. It simply served to set up the preliminary conditions—removal of the Allied pressure, stabilization of the national finances and currency, and the restoration of general confidence —which were necessary to make recovery possible. The recovery itself was due to two principal factors. One was the so-called "rationalization" of German economic life, the other was foreign loans and other importations of foreign capital. Rationalization is the very broad term which the Germans have used to describe the comprehensive reorganization of industry, commerce, and even agriculture which has taken place in recent years, especially since the inflation period, and which is still going on. In industry this reorganization has entailed the adoption of more efficient ways of utilizing existing equipment, the installation of new and better machinery, and where necessary the construction of new buildings; the devising of more effective production schemes; adopting standardized patterns, classifications, and specifications wherever possible; improvement of administrative and commercial methods; and in some cases the regrouping of entire industries, by combination or otherwise, in order to concentrate production on the better plants, to eliminate the inefficient, and to stabilize general conditions. The purpose, in a word, has been to increase the aggregate efficiency of industry in every possible way. The measures taken have often been very drastic and comprehensive, and indeed it is not far from accurate to regard the changes effected in the last few years as themselves constituting a new industrial revolution. The net result has been a great gain for the German economy as a whole. The volume of production has been increased by over 40 per cent since 1924, costs have been lowered while wages have been steadily raised, and the great majority of the companies have been making money. At the same time the country's competitive power in the world markets has been reëstablished, and the volume of manufactured exports is steadily growing.

The second major factor in the recovery has been the

importation of foreign funds. After the stabilization the German firms were confronted with a desperate shortage of working capital. During the inflation most of them had been prosperous, and had been able to borrow when necessary, but the stabilization abruptly cut off the supplies of credit, and scaled down the value of funds on hand to negligible proportions. At 1,000,000,000,000 paper marks to 1 gold mark, these funds necessarily amounted to very little in real values. The companies got through the year 1924 by various temporary devices, but after the setting up of the Dawes Plan had opened the world capital markets, a flood of foreign borrowing began. The rationalization of industry, just referred to, also required vast amounts of new capital for machinery and other fixed plant. Germany was of course in no position to provide this money herself, and had to go to the foreign markets for it. Furthermore, the local governments had been starved for ten years. They desired to make all sorts of extensions and improvements, some purely ornamental but in largest part necessary, in their street railways, harbors, power plants, and other facilities, and they too therefore appeared as large borrowers abroad.

The result of all these demands was that from 1924 to the end of 1928 Germany imported between 18,000 and 19,000 million marks (4,400 million dollars) of foreign funds. Of this enormous sum, 6,800 millions were secured by floating long-term loans abroad; between 5,500 and 6,000 millions by the sale of domestic mark securities (chiefly German shares) to foreigners; and something over 6,000 millions by short-term credits.[1] Of the long-term loans, about 60 per cent was made

[1] These estimates are as of the end of 1928 and are gross. German purchases of foreign securities, grants of credits abroad, and so on,

to governments and semipublic enterprises. But the remainder of the loans, and nearly all of the other two items—that is, nearly three-quarters of the total—were advances made to private enterprises. In largest part they were therefore made, directly or indirectly, to German industry. These foreign funds provided Germany with the life blood to start her economic organism going again, and to undertake a far-reaching program of industrial expansion, but the picture also has its reverse side. The net payments for interest, dividends, and amortization now currently due to private individuals abroad amount to not less than 1,200 or even 1,400 million marks a year (over 300 million dollars). This is a heavy burden in itself, and constitutes a most unwelcome addition to the pressure on the foreign exchanges exerted by the Reparations transfers. In addition, the disproportionate size of the short-term debt places Germany in a peculiarly vulnerable financial position, for it exposes her to very large foreign demands on little or no notice.

But despite these and other weaknesses in the present position, the main foundations of Germany's recovery have been well laid and are sound. The extraordinary scope and rapidity of the recovery itself are at bottom explained by the fact that despite the war losses, the cessions under the Treaty, and the demoralization of the inflation period, most of the country's physical equipment for production was still in operation when

reduce the *net* capital imports for the period to between 14,000 and 15,000 million marks. The United States has been much the largest lender on long-term account, but a considerable part of the purchases of mark securities and of the short credits have come from European countries, especially Holland and Great Britain. Since Jan. 1, 1929, heavy withdrawals of foreign funds have been made. (See Chap. IX, below.)

the stabilization was at last achieved, and was ready for capacity output. Under the favorable conditions which the Dawes Plan set up, the remarkable will to work of the people at large and the skill and intelligence of the leaders made recovery inevitable.

CHAPTER IV

COAL, STEEL, AND POWER

I. INDUSTRIAL REORGANIZATION

NOT quite six years have now elapsed since the end of the inflation. In that relatively short period of time many branches of German industry have been completely reorganized, and the complexion of the country's industrial life has been materially changed. Old plants have been scrapped and new ones built, old machinery has been put to more effective use, and new equipment installed; administrative and commercial methods have been revised and improved; and most of the companies have increased their efficiency and their earnings. Germany is getting a much greater volume of industrial products now than she was four or five years ago, and despite the steady increase in money wages she is getting most of them at lower prices.

The reorganization was not accomplished in a moment, nor was it due simply to a disinterested desire for progress on the part of the industrial leaders. It is principally explained by two facts, both referred to elsewhere. In the first place, the territorial cessions under the Treaty of Versailles cut off important sections of German industry, and the Armistice and the Treaty also required the delivery of large quantities of equipment, rolling stock, shipping, and so on. This made necessary both physical replacement and reorganization of the remaining industrial units on an extensive scale if anything like the pre-war volume of production was to be secured. In the second place, from 1914 to 1924 Germany was almost completely sheltered from the competition of foreign imports, first by the war and then by the inflation, while the inflation also gave German exports an enormous advantage in markets abroad. This advantage was maintained in the face of a serious decline in the average quality of the exports. At the same time the chaotic state of internal affairs made it almost impossible for the companies, except in a few branches, to achieve or even to think much about technical progress: the one great problem was the problem of staying alive. When the end of the inflation once more exposed Germany to foreign competition, she found that in many lines her industrial technique was much below the levels prevailing in other leading countries. Hers had remained virtually stagnant for ten years, while theirs had forged ahead. If she was to keep from being swamped with foreign manufactures, and still more if she was to regain her pre-war export markets, a thorough-going reorganization of the whole industrial machine was obviously necessary, and a drastic improvement in the quality of the products.

This process of reorganization and improvement, together with the simplification and standardization of patterns, specifications, forms, bookkeeping, and so on, is what the Germans themselves have described as rationalization.[1] In American parlance, it is nothing other than the endeavor to increase efficiency in every possible way—the efficiency of the worker, the plant, the industry, even of the country as a whole. In attempting to judge the merits and results of rationalization a good deal of caution is necessary, however, especially on the part of American students. The model for much of Germany's industrial reconstruction has been the United States, and American machinery as well as American

---

[1] Also see the section on rationalization in the next chapter.

methods have been imported on a large scale. But it is entirely impossible to apply American standards of efficiency directly to German conditions, and to make unqualified comparisons. The much lower level of German money wages, the smaller average volume of production, and the relatively high cost of capital have the result that it does not pay to mechanize nearly as extensively in Germany as in the United States. An elaborate labor-saving machine which is a model of technical efficiency from the American point of view, and ideally suited to American conditions, may be absolutely unable to pay for itself in Germany, and may therefore be extremely *inefficient* in the commercial sense. This fundamental difference between the two countries, which many German industrialists discovered only by costly experience, should always be borne in mind. It affects the whole character of German industrial life, makes direct comparisons with American conditions very difficult, and necessitates the application of quite different standards of judgment.

In this and the next chapter we shall trace the progress and results of rationalization in the six principal branches of German industry, as far as the available information permits, and then shall make an appraisal of the present position. These six branches are coal, iron and steel, machinery, the electro-technical industry, chemicals, and textiles. Taken together, they constitute roughly half of the total industry of Germany. About 16 per cent of the population of the country may be described as dependent on them; they employ over a third of all the workers in industry; they represent nearly half of the total share capital of the German incorporated companies, and two-thirds of that of the industrial companies alone; and their output now constitutes nearly 40 per cent of the total annual production of the country. They are thus a large and of necessity fairly characteristic section of Germany's aggregate economic life. They are also the principal exporting industries, and produce nearly 50 per cent of the value of all German exports.

The following table indicates the importance of the six divisions in industry as a whole. Figures are in percentages of all industry.[1]

Division	Workers (Census of 1925)	Persons dependent on (Census of 1925)	Share capital (Balance sheets of 1926–27)
Mining (about 70 per cent coal)	5.4	9.2	21.8
Production of iron, steel, and other metals	3.4	5.4	4.7
Machinery, etc.	10.2	10.1	10.5
Electro-technical industry	3.1	2.8	4.8
Chemicals	2.5	3.0	15.5
Textiles	9.7	7.2	7.4
Total percentage of *all* industry	34.3	37.7	64.7

II. COAL. PRODUCTION AND EXPORTS

THE two great foundations on which the industrial life of Germany have been built are coal and iron. Before the war Germany had much the largest coal reserves in Europe, and also the largest reserves of iron ore. The iron deposits were less than 150 miles from the principal coal basin, and this happy natural conjunction was at once the groundwork and the motivating force for her extraordinary industrial development after

[1] Share capital is for *Aktien-Gesellschaften* with shares listed on the stock exchanges. The low figures here for iron and steel are due to the fact that—as in mining—many companies are not organized under this form of enterprise. It is, however, the only form on which data are obtainable. It embraces about half of the total of German industry. The value of the output of the six industries listed was about

1870. Then came the war and the territorial cessions under the Treaty of Versailles, and completely disrupted the situation. Three-quarters of the iron and over a third of the coal were ceded to France and Poland, and the character of the country's whole industry was abruptly changed. The particular coal reserves surrendered, however, proved in the aggregate to be the less valuable part of the deposits, and coal production from her own mines is still the mainstay of Germany's industrial activity.[1]

The changing fortunes of the German coal industry can be measured fairly accurately by the changes in the volume of production. In the decade before the war the annual coal output had been increasing steadily, by from 5 to 8 per cent a year, and in 1913 had reached a maximum of 190 million tons. During the war, with most of the export market cut off, the output dropped

25,000 million marks in 1928 ($6,000 millions), whereas the total national production in that year was around 65,000 million marks.

The relative importance of industry as a whole in the economic life of the country is shown by these figures from the census of 1925, also in per cents:

	Persons dependent on	*Workers alone*
Agriculture, forestry, fishing, etc.	23.0	18.0
Industry and handicraft	41.4	67.7
Commerce and transportation	16.9	10.0
Other occupations	9.6	4.3
Without occupation	9.1	—
Total population	100.0	100.0

The data used here are from the *Statistisches Jahrbuch*, 1928, pp. 21–24 and 448.

[1] This coal varies widely in quality, but the average comes between the American anthracite and bituminous grades. Most of it, especially the Rhenish-Westphalian coal, makes excellent coke, although the Saar coal, coming from the mines surrendered to France, is too soft to make good blast furnace coke, and the coke it yields must be mixed with other grades. Germany has no real anthracite coal.

to an average of about 155 millions; and in consequence of the disorganization caused by the Armistice and the Revolution it fell to 117 millions in 1919. Then came the artificial stimulus of the currency depreciation, together with the reopening of some of the old export markets and the inauguration of Reparations deliveries of coal, and despite the cession of large coal-mining areas under the Treaty the production climbed to over 130 millions annually for the next three years. This revival was abruptly checked, however, by the Ruhr invasion, and in 1923 the output fell abruptly to 62 millions. This was less than one-third of the 1913 production, and was the low point for the whole period. The ending of the inflation and the gradual withdrawal of the Ruhr occupation then brought about a second and much sounder revival. Since 1924 production has again climbed steadily, and is now above 150 million tons a year. This figure is still 20 per cent below the 1913 level, it is true, but it is distinctly greater than the 1913 production *in the present area.*[1] Germany is now getting nearly 9 per cent more coal a year from her present coal basins than these same basins yielded in 1913.

[1] The annual production of coal (*Steinkohlen*) has been as follows in million tons (data from the *Statistisches Jahrbuch*):

1913, old area	190	1920	131
1913, new area	141	1921	136
1914	161	1922	130
1915	147	1923	62
1916	159	1924	119
1917	168	1925	133
1918	158	1926	145
1919	117	1927	154

1928 (estimate) 152

Including lignite, Germany produced 16.6 per cent of the world's coal in 1913, but only 14 per cent in 1927: while her aggregate production declined, that of other countries increased somewhat.

The known and probable coal reserves of the principal industrial

The volume of exports has fluctuated more widely than production itself, but the general movement is not dissimilar. In 1913, net exports totaled 24.1 million tons. During the inflation they were much below the pre-war level, and in 1924 dropped to under 6 millions. A steady recovery then began, however, and in 1926, under the influence of the English coal strike, they climbed to 35 million tons—half again as much as in 1913. This expansion was of course abnormal, but even today net coal exports, if Reparations deliveries be included, are only 10 or 12 per cent below the 1913 level. If allowance is made for the loss of coal fields under the Treaty they are some 12 per cent higher, and they take about the same fraction of the total domestic production now as before the war: 11 to 14 per cent on the average. Indeed, the principal new difficulty which the German coal exports have had to face, and one which is particularly exasperating to the Germans themselves, is the severe competition of former German coal fields

countries before the war were divided as follows, in per cents (excluding lignite):

United States	45.0
Germany	9.3
Great Britain	4.3
France	3.7
Other	37.7
World	100.0 (7,383,148 million tons)

The Treaty cessions reduced Germany's figure to 6 per cent. The surrendered areas had produced 28 per cent of the German coal in 1913. Of this ceded production, 61 per cent went to Poland, 33 to France, 6 to Belgium. See F. Fech, *Die Kohlenvorräte der Welt* (Stuttgart, 1917), pp. 22–23, 71; W. Hoffman, *Der deutsche Bergbau* (Wirtschafts-Jahrbuch, 1928/29), p. 442; A. Ströhle, *Von Versailles bis zur Gegenwart* (Berlin, 1928), p. 64; Guy Greer, *The Ruhr-Lorraine Industrial System* (New York, 1925), *passim*.

For a summary table giving the significant general data on the industry, see Appendix IV, below.

which were ceded to other countries under the Treaty of
Versailles. This is particularly true of Poland. Working
with very cheap labor, and getting the coal largely from
what had been German Upper Silesia, Poland has captured many former German markets in Scandinavia and
southern and central Europe, and even exports to England.[1] This situation, in combination with the severe
pressure to export which has frequently been operative
in other producing countries, has made the German markets abroad much smaller on the average than they
would otherwise be.

The physical volume of production and exportation
of the coal industry, although still somewhat below the
1913 level, is thus distinctly higher than the pre-war
volume in the present boundaries. The value of the output has increased even more. In 1928 it stood at nearly
2,400 million marks (570 million dollars). This is 11
per cent higher than the aggregate 1913 value in the
old boundaries, and 44 per cent higher than the value of
the 1913 output in the present boundaries. The increase
in value is in part due to the increase in the volume of
production itself, but about three-quarters of it comes
from the rise in coal prices since 1913, amounting on
the average to about 32 per cent. On the other hand,

---

[1] Exports of German coal are now about 5 times as large as imports. The principal export markets are Holland, Italy, France, Belgium; together they take over 80 per cent of the total exports. (See
Appendix XIV, below.) *Net* exports, including Reparations deliveries, were as follows:

	Million tons	*Million marks*
1913 (old area)	24.1	312
1924	5.8	—
1925	14.9	—
1926	35.2	755
1927	21.6	494
1928 (estimate)	16.5	370

however, this rise is less than the rise in prices at large in Germany, for with 1913 as 100 the general whole-sale price index now stands at about 140. In other words, coal is cheaper now relative to other commodities than it was before the war.

To repeat, the German coal industry is now produc-ing about 9 per cent more coal than was secured from the same area in 1913, and at a price which is some 6 per cent lower in terms of other commodities. The gen-eral economic effectiveness of the industry has therefore increased about 15 per cent in the present boundaries (although relative to the larger pre-war boundaries and the production in them, the decrease in total output has entailed a loss in aggregate effectiveness of about 15 per cent).[1] This gain, though not spectacular, is solid, and is really much greater than these figures taken alone

---

[1] The conception and the measure of "effectiveness" for an in-dustry as a whole are of course open to debate. What is meant here is that since output is greater by 9 per cent than in the same area be-fore the war, and prices 6 per cent lower relative to other commodi-ties, the gain to the country from increased output and decreased real cost combined is about 14 per cent, as follows: If Q_1 be output in 1913, Q_2 output in 1928; Pn the average wholesale price level in 1928, and P_2 the price of coal in 1928; all measured with 1913 taken as 100; then the relative effectiveness in 1928 is given by $\dfrac{Pn}{P_2} + \dfrac{Q_2}{Q_1} - 1$; and the amount of the change in relative effectiveness is this sum minus 1. Here we get:

$$\frac{140}{134} + \frac{109}{100} - 1 = 1.13\frac{1}{2}; \text{ minus } 1 = +0.13\frac{1}{2},$$

or roughly 14 per cent. At capacity output, say around 225 million tons, the gain would be as high as 65 per cent.

Relative to production in the pre-war boundaries, however, the present output is lower by 20 per cent, with the result that the effec-tiveness of the present industry is less than that of the aggregate in-dustry in the old boundaries by about 15 per cent. At capacity pro-duction, the increase in effectiveness would be only about 25 per cent.

would indicate. German coal-producing capacity is now about 50 per cent in excess of the present demand, and a considerable expansion in current production could take place with little or no addition to the existing plant. Should the increase appear, costs per ton would also fall materially.

III. MECHANIZATION AND CONCENTRATION

THIS increase in actual and potential efficiency has come from two principal sources. One has been the increased mechanization of the mines themselves. The other is the steadily growing concentration of production on the better mines, and the regrouping of the shafts into more effective production units.

In their attempts to increase the mechanization of the mines the German producers have encountered serious obstacles directly due to the geological conformation of the deposits. In the American coal beds much of the coal lies in broad and nearly horizontal seams which may be from 10 to 20 feet or more in height, and therefore almost ideally adapted to the use of machinery. In Rhenish Westphalia, on the other hand, which is the principal German coal area and which contains the Ruhr coal-iron-steel district, the conditions are relatively bad. The seams vary in height from 3 to 12 feet or more, but a large proportion average only about 6 feet. Moreover, instead of lying flat, the enormous pressure of the geological disturbances in post-carboniferous eras has forced them into every conceivable shape. They run up and down, twist from side to side, sometimes drop almost vertically for a hundred feet or more, and have many faults in the geological structure. The coal often stops abruptly at a blank wall of rock, and the puzzled miner discovers it again only some scores of feet above or below in the twisted mass. Finally, a considerable part of it is not "clean" coal. In a typical Ruhr seam altogether 6 or 7 feet high, there may be 18 inches of coal, 2 or 3 inches of black shale, then 18 inches more of coal, and so on to the top. In Silesia, where the other principal deposits lie, the seams are often even thinner, though those actually worked average over 6 feet.

Mechanical coal mining under such conditions obviously presents great and often insuperable difficulties, and in some seams hand mining is still the cheapest procedure. Nevertheless an average of from four to five times more machinery is used in the mines now than in 1913. The geological formation often makes the employment of the large mechanical coal cutters—saws, scrapers, and so on—a physical impossibility, but the lighter tools, such as pneumatic hammers and electric drills, are used extensively. The greatest gains, however, have come in the organization of the transportation of the coal within the mine itself, from the coal face to the pit head. In typical Ruhr mines a system of shaker screens takes the coal from the face to the central galleries, where it is collected by networks of narrow-gauge electric railways and is then moved by them to the main shaft. The loading of cars on the elevators is semiautomatic, and the elevators themselves operate at high speed. Coal-breaking and grading at the surface are also almost entirely mechanical, though no satisfactory way of separating out the black shale rock by machinery has yet been devised. In the better mines, from the time the coal leaves the mine face until it is in railway cars ready for shipment it is never touched by a human hand. By the end of 1927 over 85 per cent of the Ruhr coal was being mined by machinery, and only 15 per cent by hand.[1]

The other great factor responsible for the increase in efficiency of the coal industry has been the regrouping of the mines into a smaller number of production units, and the actual shutting down of a good many shafts. This process has usually reduced operating overhead, and has permitted production to be concentrated on the better seams. A better average of mining conditions has thus been secured, and the shifting of much equipment from the closed shafts to the ones kept running has frequently made it possible to operate more machinery from a single pit head, yet with little increase in costs. In 1913 there were 284 producing units (*Betriebe*, consisting of two or more shafts) in the present territory of Germany. By 1923, under the influence of inflation period expansion and in the face of a declining total output, the number had risen to 384. Then came the stabilization and the consequent necessity for thorough-going reorganization, and by 1927 the number had been reduced to 303—little more than in 1913, and a decrease of 21 per cent since 1923. In the Ruhr alone, some 91 shafts were closed in the years after 1923, and about 20 per cent of the Ruhr shafts which were operating in 1918 have been closed in recent years. For the country as a whole, the actual output *per unit* is now about 6 per cent higher than the 1913 output in the present boundaries, and capacity output is very much greater.

Considerable savings were also effected by the outright combination of firms with one another. Most of

[1] *Die deutsche Bergwirtschaft,* p. 51. For partial estimates on the increase in mechanization since 1913, see E. Ledermann, *Die Organisation des Ruhrbergbaues* (Berlin, 1927), p. 251; and *Die Wirtschaftskurve,* 1926, p. 296.

the larger enterprises involved in these combinations were engaged in iron and steel production as well, however, and it will therefore be convenient to postpone discussion of this question until we come to the steel industry itself.

The two principal forms which the reconstruction of the coal industry has taken in the period since the war, and especially since the inflation, were thus a four- to fivefold increase in the average amount of machinery used; and a decrease in the number of production units, relative to the high point in 1923, by over 20 per cent. The most striking measure of the gain which this reconstruction has brought is the increase in the output of coal per man per shift. Although the average working day is now only about two-thirds as long as it was before the war, in the Ruhr district output per man per shift rose from 0.943 tons in 1913 to 1.132 tons in 1927, or by 19 per cent. If one makes a rough allowance for the shortening of the working day, the increase amounted to something like 40 or 45 per cent (figures for total laborers, excluding coke and by-product plants). This shortening of the work day has been partly offset by transporting the workers from the shaft to the coal face by railway and in other ways, so that the decrease in actual working time probably averages not over 15 to 20 per cent, instead of 30 to 35 per cent. Indeed, one mining engineer estimated for the present writer that whereas a typical first-class Ruhr mine with two shafts produced 2,000 tons a day before the war, the output is now 4,000 tons.

IV. FINANCIAL RESULTS. PRESENT STRENGTH

IN spite of this great gain in technical mining efficiency, however, to date the companies themselves have not se-

cured anything like commensurate financial benefits. In
part this is due to the fact that the physical reorganization and mechanization of the mines and the shutting
down of inefficient shafts have been very costly, and
have burdened the units kept in operation with heavy
capital charges. The chief reason, however, has been the
steady increase in wages and salaries. Wage rates in
coal mining, as in other branches of German industry,
have risen on an average of over 50 per cent since 1913;
and the sum paid out for wages and salaries together
has risen, per man, by nearly 30 per cent. This increase
has been enough to offset most of the gains from the increase in technical efficiency. Indeed, the mine owners
declare that nearly all the benefits from rationalization
have gone directly into the pockets of the workers, a
complaint not without foundation. Despite the extensive
adoption of labor-saving devices, wages and salaries now
take a slightly larger share of the value of the total
product than they did before the war: 53 per cent in
1913, and 56 per cent in 1927. Moreover, government
regulation of the industry has prevented various increases in coal prices which might have offset these conditions. Between the Government on the one side and
the trade unions on the other, the mine owners have
been in a rather awkward situation.

The present general financial position of the companies themselves is very difficult to assess, chiefly for
sheer lack of data. Many of the companies are organized
in legal forms which do not require the publication of
balance sheets or other information; and the most important companies are not merely mining concerns
alone. They are usually either so-called "mixed" enterprises also producing iron and steel, or are engaged in
the chemical conversion and utilization of coal, or some-

times both; and nearly all of them also have plants for handling coke and its commoner by-products. The inadequacy of the ordinary balance sheets makes it almost impossible to separate the pure coal-mining operations from the companies' aggregate finances. A recent semiofficial report declares, it is true, that they are making inadequate allowance for depletion charges, and that they are probably losing money outright on their mining operations.[1] The number of firms investigated was very small, however, and the report is open to other criticisms. Apart from this investigation, the general evidence does not indicate that the coal enterprises as a whole are in financial straits. Earnings are fairly good, and although average dividends are low,[2] a good deal of new construction and expansion is now going on. The companies also continue to appear as borrowers for productive purposes in the long-term capital markets.

Another factor bearing on the financial position of the companies, as well as on the organization of the industry as a whole, is the so-called partial "socialization" of the coal mines under the law of 1919. In practice, this socialization has meant little more than the compulsory combination of all coal producers in territorial cartels for the purpose of regulating prices and production.

---

[1] Prof. Schmalenbach, *Gutachten über die gegenwärtige Lage des Rhein-Westfalischen Steinkohlenbergbaus* (Berlin, 1928). A minority report was also submitted by one of the members of the investigating committee, entirely disagreeing with the pessimistic conclusions of the majority.

[2] In 1925–26 the dividends paid by the incorporated companies (*Aktien-Gesellschaften*) averaged 1.86 per cent of the total nominal capital; in 1926–27, 4.29 per cent (*Statistisches Jahrbuch*, 1928, pp. 446 ff.). Later complete figures are not yet available, but most of the leading companies have maintained or increased their dividends since the latter year. See the latter part of this chapter for a general summary of the financial position of the coal and steel companies.

The cartels are simply an extension of those existing before the war. The principal one is the Rhenish-Westphalian Coal Syndicate, which is dominated by the five or six biggest "mixed" coal and steel enterprises. This cartel was threatened with complete collapse in 1925–26. Overproduction had led to the accumulation of large stocks, which could not be sold without cutting prices and thus probably breaking up the cartel, but the situation was saved at the last moment by the protracted English coal strike of 1926. The resulting European shortage permitted the exportation of the German surplus at profitable prices, and the cartel was rehabilitated. Since then production and stocks have been kept within bounds, and the cartel has not again been imperiled. The cartels in the other districts are all much smaller and less important.[1] The prices of the coal are themselves fixed by the cartels, subject to the approval of a Federal Coal Council on which labor and the consumers are also represented, and of the Federal Minister of Economics. While this arrangement has prevented various increases in price which the mine owners wanted, the relative stability of prices and production which the cartels insure has undoubtedly left the mine owners with a net gain.

Indeed, it is commonly asserted in anticartel circles that the more efficient mines make unduly large profits, and that they are really capable of supplying the entire demand themselves at much less than the prevailing levels of prices. The cartel system allows production only according to specified quotas (which can be sold,

[1] On the coal cartels, see R. K. Michels, *Cartels, Combines and Trusts in Post-War Germany* (New York, 1928), Chap. 6; Ledermann, *op. cit.;* and H. R. Seager and C. A. Gulick, *Trust and Corporation Problems,* now in press, of which Professor Seager has very kindly let me consult the relevant portions in proof.

however, to other enterprises), and by preventing prices from falling it of course keeps the poorer mines going. The critics of this *régime* declare that under free competition prices would drop, the poorer mines would go bankrupt, only the more efficient mines would be left, and the whole industry would be in a better position. But the experience of the potash industry, as well as earlier chapters in the history of the coal industry itself, make it at least uncertain that this desirable result would follow. A bankrupt coal mine is still a coal mine, and after bankruptcy has reduced its capital charges it can often produce more cheaply than the technically more efficient installations. The outcome of free competition might well be simply a period of price cutting, general disorganization and distress accompanied by severe loss to investors, and at the end the formation, in self-defense, of new and perhaps still more objectionable cartels. The case for free competition in the exploitation of natural resources is far from clear. Nor is it conclusively established that the better mines are really making undue profits. The present system undoubtedly has serious drawbacks, notably the lack of adequate and clear public accounting in the "socialized" enterprises, but it is doubtful if any other general type of system would be more advantageous for the country at large.

Taken as a whole, the German coal industry must be judged to be in a fairly strong position today, despite the frequent expressions of pessimism which emanate from it. The actual output is now some 9 per cent greater than the output secured from the present coal areas before the war, and could be increased by nearly half without substantial additions to the existing equipment; the mines have been extensively reorganized and mechanized; the general level of technique is distinctly higher than the average in England or even in the United States; and most of the companies, if not excessively prosperous, are once more making money. A few big enterprises dominate the industry, and their organization in cartels which virtually constitute a legal monopoly makes the industry itself a strong and centralized unit.

The difficulties which still face the operators are hence not those of production and organization, but of markets and of labor. The domestic market for coal is wholly inadequate to take care of the potential output, and the export market is limited. Abroad, German coal meets with heavy competition from England and Poland, which even invade the German markets, and the cessions of coal basins to other countries under the Treaty have automatically cut off another large section of the export demand. At home, the coal has encountered even more serious competition from lignite, now the principal fuel in many of the big central electric power stations, and to some extent from water power. What is hardly less important, recent advances in thermal engineering have reduced the amount of fuel necessary to produce one horsepower by a quarter to a third, relative to the pre-war position, and in some cases even more. The consequence has been a still further restriction of the market for coal. The aggregate result of these conditions is that the net domestic consumption of coal in the present boundaries of Germany has increased only 6 per cent since 1913, and offers little promise for rapid expansion in the near future. That rate of growth is of course entirely insufficient to keep the industry in a progressive and prosperous condition, while at the same time the attempt to offset the limitations on the market by mechanizing the mines and thus lowering costs has now gone almost as far as is possible in the present general state of industrial technique.

In addition to these difficulties, the industry is faced with a continuous and more or less successful effort on the part of labor to raise wages. Since the margin of profit is not great, each new wage increase usually means that the mines must endeavor to raise prices in self-protection. But more frequently than not the Government has refused to allow price increases, and in consequence profits have fallen. Moreover, even when the desired increases are granted the resulting higher level of prices necessarily restricts the possible markets still further, especially those abroad, and this again limits, if it does not actually reduce, the current rates of profit. One is therefore forced to conclude that although the actual position of the industry today is good enough, its prospects for the future are not very encouraging. The prevailing German pessimism on the subject is not entirely without foundation.

V. COKE AND COKE BY-PRODUCTS

NEARLY all of the large coal mines also have their own coking and by-products plants. These plants have been a fruitful source of profit, and have often enabled the companies to show substantial earnings on their aggregate operations even when the coal mining itself was being carried on with little profit or at an actual loss. Before the war the coke ovens took a third of the total domestic consumption of coal in Germany, and produced nearly 32 million tons of coke a year even in the present boundaries. During the war and the inflation, however, output dropped heavily, and although it has since recovered most of the loss, the average is still below the

1913 level. It again stood at over 32 million tons in 1927, but in 1928 was only 28 millions (preliminary estimate). About a fourth of the coke is now exported, as against only 10 per cent before the war. Nearly two-thirds of the exports go to France, Belgium, and Luxemburg, a situation which reflects the dependence of the French post-war iron and steel industry on German coke supplies.[1] The total value of the coke output, on the other hand, has increased somewhat because of the 20 per cent rise in coke prices since 1913.[2] In addition, the total value of the by-products secured from coking is now about 45 per cent higher. Despite the decline in the average physical volume of coke production, the gross income of the coke and by-products plants is therefore 12 to 14 per cent greater now than it was before the war in the present boundaries.

This gain has come partly from the increased market for certain by-products, especially benzol and coke-oven gas,[3] but chiefly from the enormous recent ad-

[1] See Appendix XIV, below.

[2] Output of coke is 10 to 12 per cent lower than before the war in the present boundaries, but prices are 17 per cent lower in terms of commodities in general. This can be regarded as constituting an increase in the economic effectiveness of the industry of 5 to 6 per cent. Relative to the old boundaries, however, there was a slight decrease. Absence of adequate data prevents a similar calculation for coke by-products. For general statistics on the industry, see Appendix IV, below.

[3] The chief by-products, in the order of their present importance to the industry, are benzol, coal tar, sulphate of ammonia and other ammonia compounds (including nitrate fertilizers), and coke-oven gas. The production of ammonia compounds is less important now than before the war, while the output of coal tar has increased more than twice in value, and that of benzol nearly three times.

The production of coke-oven gas is increasing rapidly. The gas is piped for long distances for industrial and municipal heating, power

vances in the design and capacity of the coke ovens themselves. These technical improvements have not materially diminished the quantity of coal necessary to produce a ton of coke, but they have greatly increased the quantity, variety, and value of the by-products secured, and have reduced the labor factor to negligible proportions. Many of the old ovens have been scrapped, and large new central cokeries have been built which are models of technical efficiency. One Ruhr cokery visited by the writer has 56 regenerative ovens of 16 tons capacity each, turns out 1,200 tons of coke a day, has its own by-product plant, and is so highly mechanized that the entire coking process, from the point at which the raw coal is received until the graded coke is ready for shipment or sale, requires only 18 men per shift! Other new cokeries are up to twice as large, and the fact that most of them are placed directly at the mouth of the coal mines eliminates almost all handling of the coal itself. Unfortunately no comprehensive data have hitherto been made available for the period since 1926, whereas most of the new plants came into operation only at or after that time, and it is hence impossible to judge the results closely as yet. That a great gain has been achieved, however, is beyond dispute. The new cokeries get a yield of 40 tons or more per man per shift, as against about 5 before the war, have a capacity

production, and so on, and is becoming a serious competitor of electricity. In the Ruhr the principal companies and the communes have combined in a big enterprise (*Ferngasversorgung Westfalen*) which is covering the district with a network of pipes, and plans eventually to reach Berlin and perhaps Switzerland. The gas is sold at very low prices on long-term contracts. The *A.-G. für Kohlenverwertung* is a similar organization, and there are also others. Local gas plants are scrapped, and the local companies become merely distributors.

of up to 40 tons per oven against 6 before, and yield even larger quantities and varieties of by-products.

On the other hand, the technical advance has of course been secured only at the expense of heavy capital outlays, incurred both by building new plants and by scrapping old ones. Some plants have recently been torn down which were only three or four years old, and which were absolutely up to date at the time they were built. The companies have therefore not yet derived profits in proportion to the increase in their operating efficiency, and it will probably be a number of years before they reap the full benefits. Indeed, there is some evidence that the new construction has been overdone, and certain companies are finding themselves in temporary difficulties. The general position, however, is strong, and the coke industry will undoubtedly become increasingly profitable as time goes on.

VI. IRON AND STEEL. ORE SUPPLY AND IRON PRODUCTION

THE history of the German iron and steel industry in the last ten years has been quite unlike that of the coal industry. Despite the Treaty cessions, Germany still retains the largest and best part of her pre-war coal reserves, but nearly three-quarters of the former iron ore reserves is gone; and with them went 20 per cent of the pre-war iron and steel making plants. In those two simple facts lies the key to most of what has happened in German iron and steel since 1918. The industry has had to reorganize its production processes on the basis of quite different ore supplies; has replaced the surrendered plant with new and better installations; and has entered on a protracted struggle to regain its former commanding position at home and abroad. By the end of 1928 the volume of production was still about 20 per cent below the 1913 production in the old boundaries, but it had been raised to a point some 15 per cent or more above the 1913 volume in the *present* boundaries. In view of the keen foreign competition which has developed since the war, this increase represents a very substantial achievement. It was secured in two principal ways: by thorough-going technical rationalization and improvement, as in the coal industry, and by regrouping and combining the firms into more efficient producing units. Technical progress, however, has played a somewhat smaller part than in coal, and the effects of the structural and financial reorganization of the industry a larger one.

The first great problem that confronted the producers after the war, however, was not internal reorganization but iron ore supply. The problem ran in simple and drastic terms. In 1913, as has been remarked elsewhere, Germany had the largest iron reserves in Europe, and very much the largest production of iron ore. The production was twice that of England, and two-thirds larger than that of France. Yet even so the German output was insufficient for the ravenous Ruhr and Lorraine blast furnaces, and nearly a fourth of the ore consumed was imported from foreign countries, chiefly Sweden, France, and Spain. Then came the war and the Peace Treaty. Most of the ore deposits had been in Lorraine, and when that province was returned to France, Germany lost 72 per cent of her total reserves. She became completely dependent on foreign ore supplies, and is now compelled to import more than three-quarters of all the ore she consumes,—again chiefly from Sweden, Spain, and France.

The production of iron ore in the principal countries is shown in the following table, in million tons :[1]

	1913	*1927*
Germany	35.0	5.6
France	21.9	45.4
Great Britain	16.2	11.4
United States	63.0	62.8

Germany's present dependence on imports of foreign ores has a double disadvantage. In the first place, the ore is more expensive, since it has to bear higher transportation charges to the furnaces; and the money paid

[1] See *Statistisches Jahrbuch*, 1928, pp. 404, 48*.
The known ore reserves of the world in 1913 were as follows (see Greer, *The Ruhr-Lorraine Industrial System*, p. 10), in million metric tons:

Germany	3,362
France	3,300
Great Britain	1,300
United States	4,257
Other	13,091
Total world	25,310

Germany lost 72 per cent of her reserves by the cession of Lorraine: they were thus reduced to about 940 million tons. (See, however, the somewhat lower figures given by Hoffman, *loc. cit.*, p. 442.)

The chief countries from which Germany imported iron ore are as follows (figures in million tons):

	1913	*1927*
Sweden	4.6	8.7
Spain	3.6	3.1
France	3.8	2.9
Newfoundland	0.1	0.8
Algeria	0.5	0.7
Other	1.4	1.2
Total imports (*net*)	14.0	17.4

Figures for France in 1927 include Alsace-Lorraine. Despite her acquisition of the Lorraine reserves, France exports less ore now than formerly because of the demands of her own greatly enlarged iron

for it, which now goes abroad, is an important debit item in the general balance of Germany's international accounts. In the second place, it puts Germany at the mercy of other countries if they should ever choose to exploit her position. The situation with respect to Sweden is particularly uneasy. Half of the German ore imports now come from Sweden, and in the last two or three years many German furnaces have been reconstructed to handle the high-grade Swedish ores. In addition, the Swedish ore trust owns large deposits in other parts of Europe, and in northern Africa and South America, and is reputed to control some 17 per cent of all the ore which can compete in Western European markets.[1] To date no major difficulties have arisen, and the German firms may be able to effect a combination with the foreign interests, but they are obviously in a weak strategic position.

The problem of iron ore supply was thus solved, so far as it will ever be solved at all, by importation from foreign countries. Much more enduring and important, as it proved, was the problem of internal reorganization, a reorganization which was absolutely essential if the German iron and steel enterprises themselves were to survive. First, the losses of ore reserves and of plant under the Treaty made it necessary to recast the physical and geographical layout of the whole industry. Before the war much of the iron had been made in blast

and steel industry. The value of the net German imports in 1927 was about 360 million marks. For 1928, preliminary figures show a net import of 13.6 million tons, valued at about 290 million marks.

The figures given in the text table are from the *Statistisches Jahrbuch,* 1928, pp. 48, 49, 404. For a summary of the general statistics on the iron and steel industry, see Appendix V, below.

[1] See, for example, an article by Dr. A. Marcus, in the *Berliner Tageblatt* for Oct. 18, 1928.

furnaces constructed directly on the Lorraine ore deposits. Now, with most of the deposits gone, the new furnaces built to replace those surrendered had to be located where Ruhr coke and imported ores could be combined most cheaply. For the industry in western Germany (the Silesian division is relatively small) this meant a concentration in Rhenish Westphalia, usually on the waterways or main railroads; and this district, of which the Ruhr is the industrial heart, now makes about 80 per cent of all German iron and steel products. Similar considerations also led to the location of most of the other new plants in the Ruhr, and to a corresponding realignment of the technical and commercial relationships between the various firms. Second, the iron and steel industry had been protected from foreign competition for almost ten years, first by the war and then by the inflation. Its general technique had made little or no progress, and the industry as a whole had drifted into a state of weak and incomplete organization. The extent of the weakness did not appear until 1924, but thereafter drastic changes took place.

In describing the reconstruction of production and technique since the war, however, it is not possible to treat the iron and steel industry as a single unit. The industry as a whole is divided into three great sections, which correspond to the successive stages in production itself: the blast furnaces, making more or less pure iron out of mineral ore; the steel furnaces, which convert the iron into a wide variety of steels; and the rolling mills, which work up the raw steel ingots, blocks, and so on into half-finished and finished products (bars, plates, wire, pipe, railway construction material, and so on). Each division has its own peculiar problems and conditions, which differ largely from those of other divisions, and each must therefore be treated separately at the start. First, raw iron production and the blast furnaces.

In 1913, Germany had the largest production of raw iron in Europe: 16.8 million tons in the old boundaries, and 10.9 millions in the present ones. After the war the output dropped to less than half of this figure, and fluctuated widely during the inflation, but since 1924 it has been steadily built up again, and in 1927 reached a peak of 13.1 millions. The general business recession of 1928 brought it down to 11.8 millions for that year, but while this is 30 per cent below the 1913 level, it is still 8 per cent above the 1913 production in the present boundaries; and is nearly half again as large as the output of Germany's nearest European competitor, France.

The output of the chief countries was as follows, in million tons (1913: pre-war boundaries):

	1913	1927
Germany	16.8	13.1
France	5.2	9.3
Great Britain	10.4	7.4
United States	31.5	37.2
Other	15.2	19.2
World total	79.1	86.2

Germany's share in the world output thus fell from 21 to 15 per cent.[1] France, in consequence of the Treaty cessions, was the principal gainer by this loss.

The average price of raw iron has risen only 6 per cent since before the war, as compared with a rise of 40 per cent in the general wholesale price level. In other words, raw iron costs about 25 per cent less in terms of commodities at large than it did in 1913. This suggests that the increase in the general technical efficiency of

[1] *Statistisches Jahrbuch,* 1928, p. 55*.

the industry since the war has also amounted to about 25 per cent. In reality, however, it has probably been much greater. There are no comprehensive statistics yet available for the period after 1926, whereas some of the most important improvements have been made within the last two or three years, but the evidence available indicates that the industry is now between 50 and 60 per cent more efficient *on the average*, from the technical point of view, than it was in 1913. This increased technical efficiency reveals itself in the relatively low level of operating costs which prevail whenever an expression of market demands permits operation at capacity.

The technical advance has been secured in two principal ways. First, many of the old furnaces have been scrapped, and the new ones built have been steadily increased in size and efficiency. The average pre-war furnace would hold less than 160 tons. In 1926 the average was 285 tons, an increase of 78 per cent, and is now a good deal higher.[1] Moreover, the best new furnaces are vastly bigger than this average. Standing over 110 feet high and 25 feet through, they hold up to 850 tons of material or more at a single charging, and can produce, depending on the ore used, 1,000 to 1,200 tons of iron a day. A single block of four such furnaces (with one always held in reserve) could produce at capacity about 10 per cent of Germany's entire present output! The

[1] Another method of calculation indicates that by the end of 1926 the average capacity of the furnaces actually in operation had increased 120 per cent since the war, as follows: Relative to 1913, output had declined by 43 per cent, but the total number of weeks of furnace operation had fallen by 70 per cent, showing a gain in average capacity per furnace of 61 per cent. In addition, however, the number of furnaces in operation had decreased by 59 per cent. The two together indicate an increase in average capacity of 120 per cent. Since 1926, still further large gains have been made.

general design and technique have also been improved, and a distinctly larger output of iron is now secured from furnaces of a given size than was possible before the war. Second, the operation of the furnaces has been thoroughly mechanized and rationalized. Transport and loading are done almost entirely by machinery, as is the handling of the products, and many of the plants have been laid out anew to secure a better organization of production. One unit of 4 furnaces seen by the writer can produce, with 1 furnace in reserve, up to 2,300 tons of iron a day; and for the whole process, including foundry and transport, only 116 men per shift are required—a mere fraction of the labor used per ton of product before the war. Some of the most recent installations are even larger. The furnaces are more solidly built than in the United States, and will work for a number of years without relining. The air is preheated with the waste gas from the furnaces themselves, and the remaining gas is then carried off for use in the steel furnaces and rolling mills. In addition, where phosphoric ores are used the slag is subsequently crushed and sold as phosphoric fertilizer (Thomas meal), and provides a substantial revenue.

The result of this thoroughgoing reorganization is that although output has increased 8 per cent and total capacity about 40 per cent, relative to the pre-war industry in the present boundaries, the number of workers, the number of separate producing units, and the number of furnaces have all declined materially, with a great resulting saving in direct costs of production. At present levels of output the economic effectiveness of the industry is about 40 per cent greater than it was before the war in the present boundaries, and at capacity operation would be from 75 to 80 per cent greater. But the output is still 30 per cent less than the 1913 volume in the old boundaries, and the effectiveness of the industry today is therefore only some 2 per cent greater than that of the aggregate pre-war industry in the old boundaries—though at capacity it would be about 30 per cent greater.[1]

Germany now has much more blast furnace capacity (by 25 to 30 per cent on the average) than the present demand requires. In consequence, the furnaces cannot operate at their most efficient and most profitable rate, and the companies have not yet secured the full financial benefits which the technical reorganization should bring. Some, indeed, find that they have overexpanded, and are having financial difficulties with this part of their operations. The capital charges they incurred for the new installations were very heavy, and much of this burden, in the absence of full utilization of the plants, is necessarily dead overhead.

VII. STEEL MAKING AND THE ROLLING MILLS

A CERTAIN proportion of the raw iron produced in the blast furnaces is sold directly to foundries and to other manufacturers. Most of it, however (on an average about 70 per cent now), goes on to the second great division in the production process and is converted into steel, chiefly by the elimination of most of the remaining carbon and the addition of small quantities of other metals such as nickel, chromium, or tungsten. Here lies the heart of the whole industry.

Before the war the German steel industry was by far the largest in Europe. Its 1913 output of 17 million tons was greater than that of all the other western European countries taken together, and was second only to

[1] For a summary table on iron production, see Appendix V, below.

the output of the United States. The war and the cessions under the Treaty cut off over 30 per cent of the production, however, and the inflation period paralyzed the industry for a time. But since 1924 it has been rapidly regaining the lost ground, and in 1927 it came within 5 per cent of the 1913 volume of production. Although a decline took place in 1928, the output in that year was only 15 per cent below the pre-war level in the old boundaries, and was 23 per cent greater than the pre-war production in the present boundaries. At the same time Germany's supremacy in Europe has been unequivocally reëstablished. She is once more producing nearly as much steel annually as her two nearest competitors combined, Great Britain and France. The recovery has been greater than that in any other division of the iron and steel industry, and in view of the difficulties which have had to be overcome is really remarkable.

The world output of raw steel has been as follows, in million tons (1913: old boundaries):

Country	1913	1927
Germany	17.1	16.3
Great Britain	7.8	9.3
France	4.7	8.3
United States	30.8	44.5
Other	15.5	22.1
Total world	75.9	100.5

Germany's share thus declined from 22.5 to 16.2 per cent, the chief gainer being again France. It is interesting to note that while Great Britain has now dropped to third place in European *iron* production, she is still second in steel.

The German recovery has been due to a variety of causes. The most important is undoubtedly the reorganization of the companies themselves, especially since 1924. This reorganization resulted in the closing down of many inefficient plants, the regrouping and concentration of production on the better ones, and the construction of many new units at strategic points. The formation of the Continental Steel Cartel in 1926 also played a substantial part. On these two questions more will be said at a later point, since they cannot be divorced from the position of the industry as a whole. Finally, a good deal of technical progress has been made. There have been no radical new departures, but the existing technique has been steadily improved. As in iron making, the steel furnaces have been increased in size and in efficiency; fuel consumption has been reduced by from 30 to 60 per cent relative to 1913;[1] improvements in the Martin (open-hearth) furnaces have permitted a much greater use of iron and steel scrap, while a better design of the crucible furnaces has enabled the quality of special steels to be controlled with extraordinary closeness; and the whole process of charging and transportation has been highly mechanized. Perhaps the greatest single gain, however, has come from combining the steel works with the blast furnaces in a single production unit, physically side by side. This makes it possible to pass the molten iron direct from the blast furnaces to the steel furnaces, and then to pass the steel, after partial cooling, direct to the rolling mills, all without reheating. At the same time the steel furnaces are able to use the waste blast-furnace gas for the further heat they require, as do the rolling mills. The saving in fuel which is thus effected is very large. The most modern production groups begin with ore and coke

[1] See the publication of the Verein deutscher Eisenhüttenleute, *Mitteilungen der Wärmestelle*, No. 100 (June 25, 1927).

in the blast furnace and then work clear through to the finished rolled-steel products with almost no additional fuel, and almost no human labor. The process is nearly automatic and nearly self-heating. Of course this ideal combination of plants does not prevail throughout the entire industry, since many older units which are physically separated from the prior and following production stages are still in operation, but it is found in most of the new installations.

The lack of recent data makes it impossible to measure very closely the extent of the advance which has been made in steel production. In 1926 the volume of production was practically the same as the 1913 output in the present boundaries. But the value of the steel produced was also practically the same; and since the wholesale price average had then risen by some 34 per cent since 1913, steel was some 25 per cent cheaper in terms of commodities in general. The increase in the economic effectiveness of the industry from 1913 to 1926 was therefore about 32 per cent in the present area. It is true that the output was 27 per cent below the total production in the pre-war boundaries. As compared with the aggregate pre-war industry in the pre-war boundaries, the industry in 1926 was therefore only about 2 per cent more effective. In 1928, on the other hand, the severe stoppage in the Ruhr during November made the year's output at least 10 per cent lower than it would otherwise have been, but despite this there was a marked improvement for the year as a whole. The volume of production rose to 23 per cent above the 1913 volume in the present area, and was only 15 per cent below the aggregate output in the old boundaries. The gain in effectiveness was therefore doubtless a good deal greater. Data are not yet available, however, on the value of the total output in 1928, and a definite conclusion hence cannot be reached.[1]

The principal difficulty the steel-making division now faces is the one also confronting the blast furnace division, excess capacity. In 1926 only 71 per cent of the steel plant was in use, and although production has increased since then, it is probable that plant capacity has been increased even more. No immediate remedy for this situation is in sight. It prevents the companies from securing the full financial benefits which they apparently should derive from the reorganization of production and from the improvement of technique, and has again placed some of them in financial difficulties from overinvestment in new plant and general overexpansion. The reasons for this limitation on the market will be examined in a moment.

The third and last great division of the industry is the rolling mills, which work up the raw steel into a wide variety of finished and half-finished products— bars, plates, tubes, rolls, wire, railway and bridge construction material, and so on. Its development since the war has necessarily been much like that of the iron and steel-making divisions. In 1913 the mills turned out over 16 million tons of products. During the inflation the output fell heavily, but since 1924 it has been increasing again, and by 1927 had reached 12.9 millions. This was still 20 per cent below the 1913 production in the old boundaries, although 11 per cent above that in the present boundaries. Data for 1928 are not yet available, but some decline, perhaps to 12 millions, undoubtedly took place. The volume of net exports has fallen even more heavily since 1913, from 3.6 million tons then to only 1.6 millions in 1928. This fall reflects both increased

[1] For general data on steel production, see Appendix V, below.

competition abroad, especially from France, and an increase in the relative size of the German domestic demand itself.

The following figures on rolling-mill production, in million tons, show the extent to which Germany has regained her supremacy in Europe (finished products only) :[1]

	1913	*1926*	*1927*
Germany	13.1	9.0	11.9
Great Britain	7.0	4.5	8.1
France	3.6	5.7	—
United States	25.2	36.1	33.4

It should be pointed out that only about 90 per cent of the raw steel produced is rolled; some of it goes direct into castings and forgings.

The recovery in the rolled products division has thus been somewhat less pronounced than that in steel making, but it is nevertheless substantial, and is due to similar causes. The principal factor has been the physical and financial reorganization of the steel industry as a whole. A number of the older rolling mills have been shut down or scrapped outright; the remainder have been provided with better and cheaper supplies of steel, on the average; and a good many new plants have been built, though expansion in this direction has not been as great as in the steel-making division itself. Nearly all the new heavy mills, and many of the old ones, have also benefited from the development of complete producing groups, already commented on, which combine iron making, steel making, and rolling in one huge unit. This enables the mills to get their steel direct from the furnaces without reheating, and such additional heat as they require is secured almost cost free from the blast furnace gas. In addition, they have made a good deal

[1] *Statistisches Jahrbuch,* 1928, p. 57*.

of technical progress in other directions, less spectacular but likewise solid. The biggest gain has probably come from lengthening the floor of the new mills in the American fashion, so that the rolled products go through directly without being turned back or at most with only one turn. The rolls themselves have also been speeded up for certain products; the manufacture of both seamless and welded tubes has been greatly improved; and a number of other advances have been made, especially in the mechanical handling of materials and products.

The tangible gains from this reorganization and technical progress in steel rolling show in various ways. The number of plants and the number of workers and employees have been materially reduced, while the output per man, taking the total of workers and employees together, had been increased by about 30 per cent to the end of 1927. On the other hand, the prices of the products have risen much less than the general average of wholesale prices since 1913. In other words, they have fallen relative to the prices of commodities at large. If this decline in real cost is combined with the increase in output, it becomes apparent that the general economic effectiveness of the industry at the end of 1926, the last year for which there are complete data, was some 30 per cent greater than that of the pre-war industry in the present boundaries. Still further progress has been made in the last two years. Relative to the pre-war industry in the pre-war boundaries, however, the much smaller output made this increase in effectiveness amount by 1926 to only some 2 or 3 per cent. At present, with a larger output than in 1926, the increase is somewhat greater, but even so is hardly striking.[1]

[1] For a summary table on rolled products, see Appendix V, below; on the principal export markets, Appendix XIV.

On the other hand, the fact that the prices of rolled products have not kept up with the rise in general prices since the war has itself restricted the financial benefits which the companies have secured from their technical advances; and the 50 per cent increase in average wage and salary rates has decreased them still further. The available data indicate that the gross income of all the companies combined, from their rolling-mill operations, was only 5 per cent higher in 1926 than it was in the present boundaries before the war, and after paying wages and salaries was only 3 per cent higher. Relative to the income of the companies in the pre-war boundaries there have been large decreases, of from 20 to 25 per cent.

VIII. PHYSICAL RECONSTRUCTION: SUMMARY

Such has been, in its broad outlines, the history of the physical and technical reconstruction of the German iron and steel industry. The gains which this reconstruction has brought both to the industry itself and to the country at large are indicated by the extent to which production has recovered from the low point of the inflation period, by the decline in iron and steel prices relative to wholesale prices in general, and—as the result of these changes—by the fact that Germany has regained a position of unquestioned supremacy among the European producing countries. Nor does the size of the actual output tell the entire story. The plants have been so expanded that in 1928 production capacity exceeded actual output by about 30 per cent for raw iron, and by 40 per cent for raw steel and rolled products.

But in spite of this progress the industry as a whole is distinctly smaller today, in the present boundaries, than it was before the war in the old boundaries. The production of steel and rolled products is from 15 to 20 per cent less than in 1913, and the output of raw iron about 30 per cent less. The situation is summarized in the following table. For comparison, the data on coal and coke are also given. The figures are for total production, in million tons:

	1913: old boundaries	1913: present boundaries	1927
Iron ore	35.0	—	5.6
Raw iron	16.8	10.9	13.1
Raw steel	17.1	11.8	16.3
Rolled products	16.1	11.6	12.9
Coal	190.1	140.8	153.6
Coke	34.6	31.7	32.3

Complete data are not yet available for 1928, but a general recession occurred in that year from the high point of 1927.

There have been several reasons for this failure of the industry to recover its former size. In the years immediately after the war, the chief explanation was of course the large cessions of ore reserves and plant required by the Treaty of Peace, and the general disorganization of the inflation period. By now, however, these influences have pretty well exhausted themselves. The losses of plant have been made good, and the industry as a whole is capable of producing a rather larger output today than it could before the war. The fact that actual production is still below the 1913 level is due chiefly to the lack of markets. Despite the considerable fall in the prices of iron and steel relative to the prices of commodities in general, the consumption within Germany is smaller now than it was before the war, while at the same time intensive competition abroad has led to a

severe decline in Germany's exports. As we shall see in a
moment, the financial position of the companies probably makes any substantial new reduction in costs impossible with the present technique; and further marked
and generally adopted improvements in the technique
itself are not likely to occur in the immediate future. It
is of course true that the abolition of the cartel system,
to be discussed in a moment, would lower prices somewhat. But the average demand for iron and steel now
seems to be rather inelastic, and it is doubtful if any
substantial and enduring increase in sales would result
from such a fall.

The limitation on the consuming power of the domestic market is in turn explained by the difficulties under
which most of the industries which buy iron and steel
are working. Since their own sales are limited, their purchases are necessarily correspondingly restricted. These
industries we shall come to in the next chapter. The even
greater reduction in German exports is due to two conditions. One is the fact that the territorial cessions under
the Treaty, as we have already seen, entailed the transfer of a good deal of the pre-war plant to other countries. Former German exports to them were thereby diminished or cut off; and some of the countries, notably
France, in turn became very large exporters. The other
is that during the war itself certain countries which had
previously been dependent on imports from Germany
were compelled, when the imports stopped, to develop
industries of their own; and these industries too, carefully protected by high tariffs, are now likewise competitors.

The effect of these conditions is shown most clearly by
the following data on net exports of rolled products
from the leading countries. Foreign trade in raw iron

and steel as such is of negligible size. Figures in million tons :[1]

	1913	*1927*	*1928*
Germany	3.6	1.1	1.6
France	—	4.3	4.0
Great Britain	1.8	1.2	1.8
Belgium and Luxemburg	1.0	2.9	3.3
United States	0.9	0.6	0.8

It is important to note in this connection the highly significant fact that despite the large exports of rolled products, its complete dependence on foreign ores gives the German iron and steel industry as a whole an adverse balance of trade. In 1927, the latest year for which full data are yet available, net exports and imports were as follows, in million marks:

Iron ore	— 361
Raw iron	— 19
Raw steel	negligible
Rolled products	+ 273
Balance	— 107

IX. CARTELS AND COMBINES

The recovery in the production of iron and steel was thus chiefly due, in the first instance, to the physical reorganization of the plants themselves and to improvements in technique. These advances in turn, however, were made possible only by a thoroughgoing reconstruction of the financial and administrative side of the industry, a reconstruction which also lowered overhead costs and thus contributed further to cheap and efficient production. This reconstruction took two princi-

[1] For sources see Appendix V, below. Figure for the United States in 1913 is the average of 1910–14. For the distribution of the German exports by countries, see Appendix XIV. The largest single buyer is Holland.

pal forms. One was the regrouping of the existing firms
into better balanced and stronger units, partly by means
of combinations and mergers; the other was the wider
development of the pre-war cartels, and the creation
through their agency of relatively limited but useful
international agreements.

Something was said in an earlier chapter of the
growth of the iron and steel combines during the inflation period. In the main these new combines were badly
designed and structurally weak, and at the crucial test
of stabilization they fell apart into their constituent elements. A period of severe competition and great general
difficulty then followed, but toward the end of 1925 a
new movement toward combination began, as the only
way of assuring the continued stable existence of the industry itself. The outstanding result was the formation
of the *Vereinigte Stahlwerke A.-G.* (United Steel Works
Co.) in 1926. It was built on the wreckage of the coal,
iron, and steel units in the gigantic combine Stinnes
had built up in the inflation, and rapidly extended its
interests. The companies which originally formed the
combine all operate in the Ruhr, but numerous subsequent agreements and outright purchases have also
given it strong positions throughout middle Germany
and in Silesia. With an original capital of 800 million
marks, it is now the dominant factor in the situation.
Including its participations in other companies, it controls practically half of the entire iron and steel production of Germany, and in addition about 25 per cent
of the coal. It has scrapped plants ruthlessly, either because they were old or because they were not strate-
gically located, has built many new units, and is now an
extremely efficient production group. But this reconstruction has been very costly, and although the com-

pany is paying a 6 per cent dividend at present, it has not yet reaped the full benefits of the reorganization. It is also said to suffer somewhat from an overcentralized and rigid form of administrative control.

The other principal concerns are all very much smaller, and a number of them are organized in legal forms which make it impossible to find out much about them. The concentration in iron and steel has been so great, however, that the four or five chief firms in this group, together with the Vereinigte Stahlwerke, practically *are* the iron and steel industry.[1] At the same time, these firms also control between them over half the production of coal. Their general position is hence very strong.

The other principal agency in the structural reorganization of the industry has been the cartels. The iron and steel cartels have a history reaching back to the origins of the industry itself. They suffered various vicissitudes during the inflation period, and were several times at the point of collapse, but at the present time the principal cartels are once more firmly established. The most important one is the pig iron cartel, which regulates both prices and production for sale, and is the exclusive sales agent of its members. Unlike the coal cartels, it has no jurisdiction at all over production for its members' own consumption, but it exercises a virtually monopolistic control over pig iron production for outside sale. In steel, the products are more varied, and the cartels are at once more numerous and weaker. The basic one is the raw steel cartel, which controls only produc-

[1] On the development of the iron and steel combines, see R. K. Michels, *Cartels, Combines and Trusts in Post-War Germany* (New York, 1928), Chap. 7; Das Spezial-Archiv, *Vereinigte Stahlwerke Aktien-Gesellschaft Düsseldorf* (Berlin, 1927); Seager and Gulick, *Trust and Corporation Problems* (now in press); etc.

tion and leaves prices alone. The general cartel for half-products, however (the *A-Produkten Verband*), is the exclusive sales agent for its members, as are the cartels for semifinished products—bars, sheets, wire, and so on. All of these are in turn combined into a central administrative association, the *Stahlwerks-Verband* or Steel Works Cartel.

This elaborate cartel system has had a number of effects, some good and some bad. First, both prices and production have been controlled and stabilized. This has eliminated cutthroat competition, and has permitted an orderly development of the industry. Since the costs of the weakest and least efficient firms are taken as the basis for setting prices, however, the consequence is that prices are kept somewhat above the levels at which they would otherwise be. This places a certain additional burden on the consumers, as does the not infrequent transfer of production quotas at inflated values, though the Cartel Law checks if it does not always prevent undue abuse in these respects. Second, the virtual domestic monopoly the cartels possess has enabled them to sell abroad at prices often 10 to 30 per cent lower than those charged at home. In the special circumstances of the iron and steel industry, it may be doubted if this means that the companies are making exorbitant profits on the *aggregate* of their operations, or that the cartels are enabling inefficient firms to survive which would necessarily be eliminated by free competition. It does mean, however, that the German consumer is penalized in order to build up the export trade, and for the benefit of the foreigner. The existence of international cartels and other agreements likewise prevents foreign competition *in Germany* from doing much, by means of cheap imports, to remedy this situation.

The fact that most of the bigger companies are also integrated vertically, and hence operate in several stages of the production process at once, also leads to a good deal of friction within the cartels, and to some unfairness. The producer of raw steel who sells chiefly in the open market, for example, is interested in seeing prices raised and production controlled, while a competing firm in the same cartel which also has its own rolling mills usually wants prices lowered, and production left to take care of itself. Since the highly integrated firms are on balance also the largest, the average result is that the cartels act in ways which are beneficial to the big firms, and which further increase their power, while the smaller producer operating in only one or at most two stages is often correspondingly injured.[1]

Finally, there are a number of international associations dealing with special products—pig iron, rails, wire, and so on—and also the comprehensive Continental Steel Cartel. In most of these international cartels Germany has taken a leading part. They have attracted public attention, however, out of all proportion to any results they have so far achieved. To date they have rendered important services to the countries affected, by stabilizing prices, production and competition, and by guaranteeing its own home market to each industry, but there is nothing as yet to show that they constitute a menace to international economic peace. They have not raised prices unduly, have not entered on destructive price wars with the producers of non-member countries, and are very far from being those tightly knit and powerful international monopolies

[1] See, in addition to the references already given, W. Krüger, *Die moderne Kartellorganisation der deutschen Stahlindustrie* (Berlin, 1927).

which the press often represents them as being. On the contrary, their continued existence is precarious, and some of them are chronically on the verge of collapse.[1]

The Continental Steel Cartel is now made up of Germany, France, Belgium, Luxemburg, the Saar, Czechoslovakia, Austria, and Hungary. The quotas vary with production. Germany's, at the maximum output, is about 43 per cent, that of France about 30. At the time the cartel was formed, in 1926, its production capacity was 38 million tons, as against 59 millions for the United States and 12 for England, while its actual output was 30 million as against 49 and 3.5 millions, respectively. It controls about 70 per cent of the total western European steel capacity. It does not attempt to fix set prices or handle sales, and merely sets the current volume of production. Germany made large concessions to the other countries in order to get them to join the cartel at all, and despite several readjustments of the quotas has been continually penalized for overproduction. In March, 1929, she gave notice of intention to withdraw, and unless she thereby forces better terms for herself, the cartel will dissolve in October, 1929.

X. COAL, IRON, AND STEEL: FINANCES; COMPETITIVE POWER

THERE remains the question of what the financial results of all this thoroughgoing reconstruction and reorganization have been for the coal and steel companies themselves. Yet it is precisely that question which, for reasons already indicated, is least capable of a satisfactory

---

[1] On the international cartels also see the U.S. Department of Commerce *Trade Information Bulletins,* Nos. 484, "Origin and Development of the Continental Steel Entente" (May, 1927), and 556, "The International Cartel Movement" (June, 1928).

answer. A large number of companies—though usually not the most important ones—are organized in legal forms for which the publication of detailed information is not required.[1] Moreover, the subtleties of German accounting, especially the common practice of adjusting published balance sheets to the current executive policy of the company rather than to the bare facts, makes the picture rather uncertain. Finally, what has been pointed out before, the coal and steel industries are both dominated by a relatively small number of firms which operate in the two divisions simultaneously, and each of which is a vertical combine. The companies which merely mine coal, or which merely make iron or steel, play only a small part in the general aggregate. Yet no two of the combines are quite alike in the scope of their activities. This complicated situation makes it difficult to get any adequate picture of the organization and financial situation of the industries.

If we take the coal, iron, and steel industries together, as is necessary in making any general statements about their finances, the position is roughly as follows. Most of the companies are making money, but at present levels of prices and production they are not making much. Although certain companies are relatively prosperous, others are running behind, and the average rate of dividends is probably not over 5 or 6 per cent— somewhat less with respect to coal-mining operations, rather more for iron and steel. In addition, however, most of the companies are accumulating published and hidden reserves of some size, so that the average net

[1] Such publication is required only for incorporated companies (*Aktien-Gesellschaften*). For a list of the other usual forms of organization see Chap. VII, below. In mining, special partnerships (*Gewerkschaften*) are also common.

earnings for the last two or three years probably run up to 8 or 9 per cent; and a number of them are now engaged in further reconstruction and expansion. But against this must be set the fact that the nominal capitalizations are often low, and do not correspond to the actual total investment. The real percentage rates of dividends and earnings on the investment, for such undercapitalized companies, are therefore smaller than the figures just given. Moreover, a number of firms, especially in the iron and steel division, have borrowed heavily at both long and short term. The borrowing has been undertaken in part to finance the physical reconstruction already described, but also in part, especially in the year 1928–29, to finance current operation itself. While the average position of the companies is perfectly sound, it therefore contains no promise of excessive prosperity in the near future. The markets for both coal and steel are still limited relative to present capacity, and until production can be permanently increased to a point well beyond the present volume, the companies will not draw much net profit from the elaborate reorganization they have effected in the last four or five years. The physical and technical sides of both industries are now in excellent shape, however, and should an expansion in world demands appear the German producers are in a position to exploit it to the full. In both, the average level of technique is now higher than in any other European country. In coal it is also well ahead of, and in iron and steel not far behind, the average technical standards in the United States.

The same factors which restrict the financial prosperity of the coal and the iron and steel industries also restrict their competitive power, both at home and abroad. At current levels of production an important part of the existing plant is not being utilized, and is hence a dead weight on the remainder, but there seems to be no immediate remedy for the situation. The present markets appear to be relatively inelastic, and the increase in orders which would follow a material decline in prices would probably not be great enough to offset the loss from the lower price level itself. Moreover, there is a nearly continuous demand from labor for higher wages, and this operates, especially in coal, as a strong deterrent to any lowering of prices in the near future. Finally, the cartel organization itself tends always, by its very nature, to make price reductions difficult. On the other side of the picture, technical improvements and general reorganization have already gone so far that no large new advances, which would permit a further substantial reduction in average costs, seem likely to develop in the immediate future.

The extent to which the conditions just described have restricted Germany's competitive power abroad at current levels of demand is made clear by the production and export figures already reviewed. In steel, the capacity of the industry is greater than it was before the war, but the actual output in 1928 was 15 per cent smaller; and Germany's share in the total European production has dropped from 50 per cent in 1913 to 35 per cent now. Net exports of iron and steel products, in spite of railway rebates and in spite of the fact that export prices are lower than domestic, have also decreased from 3.6 million tons in 1913 to 1.6 millions in 1928, or by over 55 per cent. These declines are attributed by some to the restrictive influence of the international steel cartels, but in point of fact there is nothing to prevent Germany from withdrawing at any time if she thought she could make profits at prices lower than those now prevailing, and were thus tempted to increase her production materially. As remarked above, this is the step she is now actually threatening to take with respect to the basic Continental Steel Cartel itself. The principal explanation for the steel situation is, rather, the severe competition of the French industry, much of which was built up after the war on the basis of the ore reserves and plant surrendered by Germany under the Treaty. In the coal industry capacity is also larger than before the war, but actual output is likewise 20 per cent lower than in 1913, and exports have fallen from 24 million tons then to 16.5 millions in 1928, or by over 30 per cent—again despite favorable railway treatment. Against this last must be set, however, the fact of a nearly equivalent increase in coke exports.

This evidence bears out the conclusions to which a knowledge of the restricting factors in the domestic situation, and of the post-war increase in competition from other European countries, inevitably leads. At least in the near future, it is unlikely that the German coal and steel producers will appear as aggressive seekers after new foreign and domestic markets obtained by further large price concessions. In view of the present financial and other limitations on the freedom of their action, it is far more probable that they will simply have to wait until the demand increases again. When that happens, however, they will be able to expand their output very heavily, and at or even below the present levels of prices.

XI. LIGNITE

THE progress achieved in the coal, iron, and steel industries during the last few years has thus been substantial, but to date has not enabled Germany to do much more than keep pace with the advance in other countries. In lignite mining, on the other hand, the recent development has been exceptional. From both the technical and the economic points of view the industry has become one of the most effective branches of the German economy. It is of course not of the same order of importance as coal mining, for although its tonnage output is slightly greater, the value of this output is only a fifth as large, but it is nevertheless the basis for a number of important branches of German industrial life.

The lignite, which the Germans call brown coal, is scattered in numerous deposits pretty well across the center of the country, but the two main centers of exploitation are in Middle Germany, especially the Leipzig-Halle district, and in the smaller Rhenish field southwest of Cologne. A large part of the deposits are close to the surface, from 10 to 90 feet deep, and can therefore be worked by open excavations. The seams range up to 100 feet or more in thickness, and at any ratio of thickness of seam to depth of top soil which is better than about 1 to 4, surface excavating is more effective and cheaper than underground mining.

The main facts about the industry as a whole can be stated very briefly. The total output of lignite in 1913 was 87 million tons, with a value of 192 million marks. In 1927 the output was 151 millions, an increase of 72 per cent, and the value was 424 million marks, an increase of 120 per cent. The price of lignite per ton had thus gone up, but the rise was still less than the rise of wholesale prices in general by about 7 per cent. Roughly speaking, the economic effectiveness of the industry had therefore increased from 1913 to 1927 by about 80 per cent. This is the principal measure of the progress made. In addition, however, the number of separate plants had been materially reduced, the output per man had increased by 40 per cent, and although wages and salaries were half again as high as in 1913, the labor cost per ton had diminished. Complete data are not yet available for 1928, but in that year output was further increased to 167 million tons, with little change in the number of workers employed or in prices, and large additional gains were therefore presumably secured.[1]

This great advance has been achieved by an almost ideal mechanization of the larger mines, a mechanization which provides one of the best examples of technical rationalization to be found in Germany. The top soil is removed by machine shovels and overhead-bridge scoops; the lignite itself is cut entirely by machinery, either by endless chain cutters working from below or by chain buckets working from above; and all transport and other handling is completely mechanical. From the time the first hole is dug until the lignite is ready for use in furnaces or briquet factories, no hand touches it. A big lignite mine is indeed an extraordinary sight: a brownish-black crater perhaps a mile and a half long, a mile wide, and several hundred feet deep; vast dumps of waste top soil covering the nearby land; clanking machines steadily gnawing along the sides, making the crater always wider and longer; the bottom covered with long strings of cars carrying off the product; and hardly a man in sight. As time passes, the mine moves straight across the countryside, swallowing trees and farms and even villages as it goes, and leaving behind an apparent desolation that, strangely enough, is good farm land again in a few years.

The greatest part of the lignite is used on the spot. Since it contains 45 to 55 per cent water, it cannot be

---

[1] For summary statistics, see Appendix IV.

transported profitably for any distance, and for the same reason exports and imports are of negligible size. Part of it is ground, dried, and pressed into briquets, which are then sold for domestic and industrial fuel, but a large proportion of the output is now dumped directly into the furnaces of electric power generating plants. As far as possible, both briquet factories and power plants are placed directly beside the mine itself, and all reloading is thus avoided. In the newest installations, it is said that the lignite can be delivered to the furnaces for a little over 1 mark a ton (probably excluding depletion and depreciation charges, however). This figure, if correct, is equal when converted at heat equivalent to about 5.50 marks a ton for ordinary coal—$1.30! Certain factories needing enormous amounts of fuel have also been built on the lignite deposits. Of these the largest and best known is the Leunawerke, one of the Dye Trusts' plants, which uses the lignite both as fuel and to provide hydrogen in the manufacture of synthetic nitrates, synthetic gasoline, and so on, but there are many others as well.

The lignite industry is organized in cartels substantially analogous to those in the coal industry, though they seem to have given rise to much less public criticism; and the apparent financial position of most of the companies is good. A curious and little-known situation, however, has arisen in certain Middle German districts. Sales are made largely through distributing companies owned solely by the bigger share holders in the mines as individuals, *not* by the mining companies themselves. These selling companies have bought up most of the wholesalers and retailers involved. The business is then so conducted that the selling companies pay the mines what is really too low a price for the lignite, and thus keep most of the profits. The large share-holders in the mine of course benefit, but the small holders, the mine management, and the wage earners are all frozen out of any increase in earnings. In addition, however, the more important companies are themselves frequently owned or controlled by power enterprises or manufacturing firms,—or sometimes the reverse relation prevails—and the real situation is therefore often obscure.

The principal difficulty facing the industry today is neither markets, technique, nor organization, however, but the simple and dramatic fact that the mines are rapidly eating themselves out of existence. Whereas the coal reserves will last for many centuries, the lignite has recently been exploited so intensively that at the present rate of consumption most of the deposits which are commercially workable with the present technique, and at the present levels of prices, will be gone in 50 to 60 years. There seems to be no remedy for this situation, and a drastic reorientation of the branches of German industry now dependent on lignite will eventually become necessary.

XII. ELECTRIC POWER

THE recent intensive exploitation of the lignite mines has been closely tied up with the development of large electric power stations and long-distance transmission lines. It is beyond the province of this book to go into the power situation in Germany in detail, but some idea of the growth since the war is necessary to understand the present general situation of industry as a whole. In 1907 German industry alone, in the present boundaries, used some 7.7 million horsepower of energy in the form of electric current. By 1925 the figure had risen to 18.1

millions, or 2.3 times as much, and since then a further increase of at least 25 to 30 per cent has probably taken place. Other uses of electric current, for lighting and heating, have increased even more rapidly, and although no complete statistics exist, it is safe to say that Germany is now producing at least three times as much electric power as she was before the war.

The power is generated in a number of different ways, and comes from all over the country. The great bulk of it, however, is secured from coal and lignite, in about equal proportions. Taken together, these two sources account for more than 70 per cent of the total. Water power yields only 15 per cent, and gas 11.[1] The coal-burning stations are of course chiefly in the Ruhr, as are the gas stations; the lignite stations are placed directly on the mines, throughout central Germany and on the Rhine; and the water power comes principally from the south, in Bavaria. The big plants are now in process of being tied together by high-tension transmission lines, and it is hoped that a single great net will soon cover the whole of Germany. The result will be that every district will have relatively cheap and plentiful power, and in case one station breaks down the mere

[1] The per cents were as follows in 1927 (see *Wirtschaft und Statistik*, 1929, p. 74): coal, 36.2; lignite, 34.4; water power, 15.1; gas, 10.8; other, 3.5.

The total German production in 1925 was, in million kilowatt hours, 20,328; in the United States, 81,720; in the world, 179,511. (See the U. S. Department of Commerce, *Commerce Yearbook*, 1928, I, 262.) Germany then had less than half the output per capita of the United States. By 1927, however, her output had increased to 25,135 millions. Of this total, half came from public utility plants, half from plants operated by industry to meet its own needs.

Owing to war losses and Treaty cessions Germany has only about the same number of industrial workers now that she had before the war (in 1925, roughly 14,500,000). The electric power available per worker is therefore also about three times as great as before the war.

throwing of a switch will bring in another. The net has
already been pushed up the Rhine to Switzerland, where
it taps the cheap Swiss water power, and down to the
North Sea and Denmark, while a link with Italy is now
planned. The import and export of power is now a far
from negligible factor in Germany's international accounts.

Power production, especially in the coal and lignite
plants, is extraordinarily cheap and efficient.[1] The
present problem, rather, is how to pass on the cheapness
to the consumers, and thus to insure a large and steady
demand. More than half of the current is produced and
sold by the various government bodies, which act as sales
agencies and distribute the current to the ultimate consumer. It is here that the difficulty arises. The governments find themselves in a position of virtual dictatorship. By charging much more for the current than it
costs them they often make handsome profits, with
which they meet a considerable part of their budget expenses. The writer has been told of cases in which the
price to small consumers was from ten to twenty times
the original cost of the current. This is doubtless unusual, but wherever anything more than a reasonable
commercial profit is secured the price charged for current is evidently an unavowed and uncontrolled tax, and
consumption is correspondingly restricted.[2]

---

[1] In the United States, the consumption of fuel in public utility
plants has declined from 3.2 pounds of coal per kilowatt hour in 1919
to 1.95 pounds in 1926, a decrease of 40 per cent. The writer has been
told by German engineers that their savings relative to 1913 (the war
and inflation years are hardly a fair basis for comparison) have been
even greater. There seem to be no comprehensive statistics on the
question.

[2] Of the total amount of current sold by the leading companies in
1927, private companies delivered only 14.5 per cent, "mixed" companies (in which the shareholders are both private individuals and

These obstacles, however, and others arising from matters of intergovernmental jurisdiction, will be overcome before long, and cheap and plentiful power will soon be available in almost every section. This development has already begun to have a far-reaching effect upon the country's economic life, for it greatly increases the mobility of industry. The question of local power supply becomes a matter of relative indifference, since one place is about as good as another from this point of view. The light manufacturing industries requiring labor which is cheap in proportion to what it can turn out are concentrating in the big cities, while those heavy industries which are not dependent on a particular source of raw material are moving out into the less populated districts, where the low price of land offsets the slightly higher transportation charges. Cheap power universally attainable is one of the principal factors in the state of flux now prevailing in many branches of German industrial life. The other chief explanation, it is interesting to note in passing, is the fact that wage rates, despite many local exceptions, are becoming fairly uniform throughout the country. In consequence of this leveling, many firms which had placed their plants in small towns and villages before the war because labor was then very cheap there are now in a difficult situation. They have to pay nearly the same wages as the

public bodies) 30 per cent, the Federal Government 10 per cent, the provincial governments 11 per cent, and the local governments 34.5 per cent. The total for all classes of governments was thus 55.5 per cent. Detailed figures for production are not available, but it appears that the various governments produced 60 to 65 per cent, and the private and the "mixed" companies together only 30 to 35 per cent—with the private companies having the smaller share. See the Vereinigung der Elektrizitätswerke publication, *Statistik der Elektrizitätswerke* (Berlin, 1927); also *Wirtschaft und Statistik*, 1929, H. 3, p. 74.

enterprises in the big cities, but the rural and small-town workers are not usually as efficient as the city dwellers. The real cost of labor is hence often, if not usually, higher in the country than in the city; and this provides a powerful motive for moving the industries back into the metropolitan areas.

CHAPTER V

THE CHIEF MANUFACTURING INDUSTRIES

THE coal and steel industries have thus been thoroughly reorganized since the inflation period, and most of the firms, although not prosperous, are making money. The situation of the other leading German industries is much more varied. Some are in excellent shape, and are earning large sums on their invested capital. These are industries which, like the electro-technical group, have found a steadily expanding market for their output, or which like the chemical group have developed a wide range of new and profitable products. Other industries, especially the machinery division and parts of the textile group, have been in difficulty much of the time since 1924. They had expanded heavily during the war and the inflation period, and after the stabilization found themselves with far more productive capacity than the markets would support. At the same time technical and other factors prevented any drastic consolidation or elimination of the inefficient enterprises, and the result has been recurrent waves of cutthroat competition, despite all attempts at cartel control. Except in one or two branches the majority of firms have not managed to do much better than break even, and the average rate of dividends is low. Finally, still other industries have been in a middle position, and without growing rich have earned profits that are in line with the general rate of recovery and new expansion of the country at large. In this group belong most of the remaining textile branches, the clothing, construction, potash, leather and paper industries, and so on.

Of the principal manufacturing groups, we shall deal in any detail only with the four largest, which are at the same time the most important export divisions. Ranged according to the value of their annual output, they are textiles, chemicals, machinery, and the electro-technical industry, with textiles much the biggest. The machinery industry, however, is the one most closely related to the basic iron and steel industry just discussed, and consumes about half of its current production. We shall therefore begin with machinery, and then pass on from it to the other groups.

I. THE MACHINERY INDUSTRY

THE machinery industry has many branches, and covers a wide range of products. It includes not only factory machinery, such as machine tools, textile, paper, shoe, milling, and mining machinery, but also farm machinery, locomotives, bridges, internal combustion engines and automobiles, as well as many other articles. Conditions are often extremely dissimilar in the different branches, and while some prosper others are in the doldrums, but it is nevertheless difficult to make any satisfactory practical division between them. The general statistics available usually lump a number of branches together, and many if not most of the companies operate in several lines at once. One makes both locomotives and fine machine tools, another milling machinery and trucks, and at the same time builds bridges, and so on.[1] To get a comprehensive picture, it is therefore necessary to treat the entire industry more or less

[1] This diversity of products in the individual firm has the advantage, however, that when one line is slack another may be active, and

as a unit, even at the expense of doing some violence to the details of the situation.

Before the war, Germany had much the biggest machine industry in Europe. She produced over 20 per cent of the value of the world's output, and although the American production was far larger, Germany's nearest European competitor, England, had only 12 per cent of the world total. During the war itself a rapid expansion took place in consequence of the urgent demand for ammunition and armament, while the industry suffered little loss of plant from the subsequent cessions under the Treaty of Peace; and during the inflation plants were further extended, partly because construction was cheap but partly because there was no other way of protecting funds from renewed depreciation. Trade was active, and until 1923 conditions were fairly prosperous.

With the stabilization, however, the bubble burst, and the real situation became clear. The manufacturers found that they had far more plant than they could possibly use. Productive capacity had increased nearly 40 per cent, but the markets, instead of growing, were actually smaller in the aggregate than they had been before the war. If drastic consolidation and control had been practicable, some way out of the situation might have been found, as it was in iron and steel, but to date the nature of the existing conditions has been too great a barrier to overcome. Apart from the wide variety of products, the industry is made up of a great number of relatively small firms scattered all

the company is hence usually able to maintain a more nearly even volume of production in the *aggregate* of its operations than if it specialized.

over the country—there are nearly a thousand incorporated companies alone—and it has been impossible to achieve, unified action under strong central control. During the inflation a strong movement toward vertical combination developed, to be replaced by a horizontal movement after the stabilization, and in the last two or three years a number of vertical groups have again been formed. But both the horizontal and the vertical combines are of relatively limited scope, and have as yet not been able to raise materially the general level of conditions in the industry as a whole. Moreover, many firms found themselves in severe financial difficulties after the conversion from paper to a gold mark basis, and whenever a potential market appeared anywhere they therefore jumped for it at cutthroat prices, regardless of any cartel agreements or other arrangements.

The general figures available show the situation very clearly. In 1913, the value of the total output was 2,800 million marks. By 1927 it had risen to 3,400 millions, but prices had risen even more rapidly, and the physical volume of production was therefore at least 11 per cent less than before the war. At the same time, the size and number of the plants had so increased that even in 1927, which was a good year, they were working at less than two-thirds of aggregate capacity. Complete data for 1928 are not yet available, but some recession occurred in that year. It is probable that the physical volume of production in 1928 was at least 15 per cent below the 1913 level, and that actual output was hence at less than three-fifths of capacity. Since machinery prices have risen as much as general wholesale prices or more, it follows that what we have called the economic effectiveness of the industry has also diminished by at least 15 per cent.[1]

The change in the position since the war is shown by the following data on world output and capacity, in 1913 and 1925. Electro-technical products and boilers are excluded, but locomotives are included. Output in 1913 is assumed to have been at capacity. Figures are in million marks:[2]

	1913: Output	1925: Output	1925: Capacity	Output in per cents of world total 1913	1925
Germany	2,800	2,900	5,040	20.6	13.1
Great Britain	1,600	3,000	3,450	11.8	13.6
United States	6,780	12,700	17,000	50.0	57.6
All other	2,380	3,460	4,280	17.6	15.7
World totals	13,560	22,060	29,770	100.0	100.0

The least unfavorable side of the situation is the volume of exportation. Since 1924 it has risen steadily, and in 1928 net exports reached a figure of over 900 million marks. This is nearly 30 per cent of the total production, and represents about the same physical volume as the pre-war exports. Machinery exports are extensively encouraged. Large classes of machinery receive reductions of as much as 40 to 50 per cent from

[1] The official price index for machinery for 1928, with 1913 taken as 100, stood at about the same level as the general wholesale price index. There is some evidence, however, that the average rise in machinery prices has really been distinctly greater than this. If so, the physical volume of production in 1928 was probably not more than 70 to 75 per cent of the 1913 level; but this tentative conclusion is too uncertain to use without further support.

[2] Figures from "The Machinery Industry of the World" (*Mechanical Engineering*, April, 1928). The article is a digest of memoranda submitted to the International Economic Conference at Geneva, 1927. Comparable international compilations for the period after 1925 have not yet been made. For later figures on Germany, see Appendix VI, below.

the normal railway rates when destined for export, and the manufacturers also get a rebate from the steel producers in connection with exported machinery. The latter rebate is a compensation for the high price of domestic steel. Machinery exports were also greatly stimulated for a time by the German grant of credits to Russia in 1926. They encounter relatively moderate tariffs in most foreign countries except Poland and the United States; usually around 10 per cent. Europe is Germany's best market, and takes about 75 per cent of the total exports.[1]

Despite the present unsatisfactory condition of most branches of the machinery industry a great deal of reconstruction and improvement has taken place in the last few years, and along lines roughly analogous to those followed in the iron and steel industry. A good many firms also attempted to secure American results by taking over American manufacturing methods wholesale, but the experiment was only partly successful. In most branches it has not proved possible, for a variety of reasons, to develop the enormous markets and mass production on which American results are based. The German companies loaded up particularly on special American machine tools, which are now exhibited with great pride but which in fact are too often only expensive museum pieces. Many, and perhaps the majority, cannot be used effectively under German conditions. In general, the two basic factors already noted, limited markets and the large number of separate enterprises, have hitherto prevented these and other forms of technical progress from yielding the desired results. There

[1] For summary tables on the industry and its exports, see Appendix VI and XIV, below. On tariff rates, see the summary in the Verein Deutschen Maschinenbau Anstalten, *Statistisches Handbuch*, 1928, p. 70.

is a good deal of costly and unnecessary duplication of plant, while any general consolidation, as already remarked, has hitherto been impossible to achieve. The familiar and fairly well standardized technique, and the relatively small amount of capital needed, also encourage new competition to develop at every promise of prosperity; and all these conditions, together with the adverse financial situation of many of the existing firms, make any deliberate and permanently effective control over prices and production impossible at present. At the same time the numerous cartels, although unable to hold prices up against real pressure, do make them higher on the average than they otherwise would be, and thus retard or prevent the elimination of the inefficient firms. It therefore seems fair to conclude that the machinery division still has before it a large part of that process of reorganization and rationalization of the industry as a whole which has already been carried through so successfully in the iron and steel groups.

The general situation is especially bad in locomotive building. There are some twenty-two plants in Germany, of which the largest alone or any two of the half dozen bigger ones could supply the entire normal German demand. At present the domestic market is extremely narrow, comparatively speaking, in consequence of the reduction of the Federal Railway Company's purchases to more normal volume after the inflation period expansion. Similarly much of the foreign market, very profitable before the war, has been cut off by the erection of new plants in other countries. It is estimated that the present production capacity is therefore nearly twenty times the present actual output. In the general factory machinery division the situation is better, and the firms have profited by the recent expansion of various other industries, but again the necessity of producing many different types in relatively small quantities is frequently a severe handicap. Against this, however, must be set the fact that some companies built a good deal of their plant during the inflation period or on money borrowed before the war, and therefore now have it almost cost free in terms of present values. Although indifferent technique and poor plant layout is not uncommon in these firms, they are able to compete successfully with better plants and to make respectable profits. For the same reason the characteristic general excess of production capacity over output is not as great a financial burden as it would otherwise be. Much of the excess plant cost little or nothing at present values, and the firms have only maintenance charges to meet on it.

The machine tool division is in a similar but rather better position, since it is in a position to benefit more from the manual skill, intelligence, and patience of the German workmen. Certain of its products, notably precision tools, are as good as any in the world, and usually less expensive. Many of the complicated automatic tools which American firms turn out so effectively, on the other hand, are either not made at all, or are commonly poor and dear—again because the limited demand prevents their production in large quantity, and not because the German manufacturing technique itself is backward. Finally, the fate of the automobile and motor-building companies is still in doubt. A number of them have recently reorganized and rebuilt their plants. Relative to the general state of German industrial technique and relative to the size of the output, their position seems at first glance to be excellent. But the internal market for cars is limited; foreign competition, especially from the United States, is severe; and the volume of sales is therefore comparatively small. The firms have not yet been able to secure the advantages of large-scale production, and the cars themselves, as judged by American standards, are usually both indifferent in quality and exorbitant in price. This relative backwardness of the automobile industry has also retarded the technical and commercial development of that large section of the machine tool industry which is dependent on the automobile industry for its markets.

The General Motors Corporation has recently acquired control of Opel, the largest German automobile manufacturer, and one or two other firms are said to contemplate similar arrangements. If the experiment is successful, a general reorientation and improvement may result from this direct application of American production methods. But the German market for cars is much narrower under present conditions than is sometimes realized, chiefly because of the heavy taxation involved in operating them and because of the limited purchasing power of the consuming public.[1] It will be interesting to see whether American enterprise will be able to accomplish anything more than the German makers have been able to accomplish for themselves.

Taken as a whole, however, the German machinery industry is now technically as good as, and its present capacity is somewhat larger than, that of any other European country. Except for automobiles and the related branches, it can also be compared on a nearly even footing with the much larger American industry. The Germans use more labor and less machinery, but the workers are paid far less than American labor, have quite as

[1] See the U.S. Dept. of Commerce *Trade Information Bulletin* No. 485, "The Motorization of Germany" (1927). In 1925, Germany produced 12 per cent of all European motor cars, but only 1 per cent of the *world* total. The United States produced 90 per cent of the total.

much manual skill, and the average German product, grade for grade, therefore costs no more or even less than the American.[1] The very pronounced differences which nevertheless exist between the general external characteristics of the German and the American industries are accounted for partly by this situation with respect to labor, partly by the smaller size of the average German markets. The industry can be divided roughly into two main branches, that making production goods (factory machinery, work tools, engines and motors, etc.), and that making consumption goods for household and other individual uses. Certain products such as automobiles and small motors really belong in both branches, but in general the classification is correct. With respect to the first main group, except for the automobile and allied divisions, the German and the

[1] For some extremely interesting comparisons between Germany, the United States and other countries, see *Trade Information Bulletin* No. 540, and an article in *Mechanical Engineering* for April, 1928, both already cited; also data published by the Verein Deutschen Maschinenbau Anstalten, *Statistiches Handbuch,* 1928, and an article in the periodical *Maschinenbau,* vol. 6, pt. 1, p. 24.

In the machine-building group as a whole, the Trade Information Bulletin study indicates that these ratios prevailed in 1925: taking Germany as equal to 1, in the United States the number of workers was 0.78; the value of the output was 3.24; output per worker 4.15; horsepower per worker 2.9; output per worker per horsepower 1.45, output per factory 6.6; wages for skilled labor 2.8; and for unskilled 3.27. Thus the American factories were much larger; and American wages were higher roughly in proportion to horsepower used per worker. But output per worker in the United States was nearly half again as high as the additional horsepower per worker, which presumably reflects better American management. Substantially similar conditions were found in the machine tool division taken alone in 1927. Here American money wages were as 3.5 to 1 in Germany, and real wages, allowing for cost of living, 2.5 to 1. It should be pointed out, however, that these percentages are all somewhat less favorable to Germany than those based on the unofficial German sources. The differences are due chiefly to differences in the range of the plants and products covered.

American industries are not very different. In both countries the market for any one product is usually relatively small, and only a few of each type can be turned out at a time—though standardization has gone farther in the United States, and has produced marked savings. With respect to the second group, however, the much greater wealth and income of the average individual American, which is more than three times the German average, provides a much larger potential market, and hence makes possible a much larger output of each product. Here standardized mass production and specialization have reached levels which the lack of markets has hitherto made physically unattainable in Germany, and has also encouraged the growth of much larger companies. The most conspicuous example is of course the automobile industry, but the same thing is true of nearly all branches making articles for ordinary household consumption.

The financial situation of the companies, on the other hand, is not so satisfactory as their technical position. It is difficult to evaluate, because of the lack of comprehensive and accurate information, but a recent survey indicates that in 1925 a large group of firms were earning only 1.4 per cent on their invested capital. Since then their business has improved somewhat, and average earnings probably now run from 4 to 5 per cent—which even so is not excessively high! In some branches the rate is of course better, but others are operating at a loss, and have been compelled to write down their nominal capitalizations from the arbitrary figures adopted after the stabilization.[1] The companies also have a good deal of debt. The great present difficulty, however, is

1 See the data collected in *Trade Information Bulletin* No. 540, just cited. In the plants there reviewed, however, physical assets appear to

not so much this as the lack of adequate markets and the lack of liquid capital. The market situation we have already commented on. The domestic markets, especially for articles of ordinary individual consumption, are restricted by the low average level of individual money incomes. The export markets are of about the same size as before the war, but further expansion has been checked by the post-war growth of competing domestic industries in many of the countries affected, especially in central and eastern Europe, Asia, and South America. The lack of liquid capital, on the other hand, directly limits the scale of the companies' manufacturing operations, and also makes it impossible for most of them to extend in adequate volume the long-term credits so essential in building up foreign trade.

II. THE ELECTRO-TECHNICAL INDUSTRY

THE electro-technical industry is in a much better position in every respect. It is compact, well organized, and dominated by two powerful combines; the general state of its technique is as good as that of any similar industry in the world; and it has enjoyed a steadily increasing demand for its products both at home and abroad. It is now one of the most prosperous industries in Germany.

Before the war Germany had a third of the world's entire output of electrical equipment, with a value of 1,300 million marks in 1913, and was only a little behind the United States. During the war and the inflation period the industry steadily expanded its plant, like the machinery division, and operated at a level of activity which was doubtless artificially high. When the stabili-

be enormously undervalued in the balance sheets. The general machinery builders seem to have fared badly, while the makers of special machines have done relatively well.

zation compelled a return to more normal conditions, however, the electrical firms found, in contrast to the situation in machinery, that the demand for their products had undergone a large and permanent increase. The industry had suffered little or no loss from the Treaty cessions, and by 1925 the value of the output had risen to 2,100 million marks. In 1928 it stood at over 2,800 millions, more than twice the 1913 figure. Some of the increase in value was of course due to the rise in the prices of electrical products, but even after allowing for this it appears that the physical volume of production is some 64 per cent greater now than before the war. The prices involved have increased some 6 per cent *less* than the aggregate of all wholesale prices, and the increase in the economic effectiveness of the industry since 1913 therefore amounts to about 70 per cent. It is true that Germany's percentage share in the total world output is much smaller than in 1913, but this is explained by the fact that other countries, especially the United States, have expanded even more rapidly than Germany.

The world output of electrical equipment in 1913 and 1925 was as follows, in million marks:[1]

	1913		1925	
	Value	*Per cent*	*Value*	*Per cent*
Germany	1,300	31.6	2,100	17.4
Great Britain	600	14.6	1,400	11.6
France	150	3.7	420	3.5
United States	1,400	34.1	6,800	56.3
Other	660	16.0	1,350	11.2
Total world	4,110	100.0	12,070	100.0

Finally, the volume of exportation has also risen

[1] See the Memorandum on the Electrical Industry submitted to the International Economic Conference, Geneva, 1927 (C.E.I., 16), p. 21.

steadily. Net exports, which amounted to 278 million marks in 1913, now stand at over 440 millions, an increase of roughly 60 per cent, and are growing steadily. They absorb about 17 per cent of the total production. The German firms have had especial success in the export field because they will contract for an entire job, not only supplying the equipment but installing it and taking on the related construction work. The Shannon River Dam contract is a conspicuous example. The Russian credit of 1926 also had a stimulating effect on electrical exports for a time. Over 80 per cent of the exports go to European countries, Russia, Holland, and Great Britain being the largest buyers. But although exports of electrical equipment are large, these exports depend directly on prior imports, chiefly of copper, and the net contribution of the industry to the credit side of Germany's trade balance is therefore relatively small.[1]

This generally favorable situation of the industry and of the demand for its products is due in largest part to the great post-war increase in the use of electrical equipment. It was estimated in an earlier chapter that about 3 times as much electricity is consumed in Germany now as in 1913, and in some of the export markets the growth has been even more rapid. Despite the steady expansion of demand, however, the electrical industry has had serious problems of its own to contend with. It has won to its present excellent position only by thoroughgoing reconstruction and reorganization, on a scale almost as drastic as the reorganization of the iron and steel industry. Few plants have been scrapped outright, for a factory building or a machine shop, unlike a blast furnace or a coal mine, can usually be adapted to any

[1] For summary tables on the industry and its exports, see Appendices VII and XIV, below.

one of several purposes, but most of the existing plants have been extensively remodelled and reëquipped, and a number of new ones have been built. Some striking results have been secured. In a factory making meters for measuring electric current, recent alterations have cut the working capital necessary to keep the factory going to one-third of what was required five years ago, while at capacity the output per worker is 4 to 5 times higher; and in a redesigned cable factory the working capital necessary has also been heavily reduced, and output per man increased by 5 to 8 fold.

The situation of course varies widely, however, as between different branches. As in machinery, there are two principal divisions of the industry, which deal with entirely different technical problems and have different markets: the manufacture of factory, power station, and other heavy equipment, and the manufacture of articles for ordinary individual consumption—light motors, switches, telephones, and the like. In the construction of such heavy units as turbines, large generators, and motors the "theoretical limit" of savings in production and assembly has already been pretty well reached, at least for present types and designs. The great gains have come in the manufacture of the lighter machines and other equipment, especially those for which large quantities of the same or of closely analogous types can be made. The most conspicuous examples are probably the manufacture of meters, already referred to, and such products as magnetos, small motors, switches, and miscellaneous light parts. Here production and assembly methods and apparatus have been devised which are remarkably inexpensive to run, and which are almost ideally suited to the special German conditions—particularly to the fact that the labor available is relatively cheap and plentiful, yet usually intelligent. Great improvements have also been made in the production of standard telephone and signal apparatus.[1]

Yet a curious and apparently paradoxical situation exists, which is characteristic of almost all the manufacturing branches of German industry, and indeed is found in greater or less degree in every industrial country. One plant may be highly mechanized, and may represent the last word in modern technique, while an equally successful competitor is both technically and commercially inefficient, with old buildings and equipment and out-of-date methods. The explanation is usually a double one. The highly mechanized plant, by very virtue of being mechanized, saves on labor costs but has to carry relatively heavy overhead charges on its modernized installations. The technically inefficient plant, on the other hand, has a high labor charge, but its buildings and machinery are either so old that their cost has long since been amortized, or else they were built in the inflation period. In either case the company now has them almost cost free, and in consequence can produce as cheaply as the new plant. In the long run, of course, the inefficient plants will disappear as their maintenance charges get heavier, but the process of elimination is very slow.

In addition to this physical and technical reconstruction, the general organization of the industry as a whole has been recast and tightened. Two big and powerful combines, Siemens and the Allgemeine-Elektrizitäts-Gesellschaft (the former being much the larger) now

[1] On this and other aspects of the industry, see *Trade Information Bulletin* No. 548, "Exports of Electrical Equipment from Germany" (1928).

dominate the entire situation.[1] Between them they have at least 60 to 65 per cent of the total production directly, and through numerous participations in other companies they control an even larger share. During the inflation both firms became allied with the big coal, iron, and steel combines of the period, and even took a leading part in promoting them, but when these combines broke down at the stabilization, both regained their independence. Since then they have devoted themselves chiefly to the consolidation and expansion of their legitimate electrical business, and they now play an important rôle in almost every branch. They have also formed working agreements with the two leading American firms, Siemens with Westinghouse and the A.E.G. with the General Electric. The agreements involve the exchange of patents and processes and the division of markets; and while the groups compete among themselves to some extent, the four companies taken together control much the largest part of the world trade.

The industry is thus in the hands of two comprehensive vertical combines, with a group of much smaller and more specialized firms, few of which are really independent, filling in the crevices. It follows that there is little room for any important and effective cartel organization. A number of cartels of course exist, and one or two of them (especially the cable cartel) have attracted a good deal of attention, but their real effect has been slight. The markets are dominated by the competition, sometimes very severe, between the two big con-

---

[1] The remarkable recent expansion of the Siemens concerns seems to be due both to patent and process control, and to an extremely efficient technical and administrative organization—which is open, however, to the potential dangers of overcentralization and rigidity. The A.E.G. operates chiefly in the heavy-current field, whereas Siemens operates both here and in the light-current field, and hence has a

cerns themselves, and cartel or other restrictive agreements do not work in practice. Price cutting, direct or indireçt, takes place continuously. This has been especially true in the export trade, where the direct or indirect violation of cartel agreements has, interestingly enough, been an important factor in recent increases in the volume of exportation. The survival of a certain number of inefficient firms in the industry is due not to the cartels, but to the peculiar conditions already described: chiefly the fact that, for one reason or another, many of these firms have a good deal of their plant almost cost free.

Finally, the general financial position of the industry as a whole is naturally very good. The demand for its products has increased steadily, and the thorough reorganization of plants and production technique in most branches has enabled the companies to take full advantage of the favorable market situation. The A.E.G. is now paying an 8 per cent dividend, and the two Siemens companies—though on very low nominal capitalizations—10 and 14 per cent. The inadequacy of the data makes any estimate difficult, but it seems probable that if additions to hidden reserves are included the real rate of earnings in the industry as a whole is now running at an average of from 12 to 15 per cent on the aggregate actual investment, and in some important cases much higher. One great source of the financial and tactical strength of the big companies, it may be pointed out, is the construction of power stations. Either by acquiring shares of the power companies or by making loans to them, they often get a voice in the management, and in

better balance in the aggregate of its production: when the market is slack in one field it can usually turn to the other. A union between the two companies is not unlikely to occur in the next few years.

consequence are frequently able to monopolize the power companies' purchases of equipment.

III. THE TEXTILE INDUSTRY

BY far the largest single industry in Germany, in terms of the value of its products, is the textile industry. Its total annual output is worth nearly four times as much as all the coal produced in the country, and five times as much as all the steel. But this comparison is misleading. The textile industry is made up of four or five quite different branches, which for many purposes must be treated as separate industries. The principal groups, in the order of their importance, are cotton, wool, silk, linen, and jute. Cotton is much the biggest, while linen and jute are relatively small. This division into largely unrelated groups makes it difficult to form any satisfactory picture of the textile industry as a whole. Like the machinery industry, it consists of a great number of different firms scattered all over the country, chiefly in southern Saxony and Bavaria and on the outskirts of the Ruhr. No one firm is large enough, outside of the artificial silk branch, to exercise a dominating influence. This very diversity, together with the great variety of products themselves, has prevented the development of any really effective cartel organization. In consequence, neither the industry as a whole nor its component branches have much unity of structure or of operation.

In 1913, according to a recent semiofficial estimate, the value of the total textile output was just under 5,000 million marks. Like most other divisions of industry, the textile groups expanded during the war and inflation periods, and then went through a severe crisis after the stabilization. The market for textile products has since grown steadily, however, if slowly, and in 1927 the output reached a peak figure of nearly 9,400 million marks. In 1928 a general recession developed, but even so the total was over 8,500 millions, which was 71 per cent higher than the 1913 figure. But the apparent increase was due chiefly to the rise in textile prices. When that is allowed for, it becomes apparent that the physical volume of production was really only 8 per cent larger than in 1913, a very small expansion. Moreover, prices not only rose, but rose some 12 per cent more than the general average of wholesale prices. The economic effectiveness of the industry as a whole therefore *fell* by about 4 per cent relative to the pre-war position.

The summary figures on production in the chief branches are as follows, in million marks:[1]

Branch	1913	1927	1928
1. Cotton	2,350	4,950	4,490
2. Wool	1,720	2,920	2,570
3. Silk, real and artificial	490	1,040	1,090
4. Linen and jute	420	470	410
5. Total	4,980	9,380	8,560
6. Price index: 1913 = 100	100	153	159
7. Physical volume of production: 1913 = 100	100	123	108

The development has thus been very dissimilar in the different branches. The artificial-silk division, which is closely affiliated with the chemical industry, has expanded most rapidly of all, and has been very prosperous. The cotton and wool divisions have also expanded, as has jute, but have not made much money on the average, while a number of firms have been forced

[1] Items 1–5 are from the Institut für Konjunkturforschung, *Vierteljahreshefte*, 1928, IV, B, 22; item 6 from the *Statistisches Jahrbuch*, 1928, p. 345; item 7 is calculated from items 5 and 6. For fuller statistics on the industry, see Appendix VIII below; on textile exports, Appendix XIV.

out, and linen has lost ground heavily. In order to understand the whole situation, it is therefore first necessary to treat the main groups separately.

The most important division is of course cotton. In 1913 the value of the output of cotton manufactures was 2,350 million marks, and by 1928 it had risen to 4,490 millions, or some 90 per cent. But meanwhile cotton prices had also gone up a good deal, and the increase in the actual physical volume of production since 1913 has therefore amounted to only 16 per cent. Moreover, since the war the capacity of the plants has increased much more rapidly than output, by perhaps 40 to 50 per cent.[1] The total number of spindles and looms is almost unchanged, but improvements in design, speed, and operation have enabled the newest equipment to turn out more than twice the pre-war average quantity per machine. The result of this increase in capacity relative to actual output has been an almost continuous state of underproduction. At intervals the mills work busily for several weeks or months, and even run overtime, but then long periods ensue when they have almost nothing to do. The gravity of the situation is indicated by the fact that on an average of the three years 1926–28 only two-thirds of the trade union members were fully employed, though it must be pointed out that this figure does not include men working part time.[2]

[1] The figures on cotton imports and exports are not good, but it is clear that the cotton industry has a large annual import balance. In 1927, net imports of raw cotton were about 600 million marks, and of cotton manufactures over 50 millions. The total net import excess was hence over 650 millions. In 1926 the excess was about 450 millions. On the distribution of the exports, see Appendix XIV, below.

[2] This estimate is necessarily somewhat uncertain. It is based partly on the unemployment figures, partly on observation and the varying estimates of individual mill managers. For a summary table on cotton see Appendix VIII, below.

One might expect that competition would eventually provide a solution by weeding out the less efficient firms, but it is precisely in industries like cotton that the worst effects of the cartel system appear. The cartels are numerous but weak, and although they can neither keep prices high enough nor production low enough to insure general prosperity, they nevertheless do maintain prices above the levels at which they would be under free competition. In consequence, great numbers of the inefficient firms are enabled to hold on indefinitely, and either stay outside the cartel entirely, thus securing all its advantages while incurring none of its restrictions, or join it, but break out and begin price cutting again at the first sign of a revival in demand. The cartels here would be much less open to criticism if they were actually stronger than they are. The result of all this is that the typical cotton firm does not make much money. Some firms, chiefly by a combination of lucky speculation in raw cotton and skilful merchandising of the products, have done extremely well, but a much greater number are nearly always heavily in debt and more or less on the verge of bankruptcy. The average financial position of the companies is not as bad, however, as the comparatively low relation of their actual output to plant capacity might suggest. As is also the case in the machinery industry, a good deal of the present excess equipment was installed in the inflation period, and is hence almost cost free at present values; a condition which in turn, however, helps to prevent the elimination of the technically less efficient firms.

There seems to be no immediate remedy for the general situation. The machinery now necessary for cotton manufacturing is relatively cheap, standardized, and almost completely automatic, and nearly any old building will do for a factory. It follows that little capital and relatively little technical skill is needed to enter the business. When any improvement in general conditions appears which promises to be at all permanent, a host of new companies spring into existence and drag the general level of prosperity down again. No firm is or can be much ahead of the others in the general technique of production, for any improvement—and there have been many—spreads rapidly throughout the whole industry. These conditions have also prevented the formation and successful operation of large combines and consolidations. The few that were built up in the inflation period have either disappeared, or have lost their strength in the face of new competition. Finally, the industry has suffered heavily from increased foreign competition. The development of new industries abroad since the war, and the lower levels of money wages in many countries, have not only decreased German exports of cotton manufactures but have actually increased German imports.[1] This applies especially to the narrower widths of cloth, and especially to competition from France and Czechoslovakia.

But the German cotton industry is of course not alone in its difficulties. In all the older industrial countries the cotton firms have been in a situation which has become almost proverbially bad. This situation has been due to overexpansion during and after the war, to the development of new industries in certain European countries and in the Far East, and to the competition of the various cotton substitutes, especially artificial silk. On the

[1] See Appendix VIII. The fact that the general level of technique and the machinery used is a good deal the same in the principal European producing countries makes the labor factor—output per man in comparison with rates of money wage rates—of critical importance.

average, the German industry has certainly fared much better to date than the English, where large and protracted net losses have been incurred, and probably better than the American.[1] It may be added that in point of size, as gauged merely by the number of spindles, the German industry is now less than a fifth as large as the English, and less than a third as large as the American; and its output per spindle is also smaller. Despite the loss of the important Alsatian division under the Peace Treaty cessions, however, it is larger than the French or any other Continental cotton industry.

The position of the German woolen industry has been even less favorable than that of the cotton industry in some respects, but better in others. The value of its output has risen from 1,700 million marks in 1913 to nearly 2,600 millions in 1928 (a little over half the value of the cotton output), or by roughly 50 per cent, but prices have increased even more, and the physical volume of production is therefore smaller than it was before the war. A recent survey of the spinning division alone indicates that in 1926 its volume of production was hardly two-thirds of what it had been in 1913. In the last two years some improvement has taken place, but even so nothing like the pre-war level has been at-

[1] For a review of the European situation, see an extremely interesting article in the *Manchester Guardian Commercial*, June 14, 1928, summarizing a confidential report by Mr. Arno S. Pearse. The article presents some striking comparisons of money wages and real labor costs. Money wages are about as high in Germany as anywhere except England and Holland, and real labor costs as high or higher than in any country. It may be suspected that this is usually offset, however, by lower capital charges on the German plant. In point of coöperation within the industry for the common benefit Germany, despite her difficulties, is farther advanced than any country except Italy and perhaps Belgium. Recent developments in England, however, may also produce a more satisfactory position there.

tained.[1] The lack of adequate price statistics makes it impossible to calculate the changes in physical volume of production for the industry as a whole with any degree of closeness. The average physical volume of net raw wool imports, however, is running about 15 per cent *below* the 1913 level, and this is probably a good guide to the general state of production, since most of the wool is imported. The number of spindles and looms is also substantially smaller· than before the war. As in the cotton industry, however, extensive improvements have been made in design and operation, the output per machine is very much higher, and the capacity of the industry as a whole is therefore far in excess of its previous or present actual production. Taking the three years 1926 to 1928 together, on the average only 78 per cent of the trade union members were employed at full time—a figure which gives at least some idea of the position. As gauged by the number of spindles, the German woolen industry today is only three-fifths as large as the English, but is nearly as big as the American, and is much bigger than that of any of the remaining countries. Output per spindle, on the other hand, is less than in England or the United States.[2]

With respect to its general organization, the woolen industry is much like the cotton industry. There is a relatively large number of firms, with no one of them strong

[1] See the article by Dr. G. Plum in *Wirtschaftsdienst*, Jan. 25, 1929.

[2] For general data on the wool industry, see Appendix VIII, below. The wool industry has a heavy adverse balance of imports and exports. Taking raw wool and manufactures together, *net* imports amounted to 290 million marks in 1926, and to 530 millions in 1927, as against only 163 millions in 1913. Gross exports of manufactures alone were 387 millions in 1926, however, and 423 millions in 1927: they are growing steadily. On the distribution of the exports see Appendix XIV, below.

enough to dominate; the firms are scattered through a number of districts all over the country; and they often operate in several different branches at once, so that no two enterprises are quite alike. The general technique of production is more complicated and difficult than in cotton, and the variety of products is greater, but much of the newest machinery is nearly automatic, and hence no one firm can establish a monopoly of production methods. In consequence of these conditions, all attempts to form enduring big combines have failed, and the numerous cartels have had only a limited effect. At the same time, however, the industry as it now stands seems to be rather more prosperous than the cotton industry, even in the face of the serious decrease relative to 1913 in the physical volume of its production. It may be that the wool firms are better speculators, but the more probable explanation is the very fact, just referred to, that the technique of manufacture is more difficult and more varied than in cotton. This gives the better managed firms a greater chance for success, and makes it harder for the inefficient firms to survive, despite the help given them by the cartels. It also makes it harder for new competition to spring up at each slight improvement in general conditions. There is probably less deadwood now in the German woolen industry than in cotton, and the average rate of earnings appears to be somewhat higher.[1]

The third great branch of the textile industry is silk. Whereas wool has actually lost ground relative to 1913, and cotton has not done much more than hold its own,

---

[1] In the spinning division the estimates made by Doctor Plum, already referred to, show average earnings of about 8 per cent on nominal capital for 17 of the larger companies in 1926, and of about 9 per cent in 1927. Figures for 1928 are not yet available, but some recession occurred in that year.

the silk division has expanded with great rapidity. Taking artificial and real silk together, the total value of the output in 1913 was 490 million marks, but by 1928 it had risen to 1,090 millions, an increase of 122 per cent—though this value was still less than a fourth the value of the cotton manufactures. Moreover, average prices had risen only about 15 per cent. The greatest part of the increase in value therefore came from the growth in the physical volume of production alone. At the present time this volume is nearly 100 per cent above the 1913 level.[1] The silk industry as a whole, however, is made up of two branches which in their earlier stages are absolutely dissimilar, and which have had very different histories. The real silk branch was much the largest in 1913, but has grown little or none at all since then. Indeed, it has more probably diminished in size, since the physical volume of raw silk imports is now about 30 per cent less than in 1913. Germany grows no real silk herself. The artificial silk branch, on the other hand, has had an extraordinary expansion since the war, and its output is now three or four times as large as the output of real silk products. We shall therefore deal only with it.

In 1913 Germany was the largest producer of artificial silk in the world, with an output of 3.5 million tons a year. Great Britain was close behind, while the American production was small. In 1928 the German output

[1] For summary tables on the silk industry, see Appendix VIII, below. Raw real silk is imported in considerable volume, but the exports of real and artificial silk products nearly offset this import. The industry as a whole, taking real and artificial silk together, had a net export of 20 million marks in 1926, a net *import* of 60 millions in 1927, and again a probable small net export in 1928 (complete data not yet available). *Gross* exports of manufactures are growing steadily. They amounted to 213 million marks in 1926 and to 274 millions in 1927. On the distribution of the exports, see Appendix XIV. The principal buyers have been Great Britain, the United States, and Switzerland.

was 19.5 million tons, nearly a 6-fold increase. More-over, since the money price of the product has remained almost unchanged, its real cost in terms of commodities at large has fallen considerably. Indeed, typical grades are now less than a third as expensive as the correspond-ing grades of real silk. In that fact lies the principal ex-planation of the phenomenal growth of sales and pro-duction in recent years. It is true that Germany has dropped from first to fourth place among the world producers, but that is due to the fact that other coun-tries have expanded even more rapidly than she. Since 1913, the aggregate world consumption of artificial silk has increased some 14 fold.

In this rapid development of the artificial-silk divi-sion, the type of reconstruction and reorganization which has taken place in other industries has necessarily played a rather minor part. Artificial silk is made from wood pulp and other cellulose materials by three or four different and competing processes, and the prin-cipal problems have been those of the chemistry in-volved rather than those of general industrial organiza-tion. The industry is still in a state of constant flux. The technique is changing rapidly, and many plants built even two or three years ago are already antiquated, while the possible future improvements are still very great. Until the technique is stabilized, and until new revolutionary inventions cease to be made every year or so, skilful internal organization will therefore count for much less than success in acquiring and exploiting the latest new methods. This is not to say that competition is not keen at any given time. It is. But it is a compe-tition between different chemical processes, not, as in other branches of the textile industry, between different firms using substantially the same basic technique and prospering or failing according to their skill in production and marketing under that technique. There are a number of companies in the German industry, but one big combine, the Vereinigte Glanzstoff, itself closely affiliated with the chemical trust, controls two-thirds or more of the total output. In the face of this quasi-monopoly, the question of the organization of the industry as a whole, and especially the cartel problem, has little importance. The few small independent firms sink or swim as best they may, according to their success in keeping up with the general technical advance and in capturing markets. When they succeed conspicuously enough, they are apt to be absorbed by the big combine.[1]

At the present time Germany herself produces less than 13 per cent of the world's output. The Italian and British industries are both slightly larger, and the American, with 28 per cent of the total, is as large as any two of the others combined. The greatest part of the American production, however, is controlled by European firms which own the basic patents, chiefly the British Courtaulds' and the German Vereinigte Glanzstoff-Bemberg groups. Taking this situation together with her participations in other countries, it is evident that Germany actually controls a much larger part of the world's output than her own production figures alone would indicate. The principal producers throughout the world, however, are linked together in a comprehensive if informal international agreement, and the competition between countries is therefore limited.[2]

[1] The earnings of the more fortunate companies have necessarily been high. The Vereinigte Glanzstoff now pays a dividend of 18 per cent, and is reputed to have very much larger earnings.

[2] See *Trade Information Bulletin* No. 556, "The International Cartel Movement" (1928), pp. 53–55.

If we now take the textile industry as a whole, it is clear that the present position is not very satisfactory. The production of cotton manufactures is little higher than it was before the war in terms of physical quantities, the production of wool, real silk, and linen manufactures is actually less, and the output of artificial silk, large though its growth has been, is not as yet a major factor in the aggregate textile production: it is under 10 per cent of the total even by value, and much less by weight. Except in artificial silk, the characteristic difficulty of the industry is that it has far too much productive capacity for the present markets, and too many comparatively small firms, many of them products of the inflation period, which cannot or will not coöperate effectively for the common good. In addition, the fact that the cotton and wool machinery is nearly automatic and relatively cheap makes elimination of the inefficient firms difficult and brings in new competition at every favorable turn. Moreover, the market demands change so rapidly and so widely that the ability to make quick deliveries often counts for far more, especially in cotton and wool, than a high level of technical efficiency in the actual production process itself. In cotton and wool, too, a situation exists like that prevailing in parts of the machinery and electro-technical industries. Many firms have machinery which though technically inefficient was bought in the inflation, or which is so old that it has long since paid for itself, and which in either event costs the companies little or nothing now. Unlike machinery which is more efficient but new it can be shut down in slack times with almost no loss, and can then be put back into operation when demand revives. This naturally has a disastrous effect on the stability of the industry at large. With the passage of time the bigger and better-run enterprises are apparently drawing ahead, and are consolidating their position by securing control of the markets for their output, but the process is slow. Only in artificial silk and in jute have big combines managed to get a permanent foothold. Finally, the cotton and wool branches also suffer from another difficulty similar to that prevailing in the machinery industry. The necessity of manufacturing a relatively large number of different types of goods, but usually in relatively small quantities of each type, makes it impossible to secure the benefits of standardized mass production, and also greatly impairs the stability of the markets. Again as in the machinery industry, part of the blame for this lies with the firms themselves, but much of the explanation is simply the variable and limited character of the demand for their products.

Outside of the artificial-silk branch, the technical state of the industry is less good than in England or in the United States. On the average the machines are smaller and older; the individual worker does not take care of nearly so many machines,—sometimes only a quarter as many in spinning and a third as many in weaving; and, what is often indicative of the state of an industry, a good deal of foreign equipment is used, especially English and Swiss. This last is less true, however, of the spinning divisions, and Germany now exports on balance much more textile equipment than she imports. (Curiously enough, the largest single buyer is the United States, the purchases being largely of special machinery.) The mills, especially in the wool division, are frequently badly lighted, and the machines crowded together. To date, however, this technical inferiority has been offset by cheap labor, low capital charges, and a better organization of the industry as a whole, so that the average financial position of the companies is probably distinctly better than in the English and American industries.

IV. THE CHEMICAL INDUSTRY

THE last of the big divisions is the chemical industry. In point of the value of its output, it is the second largest in Germany, and yields place only to the textile group. It is difficult, however, to form any really satisfactory picture of the chemical industry. The range of products is very wide, running from dyes, drugs and acids to fertilizers, light metals, and photographic supplies, and from lacquers and paints to soap and now even gasoline. Many of the products themselves also change frequently in their real nature, as new processes are found or as new markets open up. "The" chemical industry of today is therefore quite different from "the" industry of a few years ago, and still more unlike the one of 1913. Moreover, and even apart from these technical difficulties, the industry surrounds itself with a veil of secrecy and mystery which is almost impossible to penetrate. On many of its operations little information is ever allowed to emerge, and what does come out is often of uncertain value. One cannot do much more than indicate the general magnitude and scope of the industry's activities, without attempting any close quantitative study.

Before the war the world output of chemicals had a value of about 10,000 million marks a year. The largest producer was the United States, with 3,400 millions, and Germany came next with 2,400 millions. A considerable part of the American output, however, consisted of heavy industrial chemicals of various sorts. In the finer and more difficult products, especially dyes and drugs, the German supremacy was unquestioned. The war and the post-war developments in technique and demand brought great changes in this situation. By 1924 the value of the world's output had risen to 18,000 million marks, and of this total the share of the United States had become 47 per cent. Germany, on the other hand, had lost many of her pre-war export markets, and her output had increased much less than in proportion to the world average. In 1924 it was placed at about 3,000 million marks, or only 17 per cent of the world total.

The world output in 1913 and 1924 was as follows, in million marks:

	1913 or 1914	*1923 or 1924*
Germany	2,400	3,000
United States	3,400	8,400
Other	4,200	6,600
World totals	10,000	18,000

Since 1924 a further expansion has taken place, however, and preliminary estimates indicate that by 1928 the German production had reached some 4,000 million marks, making Germany the second largest producer in the world.[1] But general prices have also risen about 40 per cent since the war. If we apply this general price average to the value figures (there is no satisfactory price index for the aggregate of chemical products alone), it appears that the physical volume of production of the German industry is now only 20 to 25 per

[1] The little general information available on the German industry is summarized in Appendix IX. The plants are scattered all over the country. The pre-war centers were in the Rhine Valley and in Berlin, but some of the newest and biggest plants have been built on the Middle German lignite fields, for the sake of cheap power and materials. The industry suffered little loss from the Treaty cessions.

cent greater than it was before the war.[1] The volume of chemical exports, on the other hand, has increased greatly, and Germany is once more the world's largest exporter. The exports, which amounted to just over 500 million marks net in 1913, are now above 1,000 millions. In terms of physical volume, this probably represents an increase of nearly 50 per cent. About 25 per cent of the total production is now exported. The largest buyers are the United States, Great Britain, and Holland. Europe takes roughly 60 per cent of the total exports, Asia 17 per cent.[2]

In the main, the history of the industry since the war has been one of steady growth and general prosperity, and in some directions of phenomenally rapid expansion. The most striking change has been the shift in the center of gravity of the industry itself. In 1913 it was largely focused around the treatment of coal tar, and the characteristic products were the innumerable coal-tar dyes and pharmaceuticals, but since then a whole range of new commodities has been developed. At the present time the largest single branch of the industry is the one engaged in the production of synthetic nitrates, chiefly the nitrate fertilizers.[3] All the coal-tar

[1] The Reich Statistical Office computes a general price index for chemicals, which with 1913 as 100 gives 126 for 1928. The index, however, seems to be made up of heavy chemicals alone. Many coal tar products have risen much more in price than this. The real figure probably lies somewhere between 126 and the general wholesale price index, which in 1928 stood at 140. If we use 140, it appears that the increase in the economic effectiveness of the industry as a whole has amounted to only 19 per cent since 1913; if we use 126, the increase becomes 42 per cent. Presumably the truth lies in between, say around 30 per cent.

[2] See Appendix XIV for detailed figures.

[3] The German synthesis rests on liquefying air, distilling off the nitrogen, combining this with hydrogen under high pressure in the presence of a catalyst to secure ammonia, and then applying the am-

dyes, pharmaceuticals, and other coal-tar products
taken together now have a smaller total value than the
output of nitrates alone. In addition, a great number
of other synthetic products have been created or expanded in the last 10 or 15 years, notably synthetic
alcohol, gasoline, artificial silk, celluloid compounds,
and perhaps rubber; and the electro-chemical manufacture of light metals and alloys has reached very large
proportions. Although the industry is still popularly referred to as the dye industry, the term has really become a misnomer.

Much the most important company is the so-called
Dye Trust, the *I.-G. Farbenindustrie*. Formed in 1925
by a combination of the six greatest dyestuff producers,
it has an almost complete monopoly of many important
lines, produces over a third of the total chemical output
in its own plants, and, through participations in other
concerns, controls another large fraction. Its operations
run from dyes to photographic materials and silk, from
nitrates to metals; it owns its own lignite mines and steel
plants, maintains a very big research staff, and is constantly investing large sums in experimental plant;
and it has close affiliations with most of the leading
chemical companies in other countries. With a nominal
capital of 1,100 million marks,[1] it pays a 12 per cent

monia as desired to secure nitrate fertilizers, and other compounds.
Among other effects the great increase in this domestic production,
from 12,000 tons in 1913 to 800,000 in 1928 measured by nitrogen content, has reduced the net importation of mineral Chile nitrates (salt-
peter) by an almost equivalent amount, from 747,000 tons in 1913 to
only 81,000 tons in 1928.

[1] On the Dye Trust and the industry in general, see A. Marcus, *Die
Grossen Chemiekonzerne* (Leipzig, 1929); Das Spezialarchiv, *Der Far-
benkonzern 1927* (Berlin, 1928); *Trade Information Bulletin* No.
532, "German Chemical Developments in 1927" (1928), and No. 605 for
1928 (1929). The nominal capital of the companies which originally

dividend, and its earnings undoubtedly run very much higher, but at the moment one or two faint clouds are perceptible on the horizon. The great money maker in recent years has been synthetic nitrates, but the market is now becoming fairly well saturated, while at the same time new competition has developed. The prospects for making synthetic gasoline from coal on an important commercial scale now seem to be somewhat less dazzling than was once thought, the synthetic rubber process is as yet of uncertain financial value, and synthetic wood alcohol has been injured by protective tariffs set up by other countries, especially the United States. The most promising big field now is artificial silk, in the production of which the company is heavily interested through its holdings in Vereinigte Glanzstoff. It is constantly experimenting in a wide variety of other fields, however, and at any time may develop new commercial successes along new lines. The independent companies in the industry are much smaller and more specialized. Some of them have had a comparable if less spectacular history of expansion and prosperity, but a considerable number have been in distress much of the time, partly as a by-product of the prosperity of the other companies, partly because of the loss of pre-war export markets and the changes in domestic demands. Thus 115 independent companies paid an average dividend of only 6.8 per cent in 1927, as against 12 per cent for the Dye Trust. The independent companies and the Dye Trust have also entered into a considerable number of domestic cartels and other horizontal associations, how-

formed the Dye Trust amounted to only 646 million marks, but there is no evidence of watered capitalization. Quite the contrary, in fact; the balance sheets now published seem to understate the real position.

ever, which have usually been fairly effective in reducing competition and thus increasing profits.

In addition, the industry has many working agreements with the other principal producing countries, either in the guise of cartels or of less formal but probably more effective arrangements. What is really a gigantic international chemical trust was formed in 1927, centering on dyes, nitrates, and coal liquefaction and involving financial participations, the exchange of patents and processes, and the division of markets. Great Britain is not formally included, but in point of fact has a good many contacts and understandings with the trust, as have some of the American firms. Germany has taken a leading part in nearly all these movements; and her international competitive position, thanks to an early start in the field, initiative in developing new processes, patent control, and a plentiful supply of highly trained yet cheap chemists and technicians, is very strong.[1]

V. THE POTASH INDUSTRY

ANOTHER much smaller but still important division is the potash industry, which really belongs in both the

---

[1] On the domestic and international associations see *Trade Information Bulletins* Nos. 532 and 605, already referred to. The Dye Trust has also recently founded, in conjunction with the Standard Oil interests, an American subsidiary (the American I. G. Chemical Corp.) which will presumably exploit the coal liquefaction and other hydrogenation patents, and which may also serve as base for the American manufacture and sale of other important chemical products made under German processes.

An extremely interesting comparison has recently been made of German and world production of the principal heavy chemicals and electro-chemical metals, and of the electric power consumption entailed. In most cases the German consumption of power per ton of product is above the world average, which means a more highly mechanized and presumably more efficient technique of production. See the periodical *Die Chemische Industrie,* Jan. 5, 1929, p. 2.

chemical and the mining groups. Before the war Germany had a virtual monopoly of the world's potash production, and although the cession of Alsace to France entailed the loss of large deposits and thus broke the monopoly, she is still the dominant factor in the world situation. Potash is an invaluable fertilizer for many soils, and exports are therefore very large.

The German industry has made great progress since the war. Actual production is still about the same as in 1913, but capacity has been very much increased, and the price of potash has declined steadily relative to the prices of commodities in general. The industry was brought under the general socialization law of 1919, and now operates under a compulsory cartel or syndicate. Subsequent to this enactment it went through a painful process of reorganization, made much worse by the artificial stimulation and overexpansion of the inflation period, and a good many of the smaller firms collapsed. The industry is now dominated by three big combines, however, and has been brought to a high state of efficiency. The poorer mines have been shut down, the better ones have been expanded and highly mechanized, and practically the same output is secured from only 43 operating shafts now as from 152 shafts in 1913.[1] The improvements in the methods of mining have been not unlike those in coal, despite the quite different geological and technical conditions involved. The greatest gains have come from the increased mechanization of internal transport. In the better mines, loading and transport is now 85 per cent mechanized or more. Back-

[1] Under the law of 1919 and subsequent decrees many mines were shut down, but retain their cartel quotas until 1953. Most of these quotas have been sold or leased to the mines remaining in operation. The resulting aggregate charge on the latter is variously estimated at from 15 to 22 million marks a year.

filling with semiliquid waste from the refineries has also reduced costs, and permits drawing practically all pillars. At the mining face drilling by air hammers or electric motors, followed by blasting, is the usual practice: direct machine cutting does not seem to be generally feasible. Finally, concentration on the better deposits has resulted in the working of a higher grade of potash salts, the use of more equipment per shaft, and a consequent great increase in gross output per mine. The refining plants have also been rebuilt and greatly improved, so that their average capacity is something like 10 times as great as before the war, and the number of workers has been reduced by over 50 per cent since 1923. The better companies, while building up ample reserves, are paying from 10 to 15 per cent in dividends. There are few industries in Germany which can show a better record of increased efficiency, when allowance is made for the limitations on the size of the market for potash itself.

About 40 per cent of the product is exported, and it is this aspect of the situation which has naturally evoked most attention abroad. After the war France began a vigorous exploitation of her newly acquired potash deposits, and entered into violent competition with Germany for the world markets. The protracted struggle which ensued ended at last in a truce in 1924, and in the formation of a more permanent international cartel in 1926. Under this agreement each country has a monopoly of its own home market, and the export field (the largest purchaser being the United States) is divided in the ratio of 70 per cent to Germany and 30 per cent for France. This apportionment represents a considerable concession, made for the sake of commercial peace, on the part of the German producers. Prices are not controlled, but are to be "moderate" and designed to increase sales. The arrangement gives Germany and France combined an almost exclusive control of the world's present production. There is little evidence, however, that this monopoly position has been used to raise prices artificially high and thus to exploit the foreign consumer. On the contrary, the technical position of the industry makes a growing output the one vital consideration, and the aim of the monopoly has therefore been to stabilize prices rather than to increase them unduly. On the other hand, large deposits are known to exist in some sections of the United States, chiefly in New Mexico and Texas, and if explorations now under way should prove successful the European monopoly may ultimately be overthrown.[1]

Of the other principal branches of German industry, we shall say nothing here. Most of them are much smaller than any of the six big groups already described, and most of them play little or no part in the export trade. The largest is the combined food, beverage, and tobacco industry. The metal wares, construction, woodworking, and clothing industries each have nearly as many employees or more than the foodstuffs

[1] On the potash industry see the tables in Appendix IX; also W. Hoffmann, "Die deutsche Bergbau" (*Wirtschafts-Jahrbuch,* 1928–1929), p. 457; *Trade Information Bulletins,* No. 556, "The International Cartel Movement" (1928), pp. 39 ff., and No. 605, "German Chemical Developments in 1928"; and the publications of the Kali-Syndikat. I am indebted to Prof. George W. Stocking for permission to make use of his exhaustive study, now in preparation, of the world potash industry.

The economic effectiveness of the industry, if changes both in output and in relative prices are allowed for, increased about 15 per cent from 1913 to 1927. Later data are not yet available, but further progress has undoubtedly been made.

industry, but for each the total capital investment, at least as gauged by the incorporated companies, is very much smaller. The paper, leather, and rubber industries follow far behind.[1] Their general development since the end of the inflation period has been a good deal like the development of the six largest industries which we have just reviewed. The chief difference is that the process of reconstruction and reorganization has not yet been carried so far. Prices have therefore risen rather more relative to 1913, and the physical volume of production rather less, than in the big groups. We shall return to this situation and the problems it involves in a later chapter.

VI. GENERAL POSITION OF THE PRINCIPAL INDUSTRIES

THIS survey of the recent development and present position of the six great branches of German industry yields results which are extremely significant both with respect to the general strength and welfare of Germany herself, and with respect to her capacity to make payments abroad on Reparations and other accounts. In order to make the situation clear, it will be worth while to summarize the principal conclusions reached in this and the preceding chapters.

First, the most striking thing is the relatively *small* change in the aggregate physical volume of production since the war. Taken together, the six big industrial groups—coal, iron and steel, machinery, the electrotechnical division, textiles, and chemicals—had in 1913 an output which was valued at a little under 17,000 million marks. In 1927 the value of the output was

[1] See the *Statistiches Jahrbuch*, 1928, pp. 102, 443. The electricity, gas, and water supply divisions are also important. The first two were discussed briefly in the last chapter.

nearly 25,000 million marks (6,000 million dollars), an increase of 50 per cent. But the prices of practically all the commodities involved have also risen since the war. When allowance is made for this rise, we discover that the *physical* volume of production of the six industries as a whole was only 15 per cent higher in 1927 than it was in 1913. And 1927 was a boom year; since then there has been a marked recession, though complete figures are not yet available. The position is shown in the following summary table:[1]

	Value of output, in million marks		1927: Index of physical production:
	1913	1927	1913 = 100
Coal, coke, and by-products, net	2,422	2,690	83
Lignite	192	420	191
Iron, steel, and rolled products, net	2,700	2,470	84
Machinery	2,800	3,400	89
Electro-technical	1,300	2,600	155
Textiles	4,980	9,380	123
Chemicals	2,400	4,000	125
Totals	16,794	24,960	—
Weighted average	—	—	115

Second, the money value of the exports of these industries increased from 2,800 million marks in 1913 to 3,200 millions in 1927. But again prices have risen, and here more than in proportion. When allowance is made for this, we find that the physical volume of the exports has actually *decreased*, and in 1927 it was only some 85 per cent of the 1913 volume. In addition, what is even more significant, certain of the industries involved are now completely dependent on prior importations of raw materials for production, and hence for exportation. This is conspicuously true of iron and steel, textiles,

[1] For the sources and composition of the table see Appendix X. The final average is weighted according to value of production in 1927.

and electro-technical products, and indirectly of machinery as well. The principal imports involved are iron, ore, copper, and raw cotton and wool. When these raw material imports are allowed for, we find that the net export *balance* of the six industries as a whole is a half to two-thirds less than their total gross exports. In 1927, the position was as follows (figures in million marks):

	1 Net exports of manufactures	2. Direct raw material imports	3. Real export balance: 1 minus 2	4. Per cent gross exports are of production (by values)	5. Per cent raw material imports are of total raw material consumption (by values)*
Coal and coke (excluding lignite)	721	—	+721	26.8	—
Iron, steel, rolled products	273	380	–107	11.2	76
Machinery	790	—	+790	23.3	76
Electro-technical	365	245	+120	17.1	85
Textiles	132	1,570	–1,438	1.4	70
Chemicals	924	—	+924	25.3	—
Totals, and averages weighted by values	3,205	2,195	+1,010	13.0	55

This table shows the rôle exports play in production, and the degree of dependence of production as a whole on raw material importation. For every three marks of exports from these combined industries in 1927, there were two marks of necessary prior imports! Complete

* Necessarily a rough calculation. Allowance is made, in the manufacturing industries, for the fact that although the machinery group is not *directly* dependent on raw materials which are imported, it of course gets them from the iron and steel industry, which *is* thus dependent. A similar allowance has been made for iron and steel used in the electro-technical group.

figures for 1928 are not yet available. The indications
are, however, that the net export balance for the six
industries was somewhat higher in that year. Taking one
year with another, the average ratio of exports to raw
material imports is perhaps 2 to 1, instead of the 3 to
2 ratio of 1927, but even so the complete dependence
of the exports on prior importation is evidently beyond debate. Moreover, what is even more significant,
over half of the total quantity of raw materials consumed by the six industries combined was imported,
despite the fact that in coal, coke, and chemicals such
imports were either nil or relatively small. The part
the war and the Treaty played in producing this situation requires no comment. The dependence on imported
copper and raw textiles is of course nothing new, but
the dependence on foreign iron ore is the direct outgrowth of the Treaty cessions.

Third, the general technical position of the industries as a whole is very good in most cases, and the average is probably now better than in any other European
industrial country. As compared with the United States,
in coal mining, in most branches of the general iron and
steel industry, in chemicals, and probably in the electro-
technical division the level of technique actually found
in practice is as good or better than the American, after
allowance is made for the fact that because of the lower
level of money wages and the generally higher level
of interest rates, the use of a relatively greater amount
of labor is economical. In textiles the situation is somewhat less favorable to Germany; but in many branches
of the machinery industry there is little to choose
between the two countries, although Germany's backwardness in automobile building is undeniable. Moreover, in all of these divisions practically every impor-
portant plant now in operation has been partly or

completely rebuilt, reëquipped, and expanded in the last four or five years, and the average age of the industrial installations is therefore probably less than in any other country in the world. A further result is that although the aggregate physical volume of production at present levels of demand is now less than 15 per cent above the 1913 volume, the average production capacity is from 30 to 40 per cent greater, or even more.

An interesting sidelight on the general state of German production technique in the four big manufacturing industries is given by the following table of costs of production. The figures are estimates based on data secured by the writer in visiting some 40 plants in the industries listed during the winter of 1928–29. They are not exact, but they have been checked against other sources of information, and made as accurate as possible. Comparable data on coal, coke, iron, and steel were not obtainable. Overhead includes so-called "unproductive" labor, while the last column includes both this labor and the "productive" labor charged to the particular job, whenever a distinction was made in practice. Figures are in per cents of total factory costs, including depreciation, interest, and taxes, but excluding sales costs. They are not true averages, but are figures judged to be typical.[1]

	Productive labor alone	Materials	Overhead	Total labor costs
General machinery	25	30	45	30
Automobiles and motors	25	20	55	30
Electro-technical	20	30	50	24
Cotton and wool	20	30	50	22
Artificial silk	25	11	64	32
General chemicals	15	20	65	15
Chemical specialties	10	70	20	10

[1] See Appendix XI for full tables. For automobiles, accessories purchased elsewhere are *not* included in materials.

The most interesting figures here are those on labor costs. In the automobile industry the German figure of 25 per cent compares with an American average of 6 to 8 per cent, but in the other industries there is not much difference between the two countries. American money wages are two to three times higher than the German, but the average German plant uses a larger physical quantity of labor per job, and the aggregate labor costs work out about the same. This greater use of labor, be it noted, does not mean that German industry is less efficient than the American; it is not, for most of its products compete successfully with ours. The figures are merely a graphic illustration of the statement frequently made at earlier points above, that it does not pay to mechanize nearly as extensively in Germany as in the United States. In Germany low wages and high interest rates make labor relatively cheap, machinery relatively dear. The two are combined in a different proportion than is usual with us, but the commercial and technical results are not very dissimilar. Where large markets make mass production possible, the degree of mechanization and the general character of the technique used are not far different from the American.

Fourth, the financial position of the companies as a whole is usually sound. If we disregard the extreme cases on either side of the average, we find that the typical firms are not markedly prosperous, but are nevertheless making a fairly satisfactory return on their investment. Taking the six big industries together, the average dividend is now around 6 to 7 per cent on nominal capital, and net earnings (including additions to hidden reserves) probably 9 to 10 per cent.[1] In view of the extent

[1] Caution must be used, however, in drawing inferences from the ratio between dividend payments and nominal capital, since both items

to which pre-1924 debts were wiped out by the currency depreciation, and in view of the large amount of plant, built during the inflation period itself, which the companies now have almost cost free, it might have been expected that present dividends and earnings would be a good deal higher. In most cases, however, these latter gains appear to have been offset or more than offset by the heavy capital charges incurred to pay for the thoroughgoing physical reconstruction and reorganization of the past five years. There is no evidence that the capital charges on industry or the general burden of debt are any lower *now* in Germany than in other leading countries; in fact quite the contrary, though such comparisons are necessarily difficult and uncertain. Indeed, the principal financial weakness of the companies lies in precisely this indebtedness itself. Most of them now have long- and short-term debts of considerable size, often owed to foreigners, which were incurred to finance the recent reorganization, and the fixed charges involved would undoubtedly constitute a very real danger to the continued solvency of many firms should any protracted and substantial business recession develop. On these latter questions more will be said in the next chapter.

Finally, the competitive power of the six principal industries in the world markets is not nearly as great at present levels of demand as foreign industrialists have sometimes feared. Taken by and large, the burden of fairly heavy capital charges and excess plant capacity, and the continuous pressure of labor for higher wages, make it seem improbable that the German producers will attempt to capture additional foreign mar-

may be more or less unrepresentative of the real position. See the next chapter for a more detailed discussion of this question.

kets by means of large price reductions in the near future. Railway rebates and other preferential treatment for exports, and the usual practice of quoting much lower prices for export sales than at home, have already gone about as far as they can, and have fairly well exhausted their effects. It might perhaps be expected that precisely this state of excess plant capacity would induce the producers to lower prices in the hope of increasing their output. Under existing conditions, however, this course would be both difficult and of doubtful advantage. The cartel system, insofar as it is applied to exports, necessarily impedes price reductions; the markets, in terms of their capacity to absorb additional physical quantities of goods, are restricted (that is, present demands appear to be very inelastic); and in view of the high fixed charges many companies carry, this presumptive narrowness of the demand makes it probable that reducing prices would lead only to a net loss. In many industries it is true that a falling off in domestic sales is usually followed by an increase in exportation, but it is doubtful if this means that the German exporters in general can voluntarily increase their sales abroad at any desired time except by selling below cost. The increase in exports just noted, when it occurs, is ordinarily due partly to the drop in costs of production which internal depression temporarily brings, but chiefly to the necessity of keeping plants going, even at prices which entail a loss. Price cutting abroad is usually preferred to price cutting at home.

There are of course exceptions to these generalizations, especially in the electro-technical and the chemical industries; and any general drop in internal prices or in interest rates would undoubtedly be a great stimulus to exportation. As things now stand, however, the majority of the German producers will probably have to wait until the world demand for the kinds of thing they make expands. If that expansion develops, on the other hand, their excess production capacity and the generally good state of their production technique will enable them to take full advantage of it, and even to scale prices down somewhat from the present levels.

VII. THE RATIONALIZATION MOVEMENT

In all this process of industrial recovery and new growth during the past five years, an extremely important factor has been the organized rationalization movement itself, and no account of what has taken place can be complete without some reference to it. We have seen the effects of the struggle to rationalize as it has worked out in particular companies and divisions of industry, but in addition a comprehensive national machinery has been developed for the promotion of rationalization in every appropriate branch of the country's economic life.

The rationalization movement really dates back to the middle of the last century. It began with isolated attempts on the part of engineers and individual firms, chiefly in the machinery industry, to introduce technical norms and standards for a few raw materials and products. The pressure of war-time, with its urgent need for ever larger and more rapid production, gave the movement a great impetus and placed it on a national scale. In 1917 a normalization committee of machine builders was formed, and in 1921 the general National Efficiency Board (the *Reichskuratorium für Wirtschaftlichkeit*) was founded. This board rapidly grew in size and power, and is now a highly centralized organization covering the whole country. It stands at the head of a great number of subordinate organizations, partly territorial, which handle particular industries and particular problems. Much of its work is carried on by voluntary and unpaid committees of its members. It is concerned primarily with industrial and commercial problems, but there are also other boards, similarly supported in considerable part by subsidies from the Federal Government, which deal with agriculture and with construction, and important subordinate committees on technical norms, management, and production.

The aims of the formal German rationalization movement have been much like those of the analogous though less centralized movements in the United States, as have been its results. Its first great field is the standardization and simplification of products, types, specifications and materials, and the corollary attempt to reduce the number of the separate items. A second field is the promotion of what in England and the United States is more commonly called scientific management in its wider form: the making of time studies, the simplification and improvement of machinery and of the flow of production through the plant, better cost accounting, better planning, and a better adjustment of production to market demands. It also interests itself extensively, partly as an outgrowth of this work, in the vocational training and the general education of both children and the adult workers. A third field is the endeavor to secure a better organization of whole industries in ways we have already touched on, such as the elimination of duplication of plants, cross freights, and sales efforts, and in general by securing better coöperation. This aspect of the movement clearly encourages, if it does not require, the formation of cartels, combines, and outright mergers. Finally, in these and other ways it seeks to make the general production process of the whole nation cheaper, more efficient, and better coördinated.[1]

The German rationalization movement requires no defense, and no hymn of praise; its achievements speak for themselves. To it is due a very substantial part of the great increase in the general efficiency of the German production machine as a whole in recent years, as well as of the specific industrial divisions which we have discussed in the last two chapters. The only criticism to be made is that the movement as it has developed in Germany seems, at least to a foreigner, to be overorganized. Indeed, the Germans themselves speak with some humor of the necessity of "rationalizing rationalization." Despite this it has already been of great benefit to both industry and commerce, and may be expected to bring even greater gains in the future.

[1] For an excellent account of the development and aims of the movement, see two articles by Dr. Otto Bredt, "Rationalisierung als Internationaler Problem" (*Zeitschrift für Organisation*, 1929, *H.* 9), and "The German Rationalization Movement," which is to appear in *Factory and Industrial Management* in the fall of 1929.

For some examples of the countless savings effected directly by the formal rationalization movement, see the publication of the Deutsche Normen-Ausschuss for May 16, 1929; and the memoranda submitted by the German delegation to the International Management Congress held in Paris in June, 1929.

CHAPTER VI

FOREIGN CAPITAL, RECOVERY, AND THE MONEY MARKETS

I. FINANCING RECOVERY. FOREIGN AND DOMESTIC FUNDS

THE history of German industry since 1924 has thus in the main been a history of steady recovery and new development, broadly conceived and as a whole soundly based. When the present position is contrasted with the utter prostration and misery into which the country was still plunged less than six years ago, the advance which has been made since then must be regarded as really phenomenal. In comparison with the general development of the world's industry and commerce the progress achieved perhaps seems somewhat less spectacular, but even so it has been very substantial. Germany has reëstablished her industrial supremacy on the continent, and has regained the largest part of the world leadership she held before the war. On the whole she is now quite as strong economically as she was in 1913, and in some branches much stronger.

This recovery was not accomplished simply by the skill of the industrial and financial leaders, however, nor simply because the people involved struggled for it. The outlay of large sums of money was also necessary. Physical reconstruction, the shutting down of inefficient plants and mines, the reorganization of entire companies, are all very expensive operations. Yet at the close of 1923 German business was nearly bankrupt. The inflation and subsequent stabilization had wiped out most of its working capital, and not only were there no funds available for reconstruction, there was often not even enough to carry on daily operations. Where has the money spent in the last five years come from? It is not as easy to answer that question as one might expect. Obviously a good deal of the money, especially in the early stages of recovery, was secured from foreign countries, but the larger part has undoubtedly come from within Germany herself. A glance at the general facts available will show the nature of the situation.

Foreign funds began to move into Germany even before the currency stabilization was assured. When the successful issue of the German External Loan of 1924 proposed by the Dawes Plan definitely marked the re-establishment of German credit in the world money market, the inflow rapidly swelled to very large proportions. The aspect of this movement that has attracted most public attention has naturally been the flotation of long-term loans. From 1924 to the end of 1928 Germany borrowed, including the External Loan just referred to, some 6,800 million marks nominal value (over 1,600 million dollars) at long term, and nearly 70 per cent of it from the United States. After allowing for discount, commissions, and other charges, the net proceeds to Germany were about 6,200 million marks. To October 31, 1928, the distribution by classes of borrowers was as follows:[1]

	Million marks	Per cent
Federal Government (External Loan 1924)	960	14.3
States	677	10.2
Provinces and communes	812	12.1
Public and semipublic undertakings:		
(a) of the Federal Government	675	10.1
(b) of states, provinces, and communes	1,291	19.2
Private enterprises	2,166	32.4
Church organizations	117	1.7
Totals	6,697	100.0

[1] Figures rounded. There was little long-term borrowing from the

But although these long-term loans were the more conspicuous, they were also the smaller part of the total inflow of foreign money. It is estimated that at the end of 1928 Germany owed 6,000 to 6,500 million marks more to other countries on *short*-term account—borrowings which were heavily reduced, however, in the spring of 1929; and that in addition she had sold 5,500 to 6,000 million marks of domestic mark securities to foreigners since 1924. From 1924 up to the end of 1928, the gross total importation of foreign funds thus amounted to between 18,000 and 19,000 million marks (4,400 million dollars). But Germany had also made short-term advances to other countries herself, and had bought a certain quantity of foreign securities. The *net* importation of foreign funds to the end of 1928 was hence somewhat smaller than this, probably 15,000 to 16,000 million marks (3,700 million dollars). By the end of 1928 the net annual charges on this foreign capital, for profits, interest, and amortization payments owed abroad, were between 1,200 and 1,400 million marks (310 million dollars). These charges are hence a very important item in the general German balance of international accounts.[1]

early winter of 1928–29 up to the date of writing (August, 1929). The nominal total at present is probably still under 7,000 million marks. Of this total nearly 70 per cent has come from the United States, as just remarked; 14 per cent from Holland, 9 per cent from England, and the rest mostly from Switzerland and Sweden. (See the *Reports* of the Agent General for Reparations Payments, *passim*.)

Since most of the loans were issued below par, and since issuing costs were often high, the real interest charge is 0.75 to 1 per cent higher than the nominal rate. It now averages around 8.5 per cent. No detailed figures are available on other forms of capital importation, either by countries of origin or by classes of capital receivers. Some estimates on the latter question, however, will be presented later in this chapter.

[1] See Chap. IX, below.

How much of this foreign money was used for industrial reconstruction and reorganization it is impossible to say. Of the long-term loans, less than a third was floated by private enterprises; a considerable part of the domestic mark securities sold abroad were governmental or agricultural; and many of the short credits were granted in the first instance to the banks. But in a sense, from a broad financial point of view, none of these considerations makes much difference. Money secured from abroad is legally credited to particular individuals or groups, but most of it really goes into the common financial pool. If a governmental body borrows abroad instead of at home, its demands on the domestic money market are that much smaller, and the money which it would have borrowed there is thus left free for other purposes and other borrowers. Moreover, most of the funds obtained from abroad were spent in Germany, and eventually trickled back again into the banks, and hence into the money market. The industrial companies have been among the principal seekers after new money, and it is therefore probable that the biggest share of the foreign capital has gone directly or indirectly to them.

But large though the importation of money from other countries has been, the volume of new funds secured from within Germany herself has been even larger. These funds represent savings of all sorts which have been reinvested in the economic life of the country: savings of workmen and clerks, of investors and speculators, and especially of the various business enterprises themselves. It is difficult to judge their size, the more so as the question is necessarily in the forefront of present politico-economic controversy. We shall submit more detailed estimates later, however, which indicate that from 1924 to the end of 1928 the *gross* increase in German savings amounted to between 24,000 and 25,000 million marks (5,800 million dollars). Even after allowing for the losses in agriculture, the *net* increase in savings of all kinds to the end of 1928 seems to have been in excess of 20,000 million marks (nearly 5,000 million dollars).[1]

These various facts and estimates give the answer, so far as any answer at all is possible, to the question of how the German recovery after 1924 was brought about from the financial side. The first big impetus, in 1924 and 1925, came from the inflow of foreign funds. These funds produced a great and immediate increase in economic activity, and thus got the process of recovery started. Once it was fairly under way, however, the accompanying increases in wages, profits, and other earnings soon enabled both individuals and companies to build up savings of their own in ever swelling volume. It is true that the importation of foreign capital has not yet been permanently diminished by this growth of domestic savings. Industry and commerce have expanded so rapidly that to date the need for funds has far exceeded anything which the domestic markets alone could supply. But the volume of money drawn from German sources has increased steadily, and is now much larger than the volume imported from abroad. Of the total amount of new capital invested in Germany since 1924, roughly two-fifths has come from foreign countries, but three-fifths has been supplied by Germany

[1] See later sections in the present chapter, and also Chap. X, below. The Agent General for Reparations Payments remarks in his *Report* for December 22, 1928 (p. 115) that "important as foreign funds have been in rebuilding the stock of capital in Germany, the principal increase year to year has come from domestic sources." Detailed estimates on the total sums, however, are not given.

herself, and the German share is steadily rising. Indeed, in the first half of 1929 the inflow of foreign funds virtually stopped, and gave way to very heavy withdrawals. This must be regarded, however, as an essentially temporary situation directly due to doubts over the outcome of the Paris Conference. It will undoubtedly be a number of years before Germany can get on entirely without foreign capital.

The reverse side of the situation is that Germany's heavy indebtedness to foreign countries necessarily places her in a vulnerable international financial position. How far this indebtedness has really weakened her economic strength, if at all, will be considered at a later point. It is enough here to repeat that foreign funds made the first great step toward recovery possible, and that without them the recovery itself, if indeed it had developed at all, would certainly have been on a much smaller scale.

II. THE REICHSBANK AND THE CURRENCY

THE effect of the importation of foreign funds on the German credit situation and the money markets has been no less striking, if less permanent, than its effect on industry and business at large. It has sometimes led to a very real danger of credit inflation in certain directions at precisely the same time that credit was being rigorously contracted in other directions, and stock yields have been forced entirely out of line with interest rates. Moreover, while the gold basis of the country's currency and credit has been enormously strengthened by the capital importations, the mere fact that so much money is owed abroad creates, as just remarked, a position which may become acute on little or no notice. The whole money market and credit situation since 1924 has been so unusual that, although it is perhaps more familiar than some of the matters discussed in earlier chapters, a brief account of it is necessary.

The general position of the Reichsbank and of the currency is shown on the accompanying Chart IV. The total amount of currency in circulation increased rapidly from 1924 till the end of 1925, as the normal channels of the country's economic life were reopened and in response to the 1925 boom. Since then the circulation has continued to grow almost without interruption, except for the usual year-end fluctuations, but at a much slower and strikingly even rate. The circulation of the Reichsbank's own notes has expanded more rapidly, however, since they are gradually replacing the old Rentenbank notes. On the other hand, the Reichsbank's grants of credits to industry and commerce (*Wirtschaftskredit*) have fluctuated directly with the broad ups and downs of business itself. At the end of 1928 they were little above the high point of 1924, and since then a sharp decline has taken place. Finally, the Reichsbank's own gold reserves have been steadily built up, and in the last two or three years the Bank has again become one of the strongest institutions in the world. In addition to its published gold reserves, it carries a certain amount of foreign exchange cover, and at least up to 1928 held a further large quantity of gold which was not declared. From the time the Dawes Plan came into effect to the beginning of 1929 its known gold holdings increased by over 2,200 million marks (530 million dollars). This increase is attributable very largely to the importation of funds from abroad. The importations gave the Reichsbank command of considerable quantities of foreign exchange which were in excess of current market needs, and thus permitted it to

IV. CURRENCY CIRCULATION, REICHSBANK CREDITS AND GOLD RESERVES, 1924–1929

A Total currency circulation.
B Reichsbank note circulation.
C Reichsbank grants of credit.
D Reichsbank gold reserves.

ON MARKS

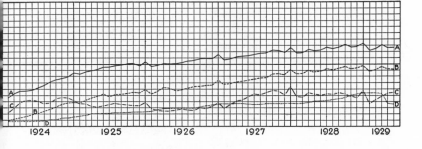

V. MONEY MARKET STATISTICS, 1925–1929

A Monthly money.
B Private discount rate.
C Reichsbank discount rate.
D Bond yields.
E Stock price index.

NDEX PER CENT

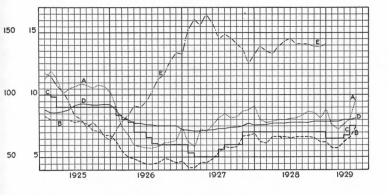

make large and continued gold purchases without creating an exchange stringency. They have also enabled it to keep its reserve ratio well above the prescribed minimum.[1]

The general position in recent months has necessarily been less favorable. A moderate business recession began in the middle of 1928, as we have already seen, and this together with uncertainty over the outcome of the Paris Conference led to heavy withdrawals of foreign funds—withdrawals which in large part could not have been anticipated. Private estimates indicate that as much as 1,500 to 2,000 million marks were taken out in the first four months of 1929. This naturally had a serious effect upon the Reichsbank itself. By the end of April, 1929, it had lost over 800 million marks of gold, which was nearly a third of the holdings at the beginning of the year, and its foreign-exchange portfolio had been virtually emptied.[2] Its domestic grants of credit were correspondingly reduced, and it was compelled to raise its discount rate. What happened is an illustration, though on a relatively small scale, of the intrinsic danger of a large indebtedness to other countries, especially when any large part of it is at short term. The movements of the foreign-exchange rates reflect the same thing very closely. Near or above par most of the time since 1924, from the beginning of 1929 until May they were continuously close to the gold export point. After the conclusion of the Paris Conference,

[1] The Reichsbank reserve ratio against its note issue has been steadily above 40 per cent. It does in point of fact pay bar gold against its notes, but is not yet legally required to do so.

The data for the charts are taken from *Wirtschaft und Statistik* and the Institut für Konjunkturforschung *Vierteljahreshefte*.

[2] For data on monthly gold movements, see Chart XI in Chap. IX, below.

however, capital once more began to flow in, and the exchanges have since been strong.

The private commercial banks have expanded steadily, and even more rapidly than the Reichsbank. They publish little information, but the trend is indicated by the growth in the deposits of the ten big Berlin banks alone from a total of under 4,000 million marks at the end of 1924 to over 10,000 millions at the end of 1928, more than double the earlier figure.[1] The largest part of this increase, however, has undoubtedly been due to the importation of foreign funds. At the end of 1928, various estimates indicated that as much as 40 per cent of the deposits of the private banks were owned by foreigners.[2] This means, if true, that at the end of 1928 the banks were placing only about 2,500 million marks more of *German-owned* funds at the disposal of business than in 1924, an increase of only 65 per cent.

III. THE MONEY MARKETS

THE general money market itself has been in a strained condition much of the time since 1924. On it has been concentrated most of the urgent demand for capital needed in the reconstruction and recovery of business, while at the same time most of the money imported from abroad has originally come into it for redistribution, as has much of the growing volume of domestic savings. In the main demand and supply have offset one another, but this has not always been true. Despite the moderat-

[1] See the Institut für Konjunkturforschung, *Vierteljahreshefte.* Other indices of the general domestic banking situation, such as the Reichsbank's clearings and the postal check clearings, show a similar and even greater expansion.

[2] See the *Report* of the Agent General for December 22, 1928, p. 119, which gives an estimate of 30 to 40 per cent. Other private estimates of the position at the end of 1928 were still higher.

ing influence of the Reichsbank many disturbances have arisen, first on one side and then on the other, and even now the market cannot be regarded as having regained a stable and "normal" position.

The principal features in its development during the last four years are shown on Chart V, above. During 1925 and 1926 all money rates dropped steadily, under the influence of foreign capital importations and of the business recession in the winter of 1925–26. The decline continued until the early months of 1927, when the revival and new expansion of business produced an upward movement in private discount rates. The Reichsbank rate was also raised shortly afterwards. During 1928 there was little change. The private discount rate, which is virtually the rate for prime bankers' bills, moved only between 6 and 7 per cent, the rate for monthly money between 8 and 9, and the Reichsbank rate held steadily at 7 per cent. At the turn of the year there was a decline, but after the Paris Conference had been running for some weeks without reaching a solution, a renewed tightening appeared. In April, apparently anticipating the breakdown of the negotiations, the Reichsbank rate was increased to 7½ per cent, and a further rise in the other rates at once followed. After the successful conclusion of the Conference some easing appeared, but until the importation of foreign funds resumes its former large volume no sustained decline can be expected.

An important and characteristic aspect of the general situation in recent years has been the relation between the money market itself and the Reichsbank. Up to the beginning of 1928 the Reichsbank, in marked contrast to its pre-war position, was never in assured control of the market, and was often entirely out of touch. The principal reason was the importation of foreign money. Germany needed additional capital very badly, and was willing to pay almost anything for it, while at the same time foreign lenders were now only too glad to provide funds at a price. The Reichsbank therefore became an unwilling competitor with foreign centers in supplying the German money market, and was often left almost helpless between two undesirable alternatives. If it lowered its discount rate to check borrowing abroad, it ran into the danger of encouraging credit inflation at home. If it then raised the rate to check the domestic expansion it attracted foreign funds in large volume, and was thus swept out of control. In 1924 and 1925 it was compelled to resort to a stringent rationing of its own grants of credit in order to break out of the vicious circle, and until 1927 its rate, though dropping, was still high relative to those abroad. A further difficulty arose from the fact that from time to time the governments and other public bodies found themselves with considerable amounts of ready money available, and appeared as lenders in the money market. This further impaired the effectiveness of the Reichsbank's action and sometimes short-circuited it, and the practice was finally stopped, partly because of the Reichsbank's protests but chiefly because of the growing scarcity of governmental funds. In the last year and a half the Reichsbank's control has become more effective, in considerable measure because higher rates in other centers produced some relaxation in the inflow of foreign funds, and has been exerted in more ordinary ways. But even so its rate has been consistently stiff, and is now (August, 1929) the highest central bank rate in the world except for Greece.[1] Moreover, it still remains largely true that the Reichsbank rate has its principal effect on the *long*-term division of the money market, whereas the short-term division is chiefly influenced by foreign borrowing, long as well as short. This is of course the reverse of the usual position.

Another important aspect of the general money market situation is the curious and paradoxical relationship which has prevailed since early 1926 between stock yields on the one hand, and bond yields and interest rates at large on the other. In any ordinary market, except in periods of intense speculative activity, the average yield of stocks is of course distinctly higher than the average yield of good bonds, since both the security and the income are less assured. But in Germany the yield of typical stocks has been less than half the yield of gilt-edged mortgage bonds at several times in the last two years, and in the opening months of 1929 was still barely two-thirds as high. In part this arises simply from the extreme narrowness of the stock market, which makes speculative manipulation relatively easy and enables stocks to be held at an artificial level, as compared with yields, for a considerable time. In part, also, it is due to the fact that the real earnings of the companies, after allowing for additions to hidden reserves, have often been much in excess of what they declared. The consequence has been that insiders who knew the true situation frequently bid up the price of the stock concerned to a point where its yield was very low. A principal explanation, however, is again the inflow of

[1] For extensive studies of the position and policy of the Reichsbank, as of the money market at large, see the various *Reports* of the Agent General for Reparations Payments.

foreign funds. To the end of 1928 nearly a third of the capital which Germany imported went directly into the purchase of German mark securities, and of these an unknown but certainly very considerable fraction consisted of corporation stocks. The largest single group of buyers, incidentally, has undoubtedly been American, partly speculators but partly the various investment trusts and other *bona fide* investors.

The effect of these various factors combined has been to force the prices of most stocks, so far as their yield basis is concerned, entirely out of line with the prices of other types of securities. This is not to say that German stock prices are necessarily too high. Many of the important stocks, however, have been carried to levels which have not only capitalized any probable rate of present earnings, but have also discounted the reasonable future prospects rather heavily. The situation reached a first crisis in the spring of 1927, when the Reichsbank intervened and compelled a drastic deflation of stock-market loans; and after some recovery in 1928 prices have again been sagging in recent months. But the general situation is still very undesirable from the German point of view. Prices are still relatively high; the stock market has absorbed a disproportionate share of the available supplies of credit; and any severe break, by precipitating the liquidation of foreign holdings, would put heavy pressure both on the banks and on the already overburdened exchange rates.

IV. DOMESTIC CAPITAL ISSUES

A THIRD major aspect of the development of the money market since 1924, and in some ways the most important one, has been the very large domestic security issues.

The greatest part of these issues come directly into the open markets, and the unceasing pressure they have exerted on the relatively limited supplies of new capital available has been one of the chief reasons for the persistently high level of interest rates. At the same time, however, a good many of the securities have been sold to foreigners. This has both relieved the market pressure, and has kept interest rates at ranges somewhat lower than they would otherwise have reached.

From 1924 to the end of 1928 approximately 10,500 million marks of domestic interest-bearing securities were publicly issued on the German markets. The volume was relatively small in 1924 and 1925, but in 1926 it reached very large proportions, and a third of the total for the whole period was floated in that year alone. In 1927 and 1928 it was again smaller, however, and in recent months few additional loans have been made. Much the largest single class of borrowers has been the land credit institutions, which up to the end of 1928 had issued over two-thirds of the total—roughly 7,200 million marks. Part of this sum represents mortgages on city property, but nearly half of it is credits granted to agriculture. Of the remainder of the total for the five-year period, the various governments issued 18 per cent, public and semipublic undertakings 6 per cent, and all private enterprises together less than 850 million marks, or 8 per cent.

In addition, a large volume of shares was floated by industrial and commercial enterprises. From 1924 to the end of 1928, after subtracting shares issued merely to consolidate existing firms, and counting only nominal paid-in capital, the aggregate was about 4,800 million marks. The distribution of the total domestic issues by

years (including preliminary estimates for November
and December, 1928) was as follows, in million marks:[1]

	Interest-bearing securities	Shares	Totals
1924	441	740	1,181
1925	994	661	1,655
1926	3,435	898	4,333
1927	2,854	1,373	4,227
1928	2,800	1,150	3,950
Totals:	10,524	4,822	15,346

The total public issue of domestic interest-bearing
securities and shares combined, from 1924 to 1928, was
thus about 15,300 million marks (3,650 million dollars). This total is of course small when compared with
American figures, and is less than half of merely the
annual issue of new securities on American markets in
any one of the past three or four years. It is large relative to the size of the German economy, however, and
seems still larger in view of the state of collapse which
Germany was in only six years ago. But the burden on
the German money markets has not been nearly as great
as the size of the total issue would suggest. As already
pointed out, a considerable part of the new securities
was sold to foreigners. Only the remainder, perhaps
9,500 to 10,000 million marks, has really been purchased out of German funds.

V. THE TOTAL SUPPLY OF NEW FUNDS. ITS DISTRIBUTION

IF the domestic security issues are now combined with
the 6,200 million marks net proceeds of loans issued

[1] See the *Reports* of the Agent General for Reparations Payments; various estimates in *Wirtschaft und Statistik*, especially 1928,
p. 485, and 1929, p. 516; and the Institut für Konjunkturforschung,
Vierteljahreshefte, 1928, III, 72.

abroad, it is clear that the total net German issue of securities on all accounts, from 1924 to the end of 1928, was in excess of 22,000 million marks (5,250 million dollars).[1] Of this total something like 12,500 millions really came from foreign countries, and only about 9,500 to 10,000 millions from domestic savings. But the pressure on the German capital supply has been so great that even today high-grade first mortgage bonds yield around 8 per cent, as against perhaps 4 or 5 per cent in most other countries, and the real yield on loans placed abroad is often still higher. In this high rate of security yields lies the measure of the size and urgency of Germany's need for capital in the past five years, to carry on and complete the process of reconstruction and recovery.

In addition to this 22,000 million marks of public security issues, to the end of 1928 Germany had borrowed over 6,000 million marks from foreign countries at short term; and in a later chapter we shall see that she had probably saved about 12,000 million marks more in ways not hitherto taken into account.[2] After allowing for 3,000 to 4,000 millions of German security purchases and short credits granted abroad, we then find that the total volume of new funds made available to Germany from 1924 to the end of 1928 was about 40,000 million marks (9,500 million dollars). Of this

[1] An estimate just published in *Wirtschaft und Statistik,* 1929, p. 516, places the total long-term issue, 1924–28 inclusive, at 28,581 million marks; and by April, 1929, at 31,085 millions. These figures are larger than the ones given in the text above: they include all land mortgages, whereas we have included only those against which securities were publicly issued and which hence came into the general markets. Total short credits outstanding at the end of 1928 are placed at 23,513 millions, but duplications between the items and with long-term credits are not eliminated.

[2] See Chap. X, below.

total, however, some 4,000 million marks was lost in agriculture,[1] and the *net* addition to capital may hence be put at about 36,000 million marks.

The distribution of the new funds within Germany, the use actually made of them, can be described only in rather general terms. At a rough estimate, on the basis of the available information, short-term loans to industry and commerce have taken about 9,000 million marks; between 7,000 and 8,000 millions have gone to agriculture; and other loans to governments and public and semipublic enterprises have taken about 7,000 millions more.[2] Of the remaining 16,000 to 17,000 millions some part has gone to commercial enterprises, but much the greatest fraction, probably 13,000 or 14,000 millions, has been invested in industry.[3] Of course not all of this sum has been spent on the industrial plants themselves. At first a considerable fraction, especially of the funds obtained abroad, went to replenish stocks of raw materials and in general to build up the working capital of the firms. But most of the larger enterprises have become increasingly able to supply their own current needs, and we shall probably not be far wrong in assuming that at least 12,000 million marks (roughly 3,000 million dollars) have been invested in the physical reconstruction and expansion of industry. Therein lies the principal explanation of the remarkable recovery of industry itself in the past five years.

[1] See Chap. VII, below.

[2] See Chap. X, below. There is some duplication between the governmental and agricultural loans, for which the figures in the text above make a rough allowance.

[3] For a study of the distribution of the long-term credits alone, see *Wirtschaft und Statistik*, 1929, p. 516, just cited. Similar figures for short credits are not given, and hence no comparison can be made with the estimates made in the text above.

The distribution of the 40,000 million marks of new funds can also be looked at in another way. How did Germany spend the money in the literal immediate sense? It has been stated above that from 15,000 to 16,000 million marks of capital, net, was imported from abroad. This means, however, that the foreign funds involved were themselves spent abroad, for foreign commodities or gold or other things and to meet German debts in foreign countries. That is, the foreign funds had to be converted into something of use to Germans in Germany. In point of fact, we shall see presently that Germany used the funds to buy raw materials, foodstuffs, and gold, to pay interest and other charges on her debts abroad, and finally to meet the Reparations charges.[1] It therefore follows that of the 40,000 million marks of new funds made available from 1924 to 1928 only the remainder, or 24,000 to 25,000 million marks (5,800 million dollars), has actually been spent *in Germany* on German products and services. That is, only the amount of Germany's own savings has been or could be spent within the country itself.[2] The funds obtained abroad were spent abroad, for commodities and other tangible objects which were then subsequently imported.

VI. THE "PRODUCTIVITY" OF FOREIGN LOANS

Two other closely related questions have recently been in the forefront of public discussion, both within Germany and abroad. One is the so-called "productivity" of foreign loans and other foreign investments in Germany, while the second is the high level of internal interest rates.

The question of the productivity of foreign loans to

[1] See Chap. IX, below.
[2] On the volume of these savings, see Chap. X, below.

Germany can be interpreted in various ways. If what is at issue is simply the financial solvency of the individual borrowers and other receivers of foreign capital, the answer must evidently be much the same as for any other progressive industrial country which carries on part of its economic life on borrowed money. In the natural course of human events companies occasionally go bankrupt, as do even governments, but the overwhelming majority continue to meet their obligations faithfully. It is undoubtedly true, and almost inevitable in the nature of the case, that some of the loans to Germany have been ill advised, and that their aggregate volume has been somewhat larger than the bare necessities of the country required.[1] There is no reason to think that the proportion of failure or repudiations, however, will be any higher in Germany than in England or the United States. So far as German foreign loans are concerned an additional safeguard also arises from the fact that so large a proportion of them are either governmental or carry a government guaranty. As a practical proposition, we must necessarily assume that Germany has *not* embarked on a policy of deliberate financial suicide, and that the capital secured from foreign countries has been invested, within the limits of human fallibility, in ways which are and will be "productive" in this sense.

The question has sometimes been given, however, another and more difficult form. It is asked whether the foreign capital placed in Germany has been so used by

[1] In a number of cases American high pressure salesmanship, interested only in commissions, has apparently forced loans on borrowers who really did not need them, and where the making of such loans was undesirable from almost every point of view. This has been especially true of the relatively inexperienced local governments, which were often dazzled by the prospect of seemingly easy money.

the Germans themselves that it will increase the volume of commodity exports (or will decrease imports), and will thereby assure a supply of foreign funds adequate to meet the necessary payments of interest and dividends to the investors abroad. It is evident that in this sense, and under any strict interpretation, a considerable part of the foreign loans to Germany is necessarily *unproductive*. Why should the reconstruction of a municipal street-car system or gas works with borrowed money, however much earnings may be increased, swell the volume of the country's exportation? Obviously it cannot; and the same thing is true of much of the large volume of government borrowing for other purposes, as well as of many foreign investments in non-governmental enterprises. On the face of it, it therefore looks reasonable to try to limit or prevent foreign borrowing of sorts which will neither swell the volume of exportation nor cut down importation. Germany has made strenuous efforts in this direction with respect to governmental borrowing.[1] But the effect of restricting access to foreign markets for loans which are "unproductive" in this sense has been to throw the borrowers back onto the domestic market. This has raised interest rates there; and the higher interest rates in turn have again attracted foreign capital! Often the result was simply that Germany increased her short-term debt abroad instead

---

[1] A *Beratungsstelle* for foreign loans, or advisory council, was set up early in 1925 in an attempt to check the first wild excesses of borrowing abroad, and is still in operation. It represents the Finance and Economic Ministries, the Reichsbank, and the States; and by common consent, though without legal powers, passes on the foreign borrowing programs of the various governmental bodies and of enterprises owned or controlled by them. Less explicit pressure has also been exerted on private borrowers. See the *Report* of the Agent General for Reparations Payments, especially for November 30, 1926 (serial p. 131), and for Dec. 10, 1927 (serial p. 217).

of her long-term debt, and of the two alternatives the former is usually much worse. The whole sum lent at short term may be called back on little or no notice, whereas long-term loans are usually held, and do not constitute a chronic threat to money market and foreign-exchange stability. It is undoubtedly true that foreign-loan control has had a desirable effect in reducing the *total* volume of governmental borrowing, taking foreign and domestic loans together. Granted that the borrower is going to borrow in any event, however, it is useless to try to keep him from borrowing abroad. Directly or indirectly, the money will be secured from wherever it is cheapest, whether in foreign or in domestic markets: the currents of international finance sift through all barriers. The real international "productivity" at issue is not that of the individual investment but of the country as a whole, which is in turn governed by the general efficiency of production, comparative price levels and the absorption power of foreign markets. These factors, to which we shall return at a later point, may be influenced just as favorably by the importation of capital for a non-exporting industry as for one which does export. The new capital affects the whole country, and the increased general efficiency which it brings about often augments the exporting power of apparently quite unrelated divisions of the national economic life.

VII. WHY INTEREST RATES ARE HIGH

A SECOND question, now especially under discussion in Germany itself, is the level of interest rates. We have already seen that prime bankers' bills have been quoted since the beginning of 1928 at between 6 and 7 per cent, while monthly money, which is roughly equivalent to the ordinary American commercial credit, has averaged be-

tween 8 and 9 per cent. Commissions, an exorbitant
charge for holding funds at disposal, and other items
make the real cost of money to the private borrower 10
to 11 per cent on the average, and sometimes much
more. It is said that so high an interest rate is unnatural; that it is a severe and even paralyzing burden on
business; and that the relationship to stock yields, already commented on, creates an unstable and dangerous financial situation.

To a certain extent the height of the interest rate, or
at least of the rates charged private borrowers, is the
fault of the banks. The leading commercial banks in
Berlin have an almost water-tight monopoly of the distribution of German credit. They have an understanding as to rates and commissions among themselves, their
innumerable branches and associated firms cover the
country, and except in a few districts they meet with no
real competition. But even if this monopoly were broken
and commissions and other charges thus reduced to
nominal figures, the interest rates actually paid would
probably not fall by more than 1 to 1½ per cent on the
average. The principal reason why rates are high is
simply the time-honored relation of supply to demand.

As we have already seen, the present supply of funds
in Germany is not small in absolute terms. The combined deposits of the six chief Berlin banks are more
than twice as large as the combined deposits of the three
big banks that dominate France's commercial credit,
and despite all England's vast international financial
business they are nearly a third as large as the combined
deposits of the London clearing banks. German interest
rates are high for no other reason than the fact that the
demand for capital is large and urgent. That is, borrowers are willing to pay high rates; and they are will-

ing to pay them because the money will earn a still higher return. This simplified statement, however, requires elaboration. It will be recalled from what was said in earlier chapters that many enterprises are earning only 8 or 9 per cent or less, and that the general average does not appear to be above 10 per cent. How, then, can it be claimed that firms can borrow at perhaps 11 per cent, and still make money? What seems to have happened is this. If Germany had been standing still economically in recent years, or even growing at only the pre-war rate, and if the rates of interest had hence been merely the rates for capital required to carry on *current* business, the supply of funds available would have been ample and interest rates would have been relatively low. But Germany has not been standing still. She has been expanding rapidly in almost every direction and planning for future growth, and she could use far more money than she has even now. At least to the end of 1928, the controlling factor in the interest rate situation, in economic terminology the "marginal" factor on the demand side, was therefore the insistent quest for more and ever more capital to reëquip and enlarge industrial plants. But much of the new plant will pay for itself in four or five years, and some in two or three. Thus an interest charge of 9 or 10 or even 12 per cent is *relatively* low. Of course not all the new plant installations are as profitable as this, but it is obviously anticipated that the great majority which are now being built on borrowed money will earn much more than even the current high interest charges. Otherwise the companies, being reasonably sane, would never have borrowed at such rates to make the installations themselves.

The high rates prevailing for this kind of borrowing, however, have naturally been carried over into other fields as well, and there often do constitute a severe burden. At first glance it seems obvious that a firm which earns only 8 or 9 per cent cannot conduct its operations on money borrowed at 11 per cent. Unless it can run on its own capital alone it must apparently go out of business. But the great majority of firms either do not borrow at all, or, what is usually the case, they ...re able to earn more than the interest charges on that part of their operations for which they do borrow. If that were not the case further borrowing would diminish or cease, and interest rates would fall. The real burden of the high interest rates is actually felt not so much in the conduct of current business itself, as in the attempt to expand the present volume and to penetrate into new markets; especially those abroad, where the exporter is expected to finance the foreign buyer and where very long credits are common. Here an interest charge of 11 per cent is almost prohibitive: carried over three years, it amounts to a third of the original cost of the exports! Paradoxically enough, the rapid reconstruction of Germany's industrial plant, through its effect on the money markets, can thus be regarded as a major obstacle to the desired expansion of the country's foreign trade.

The general interest rate situation is therefore unsatisfactory in various ways, but there is nothing unstable or unsound about it. Economic history shows over and over that a period of rapid expansion is not and cannot be a period of cheap money. In recent months, it is true, the Germans themselves have begun to feel that the average levels of interest rates were higher than the industrial expansion alone made necessary, since the rate of this expansion has been slacking off since the latter part of 1928. They say that interest rates have been held up only to check the withdrawal of foreign funds, as evidenced by the increase in the Reichsbank rate in April, 1929, and that in the absence of this influence the general levels would be much lower. In the immediate sense these conclusions are of course perfectly correct, but they do not alter the underlying facts and relationships. A *sudden* withdrawal of any large volume of foreign funds would produce a sharp credit and foreign-exchange crisis, and against this contingency a temporary increase in interest rates is the obvious safeguard. But a *gradual* withdrawal would not lead to a crisis. The real reason why foreign funds must be kept continuously in Germany and ever increased in size, and therefore the real reason why interest rates are high, is that these funds are needed to carry on the ceaseless process of expansion. The less efficient enterprises are thereby placed under a severe strain, but since the great majority of firms can pay the high rates and still make reasonable profits, the underlying situation as a whole can in no way be regarded as abnormal or unhealthy. If the demand for money is large relative to the supply, the price must necessarily be high. You cannot have your cake and eat it too.

CHAPTER VII

OTHER ASPECTS OF GERMAN BUSINESS SINCE 1924

I. THE COURSE OF BUSINESS SINCE 1924

THERE are a number of other aspects of the general position of German industry and business which are of major importance, and which must also be understood to obtain a reasonably correct impression of the present situation in the aggregate. Chief among them are the movements of prices and production since 1924, the financial position of the typical German company, the rôle of the Federal and local governments in business, and finally—a problem, however, which lies outside of the main province of this book—the nature and effects of the protracted depression in agriculture. We shall not undertake here a systematic examination of the position of industry and business as a whole, but some knowledge of the questions just referred to will bring out the salient points. The best starting point is to review briefly the general course of business itself since the end of the inflation period.

The year 1924 was necessarily a year of great uncertainty. The feasibility of the Dawes Plan had yet to be established, the economic wreckage left over from the inflation had not yet been cleared away, and there was still a paralyzing shortage of working capital. But toward the end of the year the basic conditions began to improve, and with the rapidly growing inflow of foreign funds business revived. The next twelve months were marked by extreme activity and expansion. The big industrial companies, suddenly faced anew with world

competition after ten years of protection by the war
and the currency depreciation, found it imperative to
modernize their plants at once, and the initial stimulus
thus given to the equipment and construction divisions
soon spread to all branches of business. But the expansion went much too rapidly, as was almost inevitable, and
was overdone. Before the autumn of 1925 signs of trouble were appearing, and then the real post-stabilization
crisis began. It was not so much a crisis of production
and prices, for prices dropped only about 10 per cent,
as a crisis of financial solvency and business organization. Thousands of new firms, large and small, had been
started during the inflation period and had managed to
hold on ever since, but at the first period of protracted
strain, the first real test of a general business recession,
they collapsed like so many card houses. Through the
last months of 1925 and the first half of 1926 the toll
of bankruptcies ran steadily from 1,000 to 2,000 a
month. By the end of 1926 the number of incorporated
companies had been reduced by 4,000 from the 1924
maximum, and the number of limited liability companies
by over 13,000, reductions amounting to between 20
and 25 per cent of the peak figures of 1923 and 1924.

This drastic house cleaning, however, was a blessing
in disguise, for in the main it left only the stronger and
better organized firms in existence. Even before it was
ended a general business revival began to develop. The
English coal strike of 1926 naturally had a very stimulating effect on the corresponding German industry, and
this initial impetus was greatly strengthened by the rapidly increasing inflow of foreign capital. A new expansion began in the closing months of 1926, this time on
a much sounder basis, and continued without serious
interruption until the middle of 1928. The companies

were able to carry through extensive programs of plant improvement and reconstruction, and to liquidate the large stocks of goods which had been virtually frozen since 1924–25. Prices rose somewhat, it is true, but the principal increases were in the physical volume of production itself. By the spring of 1928 production was some 40 per cent above the low point of 1926. Then in the latter part of that year a recession developed, partly because the expansion threatened to go too far and money rates were hence tightening, but chiefly because of uncertainty over the general Reparations situation and the outcome of the impending Paris Conference. The severe Ruhr strike in November, 1928, also produced a fairly severe though temporary depression, as did the foreign-exchange and money-market crisis precipitated by the threatened breakdown of the Paris Conference in April, 1929. After the successful conclusion of the Conference in May, however, a revival began, and a new period of expansion now seems to be under way.

The general position of industry and business in the first half of 1929 offered both favorable and unfavorable aspects. The physical volume of production was not far under the peak of 1927, and was distinctly *above* the volume of 1913, which had itself been a year of unusual prosperity. The average of wholesale prices was only about 40 per cent above the pre-war level, and was hence substantially on a par with prices in other countries: the rise, here as elsewhere, reflected the world-wide decline in the value of gold since the war. But some price groups had risen much more than this average, and others less; and what may be described as a state of internal price tension was thus set up, and still continues, which is far from healthy. Finally, the financial position of the companies themselves was not satisfactory in all respects. The number of separate enterprises has been greatly reduced since 1924, with the result that the general average of size and financial strength has been raised, and dividends and earnings are running at fairly satisfactory if moderate rates. But most of the companies have incurred large debts, both to finance the physical reconstruction of the past five years and to carry on current production, and an undesirably large proportion of these debts are at short term. In consequence, any severe and widespread business recession would doubtless place many of the companies in serious difficulties.

These various conditions are so important that they require somewhat more detailed comment, even though the statistical data and other concrete information available are sometimes too fragmentary to permit of very precise conclusions.

II. PRODUCTION AND PRICES

FIRST, the physical volume of production. Something has been said at earlier points with respect to the volume of production in the six biggest industrial groups. For industry as a whole, however, there is no information from which a completed picture can be constructed. The semiofficial Institute for Business Cycle Research compiles a production index which has the advantage of being up to date, but it includes only 19 industrial commodities, and the base is hence very narrow. The Statistique Générale de France also compiles an index for Germany. The results these various indices yield are as follows:

Year	Institute for Business Cycle Research[1]		Statistique Générale de France[2]	Six biggest industries[3]
	1924–26 = 100	*1913 = 100*	*1913 = 100*	*1913 = 100*
1913	—	100	100	100
1924	87.9	77	80	—
1925	106.6	94	94	—
1926	100.8	88	90	—
1927	123.7	108	117	114.9
1928	119.2	104	113	111.6

Of these indices, the one we have computed for the six chief industries includes most of the important items in the Institute index, and also several large groups which the Institute omits. It may therefore be regarded as rather more representative than the latter index. The Statistique Générale index contains fewer industrial commodities, on the other hand, but does include agricultural products, and is therefore a sample from a wider field. If we combine the evidence afforded by the several indices together, we shall not be far wrong in assuming that the aggregate physical volume of production in Germany, with 1913 as 100, stood at about 116 in 1927, and at 112 in 1928.[4] This contrasts with

[1] Institut für Konjunkturforschung, *Vierteljahreshefte*. The original series is the one with base 1924–26 = 100. For purposes of comparison, I have converted it to the base 1913 = 100 by taking the average of the Statistique Générale index for 1924–26 (88), and then multiplying the Institut figures by $\frac{88}{100}$. This conversion is necessarily dubious, but is the only way of getting a comparison based on 1913.

[2] *Bulletin de la Statistique Générale de France*, vol. 18, p. 69; prolonged on the same base by H. Quigley in the *Deutsche Volkswirt*, Feb. 22, 1929, p. 667.

[3] As computed in Chap. V above, for coal and coke, iron and steel, machinery, electro-technical, textile, and chemical products. The figure for 1928 is a preliminary estimate.

[4] Other available indices of the volume of production, consumption and exchange usually go back only to 1924 or 1925. Like the production index of the Statistique Générale, most of them indicate an increase of from 20 to 25 per cent since 1925. Thus from 1925 to the be-

about 105 for England, 125 for France, 124 for Belgium, about 113 for all Western Europe, and 166 for the United States.[1] Germany, in other words, has just about kept even with the general European average.

A second important factor is the price situation. The movements of the principal price groups are shown on the accompanying Chart VI.[2] It is noteworthy that the *general average* of prices has changed comparatively little since 1924, and since 1926 its fluctuations have lain entirely in the narrow range between 132 and 142. But the two great subgroups of prices have moved quite differently from this average. Except for a few months, the agricultural group has been consistently *below* it,—due to the world depression of agricultural prices, which the German protective tariff has not been able to overcome,—while the industrial group has been *above* it. This again, however, is not the whole story. As can be seen from Chart VII, the industrial group is in turn made up of two divisions which have also changed in different ways. The prices of raw materials and half-finished goods have nearly always lain *below* the general average of wholesale prices, while the prices of finished goods are much above it. Moreover, the spread

ginning of 1929, the volume of goods shipped by the Federal railways rose 20 per cent; electric current produced, 33 per cent; value of goods exchanged (estimated from the turnover tax returns), 27 per cent; consumption of sugar, beer, meat, and tobacco, about 18 per cent; retail sales of textiles, 7 per cent; volume of bills drawn, 16 per cent; and so on. (See the publications of the Institut für Konjunkturforschung; *Wirtschaft und Statistik;* and the *Reports* of the Agent General for Reparations Payments.)

[1] See the article by Quigley, just cited. Quigley's figure of 90 for England is probably too low, and hence also his figure of 111 for Western Europe (see Appendix X, below).

[2] Data for Charts VI and VII from *Wirtschaft und Statistik.* The group of "industrial" prices in Chart VI has been compiled by the writer by a simple arithmetic averaging of the raw material and half-finished-goods index and the finished-goods index of Chart VII.

VI. WHOLESALE PRICES, 1924–1929 (1913 = 100)
A General wholesale. B Industrial. C Agricultural.

INDEX

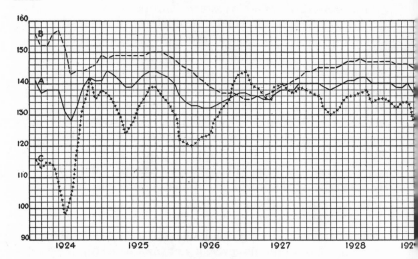

VII. INDUSTRIAL PRICES BY GROUPS, 1924–1929 (1913 = 10

A General wholesale.
D Finished goods.
E Raw and half-finished goods.

INDEX

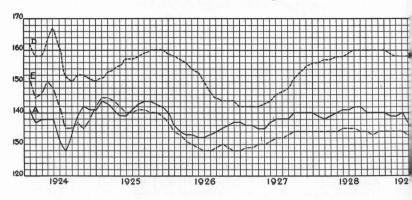

between the two groups has been growing steadily since the beginning of 1927.

This situation is extremely unsatisfactory. It means that the great gains secured from the physical reconstruction and reorganization of the basic industries are not being passed on in full to the ultimate consumer, and that a considerable part is being lost in the distributive system. The resulting high prices for consumers' goods restrict sales and production, and weaken the purchasing power of the people at large. But restricted production in turn means that a smaller total of wages and other money incomes can be paid by the industries themselves, and this itself diminishes purchasing power from the income side. It is a vicious circle.

It is not unnatural that a rise in raw-material prices should be followed by a somewhat greater rise in the prices of finished goods, since various intermediate carrying charges are also increased, but in Germany the present differential between the two groups is too large to be accounted for by that factor alone. There seem to be two principal explanations for what has happened. In the first place, the technique and methods of marketing have not yet been subjected to anything like the same drastic rationalization that has been applied to most industrial production. Distribution in Germany is still relatively inefficient and costly. A second factor, which itself in part accounts for this inefficiency, is that the cartels usually have their worst effects in precisely those industries which are nearest the ultimate consumer. Here they are most apt to raise prices without at the same time being able to increase permanently the general prosperity or the volume of output of the industry affected, despite the restraints imposed by the Cartel Law of 1923: it is here that they tend to place the greatest premium on incompetency. The reader will recall that of the six principal industries reviewed in earlier chapters, four had undergone price increases since 1913 which were *less* than the rise in average wholesale prices. Only in the textile division, which is nearer to the ultimate consumer than any of the others, and in which the cartels are both numerous and relatively weak, had prices risen distinctly *more* than the general average. This is perhaps also true of the machinery industry. Similar conditions exist in many of the remaining industries which manufacture goods for final retail consumption.[1]

III. THE BUSINESS UNIT. CARTELS AND COMBINES

A THIRD important aspect of the general business situation is the changes in the size and organization of the individual companies which have taken place since the war. The outstanding fact is the great increase in the number of separate enterprises and, since there has been nothing like an equivalent increase in the volume of business to be done, the nearly corresponding *decline* in the average size and strength of the enterprises themselves. In 1913 there were just over 5,000 incorporated companies in Germany, with a total nominal capitalization of 16,500 million marks and an average capital of 3.2 millions ($760,000). At the end of 1927, despite the wholesale bankruptcies during the post-stabilization crisis, the number of these companies was still nearly 12,000; and although the total nominal capitalization had increased somewhat, to 21,500 million marks, the

[1] See the estimates published in the Institut für Konjunkturforschung, *Vierteljahreshefte,* 1928, IV, A, 20, 21, which indicate that whereas prices of goods under cartel control rose from January, 1926, to January, 1929, by 1.8 per cent, uncontrolled prices fell by 5.3 per cent. The statistical basis of these estimates, however, is necessarily narrow.

average capital had fallen to 1.8 millions ($430,000),
little over half the 1913 level. For the incorporated companies engaged in industry alone, however, the decline
in average nominal capital was less severe: only from 2.7
to 2.1 million marks. In addition, the number of limited
liability companies increased from about 22,500 in 1913
to over 57,000 in 1927. There are no figures on the capital of these companies, but here again the available evidence indicates that a great decrease in average size took
place.[1] On the other hand, if we take the *total* of the industrial enterprises, and include all the various legal
forms, we find that the average company showed real
assets in 1927 of 228,000 marks, or $54,000. Moreover,
these figures rest on more or less arbitrary valuations,
and are somewhat too low.[2] There was an extremely
heavy concentration of assets, however, in the hands of

[1] On the incorporated and limited liability companies (*Aktien-Gesellschaften* and *Gesellschaften mit beschränkter Haftung*), see the *Statistisches Jahrbuch*, e.g., 1928, p. 443; also Appendix XII, below.

[2] See the annual *Report* of the Bank für Industrie-Obligationen for 1928 (published February, 1929), pp. 10, 11. The distribution of legal forms, number, and value of real assets of the enterprises com-ing under the Industrial Mortgage laws, which it is estimated cover over 90 per cent of all German industry, was as follows on Jan. 1, 1927:

Form	Number of enterprises	Value of real assets Million marks	Per cents
Incorporated companies	8,728	19,323	45.6
Limited liability companies	15,831	4,486	10.6
Partnerships	29,606	5,518	13.1
Kommandit-Gesellschaften	2,732	1,070	2.5
Individuals	119,612	8,517	20.1
Miscellaneous	4,099	948	2.2
Government enterprises	5,378	2,479	5.9
Totals	185,986	42,341	100.0
Average in marks	——	228,000	——

Kommandit-Gesellschaften auf Aktien are included with incorporated companies, but have little importance.

the big companies; 2.8 per cent of the enterprises apparently have 61 per cent of all the real assets.[1] This means that the average size of the remaining 97.2 per cent, in terms of physical assets, was only 91,000 marks ($21,700) per enterprise. For industrial concerns, that figure must be judged to be rather small.

But neither the small average size of the great majority of the enterprises nor the concentration in the larger firms tells the whole story. The German enterprises, as we have seen, are also linked together in a great number of cartels and other trade associations. These cartels have a wide range of activities, extending from mere regulation of the terms of purchase and sale in some cases to outright control over prices and even production in others. They thus enable their members, by uniting in common action for the common benefit, to overcome at least some of the disadvantages arising from small size. It is almost impossible to get any objective measure, however, of their real strength and effect. Although their number is large—it is variously estimated now at from 1,000 to 2,500 or more—less than a third of them make any attempt to control prices or production directly. The remainder are more like the

[1] The distribution on Jan. 1, 1927, was as follows (see the *Report* of the Bank für Industrie-Obligationen, just cited). Figures in per cents.

Groups, by value of real assets in marks	Number of enterprises	Value of real assets
20,000– 100,000	76.3	13.7
100,000–1,000,000	20.9	25.3
1,000,000 and over	2.8	61.0
Totals	100.0	100.0

There is a very large number of other enterprises not covered by these figures, with less than 20,000 marks of real assets apiece, which are of small financial importance even in the aggregate.

familiar American trade associations. Some of the
strongest price and production cartels, notably those in
coal, potash, iron, and steel, are prevented from exploiting their position unduly by government control
or by potential foreign competition, but others of almost equal strength, as in cement, brewing, and glass
bottles, escape public attention and are virtually unhampered monopolies. Still others, however, and these
probably the great majority, are relatively small and
weak, and find their members continually withdrawing
from the cartel agreements in every period of strain.
Finally, almost all of the industrial cartels, strong and
weak alike, suffer from countless evasions and violations of the agreements by their members through the
buying up of wholesale houses and the consequent securing of a hidden double profit, outright manipulation
of accounts to conceal violations, and so on. The undesirable effects which the cartels produce on the general course of economic life in Germany have been referred to elsewhere. Here it is enough to point out that
although they do lead to far-reaching coöperation between independent enterprises in certain industries, and
sometimes even to monopolistic exploitation, in most
cases their real effect upon the general pattern of industrial organization is probably not great.[1]

It is even more important in this connection to observe that the great majority of the larger German
firms have more or less extensive financial participations

[1] In the large literature of the subject, see especially M. Metzner,
Kartelle und Kartellpolitik (Berlin, 1926); R. Liefmann, *Kartelle und
Trusts* (7 ed., Stuttgart, 1927); O. Lehnick, *Kartelle und Staat* (Berlin, 1928); Seager and Gulick, *Trust and Corporation Problems* (now
in press). I am also indebted to Doctor Metzner for a very frank
verbal discussion of the whole subject.

Doctor Metzner (*op. cit.,* pp. 10–18), estimated that there were about

in other enterprises engaged in the same or in allied lines of business. The result is that what appears at first glance to be a miscellany of two or six or twenty small and independent companies is often, from the point of view of financial and even of administrative control, really a single compact group. For at least a certain number of the leading industrial divisions, the picture presented above is therefore not entirely accurate. Although the average size of the enterprises as they exist for legal purposes is small, the size of the real financial and production unit is often relatively large. The interchange of securities, the classical device of a pyramid of holding companies, and various other formal and informal practices have created a far greater concentration of control and operation than ever meets the casual eye. Nor is this concentration a matter of finance alone. The various nominally independent plants and enterprises embraced in a given group are frequently so administered, and when necessary so altered, that they directly supplement one another's activities and thus really constitute a single highly organized production

1,500 cartels in 1923, since when 300 to 500 have disappeared. A government estimate placed the number at above 3,000 in 1925, but using a much broader and less significant definition of the cartel itself.

The relative strength of the cartels may be estimated very roughly as follows in the basic industries, taking coal as 100:

Coal and lignite	100	(Big combines also very powerful)
Iron and steel	90	(Big combines also very powerful)
Machinery	40–45	(Cartels numerous, but small and weak)
Electro-technical	20–25	(Two big combines dominant)
Textiles	35–40	(Cartels numerous, but small and weak)
Chemicals	20–25	(One big combine dominant)
Potash	100	(Three big combines dominant)
Average	50–60	

These figures represent the purely personal judgment of the present writer. They have no statistical basis whatever.

unit. The lives of the German industrial financiers are blighted by no antitrust laws, and here as in the cartel field they are able to go as far as efficiency requires or their own skill permits. Their motive is often not merely the pursuit of private profit, but also the desire for power and control as such; and the movement is greatly helped by the extensive avoidance of taxes which concentration makes possible in many cases. It is also worth noting that the effect of this piling up of related enterprises is often to deprive the ordinary stockholders not only of any real influence over the affairs of the company but even of much of the increase in profits; all to the benefit, of course, of the insiders who have control. The stockholders' position in these respects then becomes more like that of the bondholders and other lenders.

We have already seen something of the nature and results of this concentration of control and organization as it has been worked out in the coal and steel complex and in the electro-technical and chemical industries. For business as a whole, the lack of information makes any general conclusion impossible. The Federal Statistical Office, however, has estimated that in 1926 the various combines, mergers, and so on held participations affecting some 65 per cent of the total nominal capital of all German incorporated companies. Of course this figure must not be misinterpreted. In some cases the participations amounted to 100 per cent, but in others to much less, and the average degree of participation was probably not over 50 per cent.[1] Even so, however, this means

---

[1] See the Statistisches Reichsamt publication, *Konzerne, Interessengemeinschaften . . . Ende 1926* (Berlin, 1927), pp. 13 ff. The percentages of the total nominal capital of the industry which were affected by the combines were, in the leading divisions: coal, 90; heavy iron and steel, 85; machinery, 47; electro-technical, 87; textiles, 37; chemicals, 83; potash, 98. By great groups the percentages

that the average size of the real financial and administrative unit was much larger than the size of the various
enterprises taken separately would suggest. If we assume that for the 65 per cent of total nominal capital
affected the average participation amounted to 50 per
cent, this indicates that the average size of the real unit
was greater than the size of the apparent legal unit by
half of 65 per cent, or by about a third. In some of the
largest divisions, however, the effective concentration
has gone so far that from one to at most three or four
big combines dominate the whole industry.

IV. GENERAL BUSINESS FINANCE

OF even greater interest is the question of the financial
position of the companies themselves. The state of affairs in the 6 leading industries has been discussed in
earlier chapters. We concluded that the average rate
of dividends in these industries was now running around
6 to 7 per cent, and net earnings, including additions to
hidden reserves, around 9 to 10 per cent. For the totality
of industrial companies no complete figures exist, and
the partial information available is not up to date. The
Federal Statistical Office, however, has made compilations which include from 75 to 80 per cent of the nominal
capital of the incorporated companies alone, a form of
organization which, it will be recalled, embraces about
half of the total assets of all industrial enterprises. For

were: raw material industries, 88.5; manufacturing industries, 56.5;
commerce, etc., 58.2.

The Statistical Office is itself the first to point out, however, that
these figures must be used with great caution. They also show nothing, of course, about forms of business organization other than the
incorporated companies.

Also see *Trade Information Bulletin* No. 556, "The International
Cartel Movement" (1928), pp. 10–23.

the year 1924–25, dividends actually paid were less than 4 per cent of the total nominal capital of the companies included; in 1925–26, 4.75 per cent; in 1926–27, 5.35 per cent. A private compilation recently made on a similar basis shows dividends in 1927–28 of 5.7 per cent; and a much smaller sample at the end of 1928 a rate of 8.5 per cent (7.8 per cent excluding banks).[1] The figure for 1928, however, seems to rest on a selection from the larger and better companies alone, and is probably unrepresentatively high. For the total of incorporated companies, industrial and commercial taken together, 6 to 7 per cent probably is a fairer average. On other forms of business organization there are no comprehensive data, but it may be doubted if their dividend and profits payments are as high as those of the incorporated companies. The average is more probably a third to a half lower.

The aggregate nominal capital of the incorporated companies has increased from 19,000 million marks in 1925, after the revision of balance sheets which followed the stabilization had been made, to about 22,000 millions now. The significance of this increase is open to debate, since the 1924–25 figures were necessarily arbitrary and uncertain, and indeed the whole question of the realty of the present capitalizations is still highly controversial today. Some of the increase doubtless represents nothing more than the writing up of figures which were originally too low, but in the absence of other evidence a good deal of it must be regarded as reflecting

[1] *Statistisches Jahrbuch,* 1927, p. 398; 1928, pp. 446–449; and the *Berliner Tageblatt,* Jan. 13, March 5, April 21, 1929. The dubiousness of most company balance sheets and the practice of building up undeclared reserves, which will be commented on in the text below, makes the published data on total earnings of uncertain value, and no attempt will be made to use them here.

genuine growth and prosperity. The situation is very uneven, however, and a good many industrial divisions have been in such difficulties that the firms have been compelled to write down their nominal capitalizations from the 1925 figure, although in most cases this figure itself seemed low at the time. Aggregate nominal capital is now less than in 1925 for the machinery, hardware, heavy metals, stone, and earth industries, in foodstuffs, beverages, and tobacco combined, and in several other important divisions.

The remaining balance-sheet items which are of critical importance are net earnings and debts. On both of these, however, the figures available must be treated with a great deal of caution. Some explanation of the situation is necessary.

In ordinary German business practice the published balance sheet is regarded as being just as appropriate a field for the exercise of executive policy as any other part of the company's activities. The management submits only what it thinks is proper for the stockholders and the general public to know, and its presentation often has little to do with the real state of the facts.[1] This is not regarded as an immoral deception; it is the customary convention, and dates back to the origins of incorporated business itself in Germany. The explanation is of course simple enough. If a great increase in earnings is announced labor demands higher wages, the stockholders want higher dividends, and the general public makes an outcry about monopoly prices. At the same time the government officials swoop down and re-

[1] It may again be pointed out in passing that the stockholder, both with respect to his knowledge of what is going on in the company and with respect to his participation in the management, and sometimes even in the profits, is usually treated more like an American bondholder than like an American stockholder: his rights here are few.

quire larger tax payments. On the other hand, if in consequence of the ordinary ups and downs of business an unfavorable statement is submitted, labor and the tax officials suspect deception; and the stockholders intimate that so bad a management should be replaced forthwith. The natural result is that the directors prefer to publish figures showing rather little change from year to year, and to accumulate in good years reserves which will carry the company over the inevitable bad years without much visible disturbance. This general practice has also been encouraged by the fact that since 1924 the companies have had to raise so large a part of the additional funds required by borrowing, especially abroad, instead of by issuing more shares. Lenders like a company whose position appears to be stable.

Of course the thing works both ways. There is overstatement as well as understatement. Certain companies are reputed to have paid pleasing dividends for years without having had a pfennig of earnings, and as long as the declared nominal capital is not impaired the government will not interfere. It is true that the increasingly severe tax control makes any large misrepresentation of physical assets to the tax authorities difficult, but the companies are *not* required to issue publicly the more accurate balance sheets they submit for tax purposes. Any amount of discrepancy may exist between the two, yet nothing can be done. There have also been certain weird cases in which the company managers literally did not know what the position of the concern really was, and had no way of finding out. Records had been destroyed or left incomplete, for example, cherished hidden reserves had been demolished by unrecorded declines in commodity prices, changes in real-estate values had been ignored, and old cost-keeping

methods had not been adjusted to new production techniques. The infiltration of the more rigorous English
and American accountancy methods is gradually alter-
ing this situation, but it is still frequently bad.

Taken as a whole, however, the position of the typical
industrial company is usually distinctly better than its
published statements show; a situation also promoted
by the fact that the character of the German corporation law encourages understatement rather than overstatement. Competent authorities familiar with the
situation believe that for the two or three hundred larger
industrial companies total reserves, taking published
and hidden items together, now average between 40 and
50 per cent of the total nominal capital. For the aggregate of *all* industrial firms the average figure is of course
lower, but even so seems to be at least 25 per cent of the
present aggregate nominal capital. In largest part these
reserves are hidden, and in good years are steadily aug-
mented, a process which the Germans describe as "self-
financing." The authorities just referred to also estimate, with respect to the better companies alone, that
for every 2 marks paid as dividends at least 2 marks
more are put into aggregate reserves, again chiefly hidden. That is, additions to reserves, *after* legitimate depreciation charges and after all taxes, are usually at
least as large as dividends. For the total of all industrial
firms the average is of course again lower, but even in
the aggregate the average additions to reserves probably
amount to between 50 and 60 per cent of dividends. The
size of the funds thus accumulated has often been
greatly exaggerated in the press, but nevertheless they
are very substantial. For incorporated companies alone
the increase since 1924 has probably amounted to over
5,500 million marks, and for the aggregate of all busi-

ness enterprises to over 8,500 millions (something over 2,000 million dollars).[1]

It has already been remarked that the larger part of these reserves, probably two-thirds or more, are hidden. The hiding takes many forms which differ in different industries, but the more important ones are worth enumerating in order to show just why the average published company balance sheet is so unreliable. The most obvious device is the undervaluation of physical plant. One large corporation reports all its machinery at a valuation of one mark; another all its buildings at practically their value as rubbish; another, which has increased its holdings some 50 per cent in the last few years, does not report the new acquisitions in its published statements at all. This form of undervaluation, however, is less common now than formerly. It has the disadvantage that nominal earnings subsequently declared may represent nothing more than the recouping of this original undervaluation, but the companies have to pay taxes on them as income, and at rates which are frequently very burdensome. Another method is the undervaluation of stocks of goods on hand and other items of inventory. A third is the writing off of excessive sums for depreciation and depletion, though here government control has some influence, since any padding in the depreciation write-off, if detected, is taxed as income.[2] Another device is the concealment of security holdings; and another, now frequently used, is the overstatement of debts, especially current liabilities. Finally, when the company balance sheets were converted from

[1] See Chap. X, below, for more detailed estimates.

[2] Difficulties under this head are especially common in mining. It is often literally impossible for the companies themselves to determine the proper charge for depletion, and the procedure is apt to be purely arbitrary.

a paper basis to gold, in 1924–25, many companies cautiously understated their general position as an entirely commendable safeguard against future contingencies, but they have never since bothered to make the corresponding correction in their subsequent published statements. The assets thus unaccounted for constitute a further hidden reserve. Against this must be set the fact that a considerable number of other companies overvalued their 1924–25 position, and in place of hidden reserves some of them are doubtless carrying hidden deficits even now.

To some extent these hidden reserves are of necessity revealed to the tax authorities, but the tax returns, as already remarked, are not published. The balance sheets issued by the companies are often defective, because of the misstatements just listed. In consequence, any really accurate evaluation of the aggregate position of all the companies taken together is impossible to make.

As far as debts are concerned, the following partial figures are submitted for what they are worth. The Federal Statistical Office compilations, covering 75 to 80 per cent of the nominal capital of the incorporated companies, show that in the year 1925–26 the total of all debts and amortization payments of these companies was over 19,000 million marks. This was 118 per cent of aggregate nominal capital, and 50 per cent of total assets. In 1926–27 the total had risen to 150 per cent of nominal capital and to nearly 57 per cent of assets. For 1927–28, on the other hand, the private compilation already referred to shows total debts as only 93 per cent of nominal capital and only 47 per cent of total assets, but these figures apparently rest on a selection from the better companies only. Of the debts over two-thirds were at short terms. The long-term debts totaled only 4,700 million marks, but the short-term debts came to nearly 11,000 millions.[1] For forms of business enterprises other than the incorporated companies, there are no comprehensive estimates.

If we now combine these various types and sources of information, and also take into consideration what has been said in earlier chapters about specific industries, it is possible to form at least a general judgment as to the present financial conditions of the German companies. In the aggregate, that position is good. Some companies are of course doing unusually well, while on the other hand a large additional number have overexpanded temporarily and are in difficulties, but the typical enterprise is sound and has limited its commitments. As we have already remarked, average dividends appear to be running at 6 to 7 per cent on the total nominal capital, and real net earnings, after taxes and legitimate depreciation but *including* hidden reserves and including dividends paid, may be roughly estimated at 9 to 10 per cent. The debts of the companies are often high in relation to nominal capital, but this is in part offset by the fact that the nominal capitalization itself is nearly always low, sometimes absurdly so. The only really weak point in the situation is the comparatively large size of the short-term debt, itself due in considerable part to the difficulties the companies have had in raising additional capital by issuing shares and to the resulting necessity of borrowing. Although this debt would put the companies affected in an exposed position should any sudden and severe business recession develop, there is no evidence that their fundamental strength has been impaired. The average company is not particularly

[1] See the *Statistisches Jahrbuch*, 1928, pp. 443–451, and the *Berliner Tageblatt*, March 5, 1929.

prosperous, but its general position is still entirely satisfactory.

In view of the extent to which debts and capital charges of all kinds were eliminated during the inflation period, it may at first glance seem surprising that average earnings do not run a good deal higher than the figures just given. The explanation, to which attention was drawn in an earlier chapter, is that the new capital charges incurred for the drastic post-inflation programs of reconstruction and reorganization have offset or more than offset the wiping out of the older charges by the inflation itself. There is no evidence, for example, that the average capital charges on the German companies are any lighter today than in other countries; indeed, quite the opposite. Even here the few apparent gains which the inflation period brought were thus purely ephemeral.

In comparing the financial situation of the German companies with the situation in other countries another fact which has also been commented on at earlier points should be remembered. The loss of plant, equipment, and material under the terms of the Armistice and the Treaty of Peace was a severe blow to German industry, and for a time a paralyzing one, but this loss, paradoxically enough, brought certain clear advantages in its train. The very necessity of replacing the surrendered installations has had the result that the average age of the German industrial plants is probably now less than in any country in the world. For at least some years to come this situation may be expected to have a marked effect on German competitive power abroad, especially if world demands increase enough to lighten the present burden of excess production capacity.

It is also interesting to observe that the companies are

now distinctly less dependent on the banks, in the aggregate, than they were before the war. The banks had of course played a very large part in Germany's pre-war industrial and commercial expansion. They brought out the principal capital issues, provided short-term funds, and even supplied a good deal of the brains that went into the companies' own central management. During the inflation period, however, most of the companies were for the moment prosperous and began to break away, while in the first year or two after the stabilization, since the banks were themselves desperately in need of funds, they were unable to do any large volume of lending. Today a good many of the leading companies are still either comparatively independent of the banks, or even, in a few cases, really own the banks themselves. They float capital issues without surrendering control to the banking institutions involved; a good deal of their short-term debt is owed abroad rather than to German lenders; and their boards of management are no longer dominated by the bank representatives. It is of course true that large numbers of companies, and doubtless the majority, are still very much under the influence of the big banks, but the average degree of dependence is clearly less than it was before the war.

V. TAX BURDENS AND SOCIAL CHARGES

A QUESTION which is closely related to the financial situation of the companies, and one which is much agitated, is that of the so-called burdens on industry. These burdens are of various sorts, but those most commonly envisaged in discussion of the subject are taxation and the social charges.

The aggregate tax burden borne by the German companies is undoubtedly severe. Four principal kinds of

taxation are involved: the Federal corporation income
tax; the Federal turnover tax; the contributions of the
companies coming under the Industrial Mortgage set
up by the Dawes Plan, which is a tax measure in all but
name;[1] and the property taxes and other levies imposed
by the local governments, from which these governments
derive the largest part of their pure tax revenues.[2] The
lack of recent data on local government finance makes
the aggregate tax situation uncertain, and the whole
question will be reviewed in more detail in Chapter X,
below. One or two figures, however, will suffice to indicate its general nature. In the fiscal year 1925–26 all
the industrial and other companies taken together appear to have paid directly, on all accounts, something
under 4,000 million marks in taxes; and in 1928–29 between 4,500 and 5,000 millions. If we take the nominal
capital of the incorporated companies alone, and assume, as is substantially true with respect to the physical assets of industry itself, that these companies constitute about half of the total value of all business enterprises, it then appears that the taxes paid amounted to
about 9.5 per cent of their total nominal capital in
1925–26, and to about 10.7 per cent in 1928–29. These
figures are of course extremely rough and will not stand
close scrutiny, but they do serve to give some idea of
the magnitudes involved. In terms of dividends, the
balance-sheet statements (here for once reliable) show
that total taxes paid usually average from 10 to 15 per

[1] It will presumably be replaced soon by an explicit tax law under
the Paris agreements. See Chap. XI, below.

[2] Another levy, which is smaller in size but which is much objected
to, is the tax on the total wages paid by the companies. This tax becomes more burdensome if the company raises its wage rates, and also
bears most heavily on companies making quality articles for which
relatively large amounts of labor are needed.

cent higher than dividends for the incorporated companies in those that pay dividends at all.

The so-called social charges arise in connection with the elaborate system of labor insurance now in force, the origins of which go back to Bismarck's struggles with the Socialists in the last decades of the nineteenth century. The insurance covers sickness, accident, provision for dependents in case of death, and since 1927 unemployment. In most cases it is compulsory, and includes not only workers but also, with respect to certain types of insurance, some classes of clerks and officials and even household servants. The payments involved are divided between the employer and the employee, each usually paying half, and in addition the Federal and local governments make contributions in certain cases.[1]

It is not easy to discover what the real burden of the social insurance system is. In 1927, before the unemployment insurance had come into full operation, total receipts were over 4,000 million marks; and for 1928 preliminary indications are that they were nearly 5,200 millions. Since nearly half of the contributions came from the companies themselves, they must have paid about 2,300 million marks—which is also roughly half their tax bill. The degree of the burden varies widely, according to the company and the industry. Inquiries throughout the principal industrial branches indicate that in the typical company the social charges on the firm itself amount to about 10 per cent of the wages bill, although in mining they may run as high as 16 or 17 per cent because of the greater danger of the occupation. Where the wages bill is a comparatively small item in total costs of production the burden is hence low, and *vice versa.*

[1] For a fuller discussion of the social insurance system, see the next chapter.

From the workman's point of view, the social charges paid by the companies are thus tantamount to an increase in effective money wages of about 10 per cent on the average, plus the amount of the relatively small contributions from the various governments. This must always be borne in mind in making comparisons with other countries. From the national point of view, however, it is probably not correct to regard the whole of the employers' contributions as simply an indirect way of compelling them to pay higher wages. To some extent they are a pure tax on the employers for the benefit of the workers. If the compulsory insurance system were suddenly abolished, money wages would assuredly rise, but it is doubtful if they would rise by the full amount of the present charges on the employers. The difference, though probably small, would measure the amount of the tax on employers which the system in effect levies. It should also be pointed out that the employers accuse the social insurance administrations of great inefficiency and waste, and assert that the present charges are absurdly high relative to the claims paid. There appears to be some foundation for this accusation, though the issue is so clouded in domestic politics that it is almost impossible to discover the truth.

The financial burdens which the social charges and taxes impose on the typical German company can be illustrated by the following rough estimate of the average distribution of net company earnings, taken after legitimate depreciation (figures in per cents):

Social charges	17
Taxes	34
Dividends	31
Carried to reserves (published and hidden)	18
Total	100

It must be emphasized, however, that these percentages show only the *average* situation as we have inferred it from the foregoing study. Probably in no one firm does precisely this relationship prevail. In a number of important industrial companies which are especially in the public eye, the percentage for social charges is at least as high as that for taxes, while in others the sums really carried to reserves are distinctly greater than the sums paid as dividends.

VI. GOVERNMENTS IN BUSINESS

ANOTHER extremely important feature of the business situation, about which rather little has hitherto been said directly, is the large rôle which the various governments themselves play in industry and commerce. This rôle takes the form both of general control and of active participation in business itself, and has been carried farther in Germany than in any other leading industrial country. It is true that in the modern state governmental supervision over certain branches and departments of economic life must now be accepted, either as a necessary evil or as a step toward the millennium according to one's philosophy. In Germany, however, the control assumes a somewhat different form from that to which we are accustomed in the United States, except for our elaborate regulation of the railroads. Trusts and combines are left free to do virtually what they please, while the cartels and other trade associations are subjected to fairly rigorous limitations. Indeed, in two industries—coal and potash—compulsory cartels have been set up by law and prices restricted. In addition, as we shall see later, the Government is given wide powers both with respect to wage determination and in the adjudication of labor disputes, while the United States has no real counterpart at all to the comprehensive German social insurance system. Finally, the whole tax machinery is necessarily more drastic than with us, and more burdensome.

Besides these essentially restrictive activities, many of the governments are also in business for themselves, and make commercial profits which, whether wisely or not, they use to defray their current expenditures. The local governments own and operate street railways, gas and electricity supply systems, waterworks, harbors, forests, mines, banks of all kinds, and a wide variety of other enterprises, and appear as part owners in public-utility companies which operate as purely private concerns. Of course there is nothing new in this type of government activity, but it has been pushed much farther in Germany than in the United States. The Federal Government itself is also in business on a large scale. Besides the railway system[1] and the post office, which are both run for profit (the post office also controls the telephone and telegraph systems and a large banking business), it owns one of the big commercial banks, an accountancy company, and also owns or has extensive participations in a considerable number of other industrial and public utility enterprises. The industrial

[1] The Federal railway system falls outside the province of this study, but it should be pointed out that it is now one of the most efficient and best managed divisions of German economic life. It has been thoroughly reorganized and modernized, and its present position offers an example of some of the best results which Germany has thus far secured from the struggle for rationalization.

Although operated as a private system, it is of course owned by the Federal Government, and is the largest company in the world. Its rate policy is used by the Government to promote approved economic purposes such as the stimulation of exports, and the company is in effect a tool for the execution of the Government's general economic program.

enterprises were largely created to meet war needs, but the Government's interest in them has never been completely liquidated. Except for the railway and the post office, these interests are all administered for the Government by a holding company, the so-called VIAG.[1] The nominal capital of this company is only 120 million marks, but the nominal value of its participations is over 250 millions (60 million dollars).

The real extent of the economic undertakings of the various governments has never yet been accurately assessed. Competent observers seem to agree, however, that of the entire economic activity of all Germany, at least 12 to 15 per cent is in the hands of the various governments. If we exclude agriculture, and take only industry and commerce, the figure is probably at least 20 per cent. In electric power the governments produce 60 to 65 per cent of all that is offered for sale; and even in banking, which is usually regarded as a field for private enterprise alone, their control runs up to 50 per cent![2]

Whatever the exact percentage for the aggregate, it is high enough so that the governments as a whole play

[1] The *Vereinigte Industrie-Unternehmungen Aktiengesellschaft.* See its annual *Report* for 1928–29, especially pp. 8–10. The enterprises involved include, besides the bank and the accountancy firm, electricity, gas, aluminum, nitrate, iron, and machinery enterprises, and a steamship company.

[2] As measured by deposits, in the spring of 1929 the governments owned 31.5 per cent of the commercial banks, 46 per cent of the mortgage banks, and *all* the savings banks, and thus had some 50 per cent of the grand total—though some caution must be used in interpreting these figures.

On the extent of government ownership in general see K. Helfferich, *Deutschlands Volkswohlstand* (7 ed., Berlin, 1917); and Hirsch and Falk, *Polizei und Staat,* Vol. V (Berlin, 1926), p. 53. A comprehensive study, to appear in the fall of 1929, is now being made by the Forschungsstelle für Wirtschaftspolitik, of Berlin.

an active and important part in the country's private
economic life. They are very large consumers of the
products of private industry, and by their entry into or
withdrawal from the markets can often determine the
prosperity or depression of entire industrial divisions.
This is conspicuously true of the Federal Railway Company, the post office, and other public utilities, and to
some extent of the remaining forms of government enterprise. The coal, iron and steel, machinery, and electro-technical industries, in particular, are all dependent
on the Federal and local governments for a considerable
part of their orders, a situation which obviously has a
number of actual and potential disadvantages. In addition, a good many of the government-owned enterprises
compete directly with private business, especially in
electricity, mining, and some branches of the machinery
industry. This is of course not objectionable in itself,
but the government concerns are free of all taxes, and
this gives them a very unfair advantage. The tax burden which must be borne by private enterprise is also
made correspondingly heavier by the exemption; and
a severe political struggle is now in progress to compel
the taxation of government undertakings, a measure
which the Socialists of course oppose.

The whole question of government ownership in Germany, however, is steeped in controversy, and lies near
the heart of the fundamental political and economic
struggle between the socialist and non-socialist groups.
From the strictly economic point of view there is of
course much to be said for government ownership under
certain circumstances. The existence of a natural monopoly often makes governmental control if not outright ownership necessary to prevent unfair private
exploitation at the expense of the general public, and

even, as in the case of German coal and potash, to prevent private enterprise from seriously injuring or perhaps destroying itself by cutthroat competition. A case can likewise be made out for government ownership wherever market demands are relatively stable, and where the industry is therefore not strongly affected by the fluctuations of the business cycle. In terms of the test of actual experience, it is undeniable that some of the German government enterprises are as efficient both technically and commercially as any private enterprises in the country. This is especially true of the big power companies, despite those difficulties over distribution which were commented on in an earlier chapter. Outside of socialist circles, however, there seems to be a general feeling that government ownership has been much overdone, and that *on the average* the government enterprises are less efficient, less progressive, and therefore more costly in every way than similar private enterprises would be. With the exceptions just noted, this is also the conclusion commonly derived from American experience.

But government ownership as it exists in Germany today cannot be gauged only by the ordinary commercial standards of private capitalism. To do so would be to misinterpret the whole situation. It is bound up with the conflict between two fundamentally opposed social political philosophies, and will be judged a success or a failure according to which of the two philosophies may be selected as a criterion. To their defenders the government enterprises seem a first great advance on the path to thoroughgoing state socialism, and therefore deserving only of praise; and this group also points out that the transition from the numerous powerful private combines and cartels to government ownership would be a small and easy step. To their critics, on the other hand, the government enterprises seem not only economically wasteful on the average, but an ominous manifestation of a policy which at the end can bring only failure and national loss. The future development of government ownership in Germany, and the judgments which are passed upon it, must therefore depend on the outcome of that struggle between socialist and non-socialist groups which dominates the whole German socio-economic state today. To these problems we shall return in the next chapter.

VII. AGRICULTURE

THE last major aspect of the general business situation which it is proposed to discuss here is the position of agriculture. Any detailed study is beyond the province of this book, but some knowledge of the main facts is essential. The agricultural depression which prevailed from the end of 1923 through 1927 had far-reaching effects on the financial and industrial life of the whole country. Although conditions improved greatly in 1928, it is doubtful whether this reflects anything more than the impermanent effects of the peak year in an agricultural production cycle.

The most conspicuous feature of the position of agriculture is the fact that in nearly all its important branches the physical volume of production is now distinctly *less* than in 1913.[1] For rye, which is the largest of the German grain crops, the average production in the past 4 years has been 22 per cent less than the average of the 4 pre-war years; for oats, 18 per cent; wheat, 14 per cent; barley, 2 per cent; potatoes, 1 per cent; and sugar beets, 23 per cent. Taking the principal crops

---

[1] For tables on agricultural production, see Appendix XIII, below.

together, the average decline has thus been about 14 per cent. Agricultural production has fallen off in other European countries as well since the war, but nowhere has the aggregate drop been as great as in Germany. The number of head of livestock, however, is only a little lower than in 1913.

There are a number of reasons for this decline in the German agricultural output. The most obvious is the cessions of territory under the Treaty of Versailles, which entailed a loss of about 15 per cent of the pre-war arable land. This percentage is substantially the same as the percentage of the decline in production itself, and means that Germany is producing now just about what she did in the *present* boundaries before the war. One is therefore apparently justified in concluding that no progress has been made in the general technique of agriculture since the war, and that this failure to improve technique is the adequate and sufficient reason for the present situation. But this is not the whole story; there is worse to come. A glance at the figures on area under cultivation and yield per acre shows that the average yield per acre is now from 5 to 15 per cent or more below the pre-war yield. In other words, the only reason why production has kept up to the pre-war volume in the present boundaries is that the area under cultivation has been increased. It therefore appears that the general level of agricultural technique, as measured by the results it yields, has not only failed to improve but has actually retrogressed. And in point of fact an examination of the situation shows that the proximate reason for the decline in crop yields per acre is largely a matter of fertilization. Relative to the amount of lime and phosphorus put in, the use of artificial nitrate fertilizers has been overdone. Most of the German soils are now acid, and need additional quantities of lime and phosphorus.[1]

What happened was substantially this. During the war and the inflation period agriculture prospered, for the farmers were masters of the food supply. They raised prices exorbitantly, paid off their debts in depreciated paper and further increased their holdings. But with the stabilization came an abrupt and stunning reversal. The reappearance of foreign competition sent grain prices tumbling, despite the protective tariff; working capital was almost wiped out by the currency conversion; and the farmers found themselves badly overextended. They borrowed, could not pay, and borrowed again. The result has been a paralyzing accumulation of debt, largely contracted at very high interest rates. Much of the money thus obtained was badly invested and did not pay for itself. In later years some of it was never put into improvement and equipment at all, but was spent for food and other things needed to keep the farm population alive, the crops themselves having been sold to meet interest charges, and to pay off previous debts. Since 1924 between 7,000 and 8,000 million marks of new money has been lent to agriculture, but it is estimated that the real value of the farms and their equipment has not been increased by more than half of this sum. The remainder, perhaps 4,000 million marks or more, has simply been lost.[2] This bad financial

[1] Also see *Trade Information Bulletin* No. 605, "German Chemical Developments in 1928."

[2] Some estimates of the loss run as high as 6,000 million marks; see the article by Doctor Baade in the Berlin *Boersen-Courrier*, Dec. 25, 1928. This figure, however, seems too large. The whole question is very difficult, and to date information is not available on which to base an accurate estimate of the loss. Where mortgages have been foreclosed, and where the proceeds of loans were spent to buy foodstuffs

situation, the pressure of existing debts and the resulting lack of working capital available at reasonable interest rates, has prevented the farmers from making many needed improvements in recent years. It has also reduced the total quantity of fertilizers they could afford to use, and on both accounts has therefore been a main cause for the decline in crop yields per acre.

But the responsibility for the general distress of agriculture cannot be laid on the financial situation alone. A good deal of the blame belongs on the farmers' own shoulders. Even where they had the capital needed, they have usually been very unwilling to climb out of the traditional ruts. The mechanization of German agriculture is still backward, the possibilities of a more elaborate rotation and diversification of crops have been ignored or viewed with distrust, and many of the less important commodities are now imported which could be grown in adequate quantities on German soil at a handsome profit if the farmers could only be convinced of the opportunity.[1] The commercial side is also bad. In

rather than productive equipment, the nature of the loss is obvious enough, but where the money was invested in improvements which *to date* have not been paying for themselves, the case is less clear. Better utilization of existing equipment or an increase in demand could easily turn present book losses into net profits. The figure given in the text above is based on the personal opinions of people familiar with the problem, but may well be wide of the mark. An elaborate study of the situation is now being made by the so-called Enquête-Ausschuss, and should be published by the end of the year. Also see current estimates of the volume of agricultural credit outstanding in the Institut für Konjunkturforschung's *Vierteljahreshefte.*

Most of the loss has hitherto fallen on the landowners themselves, but when the present value of a farm is less than the value of the mortgages foreclosed on it, as frequently happens, the lenders have evidently shared the loss. Outright loss to *short*-term lenders, however, is apparently not common; unpaid short debts are usually funded in a land mortgage.

[1] A further source of difficulty in agriculture is the heavy falling

the main the prevailing methods of selling the crops and getting them to market are costly and inefficient, and the bookkeeping practices are antiquated. In a word, that insistent struggle for reconstruction and rationalization which has characterized the basic industries since the end of the inflation period has made little impression on agriculture as yet. Attempts to induce the farmers to coöperate for their own mutual benefit also encounter continuous difficulties. The farmer is usually not a good business man, but he is independent, and suspicious of anyone who tries to teach him better ways. Before the war the large landowners took the lead in promoting the general advance of agricultural technique, but now most of them are impoverished, and some of the big estates are being broken up. This change is desirable from certain points of view, but it has seriously impaired the progressiveness of German agriculture as a whole.

The difficulties of agriculture have had consequences which are spread throughout the entire economic system. The failure to increase agricultural production means that food prices are relatively high, while at the same time Germany must continue to buy an important part of her foodstuffs in other countries. In the last four years over 40 per cent of all the wheat and barley consumed in Germany was imported from abroad, 10 per cent of the potatoes, and even some of the rye and oats, as well as a good deal of meat, fish, butter, and sugar. Nearly all of these commodities come in over heavy protective duties, which run anywhere from 30 to 60 per cent or more of the value, and in most cases the resulting increase in import prices is also reflected in domestic

off in the immigration of cheap Polish and Russian labor, which was common before the war. This has further increased production costs.

prices. Agriculture is thereby helped somewhat, but at a heavy cost to industry and commerce. The high price of foods in turn raises the cost of living of the working classes, and this entails higher money wages. Industrial costs of production are forced up to correspond, and the exporting power of the industries themselves is thus restricted, which is particularly undesirable in the present general situation of the country. Removal of the agricultural tariff would help the domestic price situation, but the current depression in agriculture itself would then be seriously aggravated. At the same time imports from abroad would be increased, and a further burden would then be placed on the already strained international financial position.

Agriculture has thus been one of the weakest spots in the German economy since 1924, and one of the principal sources of internal stress. The remedy, apart from an expansion of the demand for its products much greater than is probable in the near future, seems to lie in promoting the advance of agricultural technique as rapidly as possible, both by educating the farmer in modern methods and by securing, probably from other countries, the additional supplies of working capital which are needed. The resulting increase in domestic production, at the same or even at lower prices, would then make possible an increasing independence of imported foodstuffs, while the growth in the farmers' own consuming power would have a stimulating effect on the internal markets for industrial products. The large crops of 1928 permitted a certain amount of progress to be made in these directions, but whether the improvement was more than temporary still remains to be seen.

CHAPTER VIII

THE POSITION AND POLICY OF LABOR

IN the preceding chapters we have followed the progress of German industrial recovery from the physical and financial points of view alone, and have measured its success primarily in terms of its effects upon the companies themselves. In many respects its effects upon the working classes have been even more striking, while the general program of organized labor as a whole is now one of the most vitally important elements in the entire economic situation. To these questions, about which comparatively little has hitherto been said, we now come.

The changes in the economic welfare of the industrial working classes in the past ten years, as judged by their real incomes, have been governed by three principal factors. One is the changes in the numbers and composition of the population itself, which have materially affected the actual and the potential size of the labor supply. The second is the general volume of production. Its great increase from the low point of 1923 has made economically possible, though it of course did not directly cause, a steady rise in the rates of money wages. The third factor, and in many ways the most important, is the policy of organized labor itself. The trade unions have struggled ceaselessly not only to restore the laborers' real standard of living to the 1913 levels, but to raise it ever higher and higher.

It is not proposed to trace the interworking of these three major factors in any detail. As was shown in an earlier chapter, during the inflation period the working classes suffered severely. Despite frequent adjustments, wage rates rarely caught up with the rise in commodity prices or in the general cost of living, and by 1922 the avera*ge real* wages of labor, measured in terms of the commodities and services which the money wages would buy, were only 75 per cent of the 1913 level, which itself had not been high. By 1923 they were only 65 per cent of 1913. Certain classes of labor were even worse off than this average would indicate, and it is estimated that at times the general standard of living of the workers was hardly half of any reasonable subsistence minimum. After the stabilization conditions improved, however, as can be seen from the accompanying Chart VIII, and money wages rose rapidly. In 1913 the average tariff rate had been about 28.65 marks a week, and at the beginning of 1925 was still only 25.75 marks, but by the end of 1928 it had risen to 46.35 marks a week ($11.00), plus family allowances and other supplements. This was 62 per cent above the 1913 level, and 80 per cent higher than at the beginning of 1924. In the first half of 1929 a further slight increase developed. Costs of living had also risen, however, although somewhat less rapidly, and average real wages at the end of 1928 were therefore only some 6 per cent higher than they had been in 1913.[1] For skilled labor real

---

[1] In 1928 the official cost-of-living index, with 1913 as 100, averaged 152. This compares with a level of 140 for general wholesale prices. The greater rise in costs of living is due partly to high costs of distribution, commented on in an earlier chapter, partly to the German protective tariff on foodstuffs. Taxes on wages are not included in the index, nor are uncontrolled or competitive rentals, which are much higher than the controlled rentals. Inclusion of these items would make the index still higher relative to 1913. It is also frequently charged by labor leaders that even apart from this omission the official index figures are kept unduly low, because of political pressure

wages have actually failed to rise above the pre-war level, but for unskilled labor they are some 15 per cent higher. Relative to the beginning of 1924, on the other hand, average real wages have risen about 48 per cent. How far this very large increase during the past five years constitutes a danger to the stability of the German economy will be considered presently.

As compared with the post-war changes in other leading countries, however, German labor seems at best to have held even, and has probably lost some ground. The latest year for which comparable figures are yet available is 1927. First, taking 1913 as 100, the average index of real wages in 1927 was for Germany 98, England 102 to 105, the United States 126. France appears to have been in about the same position as Germany.[1] Second, in terms of money wages the German

from the employers against presenting too unfavorable a picture of the economic position of labor.

Data for Chart VIII from the Institut für Konjunkturforschung, *Vierteljahreshefte;* for Chart IX from the *Reichsarbeitsblatt.*

[1] The index figures of average *real* wages were as follows (comparable data later than 1927 not yet available):

Year	Germany (average)	Great Britain	France	Sweden	Denmark	U.S.A.
1913	100	100	100	100	100	100
1922	75	96–98	—	105	127	117
1923	65	93–96	—	112	118	126
1924	81	94–97	102	121	119	125
1925	97	100	99	122	139	125
1926	96	100	95	127	127	126
1927	98	102–105	—	—	128	130
1928	104	—	—	—	—	—
1928 Dec.	106	—	—	—	—	—

Data for 1913–27 from International Labor Office (German edition), *Internationale Rundschau der Arbeit,* July, 1928, p. 621. Those for Germany in 1928 are estimated by the present writer on the basis of the German official statistics on money wages and cost of living.

The influence of the social insurance system, unemployment and

VIII. WAGES AND COST OF LIVING, 1924–1928

A Weekly wages of skilled labor.
B Of unskilled labor.
C Cost-of-living index (1913 = 100)

WEEKLY
WAGES
INDEX (MARKS)

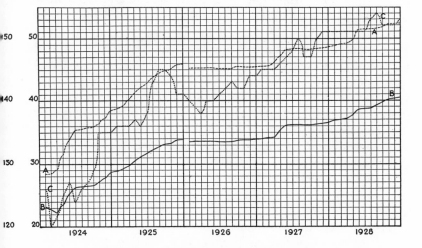

IX. UNEMPLOYMENT, 1924–1929

A Per cent of trade union members unemployed.
B Numbers receiving relief.
C Numbers awaiting work.

PER CENT OR
100,000's

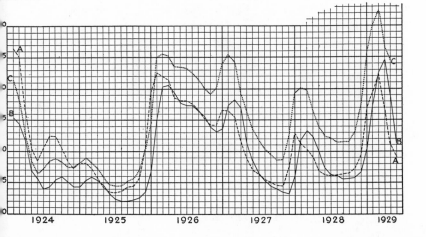

average for 1927 was about 41.25 marks a week, whereas the American was 126.50 marks, or more than three times as high. In France average money wages were about the same as in Germany; in Sweden a little higher; in Denmark still higher, or about 75.50 marks a week. Absolute figures for England, calculated on a comparable basis, are not available. It must be pointed out, however, that the significance of these international comparisons is open to a good deal of doubt. The differences in wage scales between different districts, and between different industries for even substantially the same kind of work, are often so wide as to make the meaning of any so-called national "average" rather uncertain, while the available figures themselves are too often almost worthless.

II. UNEMPLOYMENT. THE POPULATION STRUCTURE

THE continuous recent rise in the levels of real and money wage rates in Germany, great though it has undeniably been, gives a somewhat misleading impression of the economic welfare of the German laboring classes. Low wages received 52 weeks a year may leave the worker much better off on balance than high wages which because of unemployment, or for other reasons, are actually received only part of the time; and the volume of unemployment in Germany has been large during much of the last six years. During the inflation period it was very low, for business was active and most plants were running full time, but the end of the inflation brought a violent reversal and depression, and in the last months of 1923 probably over a third of all German laborers were out of work. In the first two

other factors on the effective rates of wages in Germany will be considered in a later section of this chapter.

years after the stabilization, when the process of reconstruction and recovery was getting under way, unemployment fell continuously, but the crisis of 1925–26 again forced it up to high figures. At the beginning of 1926, 20 per cent of the trade union members alone were out of work, and the figure for unorganized workers was undoubtedly much greater. Then the renewed expansion in 1927 sent the rate down, and despite marked seasonal fluctuations, it stayed at moderate levels till the end of 1928, when the depression which accompanied the Paris Conference caused it to shoot up temporarily to very high levels (see Chart IX, above). Apart from this last abnormal rise the general drift of unemployment has been steadily downward since the beginning of 1926, but even so the average rate of unemployment in the past two or three years (disregarding the spring of 1929) has been over 8 per cent of the trade union membership alone. This contrasts with an average of only 2.2 per cent for the four years 1910–13, though the much larger size of the pre-war standing army impairs the validity of a direct comparison between the two periods. The large average volume of unemployment obviously operates to deprive the laborers of a good deal of the value of the increases in money wage rates, for it seriously reduces the total annual income they receive. The elaborate system of unemployment subsidies and insurance has offset these losses only in part, for what the laborer gets under them is necessarily but a fraction of his ordinary working wage.

There are two principal reasons for the relatively high rate of unemployment which has characterized the German industrial situation throughout most of the past five years. The first has been the very process of industrial reorganization and rationalization itself. One of the most important aspects of rationalization, as we have seen, has been the endeavor to increase the mechanization of the plants, to simplify the process of production, and in general to lower labor costs. From the point of view of the companies, the result of this endeavor has usually been a great reduction in the amount of labor used. But the workers themselves have not ceased to exist merely because their services were no longer required, and the reverse side of the rationalization picture has therefore been a roughly equivalent initial increase in unemployment. Only with the much slower growth in the general volume of production, itself seriously retarded by the universal shortage of capital since 1927, and only with the accompanying renewal of the demand for labor, has the surplus gradually been absorbed again. This process of absorption is still far from complete, and the average level of unemployment will probably remain relatively high for some years to come.

The second factor in the situation has been the changes in the size and economic composition of the population itself. At the outbreak of the war the population of Germany was just under 67 millions. Nearly 2 million men were killed in the war itself, and 6½ million more persons were transferred to other citizenships in consequence of the cessions of territory under the Treaty of Versailles. But births continued to exceed deaths after 1918, and there was doubtless some immigration. By 1925, the first post-war census year, the population again stood at over 63 millions. This was only 6 per cent under the 1913 level, whereas the area of the country was smaller than in 1913 by some 13 per cent. On the face of it, this situation suggests a pressure in the direction of inadequate employment for at least a part of the population. But the change from pre-war days did not stop with this. In addition, the economic composition of the population itself has altered. The heavy infant mortality during the war and the inflation and the loss of men in the war itself cut great slices out of the middle and lower age groups, and shifted the *average* age upward. The effect of these losses is shown on the accompanying Chart X.[1] In 1907 some 30 million persons, or 48.5 per cent of the total population, fell in the age groups listed as "capable of work." In 1925, with a population of practically the same size, nearly 36 million persons were so listed, or 57 per cent of the total. This change, by materially increasing the potential labor supply and the competition for jobs, has tended to increase unemployment still more.

From the point of view of the laborer, however, this situation will probably improve steadily throughout at least the next decade or two. The reason can be seen at a glance from the population chart for 1925. The children of today are the workers of 10 or 15 years hence; and the great gaps in the present child population will be reflected in a corresponding shortage of laborers later. Whereas there were roughly 35,900,000 persons "capable of work" in 1925, there are now only 33,400,-000, and it is estimated that even in 1940 there will be only 34,700,000, which is still actually less than in 1925.[2] Assuming that Germany will continue to expand economically, the demand for labor will therefore increase steadily relative to the supply. For at least the next 15 or 20 years the average rate of unemployment

[1] Data from *Wirtschaft und Statistik,* 1928, p. 114.
[2] See *Wirtschaft und Statistik,* 1928, p. 123.

X. POPULATION, BY AGE GROUPS: 1910 AND 1925
(*In millions.*)
I. 1910 (IN *PRESENT* BOUNDARIES)

AGE GROUP

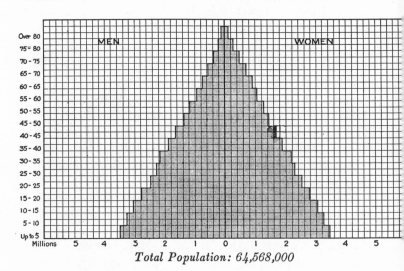

Total Population: 64,568,000

II. 1925 (DOTTED LINES: ESTIMATED "IDEAL" SIZE)

AGE GROUP

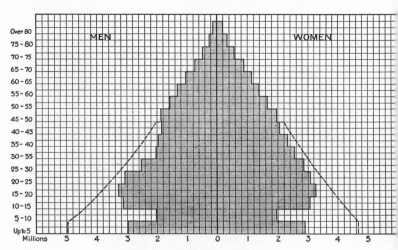

Total Population: 63,177,000

will almost certainly continue to fall, and regardless of labor policies money wages will therefore tend to rise.

III. THE SOCIAL INSURANCE SYSTEM

THE levels of wages and of unemployment are the two principal elements in the general economic welfare of the working classes, but in Germany there is a third element, which has no complete counterpart in any of the other leading industrial countries except England.[1] This is the system of social insurance. Its origins date back to Bismarck's legislation of the last century, and except for unemployment insurance the main divisions were all in force before the war.

The German social insurance system is extremely complicated, and no attempt can be made here to do more than indicate its broad outlines. It proceeds on the theory that the laborers, and certain other classes in society, are necessarily in a vulnerable position. Their incomes are small, and may be cut off completely at any time by a business depression; and they are usually in no position to protect themselves adequately against the adversities and misfortunes of modern economic life. Society itself, which is responsible for their condition, must therefore take on the task of protecting them. Experiments have been made with outright governmental subsidies of various kinds, but in the main they proved costly and ineffective. The system in force today rests primarily on the principle of compulsory insurance, supervised by the Federal Government and with governmental contributions at certain points.

[1] The English system, however, is somewhat less broad in its scope than the German, gives a larger place to compulsory compensations coming from the employers alone (for accidents arising from work), and covers a narrower range of the population.

The working classes are now protected by four principal classes of compulsory insurance, covering sickness, accident, old age, and since 1927 unemployment, which had previously been taken care of only by governmental subsidies. In addition, most clerks who have incomes of less than 6,000 marks a year are insured; and there is a special arrangement covering the peculiar position of the miners.[1] The largest division is that dealing with accidents, in which nearly 23,000,000 persons were insured in 1927. The terms of the various laws differ somewhat, but in general the insurance premium payments are divided in roughly equal proportions between the employers and the employees, each paying half. The total contribution for all the various forms of insurance taken together averages about 20 per cent of the workman's wage. In other words, the worker pays 10 per cent of his wages for insurance and the employer pays another 10 per cent. For certain hazardous occupations such as mining, however, the greater risk makes the figure run as high as 15 or 16 per cent apiece. In some cases, notably unemployment insurance, contributions are also made by the Federal and the local governments, though in most cases to cover deficits rather than as a part of the original scheme, which was designed to be self-supporting.

The total cost of the social insurance system in 1928 was nearly 5,200 million marks ($1,200 millions). Of this total the employers and the employees each paid about 2,300 millions, or 44 per cent, and the governments 12 per cent. The estimated distribution by

[1] For an excellent summary, see the pamphlet by the present Minister of Labor, R. Wissell, *Die Sozialpolitik nach dem Kriege* (Berlin, 1929). Since both the risks of the specific occupations and the terms of the various laws differ, the total number of insured persons also differs somewhat in the several branches.

sources and classes of insurance in 1928 was as follows, in million marks (numbers rounded) :[1]

Sickness insurance	1,750
Old-age insurance	1,080
Unemployment insurance	850
Accident insurance	350
Clerks, officials, etc.	315
Miners' insurance	220
Total from employers and employees	4,565
Contributions from the governments	610
Miscellaneous	5
Grand total	5,180

The social insurance institutions have great and obvious merits, but also certain defects and disadvantages. They are frequently attacked as being costly and inefficient from the administrative point of view, and as serving in considerable part simply to provide easy jobs which can be placed at the disposal of the lesser politicians. The practice of collecting the premiums in frequent small payments is also very burdensome on the employers, who must deduct the worker's contributions directly from his wages for him, and an enormous amount of bookkeeping is hence involved. In addition, there is undoubtedly a good deal of abuse of the system on the part of the workers; and, human nature being what it is, this is perhaps inevitable. Sickness insurance is sometimes used by malingering workers to provide a paid vacation, men retired on old-age pensions take an-

[1] These figures are preliminary estimates, and undoubtedly contain a considerable error. Data chiefly from Wissel, *op. cit.*, p. 11; on unemployment insurance, from the *Reichsarbeitsblatt,* 1929, Vol. VI, Appendix, p. 56, and *Wirtschaft und Statistik,* 1929, p. 349. Emergency contributions by the Reich and the local governments for unemployment relief (Krisenfürsorge) are included in the government item, though they are of course not part of the insurance system proper. In 1928 they totaled 130 million marks.

other kind of work and thus get paid twice, and so on. The employers also declare that the whole social philosophy underlying the system is paternalistic and weakens the independence and self-reliance of the workers. Social insurance has been imbedded in the German economic structure for many decades, however, and is a vital part of the general program of the Socialist parties. The future will therefore probably see no withdrawal from the present policy, but rather a further expansion.

From the point of view of the workers themselves, at least insofar as concerns their immediate economic welfare, the system is an unmixed advantage. The payments they receive under the insurance benefits are small, but they are enough to support life on. For the workers the haunting and all too familiar specter of starvation in consequence of accident, illness, or old age is fading. To some extent, also, the contributions made by the employers are really a tax for the benefit of the workers. If the system were abolished overnight wages would rise, but it is doubtful if they would rise by the full amount of these contributions. The difference would represent the amount of the tax. The same thing is also true of the largest part of the contributions from the governments. The result is undoubtedly to raise the aggregate wage rates, if we take wages actually paid in cash and the insurance contributions of the employers and the governments together, to levels somewhat higher than would prevail if a purely commercial insurance system were in force.

Since the social insurance contributions from the employers and the governments operate as a net addition to the wages received directly by the workers themselves, this means that what we may call the "effective" wages of labor are really 12 to 13 per cent higher than the wages actually paid over to the individual workers in cash. A corresponding allowance must always be made in comparing German rates with those in countries where part or all of the burden involved is left to the less comprehensive and less assured action of locally organized public and private charity. There are also various small supplementary wage payments based on the number of dependents, age, and so on, and in most cases occasional voluntary bonuses as well. The nominal tariff wage rates at the end of 1928 averaged only 46.35 marks a week, but if allowance is made for the social insurance contributions of the employers and the governments, as well as for these supplements and bonuses, the aggregate effective rate was probably close to 58 marks. This, however, is on a full-time basis. To get the real position year in and year out, we must also allow for at least 10 per cent average unemployment for the aggregate of workers, taking trade union and non-trade union members together. This reduces the effective wage to about 52 marks a week, or 2,700 marks ($645) a year.

IV. THE GENERAL ECONOMIC POSITION OF LABOR

THE general economic welfare of the working classes has been influenced by a number of other changes effected since the war. Of these perhaps the most important is the shortening of the working day to a legal maximum of 8 hours. This provision was embodied in one of the first decrees of the revolutionary socialist dictatorship, in November, 1918, and was repeated in the Weimar Constitution of 1919. Certain exceptions have since been legalized to meet situations where technical conditions make a longer shift necessary for efficient production, especially in the heavy iron and steel industries, but for the great majority of workers anything over 8 hours is treated and paid as overtime. Other forms of legislation, governing the general conditions of work, employment of women and children, safety, sanitation, and so on, have also been extended and greatly improved. On the average, working conditions in Germany are probably as good now as in any highly industrialized country on the Continent. In addition, the workers have benefited greatly from the semiconfiscatory rent laws put into force under socialist leadership. Until 1926 dwelling rents were held at only 84 per cent of the pre-war levels, and although they were then allowed to rise to 120 per cent, this is still far below the increase in building costs, and indeed in the general costs of living. To relieve the acute housing shortage, many local governments have also been compelled to go into tenement building on a large scale, and now lease houses and tenements to the workers at relatively low rentals. Despite these measures, however, the housing situation is still bad. In the larger cities the workers are crowded together like flies, and families of five or six persons or more may live in a single room.

Against the favorable changes must be set the direct tax on wages inaugurated in 1925. For an unmarried man 100 marks a month are exempt; for a married man with two children, 140 marks ($33.40). On any income above this a tax of from 7½ to nearly 10 per cent is levied. In addition, the tax (which is collected at the source) must be paid monthly. As a result, in computing and paying the tax a month of irregular employment and low aggregate wages cannot be set off against a good month. With employment fluctuating as widely as it does in Germany, this really operates to increase the charge by lowering the effective exemption; yet even assuming full employment, the exemption is only $286 a year for an unmarried man, and $400 for a married man with two children! The actual tax paid is about 1.7 per cent of the average working class income,[1] and since a good many workers pay no tax even with this low exemption, the burden on those who do pay is necessarily somewhat higher.

The workers are also hit by a wide number of indirect taxes on consumption—the customs duties, the taxes on tobacco, beer, sugar, transport, and business turnover, the alcohol and salt monopolies, and so on. These levies taken together furnish nearly 50 per cent of the total tax revenues of the Federal Government. How much of the burden actually falls on the working classes cannot be estimated from the available data, but since a considerable part of them are taxes on the necessities of life and on other articles of general consumption, it is undoubtedly heavy.

If we now bring together the results of this brief study, it does not appear that the aggregate economic position of the German working classes is much better today than it was in 1913. Average real wages, as com-

---

[1] Taking this income as 2,450 marks a year (end of 1928) per worker. Women's wages are lower than this, but men's wages higher, and the fact that many persons with low wages who pay little or no tax are also members of families operates to diminish the real burden of the total taxes paid by the family groups.

This kind of tax, collected in very small amounts (on the average 80 to 85 cents each time!), and from a large number of persons, is a relatively costly and inefficient device, though collection at the source places most of the bookkeeping burden and expense on the employers, not on the Government. At an average of 41.50 marks a year per full-time worker, allowing for 10 per cent average unemployment and assuming about 13,000,000 tax-paying workers, the yield is about 500 million marks annually, or roughly 20 per cent of the total Federal income tax revenue.

puted from the official statistics, were about 6 per cent higher at the end of 1928, but when allowance is made for 'the tax on wages, this apparent increase is reduced to little over 4 per cent. It is also significant, as has already been pointed out, that although the unskilled grades of labor have gained rather more than this average, the skilled grades are no better off than they were before the war, and perhaps worse. Relatively speaking, they have lost ground heavily. In addition, the average percentage of the workers who are employed at a given time is at least 6 per cent less than in the four years before the war; and it therefore seems probable that the total annual earnings of the average worker, measured in terms of real income, are actually smaller than in 1913. Against this must be set the direct and indirect gains derived from the extension of the social insurance system, from the rent laws and government housing programs, and from the improvements in the hours and general conditions of work. The workers also have the benefit of one of the best free school systems in the world for their children. The general standard of living of the working classes, taking all these things together, hence seems a little higher than in 1913. Relative to the position in 1924, on the other hand, the advance has been considerable. In round numbers, and after allowance for the great decrease in average unemployment since that year, it amounts to about 40 per cent.[1]

If we seek to compare German conditions with those in other countries, we immediately find that there are

[1] Another line of evidence on working-class welfare is the consumption of foodstuffs per capita, but unfortunately no compilations appear to have been made for the period after 1925–26, since when very large gains have been made. The following data, showing consumption in kilograms per capita, are from H. Ritschl, "Repara-

no comprehensive data which make an accurate judgment possible. On the basis of the available information, however, it seems probable that the economic position of the average workman in Germany is distinctly less good than in England, Holland, Denmark, Sweden or Switzerland, but is about the same as, or a little better than, in France, Belgium, or Italy, and much better than in Austria, Czechoslovakia, Poland, or the eastern Baltic countries. Germany occupies, in other words, a position at or a little below the general European average. As compared with the United States, on the other hand, Germany lags far behind. American money wages are from $2\frac{1}{2}$ to 3 times as high as in Germany, *real* wages are about twice as high, and the general economic position of the American workman, taking all the conditions of daily life into consideration, is therefore roughly twice as favorable.

V. THE TRADE UNIONS

THE principal direct cause of the progress made by the German working classes in the last five or six years has been the unceasing struggle waged by the trade unions and their political representatives to improve the general position of labor. Germany has one of the strongest trade union organizations in the world. The

tionslast und Kapitalbildung" (*Schriften des Vereins für Sozialpolitik*, Vol. CLXXIV, Pt. IV, p. 188). Consumption by animals is included for grains.

	1913–14	1925–26
Rye, wheat, and spelt	248.9	188.2
Sugar	19.0	20.5
Fish	52.0	47.9
Coffee	2.4	1.7
Cocoa	0.8	1.0
Tea	0.06	0.07
Southern (imported) fruits	4.4	6.2

total membership in 1913 was only 3,000,000, but in
the inflation period it jumped to 9,000,000, and despite a great decline after the stabilization, it is now
about 5,250,000. This is still little more than a third
of the total laboring population of the country, but
the trade unions include the great majority of the
more highly skilled and intelligent workers, and most
of the recent gains they have secured for their own
members have spread throughout the whole of the working classes. There are a number of lesser trade union
groups, the so-called "Christian" or Catholic unions,
the Hirsch-Duncker unions, a small and comparatively
unimportant communist faction, and so on, but much
the biggest is the "free" or socialist unions. These
unions, with nearly 4,700,000 workers, have about 85
per cent of the total trade union membership and dominate the entire labor situation. They play a leading
rôle in the Socialist party, itself the largest single
political party in Germany, and this in turn enables
them to employ political methods extensively for the
achievement of what are really purely economic ends.
The socialist unions are also much the wealthiest of
the trade union groups. Their total income in 1927 was
over 182 million marks, against 129 millions of expenditures, and in the four years 1924–27 they accumulated
a surplus of about 115 million marks. They are large
owners of real estate, have entered the banking business, and engage in various other profit-making enterprises on their own account.

In recent years the most conspicuous achievements
of the unions have been in the field of wages. The rise
in money wages from an average of 25.75 marks per
week at the beginning of 1924 to 46.35 marks at the
end of 1928, or by 80 per cent, is due almost entirely

to their efforts. Wage rates in Germany are governed in large part by a complex network of legally binding agreements, usually territorial within each industry, which are made between the unions on the one side and the employers, or more commonly the employers' associations, on the other. The agreements run for a stated period, and they may *not* be revised downward.[1] At their renewal the unions almost invariably fight to raise the wage schedule, and to date with marked success. In the majority of cases a peaceful compromise is reached, but all too frequently a strike or a lockout is threatened or actually begun. In order to meet this situation an elaborate machinery for arbitration has been set up under the supervision of the Federal Government. Arbitral boards are appointed by the Minister of Labor, and in addition he has recently been given power to make the arbitral awards binding at his discretion. If the employers refuse to abide by the awards their property can be seized. Appeals can be carried, however, to the Federal Supreme Court.

This arrangement undoubtedly has great advantages. It has forced compromises in a number of disputes that threatened to become very grave, notably the Ruhr iron and steel conflict of November, 1928, and has reduced the business uncertainty which accompanies a constant danger of strikes and lockouts, thus producing a highly desirable stability in the general operation of industry. But there is a reverse side of the picture. The arbitrators are appointed by a Ministry which hitherto has been dominated by the Socialists, and they have never yet been accused of undue partiality to the employers. The awards have usually lain about halfway between what the unions demanded and what the em-

---

[1] Under the decree (Verordnung) of Dec. 23, 1918.

ployers would grant voluntarily, and this has meant
that the trend of wage rates under the awards has been
persistently upward. The situation hence contains very
serious potential dangers. Raising the general standard of living of the workers to a reasonable level which
shall be comparable with those prevailing in other leading European countries requires no defense, but the
policy of granting ever higher wages which has been in
force during most of the past five years is obviously
fraught with peril for the general stability of the German economy. Wages cannot be raised indefinitely without eventually producing a severe crisis and a reaction.
Since 1924 money wages have been increased some 80
per cent, but the general volume of production has
risen only 40 per cent. This means that the share of the
aggregate national output which goes to labor has been
steadily enlarged at the expense of the employers, and
the process cannot go much farther without undermin-
ing the present organization of production itself and
thus inducing a collapse. The trade unions are becoming aware of the danger, but it still remains to be seen
how far their demands will or can be abated.

There have also been a good many conflicts, scarcely
less important, over the hours and conditions of work,
the participation of the laborers in factory administration, the right of the unions to negotiate for the totality
of the workers, and so on. The unions have usually won
part and sometimes all of what they were fighting for,
and in no important case have they actually lost ground
involuntarily. The result has been a very great improvement in general working conditions relative to 1924,
and even relative to 1913. But this advance, like the
gains in the field of wages, has been secured only at the
price of numerous strikes and lockouts. In the four and

three-quarters years from 1924 to September, 1928, there were 4,802 strikes, 829 lockouts, and a total loss of 70,000,000 working days. The average loss in working days per laborer affected has varied from 9 to 21 a year, a fairly heavy rate. The lockouts, though fewer in number, have lasted much longer on the average than the strikes, and have actually caused a greater aggregate loss in working time. But since 1926 strikes and lockouts have been much less frequent, and the loss in working time much smaller.[1]

The Weimar Constitution of 1919 and the subsequent legislation set up the forms for an elaborate system of labor representation in industrial and commercial management. In the words of the Constitution itself, "the laborers and clerks are called upon to coöperate on an equal footing with the employers in the regulation of wages and the conditions of labor, as well as in the general development of the productive forces. The organizations and associations of the respective groups will be recognized."[2] To carry out this principle factory and shop councils elected by the workers have been set up in each establishment employing 20 or more persons, with similar councils for the clerks, and the councils are given representation on the boards of management of the companies themselves. In addition, the local factory councils join with representatives of the employers and other interested parties to form District Economic Councils; and a central Federal Economic Council (Reichswirtschaftsrat) has been created, which brings together employers, workers, and consumers, as well as a number of independent experts, in a single body. All

[1] See *Statistisches Jahrbuch,* 1927, p. 343, and 1928, p. 393; and the *Gewerkschafts Zeitung,* Feb. 2, 1929, p. 25.
[2] Article 165.

important economic legislation of the Federal Government must be submitted to this Federal Economic Council for its opinion, though it has no veto power; and it can also initiate legislation, which the Government is required to introduce into the Reichstag.

In many respects, however, this comprehensive and impressive machinery has remained not much more than an empty shell. The factory councils and the central Federal Council are in operation, but their powers have been so curtailed in actual practice that they have only a limited effect upon the general course of affairs. The work of the factory councils is virtually restricted to improving conditions in the individual plants themselves, and to checking the unfair discharge of workmen. Here their influence has been considerable, it is true, and especially in the government-owned enterprises, but in the private companies the workers' representatives on the boards of management have been carefully prevented from acquiring any real knowledge of the state of the companies themselves, let alone participating in their actual direction. Similarly the Federal Council has remained an advisory body which, although it has acquired a certain amount of prestige, has little real influence. Taken as a whole, the formally organized machinery of workers' representation in Germany has yielded only a small part of what was originally expected of it, but here as in other fields the unions are constantly fighting to increase the workers' power, and later years may tell a different story.

VI. THE STRENGTH OF LABOR. SOCIALIST PROGRAMS

Despite the partial breakdown of workers' representation, the post-war changes in other directions which we have already reviewed have greatly strengthened the legal and general strategic position of the labor groups, and this largely at the expense of the employers. The gains are so important with respect to Germany's economic future that it is worth while to recapitulate them. First and most important, wage rates have been forced steadily upward, while any downward revision of wage agreements once entered into is legally forbidden. Second, the Federal Government has been given the power to intervene in labor disputes, and to make the decisions of its arbitrator binding. Under Ministries which have been predominantly Socialist, the awards have naturally not been unduly unfavorable to the workers. Third, at least some fraction of the social insurance charges must be regarded as a burden placed on the employers for the workers' benefit, though most of these charges go back to the pre-war era; and a part of the formal tax system itself, insofar as it strikes the employers, can be held to constitute a similar burden, since an ever increasing share of the aggregate proceeds is spent for social purposes. Finally, the employers have been legally compelled to recognize the trade unions and to deal directly with them. In effect, although their membership is much the smaller part of the total laboring population, the unions hence speak now for the whole body of the workers. They constitute compact, well-organized groups whose strength in negotiation is great. They have the further advantage that the Federal and most of the local governments look upon them with a favorable eye, whereas the employers must nearly always assume the burden of proof. Taking the situation as a whole, the employers still retain the supreme weapon of ownership of the plants and productive equipment, outside of the government enterprises, but they now have a far smaller share of control over those matters which directly affect the working classes themselves,than they did before the war. Nor has the movement of aggression and capture by labor in ever wider fields shown any signs of diminishing its force. The grip of the employers is being slowly but steadily weakened in almost every direction.

This increase in the immediate power of labor itself, however, is what the trade unions in every industrial country are struggling for. In the German situation there is another element, which in terms of its eventually possible effects is far more important. This is the underlying economic policy and philosophy of the leading labor groups. The nature of the ultimate goals which labor sets for itself, and its degree of success in achieving them, will necessarily dominate a large part of the country's economic and political life in the years to come, and will vitally affect, for better or for worse, the foundations of its economic strength.

Since the Socialist trade unions are by far the most important factor in the German labor situation, just as the Socialist political organization is the largest political party, we may confine our discussion to the Socialist programs alone. The aims of the relatively small Christian and Hirsch-Duncker unions are much more limited, and are centered chiefly on further improvements in wages and working conditions or on increased coöperation. The communist factions, on the other hand, have adopted most of the doctrines of Moscow, but their numbers are small, and despite violent propaganda, incessant quarrels with all other labor groups, and occasional rioting, their influence is slight. As far as anyone can foresee, the dominant labor power both of today and of the future is socialism.

To many Americans, socialism is still synonymous

with revolution, Bolshevism, property confiscation, the abolition of individual rights, and a variety of other unpleasant things, but with respect to Germany this picture is quite erroneous. German socialism as it is today in practice is rather different from what it is in theory. It is, indeed, little more than strongly organized trade unionism projected into the political as well as the purely economic field, plus an aggressive form of that kind of government ownership with which we are already familiar in the United States in our municipal street car, gas, and lighting systems. Far from being revolutionary or anarchistic, the German Socialists are inherently orderly, and have an ingrained respect for peaceful and democratic methods. The adequate proof of this is that when the collapse of 1918 put them in a position of absolute dictatorship, they submitted to the majority will, and within a few months allowed their power to be replaced by a democratic republic which, except for a few formal gestures, was based on individual capitalism and private property.

German socialism in theory, which may perhaps become the practical socialism of the future,[1] sets for its ultimate goal the outright abolition of private capitalism, and the establishment in its place of a *régime* under which the control of all the means of production, such as factories, mines, and raw materials, will be in the hands of the State. It is frankly recognized that this goal is quite beyond attainment in any immediate future, at least by those peaceful and essentially democratic means to which the Socialists themselves stand

[1] For the program and policies of the Socialist groups, see the Protocol of the proceedings of the Thirteenth Congress of the Socialist trade unions at Hamburg in September, 1928 (Allgemeine Deutsche Gewerkschaftsbund), especially pp. 170 ff.

committed, but meanwhile many things can be done to bring it nearer. The Socialists are constantly struggling to increase the participation and power of the workers in the management of industry and commerce, and in the numerous economico-political organizations; they seek always to extend the range of enterprises which are operated under government ownership; and in the main they encourage the formation of combines and monopolies, on the perfectly sound ground that the last step, the substitution of a powerful centralized organization under state control for the same organization under private control, will be easier the stronger is the original organization itself. For similar reasons, they regard many aspects of the organized rationalization movement with favor. They have also gone into business on their own account as owners of banks, cooperative stores, and other forms of enterprise, and they promote all other movements of the non-capitalist classes which seek mass action for the common economic and political welfare. In a word, they are trying by orderly and democratic methods to convert a private-capitalistic society to a condition in which unqualified socialism shall actually prevail almost unperceived. Both the restraint and in general the skill with which this program is being executed deserve great admiration.

But between the economic philosophy which underlies the immediate practical policy of the Socialists, and the prevailing opposite philosophy of private ownership and private profit, there is a ceaseless struggle for supremacy. This part of the conflict between the labor-socialist and the capital-employer groups, unlike the struggle over wages, is necessarily carried on primarily in the political field. Here the power of the two groups is more nearly evenly divided than it is at present in the industrial field itself. In the present Federal Reichstag neither group has an absolute majority. The organized Socialist party has only a third of the Reichstag seats, but when its delegates are combined with the communists and certain factions in other groups, the labor supporters as a whole have nearly half the total. The capitalist-employer representatives are scattered through 8 or 10 parties, and altogether command about two-fifths of the votes, while a smaller group of liberal and miscellaneous elements have the rest. The Socialists head the present government, but they remain in power only by virtue of an unstable coalition with other parties. Neither the labor nor the capitalist group can really dominate the present situation, and neither is strong enough to bring about those opposite changes in the Federal Constitution which they each desire, the one to increase, the other to restrict, the power of labor and the general contemporary drift toward ever more fully developed socialism. In the local government field the position of the Socialists is somewhat stronger, especially in the great cities, but here again they usually have no clear and incontestable dominance.

The eventual outcome of the conflict between such divergent political and economic ideals must be a matter of grave concern not only to Germany, but to all those who are concerned in her welfare and development. The conflict itself produces a tense internal strain, and has an obvious and vital bearing on the country's future economic strength. A number of neutral German observers predict an eventual dictatorship on one side or the other, but a more democratic method would have a greater chance of preserving and augmenting the country's economic stability and power.

Such a method would receive reënforcement from the continued economic development of Germany. The socialist movement owes some part of its influence, it is true, to the fact that many people who are not directly concerned themselves in the conflict between laborers and employers see in it the only effective weapon with which to fight the growing power of the big combines and monopolies. But it draws its strongest argument from the comparatively depressed economic condition of the great mass of the workers. In the United States, where the population is still small relative to the area and the natural wealth of the country, the workers' standard of living is high, there are opportunities for everyone, and there is no socialist movement of any consequence. In Germany just the opposite conditions prevail. The standard of living is low, opportunities are relatively few and limited, and to the great mass of the workers socialism offers the only hope for the future. It follows that if it were possible to increase the material welfare and prosperity of the working classes very substantially, say to double the present living standard, the extreme socialist movement would lose its principal appeal. Such a program looks far ahead, but the possibilities it contains provide a further cogent reason why the employers and capitalists should strive, if only in their own interest, to carry vastly farther the process of general economic reorganization which has already made such progress, and with it to raise the prosperity of the people at large.

This fundamental conflict between laborers and employers, between untrammeled private property and socialism, is of great importance for the long-run future development of Germany. The effort of the Socialists to increase the current economic welfare of the workers themselves, however, is of much greater *immediate* significance. The endeavor to improve general working conditions, which at their best are never very good in modern industrial societies, deserves all support, and the attempt to shorten the working day is justified by the steady progress in industrial technique and the resulting steadily larger output per unit of labor time. On these matters no really critical issues have arisen. The danger point, rather, is in the field of wages. As we have already seen, from the beginning of 1924 to the end of 1928 real wages have been increased by nearly 50 per cent and money wages by 80 per cent, but despite these great gains there has been no sign of a more than temporary relaxation in the trade unions' pressure for ever higher levels. Money wages have risen just twice as rapidly as the aggregate physical volume of production itself since 1924, and even real wages have gone up about 25 per cent more rapidly. In at least many cases, the increases hitherto secured have more than kept pace with the average savings the companies have themselves derived from their improvements in technique during the past five years.[1] If wages are raised much higher in the near future, prices will necessarily rise, and will rise above levels which in the field of finished goods are already too high, while the rise in prices will in turn justify a further increase in wages. If this happens, apart from the internal disturbances and tensions which will result, it is clear that Germany's exporting capacity and general international financial strength will be seri-

[1] The situation is especially difficult in certain industries where, as in coal, prices are subject to the control of the Ministry of Economics. The Ministry of Labor may order an increase in wages, but the Ministry of Economics may refuse to allow a corresponding increase in prices; and the employers, caught helpless in a cleft stick, are squeezed.

ously weakened. It is hard to avoid the conclusion that the present vicious spiral of wages and prices, if means are not found to break out of it, must eventually lead to a severe crisis. As remarked elsewhere, the labor leaders are becoming increasingly aware of the dangers involved, which it is as much to their interest as anyone's to avoid, but how far their demands can be moderated still remains to be seen.

CHAPTER IX

FOREIGN TRADE AND THE BALANCE OF PAYMENTS, 1924–29

I. THE VOLUME OF TRADE SINCE 1913

IN no field have the changes in Germany's economic fortunes since the war been more clearly portrayed than in her foreign trade and finance. Around them are centered, either as cause or as result, a large part of the events and forces with which we have been dealing in earlier chapters, and many of the effects these forces have produced have been mirrored directly in the trade and finance movements. Any detailed examination of them is unnecessary, for the dominant elements in the situation—chiefly industrial recovery, foreign loans, and Reparations—have already been discussed in other connections. We shall begin with the foreign merchandise trade itself, and then turn to the general balance of the country's international payments.

In the foreign trade situation, four facts or groups of facts are of especial importance. They are, first, the decrease in the absolute size of the trade relative to 1913, despite its rapid growth in the past five years; second, the persistent excess of imports and the conditions which have brought it about; third, the composition of the trade in terms of the principal classes of commodities; and fourth, the distribution by countries and continents.

The changes in the size of Germany's foreign trade since the war have necessarily been much like the changes in her general volume of production, but there is one great difference. Whereas the volume of production has more than regained its pre-war level, the volume of foreign trade has not. In 1913 German merchandise exports exceeded 10,000 million marks, imports were 10,800 millions, and the two together totaled nearly 21,000 millions (5,000 million dollars). This was 13 per cent of the world's total commerce, and was larger than the trade of any other country except England. Then came the war, which broke up most of Germany's existing commercial relationships, and after it the inflation period. The inflation stimulated trade in certain commodities, but by 1923 the volume of exports had fallen to less than 20 per cent of the 1913 level. With the stabilization and the Dawes Plan, however, a steady recovery began. By 1928 exports were again over 12,000 million marks, imports over 14,000 millions, and their combined total was 26,100 millions (6,200 million dollars). At first glance this looks like a large increase over 1913, when the total had been only 21,000 millions. But general prices have risen some 40 per cent or more since the war, and the mark is worth correspondingly less. When allowance is made for this, we find that the actual physical volume of Germany's foreign trade was at least 11 per cent smaller in 1928 than it had been in 1913. For exports alone the decline was even greater, though it should be pointed out that German exports in 1913 were of record size.[1] Moreover, whereas the volume of exports had been equivalent to some 25 per cent of the aggregate national production in 1913, as measured by

[1] There is no satisfactory index for export and import prices taken separately. Application of the general wholesale price index indicates that the physical volume of imports has declined 10 per cent since 1913, of exports 13 per cent. In point of fact the decline in exports is probably still greater; they consist chiefly of finished goods, and the prices of finished goods have risen more than the general average. If we take the tonnage figures alone, we find that imports have again

values, it was under 19 per cent of the national production in 1928. Finally, Germany's share in the world's trade has dropped from 13 to only 9 per cent of the total.[1] The size and importance of her commerce are thus smaller in every respect than before the war.

Relative to 1924, on the other hand, a remarkable recovery has taken place (see the accompanying Chart XI).[2] Imports have fluctuated widely, and have been declining in the last year and a half, but exports have increased almost without interruption; and the total volume of the trade, taking exports and imports together, is half again as large as it was five years ago. The expansion is similar to that which has taken place in the main branches of industry itself since 1924, and has gone forward at an even faster pace.

But despite the rapidity of this recovery the volume of the trade, as we have just seen, is still below the pre-war level in both imports and exports. The decline in imports is not altogether undesirable. It arises in part, it is true, from the loss of pre-war foreign investments,

declined 10 per cent since 1913, but exports 18 per cent. There is some evidence, however, that Germany is now exporting goods having a greater value per unit of weight than before the war.

For the general statistics on foreign trade, see Appendix XIV, below.

[1] It is also significant that in exports of finished goods taken alone, Germany had 22 per cent of the world total before the war, and only 16 per cent in 1927. Great Britain also suffered some decline. The share of Europe as a whole dropped from 80 per cent in 1913 to 68 per cent in 1927, despite the shift of much trade from the domestic to the foreign category in consequence of the break-up of Austria-Hungary and Russia. The chief gainer has been the United States. Our share of the world total increased from 11 per cent in 1913 to 16 per cent in 1927. See the article by Dr. R. W. Goldschmidt in the *Berliner Tageblatt*, December 11, 1928.

[2] Corrected data, from the *Monatliche Nachweise über den auswärtigen Handel Deutschlands*. Reparations deliveries not included in 1924–26, for lack of monthly data.

XI. FOREIGN TRADE, 1924–1929

(Basis of trade figures changed, October, 1928.)

I. MERCHANDISE IMPORTS AND EXPORTS

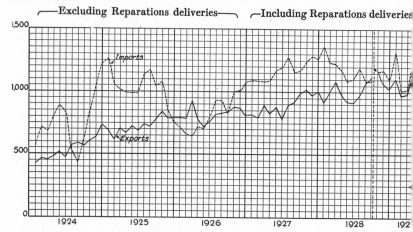

II. NET BALANCES: MERCHANDISE TRADE AND GOLD MOVEMEN

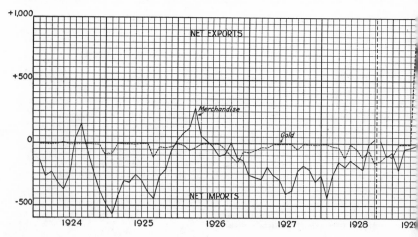

which had formerly yielded a large income; and in part from the absolute decrease in Germany's purchasing power with respect to various classes of imported goods. But in view of the continuous heavy payments Germany is now called on to make abroad, to which we shall come in a moment, this decline offers at least certain offsetting advantages.

The decline in the volume of exports relative to 1913 is a much more serious matter. It means not only that the volume of German production is smaller than it might otherwise be, and the general average of prosperity correspondingly less, but also that the country's power to make precisely those foreign payments which were just referred to is restricted. The decline is due to a variety of causes, some essentially within Germany's power to remedy but some not. One is the high level of domestic interest rates, which increases aggregate costs of production and also makes it difficult for German manufacturers to extend the long-term credits so essential in many foreign markets. Another is the fact that the prices of finished goods as a whole have risen much more than the general average of German wholesale prices, and apparently more than in most foreign countries. The largest part of Germany's exports consists of finished goods, and, despite severe price cutting in foreign trade, exportation is seriously hampered, while imports are attracted. Still another cause, though one which by now has been pretty well overcome, was the stagnation of German industrial technique during the inflation, and the consequent decline in the quality of German products as compared with the standards prevailing abroad.

Much more important than these factors in restricting German exports are the economic and political changes that have taken place in other countries since 1913. During the war itself many nations which had formerly been dependent on Germany for a wide variety of products found that their supplies were cut off, and in consequence were compelled to develop the corresponding industries within their own boundaries. This was conspicuously true with respect to dyestuffs, and to a lesser extent in textiles, and in iron and steel products. To this situation was then added the effects of the violent economic nationalism which spread over most of Europe after the war was over, and which was especially manifest in the countries created out of the ruins of the old empires. Still more domestic industries were founded, the existing ones were further encouraged, and to all was given the help of high protective tariffs, in the expectation of attaining national independence in the economic as well as in the political field. The cessions of German territory required by the Treaty of Peace had also entailed the surrender of much of the country's former coal and iron reserves and of a good deal of industrial plant, and the corresponding industries themselves were thereby also transferred to foreign ownership. The net result of these various changes has been that a wide range of countries which were excellent markets for German exports before the war now find themselves, some for one reason and some for another, able to produce part or all of the corresponding commodities in their own plants, and to compete with Germany in neutral and even in German markets. Certain European countries are the most obvious cases in point, but the same thing is true to greater or less degree of the Far East, the United States, and even South America. It should therefore be no matter for surprise that Germany's exports have hitherto failed to regain their pre-war level; the surprising thing is, rather, that the recovery could go as far as it already has. The explanation of this recovery is partly that the pre-war dependence of a good many other countries on German products still exists, whether from geographic location, habit, or for other reasons, but a great deal of credit must undoubtedly be given to the aggressiveness with which the German exporters themselves, in the face of severe handicaps, have struggled to regain their foreign markets.

II. THE TRADE DEFICIT. GERMANY'S DEPENDENCE ON IMPORTS

NEXT to these changes in absolute size, the most conspicuous feature of Germany's foreign trade since the war has been the large and persistent excess of imports over exports. The situation during the inflation was of course extremely abnormal, but even in the years since the stabilization, except for two short periods, the balance of trade has been steadily unfavorable (see Chart XI, above). The import excess has averaged over 2,000 million marks a year since 1924 (500 million dollars), though in 1928 it was reduced to only 1,700 millions; and for the five years 1924–28 combined the total excess has amounted to 10,300 millions. Interestingly enough, this is almost exactly the same as the situation which prevailed before the war. In the four years 1910–13, the average annual excess of imports was 1,370 million marks, which at present values is equivalent to 1,920 millions.[1]

There is of course nothing disturbing in the mere fact that a country's balance of trade is adverse. The excess

[1] Put in another way, the annual average receipts for 1924–28 from net capital imports and service income, less Reparations, was a little

of commodity imports may be due to receipts of income from earlier investments abroad, and may thus reflect a state of national prosperity; or it may arise from those large foreign borrowings which so often accompany the inception of a period of rapid internal expansion. In either event the import excess is more a sign of present or future strength than of weakness. In the case of Germany, however, somewhat different factors enter in. The excess has been the tangible manifestation of the effects of foreign borrowing, it is true; but in the ultimate sense a considerable part of this borrowing was not originally undertaken to finance legitimate new expansion. It was undertaken simply because the country would otherwise have been unable to meet her current obligations abroad, or at least would have been unable to meet them without severe strain. As we shall see more clearly in a moment, Germany is even now very far from being able to meet all her foreign obligations out of her own funds; that is, out of the proceeds of her own exports of commodities and services. The remainder she must still borrow. It requires no proof, however, that this cumulative borrowing cannot continue indefinitely. Each new loan increases the current payment deficit by the amount of the interest and other charges it entails, and thus makes it necessary to borrow still more the next time, a process which can end only in ultimate collapse. As time goes on, Germany must therefore shift an increasing part of the burden of meeting her current obligations abroad to her commodity and service trade. That is, exports of goods and services must expand relative to imports, and eventually by an amount suffi-

greater than the annual average for 1910–13 of income from foreign investments and services. On these balance of payments questions, see the table later in the chapter.

cient to meet the whole payment deficit. Further importations of foreign capital will then cease.

These present facts and future necessities make it of
great importance to discover just how the commodity
balance of trade is made up, since the trade deficit is now
much the biggest item in Germany's international
debits; and to see, in terms of the economic life of the
country, where this deficit comes from. To what extent
can imports be reduced and exports be increased under
present conditions? How far is the common German con-
tention correct, that exports are dependent on prior imports? What, in a word are the elements of elasticity
in the situation?

Even the most summary examination of the actual
composition of Germany's foreign trade reveals an interesting and significant state of affairs, and brings out
clearly the character of the German economic machine
from the international point of view. Over 70 per cent of
Germany's exports consist of finished goods alone. Of
her imports, on the other hand, less than 17 per cent are
finished goods. All the rest is foodstuffs, raw materials,
and half-finished goods. These are also, incidentally,
very nearly the same as the percentages which prevailed
before the war, especially in exports. The averages for
the period 1924–28 have been as follows, in per cents:

	Imports	Exports
Foodstuffs and livestock	33.5	5.5
Raw materials and half-finished goods	50.0	21.5
Finished goods	16.5	73.0
	100.0	100.0

The explanation of this situation is not far to seek.
In the first place, Germany is heavily overpopulated
relative to her own present capacity for producing
foodstuffs, and is therefore directly dependent on addi-

tional foods imported from abroad to maintain the
standard of living, itself none too high. In the last two
or three years, as we have seen in an earlier chapter,
over 40 per cent of all the wheat and barley consumed in
the country has been imported, and even for rye, oats,
and potatoes the average imports have been fairly large.
Of the foods consumed by the working classes, roughly
a quarter is imported. In the second place, Germany is
also completely dependent on foreign supplies of raw
materials to keep her industries going. The principal
commodities now imported include nearly all of those
on which modern industrial life is based except coal;
notably iron ore, copper, cotton, wool, and petroleum.
It will be recalled that the six principal industrial divisions taken together import over 50 per cent of their
aggregate raw-material supply, directly or indirectly,
and in some cases the figure runs above 85 per cent. This
double dependence on foodstuff and raw-material imports places Germany under a severe strategic handicap
in international economic competition, a handicap of
which she is keenly aware. Finally, as an almost inevitable consequence, many branches of industry are in
turn dependent on exportation for a considerable part
of their markets, and prosper or are depressed according as the foreign demand expands or contracts. We
have estimated elsewhere that some 13 per cent of the
total output of the six principal industrial divisions
combined is exported, but in certain branches exports
probably exceed 50 per cent of aggregate production.[1]

---

[1] Also see the estimates published in the Institut für Konjunkturforschung, *Vierteljahreshefte,* 1927, No. 4, p. 32. The estimates cover
a wide range of industries, but are necessarily ·rough.

Increased raw-material imports in one year tend to be reflected in
increased exports of finished goods in the next year; see a table in
Appendix XIV, below.

If we now compute separate trade balances for each of the three big classes of commodities taken separately we find that in foodstuffs, and also in raw materials and half-finished goods combined, Germany has a large and persistent import surplus, but in finished goods she has an export surplus which is larger than either of the import surpluses alone. These facts give an illuminating picture of the working of the German economic machine. From the foreign trade point of view Germany can be regarded as being in largest part a great factory, but one which is not completely self-supporting. She imports raw materials from other countries, works them up, and exports a much greater value of manufactured goods in payment. In the years 1924–28, the average excess under this head alone has been over 1,200 million marks a year. But she is also compelled to import large quantities of foodstuffs to support her industrial population. These imports far more than offset the export surplus secured directly from manufacturing operations, and leave the country with a substantial net deficit in her foreign trade as a whole, a deficit which in recent years has been and could be made good only by foreign borrowing.

It is obvious from this that the maintenance of the present volume of production and of the present standard of living are very largely dependent on importation. If imports decrease, both must fall. The same thing is necessarily true of exportation. The great majority of the products which are exported from Germany are made directly from imported raw materials. Any general decline in imports therefore entails a decline in exports, while exports cannot be permanently increased without first increasing imports, except at the price in both cases of shifting goods from domestic to foreign consumption and thus lowering the domestic standard of living. If we disregard the inevitable short-time fluctuations in trade, the statement which has so often been made in the past and so often challenged, that Germany cannot export without first importing, is hence substantially correct.

These various considerations give at least a preliminary answer to the question raised a few pages above, as to the extent to which the present deficit in the trade balance can be corrected. It is evident that the elements of elasticity which can be called into play in any relatively short period of time are not great. We have indicated at an earlier point in this chapter the nature of the existing limitations on the volume of exportation. It is now further apparent that any general and protracted increase in exportation would also entail an increase in importation, though presumably a much smaller increase. In addition, much the largest part of the present imports are "necessary," in the sense that if they were cut off, the general volume of production and the general standard of living would inevitably fall. The most promising prospect for improvement would seem to lie, rather, in cutting down the volume of those imports which are not "necessary." These are chiefly imports of manufactures, which now form nearly 17 per cent of the total of imports. They are largely articles which Germany does or could manufacture for herself. They are being brought in by the relatively high levels of the domestic German prices involved, and could be stopped by a material decline in these prices. Any enduring price reduction of this sort will be accomplished only gradually, however, and hence offers little promise of immediate help.

The very composition of Germany's foreign trade

itself thus makes it extremely unlikely that a great and enduring improvement in the existing trade deficit can be accomplished at once, or even in the near future. The correction must wait on that general readjustment of German prices relative to world levels which later years will almost certainly bring. We shall postpone further consideration of this situation, and of the critical problems it involves, until a later chapter.

III. THE DISTRIBUTION OF FOREIGN TRADE

WHEN we turn from these questions to the present distribution of Germany's foreign trade by countries and continents, and compare it with the situation before the war, we find extraordinarily little change. After the general disturbances and the abnormal stimulus to exportation of the inflation period had been ended by the stabilization Germany rapidly regained the largest part of her pre-war markets abroad, and except for those changes which are the direct outgrowth of the territorial cessions under the Peace Treaty, the main channels of her commerce today are substantially what they were in 1913.

This stability is especially conspicuous with respect to exports. There has been no evidence at all of any material permanent change in the direction or the general character of German exportation, great though the shifts in the political and economic map of the world have been. Despite all that has been written about the threat of German competition in South America and the Far East, Germany's biggest export market is still Europe, and indeed the proportion of her exports that are sold in Europe seems to be slowly increasing. In 1928 Europe took 75 per cent of the total of German exports, North and South America combined less than

15 per cent, Asia 7.7 per cent, Africa 2.3 per cent, and Australia only 0.6 per cent; and these ratios are almost exactly the same as those that prevailed in 1913. The principal individual countries also buy substantially the same proportions of the total exports that they did before the war and in the same order of importance, after allowance is made for the post-war changes in political boundaries. Great Britain remains Germany's best single customer, though she takes somewhat less now than in 1913, and is followed at some distance by Holland, the United States, France, Czechoslovakia, Switzerland, Italy, and Belgium, in order. The eight countries alone take over 50 per cent of the total.[1] There has also been little or no permanent change in the principal classes of export goods themselves. Of course many new commodities have been developed, while others have disappeared from foreign trade. But except for the phenomenal development of synthetic nitrates and artificial silk, and except for the reorientation in the coal, iron, and steel trades caused by the cession of Lorraine and the Upper Silesian territory, Germany is now exporting much the same general kinds of goods that she was in 1913 and to nearly the same markets, though on the average in somewhat smaller quantities. Relative to 1924, on the other hand, the volume of the exports has of course increased greatly, but again their character and the places to which they have been sent have altered surprisingly

[1] The principal exports to the United States are now, in order, chemicals, iron and steel products and machinery, textiles, furs, leather and shoes, paper, and toys.

For more detailed figures on the composition and direction of German foreign trade, both as a whole and with respect to the principal exported commodities, see Appendix XIV, below. The changes in the foreign markets for particular articles has of course often been much greater than for the export trade as a whole.

little. The most significant change is the fact that Germany's exports to a considerable number of the smaller countries, unlike those to the larger ones, have increased substantially in *relative* terms, though the *absolute* increase is usually not great in any one case. This growth reflects the aggressiveness with which she is seeking every possible outlet abroad.

A similar striking stability in the character and direction of the trade prevails with respect to Germany's imports. As was true before the war, Europe supplies roughly half the total, North and South America combined 30 per cent. Much the biggest single source of imports is the United States, the commodities being chiefly cotton, wheat, and copper. The next largest are Argentina, Great Britain, France, and Holland. The respective shares of the several countries involved have changed somewhat more since 1913 than has been the case with exports, but again the general lines of the distribution are similar. So far as concerns individual commodities and commodity classes, the few outstanding changes have been largely those made inevitable by the cessions of coal and iron ore reserves and of industrial plant under the terms of the Peace Treaty. The aggregate physical volume of imports is of course less than before the war, but the general kinds of things which are imported and the places from which they come are much the same.

IV. THE BALANCE OF PAYMENTS, 1924–29

THE permanent shifts that have taken place in the main currents of Germany's foreign trade during the past 15 years have thus been amazingly small, especially in view of all the kaleidoscopic changes in boundaries, populations, and general economic forces which the period has witnessed. When we turn from this to the general balance of the country's international payments, on the other hand, we find a very different and much more disturbing situation, and one quite unlike that which prevailed before the war. The elements in the present balance of payments are of such character that they make a condition of chronic strain inevitable for many years to come, and may even imperil the stability and welfare of the whole German economy itself.

Before the war Germany had very large investments abroad, amounting to nearly 28,000 million marks (6,700 million dollars) in the aggregate. The income from these investments, together with certain sums derived from services rendered to foreigners, gave Germany a net surplus in her international transactions which was of considerable size. Part of this surplus was reinvested abroad, but the rest was taken in the form of commodities, and accounted for the characteristic pre-war excess of imports over exports. The international financial position was thus strong, and reflected the rapidly growing prosperity of the country.

The war and its aftermath completely changed the situation, and eventually led to a violent reversal. Practically the entire foreign investment was wiped out, in ways we have described elsewhere, and the international surplus it had yielded of course disappeared.[1] But the German economy had been built up in the pre-war years around that very excess of commodity imports which the surplus income had permitted. After the war the surplus was no longer there, but the import excess nevertheless remained, and the resulting pressure on Germany's international financial position has neces-

[1] See Chap. II, above. On the pre-war balance of international payments, see Appendix XIV, below.

sarily been very severe. In addition, she now has the Reparations charges to carry, charges which even under the Dawes Plan schedules have been heavy. This double burden, of the persistent trade deficit and of Reparations, has been entirely beyond Germany's power to meet out of her own resources alone, and as soon as the currency stabilization and the inauguration of the Dawes Plan had restored her credit she entered on a program of large and almost continuous borrowing abroad. The proceeds of a good deal of this borrowing, as we have already seen, have been used not merely to meet the trade deficit but also to finance new industrial expansion, and the captious critic might therefore insist that that part of it was strictly speaking unnecessary. This is hardly true, however. Of course not all of the money was needed to pay for Reparations in the immediate sense, or for so-called "necessary" commodity imports. But without the industrial expansion which it has been making possible Germany would not have been able to increase the volume of her exportation on a sound basis, and in consequence would not now be on the way to securing that eventual independence of further capital imports which is the cardinal necessity of her future economic life.

The effect of these post-war events and changes has been to transform Germany from one of the world's great creditor nations, as she was in 1913, to the world's largest debtor nation on both governmental and private account. The transformation has in turn had the further consequence that to the two burdens already described, Reparations and the trade deficit, it now added a third, the interest and other service charges on the capital which has already been secured abroad. The nature of what has taken place can be seen very clearly from the summary figures on Germany's international transactions in recent years. We have presented in an earlier chapter the rather uncertain estimates for the inflation period itself, and need not repeat them here. In the five years from 1924 to the end of 1928 what happened was substantially this. In those five years taken together, on the debit side Germany paid for a total excess of commodity imports of over 10,000 million marks; bought 2,600 million marks' worth of gold and a little silver; paid about 2,300 millions to foreign countries on Reparations account in cash (that is, other than by deliveries in kind); paid about 2,700 millions as interest, dividends, and amortization on the capital secured from abroad; and finally herself invested 3,000 to 4,000 millions in other countries, at both long and short term. These are large sums, and at first glance might look like the operations of a strong and prosperous country. When we turn to the other side of the account, however, the situation appears in its true light. Germany met a small part of the payments entailed with the income from services she had herself rendered abroad, amounting to about 1,200 marks net in the 5-year period, but all the rest, some 19,000 millions, she secured by selling securities or by short-term borrowing in other countries. In that fact lies the measure of the inherent weakness in her international financial position today.

These figures are brought together in the accompanying table. Most of them are taken from the annual compilations of the Federal Statistical Office. The latter compilations, however, badly underestimate the size of the international transactions, and use has therefore also been made of information supplied from private sources.

Little information is as yet available on what has happened since the end of 1928. It is clear, however,

GERMANY'S BALANCE OF INTERNATIONAL PAYMENTS, 1924–28 INCLUSIVE[1]

IN MILLION MARKS

Credits		Debits	
1. Loans floated abroad: net proceeds	6,200	6. Commodity trade net, including Reparations deliveries in kind	10,300
2. Sales of domestic securities abroad	5,500–6,000	7. Gold and silver imports, net	2,600
3. Short credits from foreigners, outstanding at end of 1928	6,000–6,500	8. Interest, dividend, and amortization payments, net	2,700
4. Services, net	1,200	9. Reparations payments in cash, not included in (8)	2,300
5. Credit for Reparations deliveries in kind	2,400	10. German purchases of foreign securities, and German short credits granted abroad and out at end of 1928	3,000–4,000
Total in round numbers	21,000–22,000	Total in round numbers	21,000–22,000

that uncertainty over the outcome of the Paris Conference, and the expectation of a breakdown which prevailed almost universally at one time, had a very de-

[1] Item 1 from the *Reports* of the Agent General for Reparations Payments; 8.5 per cent is subtracted from the nominal amounts to cover foreign costs of flotation and discount. Items 4, 6, 7, 9, from *Wirtschaft und Statistik,* May, 1929, and other official sources. Items 2, 3, 8, 10, from information privately supplied. On the composition of Item 6, see Appendix XIV, below.

The estimates of capital movements offered here, originally made in 1929, have recently been confirmed by the Report of the Committee Appointed on the Recommendation of the London Conference 1931 (the Wiggin Committee Report, Basle, August 18, 1931). The net import of capital shown in Annex I of that Report, for 1924–28, is 14,800 million marks; the corresponding mean value in the table above is 14,700 millions.

On the pre-war balance of payments, see Appendix XIV, below; on the 1914–23 balances, Appendix III.

pressing effect. The severe fall in the foreign exchanges during the spring of 1929 was an unmistakable evidence not only that current demands for exchange to make payments abroad were far exceeding current supplies, but that large amounts of money were being withdrawn. Private estimates indicate that in the first four or five months of the year some 2,000 million marks of foreign funds—over 10 per cent of all that had been imported since 1924—were taken out, chiefly by the liquidation of short-term credits. This figure may be too high, but in addition a good deal of German money was exported in panic purchases of foreign exchange. The Reichsbank also lost gold heavily, and in April, 1929, over 900 million marks of gold were exported. Commodity imports fell off and exports increased, however, in consequence of the decline in exchange rates and prices; and when the complete figures are in they will probably show that a small export surplus, since 1924 the usual concomitant of business depression, was achieved. With the successful conclusion of the Paris negotiations, on the other hand, these conditions began to reverse themselves, and there is no reason to think that the depression will prove to have been more than temporary.

The foregoing brief analysis of the German balance of payments since 1924 gives the answer, at least in general terms, to a number of questions which have presented themselves at earlier points. They show how the adverse balance of trade has been met, and how Reparations could be paid despite this adverse balance. The explanation is of course simply the importation of foreign capital. Had confidence in Germany not been restored abroad, thus enabling her to sell her securities and to borrow in other ways in foreign money markets, she could probably not have continued the payments on Reparations account, and would certainly be a much poorer and economically smaller country today. Her remarkable industrial reconstruction and recovery would have been starved from birth. In these facts lies the evidence of the success of the Dawes Plan, for without it the whole transformation would almost certainly have been impossible.

On the opposite side of the account, the service charges on this foreign capital, the Reparations payments, and above all the chronic deficit in the trade balance form together a very heavy annual burden, which is necessarily being met by still more foreign borrowing. In addition, a considerable part of the foreign capital is money loaned at short term, which can be recalled at little or no notice and which therefore constitutes a chronic grave menace to the country's financial stability. The only permanent remedy for the situation is evidently to increase commodity exports relative to imports until a surplus is achieved sufficient to meet these annual burdens, and still leave something over with which to begin a reduction of the capital indebtedness. What the prospects are in this direction, and how they are affected by the recommendations of the recent Paris Conference, will be considered in a later chapter.

CHAPTER X

NATIONAL BURDENS AND
NATIONAL STRENGTH TODAY

I. GOVERNMENTAL FINANCES SINCE THE WAR

THE last major element in the recent economic development and present position of Germany which we shall examine in this study is the aggregate cost of government and governmental obligations, including the Reparations charges. These costs are so heavy that they visibly affect every branch of German economic life, and some knowledge of the burdens they entail is necessary in order to make a fair judgment of the real strength and weakness of Germany today.

When the position of the government finances as a whole is examined even superficially, and compared with 1913, a number of striking changes are revealed. These changes are the outgrowth of the three factors which have chiefly shaped Germany's political and economic life since the war: the Revolution of 1918 and the shift in the orientation and scope of the governments' activities which it brought about; the terms of the Treaty of Peace; and the inflation. The three factors combined have given a wholly new complexion to the German financial situation. In the first place, in 1913 Germany had a big army and navy, and both the Imperial and the local governments also had large debts. Today most of the corresponding charges no longer exist. The greatest part of the old debt was wiped out by the inflation, and the army and navy, under the stipulations of the Peace Treaty, have been reduced to very small size—

though against the latter savings must be set the large present charges for war pensions, compensation, and other expenditures directly traceable to the war.[1] In the second place, the Federal and most of the local governments have usually been dominated by the Socialists since the war, and in consequence the existing activities of the various governments in the fields of education, relief, and general social welfare have been considerably expanded. In addition, the governments have taken on themselves a number of functions which had previously either been left to private initiative or had not been performed at all. Viewed as a whole, the sphere of governmental activity is therefore much broader now than it was before the war. Finally, the charges imposed on Germany under the head of Reparations, in further execution of the Peace Treaty terms, are of course a wholly new element in the situation.

The combined result of these various changes is that the aggregate cost of government and governmental obligations in Germany, despite the reduction in the army, navy, and debt charges, is very much greater now than it was before the war. Even after allowing for the rise in general price levels since 1913, the increase, as will be shown in a moment, amounts to 65 per cent; and even after subtracting the Reparations charges it still amounts to nearly 45 per cent. A part of the latter increase arises from the fact that most of the people and political parties who have been in control since the war have had little or no previous experience in the delicate art of governing, and the resulting understandable inefficiency in administration has raised costs somewhat.

[1] The reduction of the army to 100,000 men has had the result, however, that the various police forces have been increased in size, and now total at least 100,000 men more.

Most of it, however, represents the price Germany is now paying for the execution of socialist programs and policies. There is evidently room for an interesting study of the immediate costs and immediate gains which she must charge to the latter head.

In addition to these major changes in the size and character of the governmental finances, the pattern of the financial structure itself has been altered. Under the old Empire, the financial administration of the country had been fairly well decentralized. At the time of the drafting of the new Constitution in 1919, on the other hand, strenuous efforts were made to bring the whole tax machinery into a single central system, as well as much of the general governmental administration. These efforts were only partially successful, but the local governments were nevertheless compelled to surrender a good deal of the fiscal and general political independence which they had previously enjoyed. In return they were assigned a large percentage share in a number of the Federal Government's own taxes, and the proceeds, now amounting to over a third of the total Federal tax revenues, are redistributed directly to the various local governments. This arrangement gives a peculiar complexion to the whole financial situation, and must always be borne in mind. The serious difficulties to which it gives rise will be considered in a moment.

II. POSITION OF THE FEDERAL GOVERNMENT

IT is beyond the province of this book to go into the complex problems of government finance in any detail, but the more important facts in the Federal and local government positions can be presented in fairly brief compass.

The principal items in the Federal budget and their

changes since 1913 have been as follows, in million marks:[1]

	1913–14	*1924–25*	*1928–29*
Total revenues	3,385	7,757	9,790
Less transfers to local governments	52	2,770	3,272
Net revenues available	3,333	4,987	6,518
Total expenditures, less transfers	3,469	4,805	——
Proceeds of loans	——	355	——
Current surplus or deficit	–136	+537	——

In the first two years after the stabilization, and as a consequence of the drastic financial measures which accompanied the inauguration of the Dawes Plan, the Government had a relatively large surplus. After the process of general recovery began to get under way, however, and after it became clear that the Government could stand on its own feet financially, expenditures began to grow more rapidly than revenues. In consequence, since 1926–27 there has been a chronic current deficit, which has hitherto been met out of the remainder of the previous surplus; and at the beginning of the present fiscal year an actual shortage of funds developed temporarily, necessitating short-time borrowing and the authorization of a 500 million mark loan in May, 1929.[2]

In the expenditures of the Federal Government proper for 1928–29, the largest item was general administration, which accounts for over a third of the

[1] Also see Appendix XV, below. The fiscal year begins April 1 and ends March 31. Balancing items for 1928–29 were not available at date of writing.

[2] Only 300 millions were actually put on the market originally. The proximate reason for the loan was the increase in the Reparations payments under the Dawes Plan schedule and the deficit in the unemployment funds, but these items were only the last straw. The real explanation is the cumulative budget pressure of the past 4 years.

total. The next largest was the internal charges arising directly out of the war, chiefly for pensions. They took about 25 per cent. Then came the charge on the budget for Reparations. In the year 1928–29 it amounted to 1,148 million marks, which was 17 per cent of the total. The other major heads are the expenditures for such social purposes as insurance and public relief, which taken together were barely 10 per cent of the aggregate; and for debt service, which was a little over 7 per cent. Miscellaneous expenditures account for the remaining 5 per cent. The changes in these groups since 1924 show clearly where the increase in the aggregate outlays of the Federal Government itself has come from. The debt service charge has remained almost constant, while the internal war charges are actually less now than five years ago. Three items alone are chiefly responsible for the expansion. One is the Reparations charge on the budget, which accounts for slightly over half the increase, and which is of course not within the power of the Government to control. A second is the marked growth in general administration expenditures, principally for education, a growth which has taken place despite the fact that the lower and middle ranks of officials and employees are usually pitifully underpaid. The third is the increase in social expenditures, although it is only fair to point out that these expenditures have been falling somewhat since 1926.

Excluding Reparations charges on the budget and the transfers to the local governments, neither of which it can control under the present system, the expenditures of the Federal Government proper increased by only 930 million marks from 1924 to the beginning of 1929, or by barely 20 per cent. In view of the starved condition of the Government at the end of the inflation period, and in view of the amount of relief work it has been called on to do, this increase does not seem unduly great. When converted to 1913 values, however, and again excluding Reparations and local government transfers, the present outlays are found to be some 11 per cent greater than those in 1913–14. This suggests that the present expenditures may be somewhat excessive. But the radical changes in the functions of the Federal Government since the war, and in the character of the burdens now placed upon it, make any direct comparison and any assured conclusion impossible.

The transfers to the local governments, which were not included in the figures just given, also present a really serious problem. They are not lump sum transfers, but are an agreed proportion of certain Federal taxes, of which the most important are the income and turnover taxes.[1] They increase as the proceeds of these taxes increase, and the local governments are protected against any severe decline by the guaranty of a certain minimum aggregate sum, now 2,600 millions a year. This arrangement, which in most respects is clearly disadvantageous to the Federal Government, also takes away responsibility from the local governments. They do not themselves have to answer to the actual taxpayer, and that fact frequently encourages them to make needless and wasteful expenditures: they are inclined to view the receipts as pure manna shipped prepaid from heaven. In addition, the transfers place a serious strain

[1] The transfers amount to 75 per cent of the income taxes and to 30 per cent of the turnover tax, as well as a share in certain other taxes. See the *Report* of the Agent General for Reparations Payments, Dec. 22, 1928, p. 60.

on the aggregate financial strength of the Federal Government itself by depriving it of a part of any increase in the tax yields involved, and thus restricting the elasticity of its financial resources.[1] All attempts to remedy the situation, however, have hitherto been defeated by the natural opposition of the local governments themselves.

Of the Federal revenues, not quite 45 per cent is derived from direct taxes on income and property, 50 per cent from a wide range of indirect taxes, and the small remainder from administrative revenues. The principal indirect taxes are the customs duties, the turnover tax, the transport tax, the taxes on tobacco, beer, sugar, and the spirits monopoly. It is hard to say where the real incidence of this tax system comes, but the evidence indicates that the main burden falls pretty far down in the general scale of wealth and income. The direct taxes are nominally heavy, but there is a great deal of evasion in the higher ranges of income. Moreover, many if not all of the indirect taxes are passed straight on to the ultimate consumer in the form of higher prices. Taken as a whole, the great weight of the German levies probably falls on the working class and the lower middle class. This distribution seriously impairs the general economic strength of the country, but it is doubtful if more drastic direct taxation, already very severe, could be enforced.[2]

---

[1] The weaknesses in the financial position of the Federal Government have been discussed at length in the *Reports* of the Agent General for Reparations Payments. The data on Federal expenditures and revenues presented in the text above are drawn from the excellent summaries given in these reports. See especially the *Report* for Dec. 22, 1928, pp. 55, 57.

[2] The personal income tax rate is progressive, and reaches a maximum of 40 per cent on all incomes above 80,000 marks ($19,000). The

The Federal Government also has a certain amount of indebtedness. In this item are included the German External Loan 1924 and short-term borrowing from the banks, but the chief item is the revalorized debt of the period before the stabilization. The terms of the conversion of this debt are complicated, but the effect has been to reduce the nominal principal of the obligations admitted to conversion from 74,134 million marks to roughly 5,700 millions, or to 7.75 per cent of the previous face value.[1] Since the passage of the conversion law in 1925, the total debt of the Federal Government has remained nearly constant. It has usually amounted to just under 8,000 million marks, which is equal to rather less than a single year's revenues. Shortages in working funds, however, cause occasional increases in the short-

corporation income tax reaches a maximum of 30 per cent on that part of the corporate income above 28,000 marks ($6,700), but not to exceed 20 per cent on the *total* income. The income from corporation operations, however, is taxed twice: once under the corporation income tax and once under the personal income tax. The personal exemption is only 1,200 marks for a single man ($286) and the tax begins at 10 per cent. This makes American personal income taxation seem trivial.

At least a part of the direct taxes as well as most of the indirect taxes seem to be passed on from the original payer in the form of higher prices. It is only fair to admit, however, that there is little unassailable direct evidence, and any definite conclusion must be largely a matter of individual judgment.

[1] Loans which were in the possession of the creditor continuously since July 1, 1920, were revalorized at 2½ per cent of the nominal sum, but are to be repaid by drawings until 1955 at 5 times their face value. The effective revalorization is hence 12½ per cent. The remainder, rather less than half, was revalorized at 2½ per cent, but receives neither interest nor payment of principal until the Reparations payments are finished. The revalorization as a whole was designed chiefly as some slight measure of compensation to the patriotic investors in war bonds, hundreds of thousands of whom were ruined by the inflation, but the net effect is little more than a gesture.

On the revalorization, see Reichstagsdrucksache No. 474 (1928), *Denkschrift über die Ablösung der Markanleihen des Reiches.*

term debt; and in May, 1929, as remarked above, an actual deficit necessitated the issue of part of an authorized 500 million mark loan.

III. LOCAL FINANCES. THE TOTAL COST OF GOVERNMENT

THE finances of the local governments are of even greater importance in the economic life of the country as a whole than the finances of the Federal Government, a fact which often escapes public attention even in Germany: the local revenues as a whole are now more than half as large again as the net revenues available for Federal purposes. It is hard to form any satisfactory picture of the local financial position, for most of the figures now available are several years out of date, but on the basis of partial information and estimates for 1928–29 the development of the aggregate local government revenues appears to have been substantially as follows, in million marks:[1]

	1913–14	1925–26	1928–29
Provinces, communes, and communal unions, *excluding* Hansa cities:			
Own tax revenues	2,229	3,009	3,720
Administrative revenues	1,635	2,094	3,000
Transfers from Federal Government	52	2,596	3,272
Total revenues available	3,916	7,699	9,792
Total local revenues, *including* Hansa cities	4,180	8,090	10,282

The principal source of the local governments' own tax revenue is direct property taxation, which is often very heavy. In addition to the tax revenues, however,

[1] See Appendix XV, below, for sources. Figures for 1913–14 and 1925–26 are official; for 1924–25 complete figures are not obtainable. Data for the Hansa cities are all estimates. The estimated totals for 1928–29 may contain an error of as much as 200 or 300 millions on either side.

their gross income also includes the proceeds of the many foreign and domestic loans which they have floated. These loans amounted to 2,350 million marks for the years 1924–28 inclusive. In the local government expenditures, the largest items in 1925–26, the last year for which detailed information has as yet been published, were welfare and relief work, which took 33 per cent of the total. Outlays on municipal and other housing schemes formed 26 per cent, expenditures on industry, commerce, and transportation 13 per cent, justice and police 11 per cent, and general administration only 7 per cent. As already remarked, the danger spot in the local financial situation is that the local governments receive nearly a third of their revenues directly from the Federal Government as their percentage share in the proceeds of certain Federal taxes. So far as these revenues are concerned, the local governments cannot be called directly to account by the taxpayers, and they therefore have no particular feeling of responsibility for levies or expenditures which in other countries might well be judged excessive. This is all the more true since many of the local governments are controlled by the Socialists, and are consequently interested in promoting numerous elaborate schemes for social welfare and relief, public ownership, and so on. Outlays of this sort today form nearly two-thirds of the total local government expenditures.

If we now combine the Federal and local government revenues, and add those parts of the present Reparations charges which do not fall on the Federal budget (that is, the service of the railways bonds and of the industrial debentures), we can form a fairly accurate picture of the growth in the total cost of government and governmental obligations in Germany. The figures, based on the preceding data and estimates, are as follows in million marks:[1]

	1913–14	1925–26	1928–29
Revenues available for Federal Government	3,333	5,140	6,518
Revenues available for local governments	4,180	8,090	10,282
Reparations charges not included above	——	417	960
Total	7,513	13,645	17,760
Per capita, in marks	112	216	275

The total absolute cost of government, as measured in marks, has thus more than doubled since 1913. Making allowance for the rise in prices since then, and reducing present values to pre-war values, we find that the total "real" increase amounts to some 65 per cent. Moreover, since the population is somewhat smaller today than it was before the war the tax charge per capita has increased even more than this. Many Germans, with a good deal of bitterness, attribute the increase and the resulting high tax burden chiefly to the Reparations payments. But Reparations account for only the smaller part of it. Even when all Reparations charges are subtracted the increase is nearly 45 per cent. Put in another way, the 2,200 million marks of Reparations actually paid in the government fiscal year 1928–29 formed only 12.4 per cent of the total cost of government and governmental obligations in that year.[2]

[1] See Appendix XV, below, for sources. Because of the lack of data for the local governments in 1924–25 the year 1925–26 is used, to give a complete picture. The difference between the two years is relatively small. The total estimate for 1928–29 may contain an error of 200 to 300 millions either way, but is sufficiently accurate for present purposes.

The figures for *total* income and total expenditures are somewhat higher than these revenue figures, since most of the governments have also borrowed heavily since 1924.

[2] The governmental fiscal year begins on April 1, whereas under

All the rest, or over 87 per cent, was money raised by the German governments to spend in Germany for German purposes, and no foreigner can be blamed for the magnitude of the burden thus incurred. Moreover, if the recommendations of the Paris Conference are adopted the Reparations payments, as we shall see in the next chapter, will be reduced to a figure which at the beginning is less than three-quarters as large as the sum actually paid in 1928–29. Other things equal, the percentage of the total costs of government which represents money spent for strictly German purposes will then become still higher.

If we now compare these figures on tax charges with the similar figures for other leading countries, we can form a preliminary idea as to the comparative severity of the German burden. For this purpose the charge *per capita* is evidently the most significant item. One major difficulty, however, arises immediately. The latest estimates available do not all apply to the same year, and this makes a definite conclusion impossible, but nevertheless the figures are worth presenting. Taking all central and local government costs together, and eliminating duplications between them, the *per capita* charges for the several countries in the latest years available appear to have been as follows, in *dollars*:[1]

Germany, 1928–29	$65.51
Great Britain, 1924–25	97.35
France, 1927	57.30
Italy, 1925–26	20.70
Belgium, 1926	31.40
United States, 1927	77.50

the Dawes Plan the Reparations year begins on September 1. This difference must be borne in mind in making comparisons.

[1] For sources see Appendix XV, below.

These figures make the German charge appear lighter than either the English or the American, but they do not present a complete picture. It is impossible to gauge the real burden of a tax system without knowing something about the size and distribution of the national income from which the taxes are themselves derived. When account is taken of these factors, to which we shall come in a moment, the German tax burden will be found to be one of the heaviest in the world today, and possibly the heaviest of all.

IV. THE NATIONAL INCOME

THE final test of the extent of Germany's economic recovery, the final proof of the success or failure of the far-reaching industrial and commercial reorganization which has been effected in the past few years, is the growth in the national income and the national savings. In these two magnitudes and their changes lies the best single measure of Germany's real strength and weakness today.

To get at the difficult question of the size of the national income, it is first necessary to turn back to the estimates which were presented in earlier chapters on the percentage changes in the physical volume of production since the war.[1] The principal conclusion we reached there was that if 1913 is taken as 100, in 1928 the physical volume of production stood at about 112. This figure, however, is of course only a measure of *relative* change, and must be converted into terms of absolute money value. There are two ways of doing this. First, there are a number of estimates on the size of the German national income for 1913. They range from 40,000 to 50,000 million

[1] Chaps. V–VII. See especially p. 220.

marks, but the one which has been most commonly used is Helfferich's figure of 43,000 millions. If we take this as our starting point, allow for the 40 per cent increase in average prices since 1913, and then add 12 per cent for the estimated increase in the physical volume of production, we obtain as the size of the national income in 1928 the sum of 67,000 million marks (16,-000 million dollars).[1] A second method of procedure is to start with the estimates in a recent semiofficial study based on the income tax returns, which puts the national income at 50,000 to 55,000 million marks in 1925.[2] Other evidence makes it seem probable that the higher of these two limiting figures is the better. From 1925 to 1928 the physical volume of production increased 20 per cent, while average prices declined about 2 per cent. We therefore reach a figure for the total national income in 1928 of about 65,000 million marks (15,500 million dollars). This figure checks fairly well with other sorts of information on the general situation, and is the one we shall use.[3] If it is adopted, the figure for 1913 becomes about 41,500 million marks: Helfferich's estimate of 43,000 millions seems

[1] This procedure is unsatisfactory in various respects; the more so since it is not clear what allowance should be made for the receipt of about 1,350 million marks a year before the war as income from foreign investments.

[2] Institut für Konjunkturforschung, *Vierteljahreshefte*, 1926, No. 1. Also see the same for 1927, No. 4.

[3] Most of the current German estimates run well below this figure. For references to the principal ones, see Appendix XVI, below. The present writer has also attempted to estimate the national income for 1928 on the basis of the growth in income tax yields since 1925–26. This method gives about 70,000 million marks, which seems, however, too high: it is out of line with the other evidence available.

The estimates in the text make no allowance for the small income Germany now receives from loans and investments abroad; an income which has of course increased since 1925.

to have been a little high. The composite method of calculation used here also gives the following results for
other years, in million marks:

1913	41,500
1924	49,000
1925	55,000
1926	50,000
1927	67,500
1928	65,000

These figures provide the most comprehensive measure we can obtain of the remarkable economic recovery
of Germany in the past five years, and of the change in
the situation relative to 1913. In them are brought
together the net effects of all the forces which have been
at work, so far as these forces have influenced the material welfare of the country, and in them are averaged
up all the gains and losses which have taken place in
specific directions. Since 1913, the national income as
expressed in marks has increased by 55 per cent, but
after we allow for the rise in general prices and the
corresponding decline in the value of the mark itself
we find that the total real increase, in terms of the
quantity of commodities and services produced, amounts
to only 12 per cent. The increase per capita, however,
is a little greater than this, because the population is
now smaller than it was before the war: it amounts to
about 15.5 per cent. These gains are about in line with
the general European advance relative to 1913, as we
have seen elsewhere, though of course far less than
those in the United States. Since 1924, on the other
hand, the German national income has risen by over 30
per cent. In that fact, on which no further comment is
required, lies the measure of the country's recovery,
the test of her success in climbing out of the pit into
which she was plunged six years ago.

For purposes of comparison, the latest data available on the national incomes of other countries are given in the accompanying table. They are likewise necessarily estimates, and undoubtedly contain large errors. The figures are given in *dollars:*[1]

	Total in million dollars	Per capita
Germany, 1928	$15,500	$231
Great Britain, 1924	19,400	435
France, 1927	8,900	218
Italy, 1925	5,600	140
Belgium, 1926	1,760	223
United States, 1927	76,400	652

In judging the significance of these figures, however, account must also be taken of the distribution of the wealth and income itself. In Germany this distribution seems to be especially unfavorable. Not only is the average income per capita low, but the evidence all indicates that there is a fairly heavy concentration of income in the hands of the moneyed classes, who form only a small part of the total population. The great majority of people have incomes materially *below* the numerical national average.[2] Moreover, of especial importance because of its psychological effect, the situation is much worse today than it was in 1913. As we have seen in other chapters, the inflation and its aftermath completely altered the pre-war distribution. Labor as a whole is probably slightly better off than it was in 1913, and although the farmers have lost ground somewhat, the industrial and financial capitalist groups have made very considerable gains. But these gains have been effected almost entirely at the expense of the

[1] For sources see Appendix XVI, below.
[2] In statistical terms, the modal average of national incomes appears to lie unusually far below the arithmetic average.

large middle and lower middle classes and of the old military aristocracy, and their impoverishment has seriously impaired the strength of the country at large: the middle classes especially had been the backbone of Germany's economic prosperity before the war, as well as of the national tax system. It should also be observed that in consequence of this general situation, a given average income per capita in Germany probably reflects a distinctly lower level of real average prosperity than a similar figure would in any other leading industrial country.

V. THE REAL BURDEN OF TAXATION

IF we now return to the question of the cost of government and governmental obligations, the estimates just given on the size of the national income enable us to take a further step toward discovering what the effective burden of these charges really is. In 1928, neglecting the difference of three months between the fiscal and the calendar years, the total cost of government and governmental obligations was 17,760 million marks. This was 27.3 per cent of the national income in that year, as against a figure of only 18 per cent in 1913. Put in another way, for every 10 marks earned by German individuals and companies in 1928, 2.73 marks had to be paid to the governments or to the Reparations collectors. Reparations payments, however, took less than 0.34 marks of the latter sum.

This measurement of the costs of government in terms of their relation to the size of the national income can also be compared with similar measures in other countries, and gives a better index of the real burdens involved than do the per capita costs alone. When we actually try to make this comparison, however, we are again faced with the difficulty that the most recent figures available do not all apply to the same year. These figures, given for what they may be worth, are as follows:[1]

	Total cost of government	
	In dollars per capita	As per cent of national income
Germany, 1928 or 1928–29	$65.51	27.3
Great Britain, 1924 or 1924–25	97.35	22.2
France, 1927	57.30	26.4
Italy, 1925 or 1925–26	20.70	14.8
Belgium, 1926	31.40	19.5
United States, 1927	77.50	11.8

On the face of these figures, the total real burden of government and governmental obligations is thus somewhat higher in Germany than in any other leading country, and it is doubtful if the relative positions have changed much in the interval since the years for which the estimates were made. The differences in the base years, however, and still more the virtual certainty that there is a considerable error in the various estimates of national income, make it safer to conclude simply that Germany, France, and England all fall in the same general class, with the German burden probably at least as heavy as either of the other two.

Certain other factors must also be taken into account in making a final judgment as to the severity of the German charge, and in comparing it with the charges in other countries. In the first place, the real burden of a tax system is affected not only by the question of where its main weight falls in the general scale of wealth and income, but also by the distribution of the wealth and

[1] The effects of differences between calendar and fiscal years are ignored. For sources see Appendices XV and XVI, below. When two years are given, they indicate calendar and fiscal years, respectively.

income itself. The nature of the situation in Germany has already been indicated. Because of the unevenness in this distribution, the great majority of the people have incomes distinctly below the numerical national average, which itself is low, while at the same time they probably bear the greatest part of the tax charges. This means that the real cost of government and governmental obligations, in terms of the average burden on the people at large, is even heavier than the figures presented above would indicate.

In the second place, the largest part of the money paid as Reparations goes completely out of the country and does not return. This is just opposite to the situation prevailing in the other leading countries. The United States is a creditor pure and simple in the intergovernmental account, and in the other Allied countries receipts from Reparations are now more than equal to the foreign payments being made under the Inter-Ally debt settlements. All the funds their governments receive from taxation are hence rapidly returned to internal circulation, whereas in Germany a part of the tax receipts are subtracted outright. This subtraction increases very materially the real weight of the German tax burden.

On the other hand, roughly 40 per cent of the total cost of government in Germany arises from expenditures for social welfare, relief, and other undertakings of a character which makes them regarded as desirable from the general social point of view. In other countries many of these activities are either left to private initiative, or are not performed at all. But it is doubtful whether taxation incurred to defray such expenditures, which can be regarded as in some sense "constructive" and which increase the general welfare of wide ranges of the population, can be placed on the same footing as taxation incurred to defray, for example, interest charges on internal indebtedness. The recipients of interest payments of this sort are usually only a minor fraction of the total population, and are certainly not in the lowest ranks of the hierarchy of material wealth. In most cases, taxation to defray such payments probably weighs more heavily on the country than does that for social welfare purposes, because the proceeds of the taxation are distributed less widely. Insofar as governmental costs in Germany arise from social expenditures which are greater than those carried by other countries, the real burden of any excess in the German costs must therefore be judged to be *less* severe than the bare figures alone would indicate.

It is evidently not possible to reduce these factors to concrete numerical terms, and any final conclusion must therefore be largely a matter of individual judgment. We can only point out in summary that the average income per capita in Germany today is probably less than a half of that in England, and less than a third of the American, though it is about the same as those in France and Belgium and much higher than the Italian; and can only venture the opinion, without further discussion, that the real weight of taxation and Reparations charges combined is now heavier in Germany than the tax charges in any other country in the world. The latter opinion is not altered by the virtual certainty that the recommendations of the recent Paris Conference will be carried out. The reduction in Reparations payments which Germany will secure under them, amounts, even for the first year, to only a little over 3 per cent of her present aggregate governmental charges.

VI. NATIONAL SAVINGS

THE size of the national savings during recent years also has a vital bearing upon the general financial situation, and casts further light on the extent of Germany's economic recovery since 1924. The question of the magnitude of these savings has been a highly controversial one in Germany. The estimates vary widely, and are often based on entirely dissimilar methods. No figure can be reached which is assuredly correct, and the estimate finally selected must necessarily rest to a considerable extent on individual judgment. The problem is especially complicated because of the inflow of foreign funds since 1924. These funds have penetrated into every cranny of German economic life, affect almost every item by which the volume of domestic savings might be measured, and make the task of avoiding duplication very difficult. We shall present here only the summary results of our own calculations, leaving the details of method for an Appendix.[1]

Taking the period 1924–28 as a whole, the volume of national savings—the formation of real domestic capital, as distinct from the inflow of foreign funds—appears to have been as follows, in million marks:[2]

Domestic security issues, increase in savings deposits, etc., less security exports and duplications	13,500–14,000
Corporation, bank, government, and other savings not included above	10,500–11,000
Gross total of domestic savings	24,000–25,000
Less capital losses in agriculture	4,000
Net domestic additions to capital	20,000–21,000

[1] Appendix XVI, below. Also see the data in Chap. VI, above.
[2] The loss in agriculture is placed by some writers as high as 6,000 million marks. See Chap. VII, above.

It is easier to make such estimates for a period of some length than for any one year, but it seems probable that in 1928 *gross* savings did not exceed 8,500 million marks.[1] Even if this maximum figure is adopted, the savings made in 1928 amounted to only 13 per cent of the total national income in that year, which is hardly an excessive ratio, and to only 48 per cent of the total cost of government and governmental obligations! In other words, for every 10 marks of gross income received in 1928 the average German individual or company paid out 2.73 marks as taxes, including all Reparations charges (of which Reparations, however, took only 0.34 marks in the aggregate), and was able to save only 1.30 marks. Moreover, of the savings in the past five years at least a sixth has been eaten up by agricultural losses, and has hence produced no permanent addition to the country's capital. These rough figures give an approximate measure of the burdens under which the German nation now labors. In them lies the key to an understanding of the strain in the present economic and financial position of the country.

Account must also be taken of the inflow of funds from abroad. On the basis of the estimates in this and

[1] At a guess, the distribution by years was roughly as follows, in million marks (figures for *gross* savings, without subtraction of the losses in agriculture):

1924	1,000
1925	3,500
1926	3,000
1927	8,500–9,000
1928	8,000–8,500
Gross total	24,000–25,000

These figures, except for 1928, are based purely on the writer's own judgment, and are given only to afford some idea of the rate of development.

earlier chapters, the total supply of new funds which Germany has had placed at her disposal in the 5 years 1924–28 has been as follows (dollar figures are computed from the middle values in marks) :

	Million marks	*Equivalent in million dollars*
Domestic savings, *gross*	24,000–25,000	5,800
Imports of foreign capital, *net*	15,000–16,000	3,700
Total new funds available	39,000–41,000	9,500

In interpreting these figures the losses in agriculture must also be taken into consideration, however ; and it must not be forgotten that without the impetus derived from foreign capital imports the domestic savings would certainly have been very much smaller, and might never have been formed at all. They were created out of the initial economic recovery and the subsequent sustained increase in general business activity which the importation of foreign funds itself made possible.

As with the savings figures, it is easier to make these estimates of the total volume of new funds available with respect to the entire 5-year period than for a single year alone. It seems probable, however, that in 1928 Germany had at her disposal not over 8,500 million marks gross of domestic savings, and 3,500 to 4,000 millions of additional foreign funds, or a total of about 12,000 millions of new funds (roughly 3,000 million dollars). She was therefore still heavily dependent on imports of capital from abroad.

VII. WHO HAS PAID FOR REPARATIONS?

SUCH are the burdens of government and governmental obligations in Germany, and such their relation to the national income and the national savings. The element in these burdens which has inevitably attracted the most public attention, despite the fact that their size is small relative to the total, is the charges for Reparations. The Reparations question as such is not the main focus of this book, but it will perhaps be convenient for the reader to bring together in one place the principal facts concerning the real nature and importance of the Reparations payments effected under the Dawes Plan, since 1924.

From 1924 to March 31, 1929, Germany paid altogether 6,650 million marks ($1,580 millions) on Reparations account. It is often stated that the entire sum was borrowed abroad, and that to date Germany has not paid a penny of it from her own funds. In the stricter sense, however, this statement is not true. To understand the situation as it has existed under the Dawes Plan, it is necessary to distinguish between the *payment* of Reparations by Germany, payments which are made in marks to the Agent General for Reparations Payments, and the *transfer* of the proceeds by the Agent General to the creditor Powers. So far as concerns the transfers to the creditors, Germany has hitherto borrowed directly from other countries only the principal of the German External Loan 1924, plus the foreign exchange required for actual transfers in cash (including therein the service of the External Loan itself). These items amount to 37 per cent of the total Reparations payments made up to the present time. The remaining transfers she has effected, at least in the first instance, out of her own production of commodities and services. The transfers have been made in the form of merchandise exports, and of the sale of commodities and services to the armies of occupation, commissions and other foreign organizations within German borders.

So far as concerns the mark *payments* within her own borders to the Agent General, on the other hand, Germany has borrowed directly only the principal of the External Loan just referred to and perhaps a part of the payments under the Industrial Mortgage, or less than 15 per cent of the total. All the rest has come in the first instance from her own tax and other revenues; including in these last, of course, the taxation which is in effect involved in the service of the Industrial and Railway Mortgages.

But this is only a statement of what has happened in the strict legal sense. From a broader point of view, it is fair to say that Germany has really borrowed abroad the entire sum of the Reparations payments made to date, for the importation of capital from foreign countries has amounted to nearly 3 times the total of all the Reparations payments, domestic and foreign, which have been effected since 1924. By initiating and supporting the recovery of German economic life, this capital has really enabled the German Government to secure the tax and other revenues necessary to make Reparations payments themselves. Without it the recovery would probably not have taken place, and the revenues could not have been obtained. The capital has seeped into every corner of the country, and in the economic if not in the legal sense it has directly or indirectly provided far more than the funds needed merely to meet the Reparations charges. In other words, although the great bulk of the Reparations annuities have *not* been paid out of foreign capital as such, most of the capital secured from abroad has been invested in the country, and has enabled the Germans to earn the money with which they could make the actual Reparations payments themselves. In this ultimate sense, it is perfectly correct to say that since 1924 every penny of Reparations has been paid by foreign investors and other lenders.

The real extent of the burden which the Reparations payments have thus far imposed on Germany's economic life today can be judged from the following table. For convenience, the payments effected during the government fiscal year 1928-29, ending March 31, 1929, are taken as the basis for comparison. The table shows the fraction which these payments, totaling roughly 2,200 million marks, made of certain significant economic magnitudes in 1928 or 1928-29, as we have estimated these magnitudes in earlier pages. Reparations payments made:

Of the total cost of government and governmental obligations, 1928–29	12.4 per cent
Of the national income, 1928	3.4 per cent
Of the gross national savings, 1928	26.0 per cent

The part of the Reparations charges which fell directly on the budget of the Federal Government itself, and which amounted to 1,240 million marks in 1928-29, took just under 20 per cent of the revenues available in that year for Federal purposes.

These are the salient facts about the Reparations payments as they have existed to date. The *internal* burden, though fairly heavy, has thus not been exorbitant in purely monetary terms. Its greatest weight has been psychological rather than economic, and has been the natural outgrowth of the resentment against any system of control, however well administered, which lies in foreign hands. The so-called *external* burden, the burden of making payments abroad for which no economic return is received, is another matter. In 1928-29 nearly 3.4 per cent of all that Germany produced was sent out of the country on Reparations account, with little direct current return of goods or services, and was hence lost to her economic life.[1] Until now, however, this loss has been more than offset by the gains from the importation of foreign capital. The pressure on the German standard of living which may develop from time to time when the eventual diminution of capital imports compels Germany to make Reparations payments abroad out of her own net production, and out of her own surplus of merchandise exports, has not yet begun to be felt.

Any very detailed discussion of the character and the real burden of the Reparations payments as they existed under the Dawes Plan, however, has been deprived of much of its interest by the recommendations of the recent Paris Conference. These recommendations, when they are given effect, will alter the constitution of the whole Reparations machinery. They will also materially reduce the size of the annual payments required from Germany, and will correspondingly scale down the relative weight of the payments. To these new proposals we now turn.

---

[1] Germany has benefited indirectly, however, from the restoration of economic productivity in the receiving countries which the Reparations deliveries and transfers have helped to bring about. Most of these countries are also her customers.

CHAPTER XI

THE YOUNG PLAN
AND GERMANY'S FUTURE

I. THE YOUNG PLAN

WHAT of Germany's future? Can the steady progress of the past five years be continued in the years to come, and can the country's strength and general prosperity thus be correspondingly increased? Or has the limit already been pretty well reached? Is it even possible that a period of actual retrogression and decline will set in? Few questions are of greater and more widespread interest in the world today. In them are bound up the security of the great foreign investments in Germany; the future of Reparations, and of those Inter-Ally debt payments which in fact if not in law depend on Reparations receipts; the severity of the competition to which rival industrial countries will be subjected, and a multitude of other important issues. To make detailed and specific predictions on these questions would be futile, but it is nevertheless possible to see what the broad limiting or controlling factors in the situation are, and to make a reasonable guess as to what the general drift of events is likely to be.

Of these factors the most recent is the series of recommendations of the Paris Conference held in the spring of 1929, the so-called Young Plan. Although not yet put into operation, the Young Plan will undoubtedly become the framework within which a considerable part of Germany's economic life will be conducted in future years, as the Dawes Plan has been in the period just

ending. We shall therefore begin by examining its principal provisions, with a view to determining what their
effect on the country's strength will be.

The outstanding features of the Young Plan are four
in number. First, the *total* amount which Germany is to
pay is now set, and for the first time the duration of the
payments themselves is established. Under the Dawes
Plan both questions had of necessity been left for future
determination. The controversial "index of prosperity"
is also abolished. Second, the size of the proposed annual payments is materially reduced. The average payment will amount to only four-fifths of the standard
Dawes Plan annuity, and in the opening years of the new
schedule the annuities are only two-thirds as large.
Third, most of the machinery of supervision and control which was created under the Dawes Plan is swept
away, and the largest part of Germany's financial autonomy is thus restored. In other words, Germany is now
given a definite invariable task to perform on her own
responsibility. Finally, the payments are to be made in a
form lending itself to partial mobilization or commercialization; that is, they are to be of such character that
bonds can be publicly issued and sold against a specified
part of them.[1]

The scheduled annuities run for 59 years, on a varying scale which increases gradually for 37 years and
then drops to a much lower constant level for the remainder of the period. After a 7-months' transition
period to adjust the schedule to the German fiscal year,
the annual payments begin on April 1, 1930, at 1,707,-
900,000 marks; rise fairly steadily to a maximum in
1965–66 of 2,428,800,000 marks, which is still slightly

[1] See J. W. Wheeler-Bennett and H. Latimer, *Information on the
Reparation Settlement* (London, 1931), for the text of the Plan.

less than the present standard annuity under the Dawes Plan; and then fall at once to just under 1,700,000,000 marks. This level they maintain without substantial change until the last year, when they drop again. They cease on March 31, 1988. The service charges on the German External Loan 1924 are included in them, as under the Dawes Plan. The average annuity for the whole period is 2,050,800,000 marks (490 million dollars), and the sum total of the payments is 121,000 million marks (28,800 million dollars). The so-called "present value" of the payments is estimated at about 37,000 million marks (8,800 million dollars). This latter sum is roughly twice the gross total present indebtedness of Germany to *private* creditors abroad. It is interesting in passing to compare the figure for the total of the payments with the aggregate charge against Germany which was determined by the Reparations Commission some 8 years ago. This charge was set at 132,-000 million marks, and at first glance seems little higher than the total now set. But it was merely the principal sum, and unlike the total of the Young Plan payments does not include interest. When allowance is made for this, the present figure appears to be equivalent to less than a third of the charge originally proposed.

The annuities fall into two periods of quite different character, as just remarked, the first of 37 years and the second of only 22. This division is directly traceable to the payments which most of the recipients of Reparations in turn have to make to the United States on Inter-Ally debt account, and which the Young Plan refers to merely as "out-payments." Despite the insistence of the American Government on refusing to recognize formally any connection between the two sets of transactions, the truth cannot be blinked. Reparations receipts and Inter-Ally debt payments are in fact intimately related to one another; the greatest part of the debt payments to the United States are closely dependent on the prior receipt of Reparations; and the United States, as the only large net creditor in the Inter-Ally account, will also be much the largest ultimate recipient of the money paid in the first instance under the head of Reparations.

This situation the Young Plan clothes in a few garments of euphemism, but without disguising the figure. The annuities which are scheduled for the first 37 years of the Plan cover the net Inter-Ally debt payments to the United States, and in addition leave a considerable surplus for repairing war damage, chiefly in France, but in the last 22 years they are substantially equal to the debt payments alone, leaving no surplus at all. Of the total Reparations annuities over the 59-year period as a whole, the debt payments to the United States will take roughly 65 per cent. Only the remaining 35 per cent can be applied to making good war damage. It is further provided that if the United States reduces its debt claims against the Allies Germany shall get two-thirds of the benefit in the first 37 years, in the form of a reduction in her payments on Reparations account, and the Allies one-third, but in the last 22 years Germany gets all the benefit. That is, her payments on Reparations account will be correspondingly diminished. No further proof of the actual interdependence of Reparations and Inter-Ally debts is required.

Next to these features, the most interesting aspect of the Plan is the proposal for the partial commercialization of the annuities; that is, for the issuance of bonds against at least a portion of the total stipulated payments. These bonds would be turned over to the creditor

Powers, and their public sale would then permit the creditors themselves to receive the entire principal sum of the obligation at once instead of over 59 years. Now it is obvious that if such bonds are to be issued on a commercial basis the annuities on which they will rest, and of which they will be the capitalization, cannot enjoy the so-called "transfer protection" under which Germany's Reparations payments have hitherto been made. That is, being now specific commercial obligations, they cannot be deferred every time the stability of the German foreign exchanges would be imperiled by them. Germany refused to surrender any large measure of transfer protection, however, except at the price of concessions in other directions which the creditor Powers were unwilling to make, and it was accordingly provided that only the smaller part of the annuities shall be commercialized. A flat 660 million marks a year (157 million dollars) is not postponable under any conditions, and can therefore be commercialized by the issuance of bonds. The total nominal principal of these bonds would be about 12,600 million marks ($3,000 millions), or roughly a third of the present value of the aggregate scheduled payments. Of the non-postponable part of the annuities, 500 million marks a year or the corresponding principal sum in bonds is to go to France to cover war damage, the balance being distributed among the other creditors. The remainder of each annuity is given a limited form of transfer protection, designed to secure Germany against temporary foreign-exchange difficulties but based on the assumption that she will be able to carry the total burden without a permanent breakdown.

The annuities themselves, subject to later arrangements for commercialization, are to be paid either in foreign currencies or, as under the Dawes Plan, in the form of deliveries in kind. These deliveries in kind, however, are to continue for only ten years, and are to decrease in amount during that period. The foreign currency payments are to be made directly to a new institution, the Bank for International Settlements, except when transfers are postponed. In the latter event they are to be cumulated in marks at the Reichsbank, and under certain conditions even the mark payments themselves may be postponed.

This new Bank, which is to have a capital of $100 millions, is designed in the first instance to handle the receipt, management, and distribution of the annuities, as well as to administer the transfer protection provisions. The plan for its organization is complex, but is designed to free it from all undesirable external influence, political or otherwise, within the prescribed sphere of its operations. So far as concerns its relation to the Reparations payments, it will thus be an institution combining the accountancy functions of the Agent General created by the Dawes Plan with the operations, now much restricted, of the Transfer Committee. It is also contemplated that the Bank will engage in various profit-making operations as well, and that the earnings thus made will then be applied to reducing the charge on Germany. These operations, not clearly defined as yet, will presumably be commercial transactions in international finance of the ordinary types, but conducted as far as possible in non-competitive fields, such as the opening up of new channels of foreign trade and finance and the development of new countries. Many people have also expressed the hope that the Bank would become an international institution in the widest sense, handling international payments of all kinds, both public and private, in ways much cheaper and simpler than those now prevailing; acting as an international clearing house; reducing or even eliminating gold movements and perhaps serving as depositary for most of the world's monetary gold; and so on. But its future in these respects is of course still uncertain, and it has attracted far more public attention than anything in the positive proposals for its operation or in the immediate prospects for its importance in the world's economic life can as yet justify.

The remaining provisions of the Young Plan, which are of interest chiefly to Germany herself, deal with the sources of revenue from which the annuities are to be derived. First, the present industrial mortgage is to be abolished outright, and a corresponding adjustment of the internal tax burden is to be made. Second, the railway mortgage is also to be abolished, but instead the Railway Company is to pay for 37 years a direct tax equal to the service charge on the present mortgage, or 660 million marks a year. This sum, it will be observed, is also equal to the non-postponable part of each annuity. The receipts from the tax are to be guaranteed by the German Government, and are to have priority over all other taxation imposed on the railways; and the company, which is to retain its private autonomous character, is to deposit a formal acknowledgment of the obligation involved under the tax with the new Bank. The remainder of each annuity falls on the budget of the Federal Government itself. This budget charge will be substantially less in the early years than the charge entailed by the Dawes Plan standard annuity. In 1930–31 it will be somewhat over 1,136 million marks, whereas under the Dawes Plan it would have been at least 1,540 millions. The reduction is thus very material. The charge rises to a maximum of nearly 1,769 millions in the thirty-seventh year, 1965–66. Thereafter the contributions from the Railway Company cease and the whole burden falls on the budget, but at the same time the size of the annuity itself drops heavily, to just under 1,700 millions on the average; and the budget charge therefore actually diminishes a little. The present machinery of foreign control over the so-called assigned revenues must unfortunately be continued for the present, since these revenues are pledged as collateral security for the German External Loan 1924. The control is to be simplified as far as possible, however, and its eventual abolition is contemplated.

II. ITS ADVANTAGES. PROBABLY NOT FINAL

THESE are the principal provisions of the new Plan. They represent the latest step on the way toward a solution of that bitter struggle over Reparations which began more than ten years ago, with the drafting of the Treaty of Versailles. At the date this is written the Plan has not yet been ratified by the interested Powers, but its ultimate acceptance may be confidently expected.

From the German side, the Plan evidently offers very large advantages. The size of the proposed annuities is much less than the standard Dawes Plan annuity, a fifth smaller even on the average, and a fourth smaller at the start; and the index of prosperity, under which the Dawes annuities would almost certainly have been stepped up, is abolished. Moreover, the largest part of the country's financial autonomy is restored; and for the first time the burden to be borne is definitely determined. The discouraging uncertainty of the former system is thus ended. It is also proposed to abandon completely the underlying charge on the assets of the

Federal and local governments which was set up under the Treaty of Versailles, or at least that consequence of it which gives Reparations an ultimate priority over private payments abroad; a step which would materially improve Germany's position in the world investment markets. In addition, although this is not an integral part of the Plan, early evacuation of the Rhineland is now urged, and it may be hoped will soon be achieved. Against these gains the only offset is Germany's surrender of transfer protection on roughly a third of the average annuity, a surrender far more than compensated for by the reduction in the size of the annuity itself. The first full payment, coming in 1930–31, is equivalent to less than 10 per cent of the total cost of government in the fiscal year 1928–29, and to only 2.6 per cent of the national income in 1928.[1]

The creditor Powers, on the other hand, have obviously made large concessions, and the advantages to them, apart from the commercialization of a third of the payments, are not quite so obvious. Indeed, there are many who declare that although the Paris Conference was formally successful in that a workable agreement was reached, it was in point of fact a failure. Its principal real object, commercialization of the whole Reparations obligation, was not attained, yet the creditors made very substantial reductions in their claims.[2] But

[1] A further not unimportant advantage is that Germany will have much more influence on the new Bank than she did on the old Transfer Committee. Lest the Young Plan charges be regarded as unduly light, however, it may be pointed out that the present capital value of the annuities constitutes a burden which in terms of its relation to the national income is two and a half times as heavy as the entire interest-bearing debt of the United States Government today.

[2] A change in the distribution of the annuities is also proposed, which is especially marked with respect to the non-postponable portion; and at the date of writing (August, 1929) certain countries, par-

had a materially higher schedule been demanded the attempt to enforce it might well have led to a new break-down, and a smaller but assured income is evidently better than none at all. The new arrangement, if agreed to, will also be one which Germany voluntarily accepts: no compulsion was or can be placed on her to abandon the Dawes Plan. The general security of annuities stipulated under an agreement which she makes voluntarily and carries out on her own responsibility is evidently far greater than that of annuities extracted under a *régime* of imposed foreign control and of tacit compulsion. Moreover, what was undoubtedly a compelling motive at the time the Paris negotiations were in progress, had the creditor Powers refused to concur in proposals which Germany felt she could agree to, the resulting collapse of the Conference would almost certainly have precipitated a breakdown of the Dawes Plan transfers, and quite possibly a general European crisis. The creditors had gone too far in starting the negotiations at all to draw back without risk of serious loss.

It is generally believed, and such is certainly the present writer's opinion, that the internal burden proposed by the Young Plan is one Germany can carry, and under which she can grow and prosper at a reasonable though not rapid rate.[1] If that is so, however, an embarrassing situation will arise before long. A good deal of Germany's future progress will apparently be made at the expense of those of the creditor Powers who are

ticularly England, are insisting that this new distribution is unjust to them. The absolute size of the proposed changes, however, is not very great.

[1] The cynic might also point out that a definite burden on the governmental finances such as Reparations impose, like the charges on a fairly large public debt, is a useful deterrent from extravagant and needless governmental expenditures in other directions.

also her industrial competitors. Germany's development will probably restrict the economic expansion of her neighbors, and in a few years' time we may well begin to hear complaints from them that Germany has again hoodwinked the Allies, and could have agreed to pay much more. But a materially higher level of annuities, say a half to two-thirds higher, would probably lead to continuous difficulties or even to an absolute breakdown, and to intermittent and inadequate receipts. Under the arrangement now proposed the creditor Powers who are also competitors of Germany will benefit, and to a far greater extent than they are likely to realize at the time, from the general expansion in the world's industry and commerce which her continued recovery and new progress will make possible. Germany is not only one of the world's greatest manufacturers but also one of its great markets, and one which the world can ill afford to see cut off or even seriously impaired. The fact of the matter probably is that any burden light enough to be borne now, and any schedule of future payments which seems workable from the point of view of the present, will almost inevitably seem too light later. The present moderation will doubtless prove to be not only expedient, but profitable to all concerned.

It must be also pointed out, however, that the Young Plan, great though its contributions are, is almost certainly not the last and definitive step in the solution of the Reparations problem. There are many who regard the calling of the Conference from which it came as premature, and in any event the severe personal and general political pressure under which some of the delegates unfortunately suffered cannot but have detracted from the quality of their labors. The proposals to which they finally agreed were in considerable part a forced compromise, reached because the alternative of complete breakdown was worse than any positive outcome could possibly be. In the circumstances, it is remarkable that so workable and so generally satisfactory an arrangement was arrived at. But on two major and related points the present Plan is probably not final. In the first place, it is entirely possible that further experience may lead to still another downward revision of the sum total of the payments and of the individual annuities, while any reduction in the claims of the United States on Inter-Ally debt account would of course operate automatically in the same direction. In the second place, the process of commercializing the Reparations payments is still incomplete. Two-thirds of the total is still subject to transfer protection, and is therefore postponable. Until the whole of the payments is commercialized and thus taken out of the sphere of international politics, until the issue and sale of bonds for the total sum agreed upon has converted Germany's present debt to other governments into a debt to private individuals,[1] the Reparations problem cannot be regarded as solved.

III. GERMANY'S STRENGTH AND WEAKNESS TODAY

ASSUMING that the Young Plan will come into operation in substantially its present form, let us now return to the

[1] Legally, there is nothing to prevent German individuals from eventually buying up a considerable part or even all of the prospective bond issue themselves, and thus in effect converting the German government's external debt into the much less burdensome form of an internal debt. What is more, the operation lies within the bounds of physical possibility, if spread over time. The estimated aggregate present value of the Young Plan payments, a total which would undoubtedly be materially reduced in the event of complete commercialization, is about 37,000 million marks. This sum, reduced to 1913 values, is almost exactly the same as the value of Germany's pre-war foreign investments. Some interesting possibilities are evidently involved. To the beginning of 1932, only $300 millions of the Young Plan bonds had actually been issued.

question put at the beginning of this chapter: what of Germany's future? Can she carry the large burdens which the Young Plan still entails, as well as those other internal and external burdens which it of course does not affect, or will a new breakdown occur? No one can make detailed predictions with any assurance of accuracy, but the facts and tendencies examined in earlier chapters show clearly enough the larger forces which are at work, and the limiting factors which are involved. The situation is most easily understood if we first summarize the elements of strength and weakness in Germany's position today, and then consider the probable line of development of these elements in the future.

The elements of strength in Germany's present economic position can be interpreted and classified in various ways. In ultimate material terms, the most important among them is the possession, despite the Treaty cessions, of the largest coal production of any Continental country, as well as considerable supplies of other industrial raw materials, and of a laboring population whose will to work and general adaptability to industrial pursuits are probably unsurpassed in Europe today. Looked at in terms of the actual operation of the country's economic life, on the other hand, the chief source of present national strength is undoubtedly the recent thorough reconstruction and reorganization of the basic industries. This reorganization, which is still in process, has already brought the industries affected to levels of technical and commercial efficiency which in most branches are as high or higher than in any other European country, and which are reflected in a correspondingly large volume of production. The chemical and the electro-technical industries have achieved the most clear-cut international superiority to date, but the coal, iron, and steel industries are also very strong, while machinery and textiles will develop rapidly at the first favorable turn. Another element of strength is the size of the country's export trade, although the recovery here is still incomplete, while another is the position of the Reichsbank and the currency, now among the soundest in the world. Still another element, itself largely the resultant of the ones just listed, is the remarkable increase during the past 5 years in the national income and the national savings, the former to a size now materially above pre-war levels. This increase creates an important reserve of power in the national economy with which to meet the stresses and strains of the future. Another is the rehabilitation of German credit in the world money markets, and another the stimulating influence which the Young Plan itself will undoubtedly have both at home and abroad. In general terms, the great fountainhead of Germany's economic power today is thus the size and progressiveness of her chief industrial divisions and of the related branches of her commerce and finance. It is in these directions that the skill of the leaders and the high average quality of the population produce their greatest effects.

The elements of weakness and strain in the present economic constitution of the country are of two sorts, which we may describe loosely as internal and external. The principal internal weaknesses have been discussed at some length in earlier chapters. Those which are of most conspicuous immediate importance are the distortion in the existing price structure—that is, in the relation between the prices of finished goods and the prices of raw materials—and that failure to pass on the gains from rationalization in the basic industries to the ultimate consumer which this distortion implies; the vicious spiral of rising wages and rising prices which has developed in many industrial branches; the economic friction and loss frequently resulting from the operations of the cartels; the very heavy present burden of the aggregate costs of government and governmental obligations; and above all the serious and persistent depression of agriculture. Less superficially obvious, but also a major element, is the post-war impoverishment of the old middle classes by the inflation, chiefly to the benefit of the industrial and financial capitalists. The most serious source of internal tension, however, appears to be the conflict between the socialist and the anti-socialist groups in the German state. This conflict is not a matter of political struggle alone, but vitally affects Germany's whole economic life as well.

These are the principal internal strains of today. The external weakness in Germany's international position is even more conspicuous, and is probably more critical. Germany has a large and persistent deficit in her international payment transactions, which seems likely to continue for a number of years to come. This deficit is made up of three major items. One is the excess of commodity imports over commodity exports. Even including Reparations deliveries in kind with exports, this excess has averaged around 2,000 million marks annually during the past five years. Although it is gradually being reduced, the process of reduction will almost certainly be long. Another is the payment of interest, profits, and amortization charges on the large amounts of capital secured abroad since 1924, charges probably now amounting to over 1,200 million marks a year net; and the third is the Reparations payments. Even after allowing for deliveries in kind, and even with the lower schedule of annuities prescribed by the Young Plan, the actual cash transfers abroad on Reparations account will not be far from 900 million marks annually in the opening years of the new scheme, and will increase steadily. The total international payment deficit thus amounts to around 4,000 million marks a year (1,000 million dollars), on an average of the present and immediate future prospects. This deficit can only be met, as it has been met ever since 1924, by renewed borrowing abroad; a procedure which in itself, as we have already seen, only increases the annual deficit in later years. In the second place, as has been emphasized at other points, a considerable part of the capital already secured from foreign countries has been short-term-loans borrowing. But short-term money can be recalled on little or no notice, and it therefore offers a continuous threat to the stability of the foreign exchanges and the currency.

This international financial situation as a whole is both dangerous and burdensome, and Germany can be relied on, if only in self-protection, to do everything possible to correct it. The sole major form of correction open to her, however, is to increase the volume of her commodity and service exports relative to her imports until a surplus is achieved which is sufficient to meet the current payment deficit. But an export surplus of this size cannot be developed overnight, nor merely by wishing for it, and the struggle to secure it constitutes the third external type of strain to which Germany is and will be subjected.

IV. CRITICAL FACTORS. CAPACITY TO PAY

THESE are the principal factors which will govern Germany's economic development in the coming decades. Of the two conflicting sets, one of weakness and the other of strength, which will eventually prevail? Will Germany continue to grow and prosper, or will the burdens placed upon her prove so heavy that they prevent all further expansion, and even force her backward?

If it were not for Germany's public and private obligations to other countries, on account of Reparations and for capital already obtained abroad, the answer could be given with a considerable degree of confidence. The present internal strains would almost certainly be overcome in time, and the internal development of the country would then go forward rapidly. The international payment deficit would be steadily reduced, while such further foreign borrowing as was needed to meet it in the transition period would probably not entail burdensome charges; and the increasing level of general prosperity would postpone or even end the socialist-capitalist conflict. Unfortunately for Germany, however, she could not have reached her present position at all without very large prior importations of foreign capital; and the Reparations charges cannot be avoided. In the last analysis, these are therefore the two principal controlling factors. If Germany can carry the burdens they entail and still prosper, she probably has little to fear from the future. What are the prospects for her success? Can she continue to make the scheduled Reparations payments, and at the same time meet the charges on her foreign borrowing?

At the outset, it is necessary to make a clear distinction between her internal capacity to pay, whether on account of Reparations or for the current service charges on capital obtained abroad, and her external capacity to pay. That is, it is necessary to distinguish between her power to raise the necessary sums in marks, within her own boundaries, and her power to convert these marks into foreign currencies or other things having value in the creditor countries. The first kind of capacity is largely dependent on the correctives which may be found for the conditions of internal weakness and strain recapitulated a few pages above. It can be stated summarily that the general outlook here is good. Despite the grave problems with which she is faced, there is no reason to expect that Germany will be unable to meet the internal charges involved in her public and private obligations abroad; and it is also to be anticipated that if the external burdens can be carried at all she will become steadily stronger.

The critical question is therefore the problem of her *external* capacity to pay. It is the external burdens involved in Reparations and the foreign-capital charges combined which will weigh most heavily on the country, and which are potentially the most dangerous to her general economic stability. Three ways of making these payments are open. Germany can increase her commodity exports relative to imports, until a permanent surplus of the necessary size has been developed. She can similarly increase her exports of services. Or she can borrow the funds abroad, as she has been doing since 1924. In point of fact, she will make use of all three methods.[1] But further borrowing abroad, as we have already seen, has the conclusive disadvantage that it increases the foreign payments which must subsequently be made, and in the long run thus makes the international financial situation worse rather than better. As time goes on, Germany therefore will

[1] Exporting gold is another method, but all the monetary gold in the country would be insufficient to meet the present payment deficit for a single year.

and must effect a steadily larger part of the payments out of her own resources; that is, out of her own production and exportation of goods and services. The importation of foreign capital must steadily diminish, and eventually cease. Both self-interest and the working of international economic forces will impel her to this course.

These far-reaching changes will not be brought about at once, nor without a protracted struggle. Exports of services already show a small net surplus, which in the past four years has lain between 200 and 300 million marks annually, and seems likely to grow steadily in the future. Germany is making extraordinary efforts to build up her merchant marine again, and her net freight receipts have nearly doubled since 1924. She is also trying to attract the profitable tourist traffic by fairs, exhibitions, and festivals, while the volume of banking and insurance business that she does on commission for other countries is increasing. But all these service items taken together are as yet a comparatively small factor in the general aggregate of Germany's international transactions. The principal share in overcoming the international payment deficit must almost certainly be borne by the commodity balance of trade. The present large excess of imports must be converted into an excess of exports, and quite possibly one of even greater size.

The only way in which this transformation can be accomplished is to bring about a decline in the prices of exported and imported articles within Germany, relative to the prices of similar commodities in the world at large. German exports will then be stimulated and imports checked, and eventually the necessary surplus of exports will be obtained. It is probable, however, that such a change could not be enforced abruptly. Any sudden decline in prices of the scope here involved could be produced only by a severe contraction of currency and credit. This would in turn necessitate raising discount rates still higher; the rise would attract more foreign capital; interest rates would fall again; and prices would be more apt to increase than to drop. Measures powerful enough to prevent the importation of funds from abroad, on the other hand, would be apt to precipitate the withdrawal of foreign capital already in Germany, and the resulting severe crisis could only leave matters worse than before. In addition, a rapid drop in prices at large would almost certainly force down the general standard of living. Wage rates might be held up, but employment would decline, and most money incomes would fall. Since the prices of imported foodstuffs would not be affected, they would then seem high in comparison with the general average of German prices; and the consumption of these foodstuffs, on which Germany is heavily dependent, would fall.

But a *gradual* expansion of exports relative to imports would not necessarily entail these consequences, and seems sure to develop. It will come from a number of sources. With the passage of time the present high levels of interest rates will fall somewhat, while tax charges per mark of individual and corporate income will diminish, even if the total burden remains unaltered in absolute terms. Both changes will materially increase Germany's competing power in the world markets. At the same time, partly in consequence of these factors but chiefly as a result of the ever wider spread of rationalization, the prices of finished goods will undoubtedly fall a good deal relative to other classes of

German prices and relative to world levels. The corresponding exports will then be stimulated, and imports will be checked. Two factors of more general influence and importance will also be at work. One is the future policy of the Reichsbank. In view of the continuous economic pressure under which the country must labor, the Reichsbank may be expected to prevent any inflationary excesses, as it has during the past five years, and to exert as restrictive an influence on credit and prices as is consistent with the conservation and sound expansion of the country's economic strength. The other is the progress of German industrial technique. There is no reason to think that this progress has now reached its limit. On the contrary, it may be expected to continue indefinitely, and to bring with it either steadily decreasing costs of production or improved quality, or both. In so far as the German technique advances more rapidly than the technique of other countries, which it seems likely to do in many lines, Germany will then have a corresponding advantage in world competition, and her exports of the products involved will increase. Many Germans feel that the best prospects here lie not so much in the direction of standardized mass production as of high quality work, and much is now being done along this line, but in both fields the outlook is good.

When we turn from conditions within Germany to the export markets themselves, on the other hand, the prospects for a large and sustained growth of her exports appear somewhat less encouraging. Both the capacity and the willingness of other nations to absorb large additional quantities of German goods are clearly limited at present. Most of the countries to which the exports now go maintain protective tariffs, of varying severity but of unquestioned effect, and despite the moderating influence of the numerous commercial treaties Germany has negotiated, the tariffs would probably be raised still higher if her exports showed signs of any sudden large expansion. With the partial exception of England, this is true of practically all the countries which are creditors of Germany on Reparations account, as well as most of those which are creditors on private account, for they are also her principal industrial competitors. In effect, Germany is therefore in the painful position of offering payments against her obligations abroad which the creditors insist on receiving, yet at the same time refuse to take. Nor is there any group of neutral third countries to which she could increase her exports, whose demands for the commodities she produces are now large enough to absorb more than a part of the total increase at which she must aim.

But as time goes on, these limitations will probably diminish in importance. The effects of the prospective changes in conditions within Germany just referred to will begin to be felt, and her aggressiveness in seeking foreign markets, the results of which have thus far been manifested chiefly in her trade with the smaller nations, will yield ever greater fruits. She would probably also benefit from any unexpectedly rapid development of the economically newer countries. Her best future prospects, however, are apparently in Russia. Germany was well established there before the war, and when conditions in Russia have been stabilized sufficiently to permit the entrance of foreign capital and foreign enterprise on a large scale, she will probably be in a better position than any other country to supply the knowledge, the equipment, and the managers that will be necessary.

Taking the foreign trade situation as a whole, it can thus be stated with a good deal of assurance that commodity exports will expand steadily relative to imports. How long a period must elapse before an actual surplus of exports can be achieved, and one which when added to the net service exports will be large enough to cover both Reparations payments and the charges on foreign capital, is not equally clear. Of course wide fluctuations will occur, and occasionally the trade balance may remain favorable for a number of months together, but it is extremely unlikely that a lasting surplus of the necessary size can be developed in the near future. A transition period, of perhaps 20 or even 30 years if things move slowly, must intervene. This seems the more probable when one recalls that Germany's exports, and indeed her production in general, are dependent to an unusually high degree on prior imports of raw materials and foodstuffs. Except at the price of diverting current production from the domestic markets to exportation, and thus reducing the domestic standard of living, exports cannot be increased without also increasing imports, though of course in lesser degree. Nor can imports be reduced without reducing exports much more than in proportion, except by lowering the living standard and except with respect to the narrow range of manufactured goods which fall in the import category. It follows from this that a sustained absolute increase in the volume of exportation can bring only a less than proportionate increase in these exports *relative* to imports. The attainment of an export surplus of a given necessary size will therefore be deferred longer than might at first seem probable.

I⊤ will thus certainly be a number of years, and possibly two or three decades, before Germany develops a surplus of commodity and service exports large enough to meet both Reparations and foreign capital charges. In this critical transition period, how can she make the large and sustained volume of payments to other countries which will be necessary?

Clearly she must continue to do what she has been doing since 1924. By the sale of securities and tangible property and the negotiation of short credits abroad, she must obtain in other countries the funds required to meet all the current foreign obligations which her own commodity and service exports are inadequate to offset. Even apart from the need of such capital imports to carry out her ambitious programs for further internal expansion, there is no other way in which the international deficit itself can be met. In other words, during these years Germany's capacity to *pay* abroad will be determined largely by her capacity to *borrow* abroad, or to secure the necessary funds from foreign countries in other ways. As time goes on, a steadily larger part of the total payments will come from her own production and sale of goods and services, but the critical remainder must be derived from further importations of capital.

Neither Germany nor the foreign investor need regard this prospect as dangerous, nor even as undesirable; on the contrary. The money obtained abroad since 1924, taken as a whole, has earned far more than the charges it has entailed. The evidence all indicates that the large additional sums which will be required in the future will not only pay for themselves, but will produce a considerable surplus. The investments involved will be safe and profitable in the aggregate, while at the same time they will augment both the country's general economic strength and her power to make foreign payments. Germany will not only grow steadily, but will grow at a rate distinctly more rapid than if she had to rely on the accumulation of domestic savings alone. Despite the increase in domestic and foreign charges which this new capital will entail, it will make Germany substantially more prosperous and in general better off, in terms both of individuals and of the nation as a whole, than if the capital itself had never been imported at all.

Yet there are conspicuously unfavorable features of this prospective situation, and serious though probably temporary difficulties may well develop. These difficulties center around the fact that the supply of new funds coming currently into the world's long- and short-term markets is necessarily limited at any one time. The supply is large, but it is not inexhaustible. If Germany appears year after year as an important borrower abroad, the markets will be placed under more or less chronic strain, and at times it may be entirely impossible for her to raise funds at any reasonable terms. It is under such circumstances, incidentally, that the postponement provisions of the Young Plan would be called into operation. In due course an international payment crisis of this sort will adjust itself through the working of the forces which maintain the general international economic equilibrium, but only at the cost to Germany of credit contraction, falling prices, and probably a general depression. A further undesirable feature is that simply by virtue of being a large and continuous borrower, Germany will have to pay much

higher rates for money than either her own credit
standing or the security of the particular transactions
involved would themselves justify, and the burden of
the resulting charges will be correspondingly heavier.

The magnitude of these prospective borrowing operations has already been indicated. Even in the opening years of the Young Plan, actual cash transfers on
Reparations account will come to nearly 900 million
marks annually, and will grow steadily. The service
charges on the capital hitherto obtained abroad amount
to at least 1,200 millions more, and will increase each
year as long as net imports of capital continue to be
necessary, except in so far as refunding at lower interest
rates can be effected. When to these sums is added the
current excess of merchandise imports, we reach a total
international payment deficit which on an average of
the present and immediate prospects is not far from
4,000 million marks annually, or roughly 1,000 million
dollars. Yet the entire new foreign investment of the
United States in 1928 (excluding short credits)
amounted to only 1,250 million dollars. The aggregate
requirements of Germany alone would have absorbed
four-fifths of this, though of course not all her borrowings were at long term.

Moreover, to these recurrent demands for capital
will now be added those involved in the Young Plan
proposal to commercialize a part of the Reparations
payments by selling bonds against them. The capital
sum of the issue will probably be about 3,000 million
dollars. How soon these bonds will be brought out, and
in what form, still remains to be decided. It is clear,
however, that the quantity is far larger than the world
markets can absorb at any one time, and their sale
will probably have to be spread over a number of years.

A situation threatens to develop in which the whole financial world will be badly overbought on German securities, and skilful handling will be required to prevent a breakdown.

The principal country in which Germany has borrowed in the past five years has been the United States, and indeed a chief factor in her current financial welfare has often been the New York money rates. Although the participation of other countries is increasing steadily, as they become stronger and more prosperous, this dependence will doubtless continue for a number of years. It is now generally anticipated, for example, that a large part of the German foreign issues which have been held back since before the recent Paris Conference will be offered in the United States during the fall and winter of 1929. These prospects give everything connected with Germany an especial significance in American eyes, and make it important that her real situation should be correctly understood. Borrowing may sometimes be a sign of weakness, it is true, but in the case of Germany it represents the building up of the country's general economic strength, and may be expected to yield rich returns in future years.

VI. CONCLUSION

THE history of Germany since the war thus falls into two distinct periods. In the first period, the movement of events was ever more rapidly downward. The cycle of catastrophe which began with military defeat and internal revolution carried the nation into the black maelstrom of currency inflation, swept on to the Ruhr disaster, and ended only with the utter collapse of 1923. In the second period, the trend has been upward. Under

the aegis of the Dawes Plan, and with the help of very
large amounts of foreign capital, the skill of the leaders
and the patient determination of the people have combined to bring about a recovery which is without parallel
in the world's history. In most respects, with the exception of agriculture and foreign trade, German economic
life has now regained or more than regained the pre-war
levels. Despite the loss of territory under the terms of
the Treaty of Peace, the aggregate volume of production is materially larger than it was in 1913, the average prosperity of the people as a whole is a little greater,
and Germany's industrial leadership on the Continent
has been conclusively reëstablished.

The prospects for the future are good. It is true that
any period of sustained general prosperity such as prevailed in the years just before the war is probably still a
long way ahead. From the economic point of view, Germany is and will be a country working under burdens
which by every standard must be judged severe, chiefly
the burden of Reparations and of the service charges on
foreign capital. The *internal* weight of these burdens is
not likely to prove dangerous. But the necessity of
making continuous payments abroad which they entail
will exert a downward pressure on German prices; and
by limiting the share of the total domestic production
which can be assigned to domestic consumption, it will
likewise retard or at times even prevent further increases
in the general standard of living. The conflict between
the socialist and the non-socialist groups also injects an
element of serious strain into the situation, although how
far and how enduringly the country's real economic
strength is likely to be impaired must remain a matter
for individual judgment. These and other factors will

hinder future growth in a number of directions, and discourage too roseate predictions.

But that Germany's expansion will continue in coming years seems assured. The expansion will go forward at a less spectacular rate than since 1924, except for the temporary boom which is likely to follow the ratification of the Young Plan, but it will be none the less genuine and sustained. The great source from which it will come is the progress of the German industrial and commercial techniques, techniques which are already as good on the average as the standards prevailing in other European countries or better, and which there is every reason to think will continue to advance. From the financial side, for a number of years the expansion will still be based to a considerable extent on the importation of foreign capital, but domestic savings will play an ever larger rôle. This growth in internal strength will also bring with it a steady growth in Germany's power to make payments abroad. Commodity and service exports will increase relative to imports until the present international payment deficit is wiped out, and the present hampering dependence on foreign borrowing will at last cease. The road marked out for Germany through the coming decades is not easy, but it is a road which climbs steadily upward, and at its end lies the prize of assured national strength and prosperity.

CHAPTER XII

1929–32: A POSTSCRIPT

I. THE WORLD DEPRESSION

THE preceding chapters were written in the summer of 1929. The ink was hardly dry on their pages when the course of world business began to turn downward; and the downward movement has now continued with almost uninterrupted force for two and a half years. At the present time (February, 1932), the world is plunged deep in the most severe and most ominous economic depression of recent decades, with little assurance that the end is even yet in sight.

The fundamental explanation of the origin and scope of the world depression must undoubtedly run in terms of the world economic situation created by the World War. In some directions the conditions of the war and post-war periods exerted an abnormal economic stimulus, in others an abnormal economic pressure; and in the post-war years the possibility was always present, as we now look back on the situation, that any severe strain might precipitate a general collapse. Had everything gone well, it is not improbable that these maladjustments would have smoothed themselves out in time. But beginning in 1929, the world's financial mechanism was subjected to a series of major shocks, shocks which had a cumulatively depressing effect on general business activity in all the leading countries. The unrolling of the present era of world-wide liquidation, self-propagating deflation, and international crises followed with almost the inevitability of a Greek tragedy.

The inception of this series of financial shocks really

dates back to the negotiations over the drafting of the Young Plan, in the spring of 1929. The negotiations eventually proved successful, and at the beginning of 1930 the Plan itself was formally ratified.[1] But the procedure was long drawn out, and in the earlier stages a great deal of unrest and even fear was aroused in the world money markets over its possible outcome. The tangible expression of this fear was the cessation of new loans to Germany, and the withdrawal of large blocks of funds already placed with her. This in turn led to severe pressure on Germany's foreign exchanges, as remarked in an earlier chapter,[2] and to serious difficulties, in April of 1929, over Germany's current payments abroad for Reparations and other purposes. The crisis itself was quickly surmounted, but a serious blow had been dealt to the world's business and financial structure, the first in some years. Then a few months later came the collapse of the New York stock market. At the same time, it was suddenly realized that world business had been slowly falling off for a number of months past, in considerable part as a result of the German situation. Pessimism began to take the place of optimism, and with the help of the initial fall in American security prices, a vigorous decline in the world's general economic activity rapidly got under way.

The downward world movement continued until the

[1] For the text of the Young Plan and of the subsequent Hague agreements of 1929 and 1930, see Denys P. Myers, *Reparations in 1930* (Boston, 1931); and J. W. Wheeler-Bennett and H. Latimer, *Information on the Reparation Settlement* (London, 1930). The Final Act of the Second Hague Conference was signed January 20, 1930, and formal government ratifications were given in the ensuing months. The Young Plan provisions were made retroactive, and were treated as being in effect from September 1, 1929.

For a penetrating discussion of the whole Reparations question, see Sir Andrew McFadyean, *Reparation Reviewed* (London, 1930).

[2] See p. 218, above.

spring of 1931, when it showed some signs of abating, and even of giving way to revival. But then came a new series of adverse events in Europe. The ill-timed proposal for an Austro-German customs union, which came to a head in May of that year, encountered determined opposition from France; and France expressed her disapproval by suddenly withdrawing a considerable part of the money she had previously placed in Germany. This action at once renewed the pressure on Germany's foreign exchanges. The tariff union proposal was referred to the League of Nations, and by it to the World Court, where it was eventually vetoed. But this procedure, too, required time, and before it was completed the damage had been done. The intervening delay allowed distrust of the mark to spread to other countries, and they likewise began drawing steadily larger quantities of money out of Germany. Then the Austrian Kredit-Anstalt, which was the largest bank in Austria and reputed to be above suspicion, suddenly failed; and the nervous fear of the world money markets was still further increased. Next came President Hoover's proposal, in June, 1931, for a one-year moratorium on the Reparations and Inter-Ally debt payments. The proposal was excellent in itself, and of course its adoption eventually brought much-needed relief to Germany. But it was apparently advanced without adequate preliminary stage-setting in certain European chancelleries, and again there was a disastrous delay before it could be put into effect. Bear speculators all over the world took advantage of this period of uncertainty to sell German currency; banks and investors abroad became frightened; a real foreign exchange panic developed within Germany itself; and the long-threatened financial deluge at last descended.

In order to save the German mark and the rapidly dwindling gold reserves of the Reichsbank, the German Government was compelled to step in. Foreign exchange dealings were placed under strict control, and were rationed. The stock markets were closed, and other similar protective measures were initiated. Two of the largest banks got into difficulties, and to prevent nation-wide bankruptcy had to be helped out. Finally, foreign balances and short credits in Germany were virtually frozen, at first by the action of the German Government itself and then by the acceptance, on the part of the foreign creditors, of the recommendations of the Wiggin Committee at Basle.[1] In substance, the creditors agreed that the short credits should be extended for six months instead of being paid at maturity, and that foreign-owned cash balances in Germany should be withdrawn only in limited amounts during this interval. The total sums involved were estimated at nearly two billion dollars.[2] This so-called *Stillhaltung* or standstill agreement, together with the Hoover moratorium, at last relieved Germany of a large part of her current demand obligations abroad,

[1] The formal designation of the so-called Wiggin (Basle) Committee is the "Committee Appointed on the Recommendation of the London Conference 1931." The Report of the Committee, dated Basle, August 18, 1931, has been privately reprinted in New York.

[2] This agreement expired February 29, 1932. Before its expiration it was renewed, with numerous additional safeguards and alternative options, and with provision for repayments only as Germany's financial situation might warrant rather than with specifications of times and amounts. See the *New York Times* for January 24 and February 2–4, 1932. It is estimated that the second agreement covered sums totaling about one and a half billion dollars.

Even with these safeguards, in the latter part of 1931 the Reichsbank found it necessary to negotiate large short credits with other central banks and with the Bank for International Settlements, to protect its own reserve position.

and gave her a breathing spell in which to rectify her position.

But a second severe blow had been dealt to the world's financial structure by this new German crisis, and despite all efforts, its effects spread quickly to other countries. The position of England was especially serious. The freezing of the German short credits and balances embarrassed a number of the London banks, for they had made large advances to Germany. In addition, through the summer a steadily growing volume of sterling balances was withdrawn from London by frightened foreign holders. England was thus compelled to meet large demand claims against her with a seriously impaired supply of quick assets, and although large emergency loans were secured in France and the United States, the odds were too great. On September 21, 1931, England suspended gold payments. Some eleven other countries were forced off the gold standard at about the same time, largely in consequence of England's action; and in almost every western nation the current financial tension was seriously increased. Such was the chain of consequences which the trigger-like action of the second German crisis set in motion. At the beginning of 1932, France and the United States were left as the only major gold-standard countries in the world; and although France had till that time remained comparatively immune from the international contagion, the financial situation within the United States had become acute.

Nor was the severity of the financial distress confined to western Europe and the United States. Australia, China, India, all the major South American countries, and indeed every large area of the world where modern international finance has found a foothold, suffered financial reverses of more or less serious character. To cite only a single illustration, from the end of 1928 to the beginning of 1932 not less than 216 government bond issues which had been floated abroad went into default,[1] either because of the internal bankruptcy of the governments concerned or because of foreign exchange difficulties. As these pages are written, it is by no means clear that the end of the chapter of disasters has been reached even yet.

II. ECONOMIC GERMANY AT THE BEGINNING OF 1932

THE most spectacular features of the world depression have been these financial aspects, with their striking though gloomy record of crises, bankruptcies, defaults, and suspensions of gold payments. Far more serious, however, has been the toll of the depression in terms of general economic activity and human welfare in the leading industrial countries, especially in Germany. The *relative* declines in economic activity have been roughly the same in the United States, England, and Germany. Measured from the peaks of 1928 and 1929, the fall has averaged around 35 per cent.[2] But even at the 1929 peaks Germany was less prosperous than England, and far less prosperous than the United States; and the suffering inflicted by the depression has been correspondingly greater in Germany than in any of the other leading countries.

Both for lack of space and for lack of comprehensive information, it is impossible as yet to give a detailed account of what happened in Germany from 1929 to the

---

[1] Max Winkler and Maxwell S. Stewart, "Recent Defaults of Government Loans" (Foreign Policy Association, *Reports,* January 6, 1932).

[2] To the beginning of 1932, France, Italy, and Belgium had suffered less severely.

beginning of 1932. A few basic figures, however, when compared with the data presented in earlier chapters, will serve to give a fairly adequate picture of the general course of recent events.

General wholesale prices, with 1913 as 100, declined from 140 in March, 1929, to 103 in December, 1931, a fall of 26 per cent.[1] On the other hand, agricultural prices taken alone fell by 30 per cent, and the prices of raw materials and half-finished industrial products by 29 per cent, whereas the prices of finished goods fell only 19 per cent. Thus the pre-depression distortion in the German price structure, arising from the relatively high level and the very marked inflexibility of finished-goods prices, has still not been corrected. The cost of living has also been comparatively inert, and in the same period declined only 16 per cent.[2] The drop in the physical volume of industrial production, on the other hand, has been severe. From the high point reached in June, 1929, to December, 1931, production declined by 41 per cent. The comparable figure in the United States is almost exactly the same, 43 per cent.

The position of German labor has in many districts been pitiful. Nominal tariff wage rates held up fairly well until the emergency decrees of December, 1931, when they were substantially reduced; and the cost of living, as just remarked, has fallen. But the number of workers unemployed has been so enormous that both nominal money wages and nominal real wages give a wholly inaccurate picture of the true situation. German official sources report that in October, 1931, 39 per cent of all trade-union members were wholly without employment, while 24 per cent more were on part time;

[1] See the charts on p. 222, above. The same sources are used here.
[2] See the chart on p. 257, above.

and an American observer estimated that at the end of December, 1931, some 5,670,000 workers were out of jobs.[1] This figure was just twice as large as the then current estimate for Great Britain. The serious restrictions on German unemployment relief necessitated by government budget difficulties mean that the cost of this unemployment, in terms of human health and welfare, has been very grave.

Germany's international financial position, as pointed out in the preceding section, has been critical, and a complete breakdown was prevented only by the Hoover moratorium and the standstill agreements on private credits. The net inflow of foreign funds, by which Germany had previously met the current deficits in her international payments, virtually ceased after 1929; and the successive large withdrawals of short-term funds which then took place, until these withdrawals were stopped by the government controls and the first standstill agreements (July and August, 1931), imposed a severe burden on the German reserves of gold and foreign exchange.[2] On the other hand, Germany brought home some part of her own relatively small placements abroad,[3] and the favorable turn in her balance of commodity trade provided additional funds with which to meet a part of the current international deficits. It is

[1] See *Commerce Reports,* Jan. 18, 1932.

[2] See the Report of the Wiggin Committee, already cited: Annex III. In 1930 and the first half of 1931, 2.5 milliard marks of foreign funds were withdrawn. On the danger of Germany's short-term foreign borrowing in general, apparent even in 1928, see Chap. IX and pp. 305, 348, and 357 ff., above.

[3] The Wiggin Report estimates that from the end of 1929 to July, 1931, about 1.5 milliard marks of German funds were repatriated. After the latter date, however, there was apparently an extensive flight of capital from Germany, despite all government restrictions; in particular, when possible German exporters left their balances abroad instead of bringing them home.

noteworthy, however, that while Germany secured a surplus of exports of nearly three milliard marks in 1931, she did so not by increasing the money volume of her exports—on the contrary, exports fell off substantially—but by cutting her imports almost in half. This reduction in imports was primarily a product of the depressed state of industry within Germany. It therefore seems probable that when business revives, imports will expand, and that the favorable trade balance will then be correspondingly reduced.[1]

In the course of 1931, as remarked above, Germany took very drastic steps to improve her own financial position, and to protect the interests of her foreign creditors. Sweeping reductions in government expenditures and severe increases in the scope and rate of taxation restored substantial equilibrium in the Federal budget. The measures taken by the Government and the Reichs-

---

[1] See pp. 293–297 and 355, above. The figures on the balance of trade have been as follows, in million marks (data from *Wirtschaft und Statistik*):

	1929	1930	First 11 months of 1931
Imports	13,600	10,600	6,200
Exports	13,600	12,100	8,800
Balance	0	+1,500	+2,600

Two further observations on the trade balance are in order, however. First, the export figures declined steadily in the closing months of 1931, due to the increasing severity of the world depression, currency depreciations abroad, and especially the increases in foreign protective tariffs instigated by the depression itself. The export *surplus* also declined, since exports fell more rapidly in these months than imports. Second, a considerable part of the 1931 exports were shipments to Russia on long credits, for which actual *payments* will not be received in full for two or three years. The effect of these exports on Germany's current international financial position is hence much less than might at first appear.

On both counts, the immediate outlook for Germany's export trade is not encouraging, though the long-run prospects are good.

bank have stabilized the foreign exchanges, and have prevented that precipitous currency depreciation which at one time seemed imminent. In addition, at the end of 1931 a new set of government decrees prescribed a long series of compulsory reductions in commodity prices, wages, rents, interest rates, and freight schedules, and thus abruptly forced Germany's internal economy more nearly into line with international conditions. It is difficult to see what more could have been done; and it is noteworthy that the German people have borne these new restrictions and burdens with extraordinary fortitude and patience.

III. SHORT CREDITS, REPARATIONS, AND INTER-ALLY DEBTS

At the beginning of 1932, the internal economic distress in Germany was undoubtedly greater than that in the United States and England, but it was still of the same general order of magnitude. In all three countries, the depression had reached unprecedented depths. What made the German situation so much more acute than that of the other leading nations was Germany's international financial position, first with respect to foreign short credits, and second with respect to Reparations. In January, 1932, as remarked above, an international committee which had been meeting at Berlin, again under the chairmanship of Mr. Albert H. Wiggin, finally negotiated an indefinite prolongation of the standstill agreement on foreign short credits and balances, subject to various restrictions and modifications of the original arrangement.[1] Any immediate danger of a new foreign exchange crisis, precipitated by endeavors to withdraw these credits and balances, was thus

[1] Also see the first section of this chapter.

averted. But until they can be either paid off or converted directly into long-term obligations, or until a revival of new foreign investment in Germany ends the present desire of Germany's foreign short-term creditors to repatriate them, these semi-frozen credits and balances will of course always be hanging over the exchange market, and will constitute an essentially abnormal source of strain. Until they are taken care of in one way or another, German international finance cannot resume its ordinary course, for any temporary surplus that may appear will at once be captured to help pay off the short credits and balances.

For the Reparations question, on the other hand, no definitive line of solution whatsoever has yet been found. In the preceding chapter, I expressed my conviction that Germany could carry the Young Plan charges and still prosper. At the time that chapter was written, in the middle of 1929, some observers thought that a mild recession in world trade might develop from the uncertainties incident to the negotiation of the Young Plan, but I know of no competent student who anticipated a world depression of such cataclysmic magnitude as the years 1930–32 actually brought. The depression has naturally altered the complexion of the Reparations problem very substantially. I believe, however, that after the depression has passed it will still be economically *possible* for Germany to carry, year in and year out, the *real* burden which the Young Plan contemplated. That means, of course, that the Young Plan charges would have to be scaled down at least in proportion to the decline in world prices, since this decline has increased the value of money, and has hence increased the real human effort required to produce a dollar's worth of payments. If the price levels prevailing at the beginning of 1932 prove permanent, this reduction in the scheduled money payments would amount to at least 30 or 35 per cent.[1]

Whether it is *desirable* that Germany should continue to carry the Young Plan charges, even when scaled down in this manner, is another question, and a question which will not be decided on purely economic grounds alone. Germany's own economic capacity is no longer the sole or even, at the moment, the dominant factor in the Reparations problem. Two other factors have become of controlling importance, one psychological and one essentially political. The effect of the psychological factor has been clear. Germany continued to make the Young Plan payments through nearly two years of depression; and when she finally suspended them in the middle of 1931, under the Hoover moratorium, the suspension was not due to Germany's own inability to raise the sums involved within her own borders, in marks. The suspension was due primarily to foreign exchange difficulties arising out of the world financial crisis. To put it in a word, it was not Germany's own lack of ability which was responsible: it was the growing lack of world *confidence in* her ability. At the beginning of 1932, this so-called crisis of confidence was still dominant in world finance. Another international Committee had been convoked at Basle in November, 1931, to examine the existing situation within the framework of the Young Plan provisions;

[1] Provision for an adjustment of Germany's Reparations payments in accordance with the movements both of the value of gold and of an "index of prosperity" was contained, it will be recalled, in the Dawes Plan, but was omitted from the Young Plan in order to facilitate commercialization of the Reparations obligation. Neither the framers of the Young Plan nor the authorities within Germany contemplated as a possibility any such drastic decline in world prices and world business activity as actually developed from 1929 to 1932.

but although this Committee adumbrated the possibility of a permanent readjustment of the Reparations obligation, it was confined by the Young Plan to recommending temporary measures for the immediate relief of Germany.[1] In other competent circles it was widely felt that the wisest thing to do, from the psychological point of view, would be to scale down the Reparations payments drastically and permanently, or even to abolish them entirely, and thus to end the uncertainty once for all. But this line of attack has been strenuously opposed by France, and at the date of present writing (February, 1932) no definite action had been taken by the creditor governments concerned.

As the downward movement of world trade loses its momentum, and as the elements of recovery begin to appear, the importance of this psychological factor will steadily lessen. The political factor, on the other hand, will grow rather than diminish in influence. This political factor has two components. One is the continued tension between France and Germany, which has made France unwilling to grant permanent concessions to Germany on the Reparations question except at the price of German concessions in other directions which have been greater than Germany herself would consider. The second component is the relations between the European Reparations creditors as a whole and the United States. The important Reparations creditors are all, in turn, debtors of the United States on Inter-Ally debt account. Although most of them would themselves be willing to make large concessions to Germany, and perhaps even to wipe out the whole Reparations obligation, they find themselves financially unable to do

---

[1] See the *New York Times,* Dec. 19, 1931. The American member of the Committee was Mr. Walter W. Stewart.

so unless the United States will make substantially equivalent concessions in the Inter-Ally debt claims. To date the matter has not come up for formal consideration, but the American Government has clearly indicated its unwillingness to contemplate any further permanent reductions in the Inter-Ally debts as they now exist.

It is not possible here to review in detail the long controversy which has been waged over the question in this country. The opponents of reduction or cancellation point out, quite properly, that the United States made very large initial concessions at the time the present debt agreements were made; and that to wipe out these agreements now would in effect place on our shoulders the whole remaining cost of the World War, in so far as this cost was met by international borrowing (and excluding, of course, the uncollectible loans to Russia). They can find no reason for our assuming in this way a still larger part of the burden of what was after all an essentially European conflict. The advocates of reduction or cancellation, on the other hand, call attention to the fact that we entered the war in full partnership with the European Allies, and that because of our military unpreparedness we were unable to put any troops on the firing line for a full year after our entry. They declare that our loans to the Allies in effect took the place of the soldiers we were unable to supply, and that there is hence no tenable moral ground for asking the repayment of these loans: as well demand the return of the American soldiers who were killed in battle. They also assert that in the present world depression large reductions or cancellation would give a great impetus to world trade, and would thus return to our citizens, through the channels of industry

and commerce, many times more than the sums which
our Treasury would relinquish.[1] Still a third group has
desired to link reduction or cancellation of the debts
with reduction in world armaments, making one the
price of the other. This proposal, which has much to
commend it in principle, has, however, been difficult to
translate into terms of concrete formulae or ratios of
reduction.

No special pleading for one or another of these
views will be advanced here. It is evident, however, that
in 1932 just as in 1929, the critical factor in the future disposition of the Reparations problem is the
policy and the possible action of the United States with
respect to the Inter-Ally debts. The world depression
has made Reparations once more the most important
unsolved problem in Germany's general economic situation, while Germany herself remains the critical factor
in the economic position of the European continent.
There is thus a clear line of connection running from
American financial policy to the general economic welfare of Europe.[2]

It is still too soon to see with any clarity what Ger-

[1] See the present writer's article, "Reparations and the Inter-Ally
Debts in 1931" (Foreign Policy Association, *Reports,* April 29, 1931;
revised edition August, 1931).

[2] It is also relevant to point out here that the high American tariff
makes it still more difficult for foreign debtors to pay their obligations to us. Apart from the Inter-Ally debts due the American Government, which have a "present value" (at 4 per cent compound interest) of 7.7 billion dollars, American citizens now have some 15
billion dollars of long-term investments abroad, which yield roughly
900 million dollars a year. Of the total, nearly 5 billion is in Europe. The struggle to pay both the current charges on this investment
and the Inter-Ally debt charges, in the face of the American tariff,
has been a source of serious tension in Europe's international financial position in recent years, even apart from the Reparations situation.

many's economic position is likely to be when the world depression has begun to lighten. I can find, however, no grounds for pessimism. Germany still has the best industrial equipment in Europe, she has an outstandingly effective industrial technique, and she has a people who have shown themselves extraordinarily courageous and stable in the face of adversity. To date Germany has allowed no international default to take place in her private obligations, nor is she likely to, and she will fight to the last ditch to maintain her currency and her international credit standing. When the acute stage of the world depression has passed, and when a permanent and reasonable adjustment of the Reparations obligation has been effected, Germany will embark on a new and soundly based era of recovery and prosperity.

APPENDICES

GENERAL NOTES

IN the main, statistics which are easily accessible in official publications are not reprinted here. Most of the material consists of the writer's own compilations from these and other publications; estimates; and source references on specific questions. The principal exception is the inflation period. No comprehensive study of the years 1919–23 has yet been made by German writers, and it seems worth while to bring together in one place the more important and more reliable general data.

Throughout the Appendices, 1913a signifies the magnitude involved taken within the *old* boundaries, and 1913b within the *new* boundaries. Figures in parentheses are provisional. Tons are metric.

The following abbreviations of source references are used:

I.K.F.=Institut für Konjunkturforschung.
Mon.Nach.=Monatliche Nachweise über den auswärtigen Handel Deutschlands.
Stat.J.=Statistisches Jahrbuch für das deutsche Reich.
W.u.S.=Wirtschaft und Statistik.

Since the sources of materials and estimates, apart from those cited directly at particular points, are almost entirely company balance sheets and reports, personal observation, and the writer's own conversations with a fairly wide range of people in public and private economic life, there is little point in drawing up a bibliography. A general bibliographical study is much needed, but this is not the place for it.

APPENDIX I

WAR AND TREATY LOSSES

1. POPULATION. In the war itself 1,885,000 men were killed and 4,248,000 were wounded. The territorial cessions under the terms of the Treaty of Peace entailed the loss of 6,475,700 persons in Europe (Saar 652,000), and 12,293,000 in the colonies (under 29,000 white, the rest native). The population of Germany in 1913 had been 66,978,000 (Europe only), and the losses were hence 12.4 per cent of this; or after reduction of war wounded to terms of 100 per cent incapacity, 13 per cent.

Sources: Stat.J., 1924–25, pp. 2, 14, 23; W.u.S., 1927, p. 348. Also see A. Ströhle, Von Versailles bis zum Gegenwart (Berlin, 1928).

2. TERRITORY. The cessions under the Treaty entailed the loss of 70,580 square kilometers of territory (Saar 1,992) in Europe, or 13 per cent of the pre-war area of 540,858 sq. km. The area of the surrendered colonies was 2,952,900 sq. km. Of the arable land in European Germany (itself 64.5 per cent of the total area of the country) the following percentages were lost: farm land, 15.5; garden land, 10.9; meadowland, 10.5; pasture, 11.5; orchards, 5.6; vineyards, 23.9; total, 14.3.

Sources: Stat.J., 1924–25, p. 33; 1927, p. 53; W.u.S., Sonderheft 2, pp. 69, 72.

3. PRODUCTION. The following figures give for certain industrial branches the percentage which the output of the districts later ceded under the Treaty made of the output of the country as a whole in 1913. For each branch, the first figure given is the percentage in terms of *weight* (tons); the second that in terms of *value* (marks):

Coal, 19 and 15.7; lignite, negligible; coal briquets, 7.2 and 7.1; coke ovens, 3.4 and 3; iron ore, 74.5 and 48.2; blast furnaces, 26.7 and 22.6; iron and steel foundries, 4.6 and 4; raw iron and steel, 19.2 and 17.5; rolling mills, 15.8 and 13.6; zinc mining, 68.5 and 59; zinc foundries, 60.2 and 59.4; lead mining, 26.3 and 25.6; lead foundries, 22.8 and 23.2;

potash and rock salt, 2.6 and 4.5; refineries for same, 15.7 and 13.7; sulphur, 14.3 and 12.

Losses of livestock, per head, in per cents: horses, 16; cattle, 11.6; sheep, 9.6; swine, 11.8; goats, 9.2; poultry, 12.

Sources: Stat.J., 1915, p. 59; 1924–25, pp. 21, 22, 64; 1927, pp. 97–105.

4. On the loss of foreign investments, see Appendix III, section 7, below.

APPENDIX II

POPULATION

1. Size and rate of growth are shown in the following table, in thousands:

Year (mid-year)	Population	Period	Annual average net change
1870	40,805	——	——
1880	45,095	1870–80	+429
1890	49,241	1880–90	+414
1900	56,046	1890–1900	+680
1910	64,568	1900–10	+852
1913	66,978	1910–13	+803
1919	62,897	1913–19	−680
1920	61,797	1919–20	−1,100
1921	62,469	1920–21	+672
1922	62,035	1921–22	−434
1923	62,450	1922–23	+415
1924	62,846	1923–24	+396
1925	63,177	1924–25	+331
1926	63,644	1925–26	+467
1927	64,038	1926–27	+394
1928 (est.)	64,500	1927–28	——

Source: Stat.J., 1928, p. 7.

The population within the *present* boundaries was, in 1910, 57,798,427; in 1913, about 60,000,000.

2. Data on the distribution of the population by age groups in 1910 and 1925, presented in Chart X above (Chap. VIII), are given in W.u.S., 1928, p. 114. Also see the forecast, 1929–40, in *ibid.*, p. 123.

3. Data on births, deaths, and emigration are given in Stat. J., 1915, p. 24; 1924–25, p. 28; 1928, p. 30.

4. Data on the distribution of the population by occupations in 1882, 1895, 1907, and 1925 are given in Stat.J., 1927, p. 25; 1928, pp. 21–24.

APPENDIX III

THE INFLATION PERIOD, 1919–1923

1. INDICES OF FOREIGN EXCHANGE, PRICES AND ORDINARY CURRENCY CIRCULATION

(monthly averages)

Year and month	1. Foreign exchange: marks per dollar (Par = 1)	2. Wholesale prices (1913 = 1)	3. Ordinary currency circulation (1913 = 1)	4. Cost of living (1913–14 = 1)
1919				
1	2.03	2.62	5.69	——
2	2.21	2.70	5.81	——
3	2.48	2.74	6.14	——
4	3.05	2.86	6.35	——
5	3.10	2.97	6.58	——
6	3.36	3.08	7.04	——
7	3.57	3.39	6.90	——
8	4.70	4.22	6.74	——
9	6.35	4.93	7.00	——
10	6.55	5.62	7.15	——
11	9.40	6.78	7.48	——
12	11.40	8.03	8.27	——
1920				
1	15.4	12.6	8.4	——
2	23.7	16.9	9.0	8.5
3	20.0	17.1	9.8	9.6
4	14.2	15.7	10.3	10.4
5	11.1	15.1	10.6	11.0
6	9.3	13.8	11.3	10.8
7	9.4	13.7	11.5	10.7
8	11.5	14.5	11.9	10.2
9	13.8	15.0	12.5	10.2
10	16.2	14.7	12.8	10.7
11	18.4	15.1	12.8	11.2
12	17.4	14.4	13.5	11.6

Year and month	1. Foreign exchange: marks per dollar (Par = 1)	2. Wholesale prices (1913 = 1)	3. Ordinary currency circulation (1913 = 1)	4. Cost of living (1913–14 = 1)
1921				
1	15.5	14.4	13.0	11.8
2	14.6	13.8	13.2	11.5
3	14.9	13.4	13.3	11.4
4	15.1	13.3	13.4	11.3
5	14.9	13.1	13.5	11.2
6	16.5	13.7	14.0	11.7
7	18.3	14.3	14.3	12.5
8	20.1	19.2	14.6	13.3
9	25.0	20.7	15.6	13.7
10	35.6	24.6	16.4	15.0
11	62.5	34.2	18.0	17.8
12	45.5	34.9	20.3	19.3
1922				
1	45.5	36.7	20.5	20.4
2	49.0	41.0	21.3	24.5
3	67.5	54.3	23.2	29.0
4	69.0	63.6	24.8	34.4
5	69.0	64.6	26.8	38.0
6	76.0	70.3	29.8	41.5
7	118.0	100.6	33.5	53.9
8	270.0	192.0	41.7	77.7
9	350.0	287.0	54.8	133.2
10	760.0	566.0	79.9	220.7
11	1,710.0	1,154.0	126.8	446.1
12	1,810.0	1,475.0	213.4	685.1
1923				
1	4,300	2,785	329	1,120
2	6,700	5,585	583	2,643
3	5,050	4,888	913	2,854
4	5,850	5,212	1,088	2,954
5	11,400	8,170	1,424	3,816
6	26,200	19,385	2,865	7,650
7	92,000	74,787	7,231	37,651
8	1,110,000	944,041	110,181	586,045
9	23,600,000	23,948,898	4,653,115	15,000,000
10	6,000,000,000	7,094,800,000	413,000,000	3,657,000,000
11	530,000,000,000	725,700,000,000	65,954,000,000	657,000,000,000
12	1,000,000,000,000	1,261,600,000,000	81,810,000,000	1,247,000,000,000

Sources: Foreign exchange: 1919 from daily quotations of Commerz und Privatbank, Berlin; 1920–23 from the Deutsche Bank publication, *Die Dollar Kurs* 1920–23; all converted to par = 1. Wholesale prices: W.u.S., 1925, Sonderheft "Zahlen zur Geldentwertung," pp. 16, 17. Currency circulation (see next section): *ibid.*, pp. 45–47. Cost of living: *ibid.*, pp. 5, 33.

2. CIRCULATION OF ORDINARY CURRENCY, AND REICHSBANK CREDITS

(in million marks; end-of-month figures)

Year and month	1. Reichsbank notes	2. Total ordinary currency	3. Gold equivalent of total	4. Private Reichsbank credits	5. Gold equivalent of credits
1919: 1	23,648	34,536	17,693	16,406	8,405
2	24,103	35,254	16,216	16,888	7,768
3	25,491	37,327	15,045	18,118	7,321
4	26,629	38,518	12,835	18,780	6,258
5	28,245	39,917	13,045	19,346	6,322
6	29,968	42,701	12,796	21,425	6,420
7	29,269	41,905	11,669	21,100	5,876
8	28,492	40,881	9,117	21,569	4,587
9	29,784	42,299	7,376	21,534	3,711
10	30,929	43,405	6,794	21,618	3,384
11	31,906	45,417	4,979	23,150	2,538
12	35,698	50,173	4,504	25,397	2,281
1920: 1	37,443	51,079	3,311	25,176	1,632
2	41,034	54,456	2,308	26,498	1,123
3	45,170	59,607	2,984	29,662	1,485
4	47,940	62,424	4,396	32,662	2,300
5	50,017	64,296	5,810	35,362	3,195
6	53,975	68,310	7,332	36,955	3,966
7	55,769	69,824	7,428	37,249	3,963
8	58,401	72,404	6,370	37,551	3,304
9	61,736	75,831	5,493	38,697	2,803
10	63,596	77,379	4,767	39,700	2,446
11	64,284	77,429	4,210	37,033	2,014
12	68,805	81,628	4,696	38,538	2,217
1921: 1	66,621	78,764	5,096	36,976	2,516
2	67,427	79,995	5,480	35,579	2,375
3	69,417	80,412	5,408	36,340	2,443
4	70,840	81,220	5,370	35,812	2,273

Year and month	1. Reichsbank notes	2. Total ordinary currency	3. Gold equiva- lent of total	4. Private Reichsbank credits	5. Gold equivalent of credits
5	71,839	81,735	5,510	25,284	1,678
6	75,321	84,902	5,141	18,640	1,042
7	77,391	86,664	4,745	14,948	778
8	80,073	88,833	4,425	11,926	580
9	86,384	94,941	3,801	11,919	433
10	91,528	99,812	2,791	12,868	299
11	100,944	109,261	1,744	13,366	229
12	113,640	122,963	2,690	16,378	374
1922: 1	115,376	124,426	2,723	15,480	323
2	120,026	129,017	2,606	14,536	268
3	130,671	140,494	2,075	17,237	237
4	140,420	150,752	2,175	15,719	233
5	151,949	162,546	2,352	17,872	271
6	169,212	180,767	2,391	29,894	335
7	189,795	203,246	1,730	33,686	211
8	238,147	252,858	936	58,606	143
9	316,870	332,563	952	86,231	219
10	469,457	484,685	640	156,925	146
11	754,086	769,500	450	390,080	214
12	1,280,095	1,295,228	717	675,052	378
	In 1,000,000,000			In 1,000,000,000	
1923: 1	1,985	2,000	171	1,173	101
2	3,513	3,536	654	2,564	474
3	5,518	5,543	1,109	3,521	705
4	6,546	6,605	930	4,471	630
5	8,564	8,644	522	5,968	361
6	17,291	17,393	473	9,970	271
7	43,595	43,893	168	24,854	95
8	563,200	668,798	273	204,081	83
	In 1,000,000,000,000			In 1,000,000,000,000	
9	28,228	28,244	741	4,700	123
10	2,496,823	2,504,956	145	1,215,000	70
11	400,267,640	400,338,326	400	———	——
12	496,507,425	496,585,346	497	———	——

Notes: "Total ordinary currency" includes, besides Reichsbank notes, Darlehnskassenscheine, Reichskassenscheine, pri-

vate bank notes, and metal coins. Emergency currency issued in 1923 is *not* included: see next section for this. Local currency issues are also not included, since no complete data on them exists. "Gold equivalents" are at the dollar rate of exchange, end of the month. "Private Reichsbank credits" are the Bank's grants of credit to industry and commerce (Wirtschaftskredit) as distinct from its advances to the Government (on which see a later section in this Appendix).

Sources: W.u.S., 1925, Sonderheft, "Zahlen zur Geldentwertung," pp. 45–47, 50, 52; cols. 4 and 5, Nov. and Dec. 1923 from Deutsches Reich, *Deutschlands Wirtschaft, Währung und Finanzen* (Berlin, 1924), p. 22.

3. GOLD VALUE OF ORDINARY AND EMERGENCY CURRENCY CIRCULATION IN 1923

(in million marks)

1923	Paper money and coins Ordinary (Sec. 2 above)	Emergency	Total	Fixed value money Rentenmarks	Total	Grand Total
Jan. 31	171.3	1.3	172.6	——	——	172.6
Feb. 28	654.0	3.0	657.0	——	——	657.0
Mar. 29	1,109.4	3.1	1,112.5	——	——	1,112.5
Apr. 30	930.4	1.7	932.1	——	——	932.1
May 31	522.1	0.6	522.7	——	——	522.7
June 30	472.6	0.2	472.8	——	——	472.8
July 31	167.5	small	167.5	——	——	167.5
Aug. 31	272.6	9.4	282.0	——	——	282.0
Sept. 29	741.1	10.7	751.8	——	——	751.8
Oct. 31	145.0	31.2	176.2	——	124.1	300.3
Nov. 30	400.3	118.2	518.5	501.3	969.3	1,487.8
Dec. 31	496.5	111.3	607.9	1,049.1	1,665.7	2,273.6

Notes: "Fixed value money" includes, besides Rentenmarks, gold loan certificates (first floated in September) that were used directly as currency; emergency currency issued against these certificates; and fixed value emergency currency issued by the railways. Local currency issues are *not* included.

Source: W.u.S., 1925, Sonderheft, "Zahlen zur Geldentwertung," pp. 47–49.

4. MONEY MARKET STATISTICS; UNEMPLOYMENT

| Year and month | Money rates | | | Unemployment 4. Trade union-members unemployed: per cent | 5. Receivers of relief: 1,000's |
	1. Day-to-day money	2. Private discount	3. Reichs-bank		
1919: 1	——	3.20	5	6.6	——
2	——	3.13	5	6.0	——
3	——	3.11	5	3.9	——
4	——	3.08	5	5.2	——
5	——	2.93	5	3.8	——
6	——	2.87	5	2.5	——
7	——	2.69	5	3.1	——
8	——	2.71	5	3.1	——
9	——	2.99	5	2.2	——
10	——	3.64	5	2.6	——
11	——	4.00	5	2.9	——
12	——	3.96	5	2.9	——
1920: 1	4.52	3.88	5	3.4	455
2	4.50	3.85	5	2.9	431
3	4.57	3.75	5	1.9	370
4	4.35	3.75	5	1.9	330
5	4.35	3.55	5	2.7	292
6	4.37	3.53	5	4.0	272
7	4.34	3.57	5	6.0	323
8	4.48	3.50	5	5.9	404
9	4.33	3.50	5	4.5	415
10	4.29	3.45	5	4.2	393
11	4.47	3.43	5	3.9	361
12	4.37	3.37	5	4.1	350
1921: 1	4.37	3.40	5	4.5	410
2	4.36	3.46	5	4.7	423
3	4.28	3.43	5	3.7	427
4	4.26	3.45	5	3.9	413
5	4.29	3.33	5	3.7	394
6	4.35	3.35	5	3.0	357
7	4.28	3.38	5	2.6	314
8	4.34	3.38	5	2.2	267
9	4.25	3.38	5	1.4	232
10	4.36	3.56	5	1.2	186
11	4.38	3.58	5	1.4	150
12	4.32	4.18	5	1.6	149
1922: 1	4.27	4.37	5	3.3	165
2	4.51	4.00	5	2.7	203

Year and month	Money rates			Unemployment	
	1. Day-to-day money	2. Private discount	3. Reichs-bank	4. Trade union members unemployed: per cent	5. Receivers of relief: 1,000's
3	4.61	4.24	5	1.1	213
4	4.38	4.36	5	0.9	116
5	4.35	4.55	5	0.7	65
6	4.52	4.58	5	0.6	29
7	4.75	4.85	5.13	0.6	20
8	5.77	6.12	6.13	0.7	15
9	6.89	7.32	7.5	0.8	12
10	7.50	8.15	8	1.4	17
11	8.41	8.92	9.5	2.0	25
12	8.88	9.77	10	2.8	43
1923: 1	12.00	——	11	4.2	85
2	14.50	——	12	5.2	150
3	15.17	——	12	5.6	190
4	16.93	——	15	7.0	222
5	27.75	——	18	6.2	267
6	33.23	——	18	4.1	254
7	129.69	——	18	3.5	186
8	417.00	——	30	6.3	139
9	1,058.00	——	75	9.9	249
10	1,370.00	——	90	19.1	534
11	2,880.00	——	90	23.4	955
12	360.00	——	90	28.2	1,474

Notes and Sources: Day-to-day discount rate from Stat.J., 1923, p. 269; private discount rate from Stat.J., 1924–25, p. 1*. Both are of dubious value, and are almost certainly too low (the private discount figures for 1923 are worthless and hence not given here), but they are the least questionable consecutive figures. Reichsbank rate from the Bank's own publication, *Die Reichsbank 1901–1925*, Table 48. Unemployment figures from *Reichsarbeitsblatt, 1925*, pp. ii, 3, 732. Receivers of relief (*Arbeitslosenunterstützungsempfänger*) are those fully unemployed who received subsidies from the Government. Data from *Reichsarbeitsblatt, passim*. In and after October 1922, figures include those receiving subsidies who were only partially unemployed.

5. FEDERAL FINANCES

(during or at end of month)

Year and month	Receipts and expenditures: Million gold marks		Floating debt: 1,000,000,000 paper marks Treasury certificates discounted		
	1. Receipts	2. Expenditures	3. At Reichsbank	4. Total	5. Total floating debt
1920: 4	60	308	—	—	—
5	110	695	—	—	—
6	202	1,442	—	—	—
7	264	1,279	—	—	—
8	200	792	—	—	—
9	185	817	—	—	—
10	206	349	—	—	—
11	249	629	—	—	—
12	419	723	—	—	—
1921: 1	443	614·	51	155	174
2	468	899	54	162	176
3	469	783	65	166	184
4	356	773	59	173	190
5	416	686	63	177	199
6	354	862	80	185	214
7	309	618	80	191	219
8	260	863	84	203	219
9	201	506	98	210	229
10	177	385	99	218	233
11	117	255	114	226	242
12	179	627	132	247	264
1922: 1	197	388	126	256	270
2	198	342	134	263	277
3	212	347	147	272	281
4	192	322	156	281	289
5	257	377	168	289	300
6	237	314	186	296	312
7	185	209	208	308	329
8	118	205	250	331	356
9	93	435	350	451	528
10	68	270	478	604	721
11	62	200	672	839	1,166
12	75	438	1,184	1,495	2,093
1923: 1	68	205	1,609	2,082	2,781
2	53	279	2,947	3,588	4,628
3	102	699	4,552	6,601	8,274

Year and month	Receipts and expenditures: Million gold marks		Floating debt: 1,000,000,000 paper marks Treasury certificates discounted		5. Total floating debt
	1. Receipts	2. Expenditures	3. At Reichsbank	4. Total	
4	151	467	6,225	8,442	10,291
5	123	285	8,022	10,275	12,901
6	48	496	18,338	22,020	24,926
7	48	474	53,752	57,849	63,686
8	98	1,013	987,219	1,196,300	1,235,100
9	98	1,662	45,216,224	46,716,610	46,844,781
10	22	882	6,578,650,939	6,907,511,103	7,019,640,165
11	96	1,331	———	———	———
12	334	669	———	———	———

Sources: Stat.J., 1923, p. 270; 1924–25, p. 348; W.u.S., 1921–23 *passim*. No data available for 1919, and on the floating debt none for 1920.

6. FOREIGN TRADE

Year	In million gold marks, at 1913 prices			In thousand tons		
	Import	Export	Excess	Import	Export	Excess
1913	11,207	10,198	−1,009	72,832	73,714	+882
1920	3,947	3,724	−223	18,842	19,838	+998
1921	5,751	3,003	−2,748	25,663	13,804	−11,859
1922	6,312	6,199	−113	45,868	21,561	−24,307
1923	4,819	5,352	+533	46,685	12,740	−33,945

Notes: No data exist for 1919. For 1921, May to December only. These are the official figures (see Stat.J., 1923 and 1924–25), but because of the currency depreciation and the general disorganization then prevailing, those for 1920–23 are uncertain. The figures for 1923, indeed, are almost worthless: the Ruhr invasion of that year opened a great "hole in the west" through which unknown but very large quantities of illegal imports and exports passed.

7. THE BALANCE OF INTERNATIONAL PAYMENTS AND
   THE LOSS OF FOREIGN INVESTMENTS, 1914–1923

(*a.*) *The balance of payments, Aug. 1, 1914—Dec. 31, 1918:*
        totals, in million gold marks.

    Credits

Gold exported	1,000
German-owned foreign securities sold abroad	8,000
German mark securities sold abroad	1,000
Interest receipts from neutral countries	2,000
Requisitions in occupied territories affecting the balance of payments	1,000
Credits in foreign currencies outstanding Dec. 31, 1918	1,000
Payments and credits in marks	2,000
Total, in round numbers	16,000

    Debits

Commodity trade, *excluding* gold, net	11,000
Payments for imports of German Allies	4,000
Unrecorded imports, etc.	1,000
	16,000

(*b.*) *The balance of payments, 1919–23:*
        totals, in million gold marks.

    Credits

Foreign securities privately exported	1,000
Shipping, tourists, transit traffic, commissions	1,500
Gold exports by the Government and the Reichsbank	1,500
Sale of mark currency, bank deposits, securities, houses, land, forests	11,000
Other credits (charity; short-term loans net, etc.)	2,000–3,000
Total, in round numbers	17,000–18,000

    Debits

Commodity balance of trade, net[1]	8,000
Reparations: cash payments actually transferred	2,000
The "flight of capital," net[2]	6,000–7,000
Foreign bank notes imported, net	1,200
Total, in round numbers	17,000–18,000

[1] This item is much greater than that indicated by the figures in section 6, above. The difference represents an estimated allowance for unrecorded imports, net.

[2] This item is the total German holdings abroad at the end of 1923,

(c.) *The foreign investment balance sheet, 1914–23:*
in million gold marks.

Credits

Total assets abroad in 1914	28,000

Debits

Total loss, 1914–18, by sequestration and liquidation abroad, depreciation, etc.[1]	16,100
Securities surrendered under the Treaty of Peace	800
Securities seized and exported by the Government	800
Securities privately exported	9,500–10,500
Total loss, 1914–23, in round numbers	27,500–28,500
Pre-war holdings left at end of 1923	0–1,000
Total, in round numbers	28,000

Notes and sources: The foregoing tables are necessarily very rough estimates, but are believed to be good enough to give some idea of what was happening. They are based on various sources, of which the chief ones are:

Otto von Glasenapp, "Die deutsche Zahlungsbilanz," in *Wiederaufbau in Europa,* Apr. 20, 1922 (the German edition of the *Manchester Guardian* Reconstruction Supplements); J. M. Keynes, "Die Spekulation in Mark und Deutschlands Bilanz in Ausland," in *ibid.,* Sept. 22, 1922, and "Der Mc-Kenna Bericht," in *Wirtschaftsdienst,* Apr. 25, 1924; R. Meerwarth, "Über die deutsche Zahlungsbilanz," in *Schriften des Vereins für Sozialpolitik,* vol. 167, part 1 (1924); H. G. Moulton and C. E. McGuire, *Germany's Capacity to Pay* (New York, 1923); the report of the McKenna Committee, Apr. 9, 1924 (reprinted by the Reparations Commission in *The Ex-*

estimated at 5,700 to 7,800 millions, less a maximum of about 1,000 millions estimated to have been left over from the pre-war holdings.

[1] Under an act of Feb. 28, 1929, the United States is now returning about 1,000 million marks of this as compensation, adjustment, etc.

No account is taken of the pre-war investments by foreigners in Germany, since these were virtually all lost in the war or in the currency depreciation.

pert's *Plan for Reparations Payments*, Paris, 1926); and W.u.S., 1923, p. 318.

For an estimate of the pre-war balance of payments, also based on these sources, see Appendix XIV, below.

APPENDIX IV

COAL, COKE, AND LIGNITE

1. COAL: SUMMARY TABLE (1913a IS OLD BOUNDARIES, 1913b IS PRESENT BOUNDARIES)

Item	1913a	1913b	1924	1925	1926	1927	1928
1. Production: million tons	190.1	140.8	118.8	132.6	145.3	153.6	150.9
2. Value of production: million marks	2,136	1,641	2,072	1,903	2,039	2,205	2,370
3. Net exports, including Reparations: million tons	24.1	17.8	5.8	14.9	35.2	21.6	16.5
4. Value of net exports: million marks	312	—	—	—	755	494	324
5. Value of coal per ton: marks (2 ÷ 1)	11.2	11.6	17.5	14.3	14.0	14.4	15.7
6. Number of production units (*Betriebe*)	350	284	376	343	314	303	—
7. Number of workers and employees: 1,000's	654	491	559	557	515	542	—
8. Output per man per year (total of workers and employees): tons	290	286	212	238	281	283	—
9. Wages and salaries paid: million marks	1,095	870	949	1,102	1,125	1,235	—
10. Wages and salaries per man per year: marks	1,675	1,770	1,695	1,980	2,180	2,270	—
11. Per cent wages and salaries are to value of product	51	53	46	58	55	56	—

Sources: Stat.J., 1928, *passim*; W.u.S., 1929, p. 82; Mon.Nach., *passim.*

Notes: The length of the legal working day is now only about two-thirds the pre-war average, but this is partly offset by quicker transport of the workers within the mine.

Output per worker per shift, excluding coke and by-product plants, was for total and for underground workers alone, respectively, in metric tons: 1913, 0.94 and 1.16; 1923, 0.35 and 0.47; 1927, 1.13 and 1.39. It is now still higher, though complete figures are not available.

2. COKE AND BY-PRODUCTS: SUMMARY TABLE

Item in million marks, unless otherwise indicated	1913a	1913b	1924	1925	1926	1927	1928
1. Production of coke	607.5	555.6	626.5	609.3	546.8	(650)	(575)
2. Value of coke per ton: marks	17.5	17.5	25.0	21.4	20.0	—	—
3. Production of coal tar, etc.	27.1	24.1	31.1	42.9	58.8	—	—
4. Production of benzol	32.1	29.1	52.7	78.8	80.6	—	—
5. Production of sulphates of ammonia, etc.	116.1	107.2	62.4	77.8	69.7	—	—
6. Total value of coke and by-product	782.8	716.0	772.7	808.8	755.9	—	—
7. Per cent wages and salaries are of item 6	15.5	15.7	14.9	12.9	12.6	—	—
8. Production of coal briquets	98.2	91.2	98.3	101.6	111.7	—	—
Coke alone							
9. Coke production: million tons	34.6	31.7	24.9	28.4	27.3	33.2	33.9
10. Per cent coke is of coal consumed	78	78	79	79	79	—	—
11. Persons employed: 1,000's	31.9	27.5	28.8	28.4	24.8	—	—
12. Output per man per year: tons	1,080	1,150	860	1,000	1,100	—	—
13. Number of plants	202	182	177	174	168	—	—
14. Net exports: million tons	3.8	—	—	3.7	10.3	8.7	8.6

Sources: Stat.J., 1928, 113; W.u.S., 1929, p. 82; Mon.Nach., *passim.*

IV. Coal and Lignite 395

3. LIGNITE: SUMMARY TABLE

Item	1913a	1926	1927	1928
1. Production: million tons	87.2	139.2	150.5	166.2
2. Value of product: million marks	191.9	387.8	423.9	——
3. Value per ton (2 ÷ 1): marks	2.20	2.78	2.82	——
4. Workers and employees: 1,000's	59.0	76.7	72.3	——
5. Output per _man per year (1 ÷ 4): tons	1,475	1,815	2,080	——
6. Wages and salaries: million marks	79.6	150.2	149.3	——
7. Wages and salaries per man	1,350	1,960	2,060	——
8. Per cent wages and salaries are of production (2 ÷ 6)	41	39	35	——
9. Number of plants	468	364	338	——

Sources: Stat.J., 1928, p. 110; W.u.S., 1929, p. 82. Foreign trade negligible; net imports in 1927 were 2.8 million tons.

4. WORLD PRODUCTION OF COAL, INCLUDING LIGNITE AT COAL EQUIVALENTS

(in million tons)

Year	Germany	Great Britain	France	Belgium	U.S.A.	World
1913	209.5	292.0	40.3	22.8	517.1	1,258.2
1919	137.5	233.5	21.8	18.5	502.5	1,083.5
1920	156.2	233.2	24.6	22.4	597.2	1,215.4
1921	163.6	165.9	28.5	21.8	459.4	1,021.8
1922	160.5	253.6	31.4	21.2	432.7	1,100.1
1923	88.7	280.4	38.0	22.9	596.8	1,252.4
1924	146.5	271.4	44.3	23.4	518.6	1,233.8
1925	163.7	247.1	47.4	23.1	527.9	1,242.3
1926	176.2	128.3	51.8	25.3	596.8	1,238.5
1927	187.0	255.3	52.1	27.6	544.8	1,340.1
1928	187.7	——	——	——	——	——

Notes: 1927 figures provisory except for Germany. Lignite is converted into coal at the ratio for Germany of 9:2; for France and world totals, at 9:3. Small quantity of lignite in figures for U.S.A. not converted. No distinction made between anthracite, bituminous, and intermediate grades of coal.

Sources: Stat.J., 1919, p. 47*; 1928, p. 44*; W.u.S., 1929, p. 82.

APPENDIX V

IRON AND STEEL

1. IRON ORE: SUMMARY TABLE
(1913 figures exclude Luxemburg)

Item	1913a	1924	1925	1926	1927	1928
1. Domestic production: million tons	35.0	3.8	5.0	4.0	5.6	—
2. Net imports: million tons	11.4	—	11.3	9.4	17.2	13.6
3. Net imports: million marks	219	—	—	173	361	(244)
4. Domestic consumption: million tons	46.4	12.4	16.3	13.4	22.8	—
5. Per cent net imports are of consumption (2 ÷ 4)	24.5	—	69.0	70.0	76.0	—

Sources: Stat.J., 1928, pp. 114, 104; Mon.Nach., *passim.*

2. RAW IRON AND BLAST FURNACES: SUMMARY TABLE

Item	1913a	1913b	1924	1925	1926	1927	1928
1. Production of raw iron: million tons	16.8	10.9	7.8	10.1	9.6	13.1	11.8
2. Value of products: million marks	1,088	760	719	879	714	(930)	(880)
3. Value per ton: marks	65	70	92	87	74	(71)	(74)
4. Per cent of product to total consumption of raw material, by weight	25.0	27.5	30.5	30.4	31.4	—	—
5. Number of plants (*Betriebe*)	93	70	55	56	51	—	—
6. Furnaces available (end of year)	330	216	193	200	183	—	—
7. Furnaces in operation (end of year)	313	204	138	141	127	—	—
8. Total weeks of operation: 1,000's	15.1	9.7	4.7	5.4	4.5	—	—
9. Workers and employees: 1,000's	41.9	—	24.3	23.8	(23.0)	—	—
10. Product per man (1 ÷ 9)	400	—	320	435	(420)	—	—
11. Average capacity per furnace: tons	150	—	225	—	285	—	—

Sources: Chiefly Stat.J., 1928, pp. 55, 104, 114*; Stahlwerks-Verband, *Statistische Mitteilungen,* 1927.

3. RAW STEEL: SUMMARY TABLE

Item	1913a	1913b	1924	1925	1926	1927	1928
1. Production: million tons	17.1	11.8	9.7	12.1	12.2	16.3	14.5
2. Value of product: million marks	1,603	1,098	1,058	1,300	1,173	—	—
3. Value per ton: marks	94	93	109	107	106	—	—
4. Consumption of raw iron: per cent of total raw materials	64	59	—	—	55	—	—
5. Consumption of scrap iron, ditto	26.5	32	—	—	36	—	—

Source: Chiefly Stat.J., 1928, p. 115. Foreign trade negligible.

4. WORLD PRODUCTION OF RAW STEEL
(in million tons)

Year	Germany	Great Britain	France	Belgium	Luxemburg	U.S.A.	World
1913	17.1	7.8	4.7	2.5	1.3	30.8	75.9
1919	6.9	8.0	2.2	0.3	0.4	34.2	58.0
1920	8.4	9.2	2.7	1.3	0.6	41.5	72.3
1921	9.9	3.8	3.1	0.8	0.8	19.5	45.3
1922	11.2	6.0	4.5	1.6	1.4	35.1	66.8
1923	6.2	8.6	5.3	3.0	1.2	44.2	78.3
1924	9.7	8.3	6.7	2.9	1.9	37.4	78.5
1925	12.1	7.5	7.5	2.5	2.1	44.8	90.6
1926	12.2	3.7	8.4	3.3	2.2	47.7	93.0
1927	16.3	9.3	8.3	3.7	2.5	44.5	100.5
1928	14.5	—	—	—	—	—	—

Sources: Stat.J., 1927, p. 57*; 1928, p. 56*.

V. Iron and Steel   399

5. ROLLED PRODUCTS: SUMMARY TABLE

Item	1913a	1913b	1924	1925	1926	1927	1928
1. Production: million tons	16.1	11.6	9.1	11.5	11.7	(12.9)	—
2. Value of product: million marks	2,178	1,629	1,452	1,877	1,710	—	—
3. Value per ton: marks	135	140	160	163	146	—	—
4. Net exports (+) or imports (−): million tons	+3.6	—	-0.1	+1.3	+2.6	+1.1	+1.6
5. Value of net exports or imports: million marks	+531	—	—	—	—	+273	+339
6. Number of plants	174	—	162	161	156	—	—
7. Number of workers and employees: 1,000's	129	—	91	74	78	(80)	—
8. Output per man per year (1÷7): tons	125	—	100	122	150	(161)	—
9. Wages and salaries: million marks	205	—	174	221	190	—	—
10. Per cent wages and salaries are of value or product (9÷2)	9.5	—	12	11.7	11.1	—	—

Sources: Stat.J., 1928, p. 116; Stahlwerks-Verband, *Statistische Mitteilungen*, 1928; Mon. Nach., *passim.*

6. EXPORTS (NET) OF ROLLED PRODUCTS FROM
LEADING COUNTRIES
(in million tons)

Year	Germany	France	Belgium-Luxemburg	Great Britain	U.S.A.
1913	3.6	——	0.99	1.85	0.93[1]
1927	1.1	4.35	2.87	1.16	0.62
1928	1.6	3.95	3.25	1.77	0.75

[1] Average of 1910–14. For Great Britain, average of 1910–13 is 1.99.

Sources: I.K.F., 1927, *Sonderheft* 1, pp. 97, 98; Mon.Nach., *passim; Commerce Extérieur de la France,* Dec., 1928, pp. 16, 34; *Bulletin mensuel du Commerce spécial avec les pays étrangers* (Belgium), Dec., 1927, and Dec., 1928; *Survey of Metal Industries* (England), 1928, pp. 122 ff.; *Statistical Abstract of the United States,* 1928, pp. 501 and 543; *Monthly Summary of Foreign Commerce* (U.S.A.), Dec., 1928, Part 1.

APPENDIX VI

MACHINERY

SUMMARY TABLE

Item	1913a	1924	1925	1926	1927	1928
1. Production: million marks	2,800	2,200	2,900	2,500	3,400	—
2. Price index: 1913 = 100	100	128	135	136	136	141
3. Index of physical volume of production (from 1 and 2): 1913 = 100	100	62	77	66	89	—
4. Domestic consumption: million marks	2,150	1,680	2,240	1,750	2,610	—
5. Net exports: million marks	650	520	660	750	790	910
6. Per cent of net exports to production (5 ÷ 1)	23	23.5	22.5	30	23.2	—
7. Capacity: million marks	2,800	—	5,038	4,940	5,350	—
8. Per cent of production to capacity (1 ÷ 7)	100	—	58	51	64	—
9. Number of workers: 1,000's	460	—	452	—	—	—

Sources: Verein Deutschen Maschinenbau Anstalten, *Statistisches Handbuch*, 1928; *ibid., Memorandum* to the International Economic Conference, Geneva, 1927 (C.E.J., 15); Stat.J., 1928, *passim;* Mon.Nach., *passim.*

Item 2 is the official price index, but there is some evidence, not yet complete, that it is too low. The figures for 1927 and 1928 may be as high as 165 or 170. If so, the index of production for 1927 (item 3) would be lower, perhaps only 78 or 74.

APPENDIX VII

THE ELECTRO-TECHNICAL INDUSTRY

SUMMARY TABLE

Item	1913a	1925	1926	1927	1928
1. Production: million marks	1,300	2,100	—	(2,600)	2,800
2. Price index: 1913 = 100	100	120	—	(129)	132
3. Index of physical volume of production (from 1 and 2): 1913 = 100	100	134	—	(155)	163
4. Net exports: million marks	278	309	346	365	443
5. Per cent of net exports to value of production (4 ÷ 1)	21	15	—	14	16

Sources: Stat.J., *passim;* Mon.Nach., *passim;* International Economic Conference (Geneva, 1927), *Documents on Electrical Engineering* (C.E.J., 16); *Trade Information Bulletin* (U.S.A.) No. 548; Verein Deutschen Maschinenbau Anstalten, *Wirtschaftskurven;* estimates supplied by the research bureau of the Allgemeine Elektrizitäts-Gesellschaft.

APPENDIX VIII

TEXTILES

1. COTTON: SUMMARY TABLE

Item	1913a	1924	1925	1926	1927	1928
1. Value of production: million marks	2,350	3,720	5,080	3,390	4,950	4,490
2. Augsburg price for yarn: 1913 = 100	100	238	219	155	158	164
3. Index of physical production, estimated chiefly from 1 and 2: 1913 = 100	100	64	99	93	134	116
4. Imports, raw and combed: million marks	664	—	886	598	833	(795)
5. Exports, raw and combed: million marks	87	—	124	130	172	(186)
6. Imports, manufactures, million marks	188	599	597	246	500	—
7. Exports, manufactures, million marks	508	426	471	268	446	—
8. Net imports, raw, combed, and manufactured together: million marks	157	—	888	451	715	—

Sources: Stat.J.; W.u.S.; I.K.F., *Vierteljahreshefte*, 1928: IV B, p. 22; Mon.Nach. The foreign trade figures are not good. On foreign trade also see, the Department of Overseas Trade (Great Britain) annual publication, *Economic and Financial Conditions in Germany.*

2. COTTON: WORLD COMPARISONS

Principal countries and regions	Spinning spindles: 1,000,000's		Looms: 1,000's	
	1913	*1927*	*1913–14*	*1924–25*
Great Britain	55.7	57.3	805	792
Germany	11.2	10.8	230	240
France	7.4	9.6	108	182
Russia	7.7	6.9	213	200
Austria-Hungary	4.9	2.9	170	147
Total Europe	99.5	103.6	1,877	1,959
United States	32.1	36.7	696	763
Brazil	1.2	2.6	50	66
Canada	0.9	1.2	31	35
Total Americas	34.9	41.3	807	907
British India	6.1	8.7	94	151
Japan	2.3	6.0	21	64
China	Unknown	3.6	5	22
Total Asia	8.4	18.2	120	241
World totals	143.5	164.6	2,807	3,110

Notes: Russia excluding Poland; "Austria-Hungary" after the war is the sum of the Succession States, Czechoslovakia having much the largest share.

Sources: On spindles, *International Cotton Bulletin* estimates, reprinted in Stat.J., 1928, p. 42*; on looms, *Deutsches Baumwollhandbuch* estimates, reprinted in Verein Deutschen Maschinenbau Anstalten, *Statistisches Handbuch*, 1928, p. 90.

3. WOOL: SUMMARY TABLE
(in million marks)

Item	*1913a*	*1924*	*1925*	*1926*	*1927*	*1928*
1. Value of production	1,720	2,390	2,610	2,550	2,920	2,570
2. Imports, raw and combed	520	758	627	597	810	(621)
3. Exports, raw and combed	147	133	138	130	177	(56)
4. Imports, manufactures	152	349	328	212	368	—
5. Exports, manufactures	362	308	347	387	423	—
6. Net imports, raw, combed, and manufactured together	163	666	470	292	578	—

Sources: I.K.F., *Vierteljahreshefte,* 1928, IV B, p. 22;

Stat.J., *passim;* Mon.Nach, *passim.* The foreign trade figures
are not good.

4. WOOL: WORLD COMPARISONS "AFTER THE WAR"

Country	Spindles: 1,000's	Looms: 1,000's
Great Britain	8,073	121.0
United States	5,000	85.5
Germany	4,771	72.0
France	3,000	65.5
Italy	1,200	21.0
Czechoslovakia	1,200	34.0
Belgium	670	12.0
Russia (U.S.S.R.)	490	23.2
Japan	400	12.0
World totals	26,289	474.0

Source: Verein Deutschen Maschinenbau Anstalten, *Statistisches Handbuch,* 1928, p. 91.

5. SILK, REAL AND ARTIFICIAL: SUMMARY TABLE
(1928: provisory estimates)

	1913a	1924	1925	1926	1927	1928
Artificial silk						
Production: million tons	3.5	10.7	11.8	14.0	16.0	19.5
Real silk, raw						
Imports: million marks	172	111	140	105	165	—
Exports: million marks	27	6	7	4	7	—
Real and artificial silk manufactures						
Imports: million marks	92	92	131	92	176	—
Exports: million marks	17	171	222	213	274	—
Net imports or exports, raw and manufactured, of real and artificial together: million marks	−220	−26	−42	+20	−60	—
Value of real and artificial production: million marks	490	500	630	640	1,040	1,090

Sources: Stat.J., 1928, p. 348; I.K.F., *Vierteljahreshefte,*
1928, IV B, p. 22.

6. ARTIFICIAL SILK PRODUCTION: WORLD COMPARISONS

(in million tons)

Country	1913	1924	1925	1926	1927	1928
United States	0.7	17.5	23.2	2£.1	34.1	42.4
Italy	0.15	10.5	13.9	16.0	23.0	20.3
Great Britain	3.0	10.9	12.7	11.6	17.6	23.5
Germany	3.5	10.7	11.8	14.0	16.0	19.5
France	1.5	5.6	6.5	9.0	12.0	13.6
Holland	—	1.5	4.0	6.5	8.0	——
Belgium	1.3	4.0	5.0	5.5	6.0	——
Japan	—	0.5	1.4	2.5	4.7	——
Switzerland	0.15	1.8	2.8	4.0	4.5	——
World totals	11.0	65.9	85.2	102.7	132.9	154.3

Sources: 1913–27, Stat.J., 1928, p. 43*; 1928, estimates by Schaffenhausenscher Bankverein, as quoted in Paris edition of New York *Herald,* March 8, 1929 (probably somewhat too low).

APPENDIX IX

THE CHEMICAL INDUSTRY; POTASH

1. CHEMICALS: SUMMARY TABLE

(1928 provisory)

Item	1913a	1924	1925	1926	1927	1928
1. Production: million marks	2,400	3,000	—	—	(4,000)	4,000
2. Partial price index: 1913 = 100	100	130	127	123	124	126
3. Index of physical production: 1913 = 100	100	—	—	—	(126)	125
4. Net exports: million marks	517	—	807	936	924	1,013

Notes: The price index is the official one (see Stat.J., *passim*), but is based chiefly on heavy chemicals, and is apparently too low. In computing the production index, figures were used halfway between this chemical price index and the general wholesale price index, which in 1928 stood at 140.

Sources: Stat.J.; Mon.Nach.; memorandum on *The Chemical Industry* to the International Economic Conference (Geneva, 1927); private estimates for item 1 in 1928. Also

see *Trade Information Bulletin,* No. 605, "German Chemical
Developments in 1928."

2. PRODUCTION OF PRINCIPAL CHEMICALS IN 1928

Products	Metric tons	Million marks	Approximate per cent exported
Nitrates (pure N content)	800,000	750	40
Coal-tar dyes	75–80,000	400	65
Potash (pure K_2O content)	1,400,000	230	40–45
Pharmaceuticals	10,000	200	50
Soda ash	800,000	85	?
Coal tar	1,235,000	81	70
Basic slag (Thomas meal)	1,500,000	70	–55
Sulphuric acid, concentrated	1,240,000	54	?
Superphosphates	700,000	40	?
Total	———	1,910	—

Source: Trade Information Bulletin, No. 605, "German
Chemical Developments in 1928," p. 9; export percentages
estimated from private and official sources. Basic slag is imported; figure for it in last column is per cent imports are of
consumption.

3. POTASH: SUMMARY TABLE
(in thousand tons)

Year	Quota bearing shafts	Operating shafts	Output of crude salts	Output per quota shaft	Output per operating shaft	Output of pure salts (K_2O)	Price index: 1913 = 100
1913	164	152	11,608	70.8	76.4	1,189	100
1924	221	93	8,104	33.7	87.1	896	95
1925	224	85	12,086	54.0	142.2	1,353	99
1926	228	45	9,415	41.3	209.2	1,089	102
1927	228	43	11,080	48.6	257.7	1,269	115
1928	—	—	(14,273)	—	—	(1,400)	—

Sources: Price index from Stat.J., *passim.* Other data taken
from George W. Stocking, *The Potash Industry* (New York,
1931).

4. POTASH: WORLD OUTPUT OF PURE POTASH (K₂O)
(in thousand tons)

Year	Germany	France	Poland	U.S.A.
1913	1,232	—	—	—
1919	838	97	—	30
1920	1,074	194	—	44
1921	933	145	2.7	9
1922	1,302	212	10	11
1923	1,060	249	10	18
1924	895	272	16	21
1925	1,353	312	29	23
1926	1,089	367	31	21
1927	1,269	372	34	—

Source: Stat.J., 1927, p. 55*; 1928, p. 53*.

APPENDIX X

GENERAL PRODUCTION STATISTICS

1. SOURCES OF DATA

The principal statistical series which bear on the general volume of production in Germany are all available in official publications (I.K.F., *Vierteljahreshefte;* W.u.S.; Stat.J.; and the *Reports* of the Agent General for Reparation Payments), and need not be reprinted here. In addition to those already used or referred to in the text, or in earlier Appendices, see the monthly series on coal, raw iron, raw steel, electrical current, goods shipped by rail, cars at disposal of shippers; and quarterly data on the value of goods exchanged, retail and coöperative store sales, and consumption of sugar, meat, beer, and tobacco.

A table was presented in Chapter V, above, presenting estimated indices of physical production in the six principal industries. The following notes should be added as to method of compilation: (1) The value of "coal, coke and by-products, net" is coal plus coke, less estimated value of coal used in coking, plus 174 million marks in 1913 for estimated value of by-products and 200 millions in 1927. (2) The index of physical production for this group is an average weighted by values of the coal and coke figures. (3) The value of "iron, steel and rolled products, net" is the value of rolled products, plus 30 per cent of the value of raw iron assumed not used for steel, plus 10 per cent of the value of raw steel assumed not used for rolling. These allowances are of course rough estimates, and the latter one especially may be too low. (4) The index of physical production for the iron and steel group is an unweighted average of the three constituents; weighting by values gives an unrepresentatively low figure, for the increased use of scrap has diminished the use of iron in steel making. (5) As remarked at other points, the index of physical production for machinery may be too high, in consequence of the fact that the machinery price index used in computing it may be as much as 15 or 20 per cent too low.

In general these methods of calculation are rough and sometimes arbitrary, but it is believed that they yield a reasonably fair picture of the general situation.

2. PRODUCTION INDICES OF PRINCIPAL COUNTRIES

Year	Germany	England	France	Belgium	Italy	West Europe	U.S.A.	Canac
1913	100	100	100	100	100	100	100	—
1914	74	—	—	—	91	—	92	—
1915	63	—	—	—	105	—	103	100
1916	73	—	—	—	112	—	121	—
1917	74	—	—	—	116	—	123	128
1918	73	—	—	—	92	—	121	131
1919	53	—	57	45	83	59	117	124
1920	62	90	62	88	77	68	125	123
1921	78	63	55	54	69	ʋծ	97	119
1922	89	79	78	72	81	83	127	130
1923	56	84	88	84	111	73	152	145
1924	80	89	109	94	103	92	141	138
1925	94	86	108	86	130	104	156	147
1926	90	67	124	114	127	108	163	192
1927	117	92	109	116	114	114	160	194
1928	113	90	125	124	—	111	166	224

Source: H. Quigley, "Productionsindex," in the *Deutscher Volkswirt*, Feb. 2, 1929. 1928: first 9 months only; for Belgium and West Europe first 6 months. The estimates for England are much too low. The estimates of the Board of Trade, the *Economist* and Professor Flux all agree in placing the figure for 1924 at 100, and for 1927 at 105 to 107.8. The remainder lie reasonably close to other estimates.

APPENDIX XI

DATA ON COSTS OF PRODUCTION

For plants visited by the writer in November and December, 1928. Since part of the information was confidential, and most of it based on individual estimates of officials and employees, only upper and lower limiting figures are given here. The "typical" figures on costs of production were given in a table in Chapter V, above.

Data apply to factory operations only: excluding all selling costs, but including interest, depreciation, and taxes. Wages and earnings in marks.

Industry	Number of plants visited	Number of workers	Current output in per cent of capacity	Turnover per year	Productive labor only — Per cent of total	Productive labor only — Hour wage	Costs of production in per cents — Productive labor	Costs — Materials	Costs — Overhead	Earnings of all labor — Per hour	Earnings — Annual	Per cent total labor cost is of all factory costs
Coal	1	—	—	—	—	—	50	5	45	—	—	—
Lignite	5	—	—	—	—	0.92	25-45	55-75		—	—	—
Potash	1	—	—	—	—	0.88	40	25	35	—	—	—
Blast furnaces	2	—	—	—	—	1.00	5-15	25-35	55-65	—	—	—
Open hearth furnaces	1	—	—	—	—	—	15	30	55	—	—	—
Rolling mills	3	—	—	—	—	1.00	25-35	25-35	35-45	—	—	—
Machinery	14	1,650-12,000	55-100	0.9-2.0	67-80	0.90-1.30	13-27	18-40	37-55	0.85-1.15	2,120-2,880	27-36
Electro-technical	8	1,400-65,000	55-100	1.7-2.0	70-75	1.00-1.15	15-22	20-50	30-60	0.90-1.05	2,250-2,620	19-26.5
Cotton	1	3,300	67	2	85	0.81	19	30	51	0.75	1,870	20.5
Wool	4	750-3,000	95	1.7-4.0	85-100	0.65-0.85	15-30	40-80	22-40	0.62-0.85	1,550-2,125	15.6-30
Artificial silk	2	2,000-4,000	100	2-4	75	0.75-0.83	25	8.5-12	63-66.5	0.72-0.82	1,800-2,050	26-32
Chemicals	8	160-20,000	90-100	1.7-4	100	0.75-1.05	6-20	20-77	17-70	0.75-1.05	1,750-2,950	6-15

Notes: "Productive" labor is that directly charged to the particular job. "Unproductive" labor is included in overhead.

APPENDIX XII

CORPORATION STATISTICS

1. SUMMARY TABLE

Incorporated companies

End of year	Number	Nominal capital: million marks	Average capital: million marks	Limited liability companies: number
1913	5,139	16,527	3,216	22,500
1919	5,710	——	——	33,975
1920	5,657	——	——	39,152
1921	6,636	——	——	47,911
1922	9,490	——	——	58,934
1923	16,380	——	——	71,343
1924	17,074	——	——	70,631
1925	14,978	19,121	1,470	64,398
1926	12,343	20,655	1,675	57,338
1927	11,966	21,542	1,800	——

Incorporated companies: *Aktien-Gesellschaften*. Limited liability companies: *Gesellschaften mit beschränkter Haftung*. Figure for latter in 1913 is approximate only.

Source: Stat.J., *passim.*

2. OTHER DATA

The summary figures for incorporated companies just presented can also be obtained by principal industrial and commercial groups, as can data on long- and short-term indebtedness; earnings and dividends; foundings, dissolutions, and changes in capitalization; etc. See Stat.J.; and *Vierteljahreshefte zur Statistik des deutschen Reichs*. The figures on debts and earnings, however, are of uncertain value. There are practically no usable data for limited liability companies except on their numbers.

APPENDIX XIII

AGRICULTURE

1. PRODUCTION

(annual totals in million metric tons; yields per hectare in tons)

Year or average	Rye		Wheat		Barley		Oats		Potatoes		Sugar Beets	
	Total	Per Hect.	Total	Per Hect.	Total	Per Hect.	Total	Per Hect.	Total	Per Hect.	Total	Per Hect.
1909–1913	9.6	1.9	8.8	2.3	2.9	2.1	7.7	2.0	38.0	13.8	14.0	30.0
1919	6.1	1.4	2.2	1.7	1.7	1.5	4.5	1.5	21.4	9.9	5.8	19.3
1920	4.9	1.2	2.2	1.7	1.8	1.5	4.8	1.5	27.9	11.5	7.9	24.4
1921	6.8	1.6	2.9	2.0	1.9	1.7	5.0	1.6	26.1	9.9	8.0	20.5
1922	5.2	1.3	2.0	1.4	1.6	—	4.0	1.3	40.7	14.9	10.8	25.9
1923	6.7	1.5	2.9	2.0	2.4	1.8	6.1	1.8	32.6	12.0	8.7	22.7
1924	5.7	1.4	2.4	1.7	2.4	1.7	5.7	1.6	36.4	13.2	10.3	26.0
1925	8.1	1.7	3.2	2.1	2.6	1.8	5.6	1.6	41.7	14.9	10.3	25.6
1926	6.4	1.4	2.6	1.6	2.5	1.7	6.3	1.8	30.0	10.9	10.5	26.1
1927	6.8	1.5	3.3	1.9	2.7	1.9	6.3	1.8	37.6	13.4	10.9	25.0
1928	8.5	1.8	3.9	2.2	3.3	2.2	7.0	2.0	41.3	14.5	11.0	24.2

Source: Stat.J.

The number of head of livestock was as follows in 1913 (*present* boundaries) and 1928 respectively, in millions: horses, 3.8 and 3.7; cattle, 18.5 and 18.4; swine, 22.5 and 20.1; sheep, 5.0 and 3.6; goats, 3.2 and 2.9; poultry, 71.9 and 84.3.

The quantity of artificial fertilizers delivered to German agriculture was as follows in 1924 and 1927 respectively, in thousand tons: potash, 446 and 684; phosphorus, 323 and 473; nitrates, 278 and 403; lime, 895 and 1,433 (all in terms of pure content except lime). Net imports of Chile nitrates were, in thousand tons: 1913, 747; 1924, 4; 1928, 81. The latter figure reflects the new fight of the Chile producers to regain their foreign markets.

2. FOREIGN TRADE

(excess imports (−) or exports (+) in thousand metric tons, and per cent each is of domestic production)

Year	Rye Excess	Rye Per cent	Wheat Excess	Wheat Per cent	Barley Excess	Barley Per cent	Oats Excess	Oats Per cent	Potatoes Excess	Potatoes Per cent
1913	+582	+5.7	−2,008	−49.7	−3,232	−109.8	+157	+1.8	−50	−1.1
1922	−538	−10.3	−1,388	−70.9	−264	−16.4	−85	−2.1	−100	−2.5
1923	−949	−14.2	−474	−16.4	−313	−13.2	−32	−5.2	−154	−4.7
1924	−473	−8.3	−707	−29.1	−535	−22.3	−22	−3.9	−227	−6.2
1925	−184	−2.3	−1,466	−45.6	−920	−35.4	−340	−6.1	−126	−3.0
1926	+35	+0.5	−1,886	−72.6	−1,735	−70.4	−175	−2.8	−335	−11.2
1927	−663	−9.7	−2,531	−77.4	−1,996	−72.9	−180	−2.8	−570	−15.2
1928	+65	+0.8	−2,200	−56.9	−1,927	−57.6	+163	+2.3	−307	−10.8

Source: Teken or computed from Stat.J.

8. PRODUCTION IN PRINCIPAL COUNTRIES

(average of 1909–13, and 1927, in hundred thousand metric tons)

Country	Rye 1909–13	Rye 1927	Wheat 1909–13	Wheat 1927	Barley 1909–13	Barley 1927	Oats 1909–13	Oats 1927	Potatoes 1909–13	Potatoes 1927	Sugar beets 1909–13	Sugar beets 1927
Germany	95.9	68.3	37.7	32.8	28.7	27.4	76.8	63.5	379.6	375.5	139.9	108.5
France	13.3	9.3	88.6	77.4	11.5	12.1	53.5	54.1	143.4	171.5	59.0	55.7
Great Britain	—	—	15.9	15.2	12.6	9.7	23.6	12.6	47.2	49.9	—	17.3
Italy	1.4	1.5	49.9	53.3	2.2	2.1	5.4	4.5	16.5	17.5	18.0	20.3
Russia	189.1	246.0	206.0	204.0	90.5	47.0	143.3	130.0	202.0	546.8	99.1	99.0
U.S.A.	9.2	14.9	187.8	237.2	40.2	57.8	166.0	173.5	97.4	109.4	44.1	70.2
Canada	0.5	3.8	53.6	119.8	9.9	21.1	54.2	67.8	21.2	21.1	1.4	3.5
Argentina	—	—	40.0	65.1	—	—	7.9	7.6	—	—	—	—

Note: 1927 seems to have been a fairly representative year for most crops in most countries. The 1928 figures, so far as now available, appear to have been well *above* the average in most cases.

Sources: Stat.J., 1928, p. 29*; *International Yearbook of Agricultural Statistics, passim.*

APPENDIX XIV

FOREIGN TRADE SINCE 1924

1. MERCHANDISE TRADE BY VALUES
(in million marks, excluding gold and silver)

	Average: 1910–13	1924	1925	1926	1927	1928
Imports	10,026	9,083	12,362	10,002	14,228	13,995
Exports excluding Reparations	——	——	8,799	9,784	10,222	11,641
Reparations deliveries	——	——	492	631	579	658
Total exports	8,659	6,552	9,291	10,415	10,801	12,299
Balance excluding Reparations	–1,367	–2,531	–3,563	–218	–4,006	–2,354
Balance including Reparations	——	——	–3,071	+413	–3,427	–1,696

Note: Corrected figures. Post-war figures include proceeds of ship sales, fisheries, and the improvement trade. For 1913 alone: imports 10,770 millions; exports 10,097 millions; balance, –673 millions.

Sources: Mon.Nach.; W.u.S., especially May, 1929, p. 409; *Statistik des deutschen Reichs,* No. 351. Monthly figures used for Chart XI above (Chap. IX) from same sources. On the inflation period, see Appendix III, above.

2. GOLD AND SILVER

	Average: 1910–1913	1924	1925	1926	1927	1928
Imports	360	182	718	615	238	967
Exports	133	33	40	36	22	32
Balance	–227	–149	–678	–579	–216	–935

Sources: Same as for Section 1.

3. FOREIGN TRADE OF PRINCIPAL COUNTRIES
(in million marks)

		1913	1924	1925	1926	1927	1928
England:	Imports	13,466	21,101	23,660	22,775	22,423	21,954
	Exports	10,729	14,859	15,684	13,328	14,503	14,752
Germany:	Imports	10,770	9,083	12,362	10,002	14,228	13,995
	Exports	10,097	6,552	9,291	10,415	10,801	12,299
France:	Imports	6,821	8,796	8,933	8,132	8,728	8,783
	Exports	5,573	9,279	9,342	8,143	9,119	8,438
U.S.A.:	Imports	7,375	15,015	17,540	18,514	17,534	17,111
	Exports	10,278	18,891	20,238	19,789	20,018	21,119

Sources: Official; chiefly Stat.J. and I.K.F., *Vierteljahres-hefte*. Figures for Germany include Reparations deliveries.

4. GERMAN MERCHANDISE TRADE BY WEIGHT
(in million metric tons)

Year	Imports	Exports
Average 1910–13	69.2	63.2
1924	38.6	15.9
1925	52.0	38.3
1926	43.3	60.6
1927	68.1	60.4
1928	66.0	60.9

Sources: Stat.J.; Mon.Nach. Figures for 1924 and 1925 uncertain. Horses and ships not included.

5. DISTRIBUTION OF GERMAN TRADE BY CHIEF COMMODITY GROUPS

(excluding gold and silver, including Reparations)

	Million marks						Per cents					
	Average 1910–13	1924	1925	1926	1927	1928	*Average* 1910–13	1924	1925	1926	1927	1928
Imports												
Foods and animals	2,981	2,759	4,145	3,691	4,497	4,341	29.2	30.3	33.5	36.9	31.8	30.9
Raw materials and half-finished goods	5,744	4,602	6,212	4,948	7,192	7,246	57.3	50.8	50.3	49.5	50.5	51.6
Finished goods	1,350	1,722	2,005	1,363	2,539	2,458	13.5	18.9	16.2	13.6	17.7	17.5
Exports												
Foods and animals	850	452	542	529	470	650	9.8	6.9	5.8	5.0	4.4	5.4
Raw materials and half-finished goods	2,279	910	1,996	2,732	2,608	2,703	26.3	13.9	21.7	26.3	24.1	22.4
Finished goods	5,529	5,190	6,753	7,154	7,723	8,700	63.9	79.2	72.5	68.7	71.5	72.2

Sources: Stat.J.; W.u.S.
1928: preliminary uncorrected figures.

6. DISTRIBUTION OF GERMAN TRADE BY CHIEF COUNTRIES AND CONTINENTS
(in per cents of total)

Imports from:	1913	1924	1928	Exports to:	1913	1924	1928
U.S.A.	15.9	18.8	14.4	Great Britain	14.2	9.3	9.8
Argentina	4.6	5.7	6.6	Holland	9.9	6.9	9.8
Great Britain	8.1	9.1	6.4	U.S.A.	7.1	7.5	6.6
France	5.4	7.7	5.3	France	7.8	1.8	5.7
Holland	3.1	4.7	5.1	Czechoslovakia	—	5.9	5.4
British India	5.0	4.3	5.0	Switzerland	5.3	5.7	4.8
Czechoslovakia	—	4.8	3.8	Italy	3.9	3.7	4.5
Italy	3.0	4.1	3.3	Belgium	5.5	1.4	4.1
Belgium	3.2	1.8	3.8	Sweden	2.3	4.4	3.6
Dutch Indies	2.1	2.7	2.8	Denmark	2.8	4.4	3.6
Russia (U.S.S.R.)	—	1.4	2.7	Austria	—	4.8	3.5
Europe	54.7	54.6	51.1	Europe	76.1	72.0	74.8
N. and S. America	27.8	28.2	29.4	N. and S. America	15.3	16.8	14.6
Asia	9.8	10.0	11.8	Asia	5.4	8.6	7.7
Africa	4.6	4.2	5.1	Africa	2.1	2.1	2.3
Australia	3.0	3.0	2.6	Australia	1.0	0.4	0.6
Totals	100.0	100.0	100.0	Totals	100.0	100.0	100.0

Sources: Stat.J.; W.u.S. For 1928: Great Britain, excluding Irish Free State; Belgium, including Luxemburg.

7. EXPORTS OF PRINCIPAL COMMODITIES OR COMMODITY CLASSES BY CHIEF COUNTRIES AND CONTINENTS, IN 1928

(million marks, and per cent of total for each commodity or class; for each, only the seven most important countries; data not always complete, hence totals do not always agree; value figures rounded)

Country or continent	Coal		Coke		Rolled iron and steel products		Machinery		Electro-technical products		Chemicals		Cotton		Wool		Silk	
	Marks	Per cent	Marks	Per cent	Marks	Per cent	Marks	Per cent	Marks	Per cent	Marks	Per cent	Marks	Per cent	Marks	Per cent	Marks	Per cent
Great Britain	—	—	—	—	49	8.9	52	4.7	32	6.5	68	7.5	67	10.2	77	11.3	68	21.0
Holland	111	23.6	6	2.6	105	18.9	75	6.8	43	8.8	55	6.1	56	8.6	49	7.2	19	5.8
U.S.A.	—	—	98	39.8	22	3.9	—	—	—	—	86	9.5	62	9.5	—	—	35	10.6
France	100	21.1	—	—	—	—	64	5.8	—	—	—	—	—	—	76	11.2	—	—
Czechoslovakia	27	5.6	15	6.3	—	—	59	5.3	—	—	42	4.7	65	9.9	—	—	—	—
Switzerland	12	2.6	7	2.9	—	—	—	—	28	5.7	47	5.2	—	—	44	6.5	26	7.9
Italy	101	21.3	56	23.8	—	—	48	4.4	—	—	46	5.1	26	4.0	—	—	—	—
Belgium	81	17.2	15	6.4	—	—	—	—	25	5.1	—	—	—	—	48	6.5	14	4.2
Sweden	—	—	—	—	—	—	—	—	—	—	—	—	29	4.4	29	4.3	14	4.3
Denmark	—	—	—	—	—	—	—	—	20	4.2	—	—	—	—	33	4.9	12	3.8
Austria	—	—	10	4.4	—	—	—	—	—	—	—	—	—	—	—	—	—	—
Russia (U.S.S.R.)	—	—	—	—	19	3.5	117	10.6	48	9.9	38	4.1	—	—	—	—	—	—
Poland	—	—	—	—	20	3.5	61	5.6	—	—	—	—	54	8.3	—	—	—	—
Dutch Indies	—	—	—	—	34	6.1	—	—	—	—	—	—	—	—	—	—	—	—
Japan	—	—	—	—	—	—	—	—	—	—	—	—	—	—	—	—	—	—
Argentina	6	1.2	—	—	49	8.8	—	—	27	5.6	—	—	—	—	—	—	—	—
Europe	450	95.2	222	94.8	324	58.3	831	75.8	383	78.5	523	57.6	492	75.4	555	81.9	224	68.3
N. and S. America	6	1.2	1	0.6	110	19.9	146	13.3	55	11.2	156	16.3	94	14.4	51	7.6	54	16.4
Asia	—	—	—	—	82	14.8	63	5.7	34	7.0	152	16.8	28	4.2	55	8.2	20	6.1
Africa	3	0.7	—	—	20	3.6	20	1.8	5	1.1	12	1.3	14	2.1	10	1.5	5	1.4
Australia	—	—	—	—	—	—	7	0.6	3	0.6	5	0.5	5	0.8	2	0.2	6	1.7
Totals	472	100.0	234	100.0	555	100.0	1,096	100.0	489	100.0	907	100.0	653	100.0	678	100.0	328	100.0

Source: Compiled from data in Mon.Nach., Jan., 1929. Figures on textiles include raw, combed, and manufactured goods (chiefly manufactured) but exclude clothing.

8. THE BALANCE OF INTERNATIONAL PAYMENTS, 1909–1913

(annual average, in million marks)

Credits

Interest, dividends, other capital service items, net	1,350
Freights	500
Bank services, other commissions	250
Merchandise transit services	100
Short-term loans from abroad, miscellaneous	50
Total	2,250

Debits

Commodity trade, including gold and silver, net	1,675
Savings of migratory laborers, tourists, miscellaneous	300
New long-term investments abroad	275
Total	2,250

Sources: The trade figures are official. The remainder are estimates based on the references cited in Appendix III, section 7.

APPENDIX XV

PUBLIC FINANCE

1. SOURCES OF DATA

The data presented in Chapter X above on the Federal budget are taken, up to 1928–29, from Stat.J.; those for 1928–29 from the *Reichsgesetzblatt,* June 30, 1929, pp. 443 ff. Data for local government finance in 1913–14 and 1925–26 from W.u.S., 1929, Supplement No. 1; and on the Hansa cities from W.u.S., 1928, No. 10. Estimates on local finance for 1928–29 secured by assuming roughly the same percentage of increase over 1925–26 (24 per cent) as for the Federal finances; a procedure also supported by the figures compiled by Dr. H. Fischer, Member of the Reichstag, in the *Berliner Tageblatt,* Feb. 26, 1929.

2. FEDERAL DEBT, BY CLASSES

(in million marks, at end of year. 1928: July)

Class	1923	1924	1925	1926	1927	1928
Long term	——	——	5,500	5,443	5,718	5,748
Treasury notes	1,062	376	153	21	21	21
Bank loan	1,336	1,436	1,249	1,164	1,025	921
Foreign loan	——	974	951	929	903	901
Other	495	144	83	173	324	308
Totals	2,993	2,929	7,936	7,728	7,984	7,898

Sources: Partly W.u.S., partly information supplied by the Federal Statistical Office and calculations therefrom. These are corrected figures.

Notes: Increase in 1925 due chiefly to the revalorization of the old paper mark debt, coming into effect in July, 1925. Differences in totals due to rounding.

3. INTERNATIONAL COMPARISONS

(sources of figures presented in Chapter X)

General: Stat.J., 1928, p. 170*; *Die Wirtschaft des Auslandes,* 1900–27 (Einzelschriften zur Statistik des deutschen Reichs, No. 5).

Great Britain: *Statistical Abstracts,* 1928 (calculated from data there given).

France: *Bulletin de Statistique,* 1928, I and II; *Budget général,* pour l'Exercise 1929; article by M. Michel in *Journal de la Societé Statistique de Paris,* 1926, No. 4.

Italy: *Resumé du Compte du Trésor,* 1926; *Statistica Financa Locali,* 1925.

Belgium: *Annuaire Statistique,* 1928; *Moniteure Belge,* Nov. 26, 1927; M. Boudhuin, *La Stabilisation et ses Conséquences,* 1928.

United States: National Industrial Conference Board, *Cost of Government in the United States, 1926–1927* (New York, 1928).

I am indebted to the German Federal Statistical Office for permission to use their unpublished compilations of the data from these sources.

APPENDIX XVI

NATIONAL INCOME AND NATIONAL SAVINGS

1. NATIONAL INCOME: OTHER ESTIMATES

Nearly 40 separate estimates have been made of Germany's national income for various times in the years 1913 to 1928, but lack of space prevents any detailed review of them here. For 1913 and 1914, the best known are those of K. Helfferich, *Deutschlands Volkswohlstand 1888–1913* (7 ed., Berlin, 1917); and E. Rogowski, *Das deutsche Volkseinkommen* (Berlin, 1926). For the period since 1924, see especially I.K.F., *Vierteljahreshefte,* 1926, I, and 1927, IV; Allgemeiner Deutscher Gewerkschaftsbund, *Gegenwartsaufgaben der Wirtschaftspolitik* (1926); F. Naphtali, in *Vorwärts,* Dec. 25, 1927, and in the *Frankfürter Zeitung,* Jan. 1, 1928; and E. Welter, *Belastungsprobe* (Berlin, 1929).

2. INTERNATIONAL COMPARISONS OF NATIONAL INCOME

(sources of estimates presented in Chapter X)

Great Britain: Bowley and Stamp, *The National Dividend in 1924,* (Oxford, 1927).

France: Article by M. Michel in *Journal de la Societé Statistique de Paris,* 1926, No. 4.

Italy: S. Mortara, *Movimento Economico dell' Italia* (in the publication of the Banca Commerciale Italiana, 1928, p. 387).

Belgium: M. Boudhuin, "Quel est le revenue actuel de la Belge," in the Banque Nationale de Belgique publication, *Bulletin Hebdomaire,* July 3, 1927.

United States: National Industrial Conference Board, *Cost of Government in the United States, 1926–27* (New York, 1928).

Also see the general summaries in the Reichs-Kredit-Gesellschaft publication, *Deutschlands Wirtschaftliche Lage.*

3. NATIONAL SAVINGS, 1924–1928

The following table presents the estimates made by the writer on the volume of German savings in the five years 1924–28 taken together. Some of the items are evidently debatable, but the general evidence available indicates that the final total is reasonably correct, and probably a little low rather than too high. Figures in million marks.

1. Internal public security issues, less 40 per cent sold abroad	9,500
2. Mortgages on farm and city land	10,400
3. Estimated savings of incorporated companies (*A.-G.'s*)	5,500
4. Estimated savings of other forms of business enterprise, including banks	3,000
5. Increase in Sparkassen savings deposits since beginning of 1925	6,000
6. Other (excess of insurance premiums over payments, savings in government departments, savings deposits not included in 5, etc.)	3,000–4,000
7. Gross total in round numbers	36,000–37,000
8. Less estimated duplications above (chiefly 5 and 6 in 1 and 2)	12,000–13,000
9. Net total domestic savings	24,000–25,000
10. Less estimated losses in agriculture	4,000
11. Net domestic addition to domestic capital, 1924–28	20,000–21,000

Notes: Item 3 is based on the assumption that hidden reserves of incorporated companies now amount *on the average* to about 25 per cent of total nominal capital (see Chapter VII, above), which at the end of 1928 was about 22,000 million marks. Adding to this the increase in published reserves (about 900 millions) and subtracting the rather small volume of hidden reserves held at the beginning of 1924 (probably not over 5 or 6 per cent of nominal capital then *on the average,* after allowance for assets then included in such hidden reserves which subsequently proved to be overvalued), gives the figure in the table.

Item 5 is based on the assumption that the increase in these deposits during 1924 reflected merely the revival of confidence in the currency, not genuine saving.

Sources: Item 1 from sources cited in Chapter VI, above; item 2 from W.u.S., 1929, p. 516; item 5 from the official returns; item 10 from Chapter VII, above; items 4, 6, 8 estimated from partial data.

A number of estimates for part or all of the period here considered have been made by German writers. See especially K. Singer, "Kapitalbedarf und Kapitalbildung in Deutschland" (*Schriften der Vereins für Sozialpolitik,* Vol. CLXXIV, 1929); E. Welter, *Belastungsprobe* (1929); various calculations by F. Naphtali, in the *Frankfürter Zeitung* and elsewhere; and the Reichs-Kredit-Gesellschaft periodical, *Deutschlands Wirtschaftliche Lage.*

INDEX

Agriculture, 77, 78, 85n, 178, 188, 193, 220, 245, 248–253, 360, 413–415; fertilizers and, 249–250, 251, 413; financial state of, 36, 39, 194, 204, 207, 207n, 216, 250–251, 250n, 321, 326, 327, 328, 347, 424; and foreign trade, 252, 253, 293–294, 295, 355, 414, 418; and inflation, 33, 36, 38, 39, 57; production in, 248–251, 413, 415; protective tariff for, 221, 250, 252, 253, 255n; prices, 222, 368
See also Food; Land; Live-stock
Algeria, 105n
Allgemeine Elektrizitäts Gesell-schaft, 54, 154–156
Allies, 10, 55, 73, *and passim;* aims of, 29; budget deficits of, 32; Commissions of, 74; debts of, 18, 324, 333, 335–336, 344; demands of, 4, 7, 11–12, 16, 59–60, 62, 77; discord amongst, 21; occupation of territory by, 8, 9, 9n, 10, 64, 71n, 74, 329, 390; war losses of, 13
Alsace, 2, 8, 9, 10, 105n, 162, 176
Alsace-Lorraine, 8, 105n
See also Alsace; Lorraine
American I. G. Chemical Corp., 175n
Animals, *see* Livestock
Argentina, 299, 364, 415, 419, 420
Aristocracy, military, 4, 5, 6, 7, 77, 322
Armistice, 4, 12, 82, 87, 238; terms of, 8
Army, 306, 307n
Austria, 126, 271, 419, 420
See also Austria-Hungary

Austria-Hungary, 55, 287n, 404
See also Austria; Hungary
Automobile industry, 146–147, 148–149, 182, 183, 184

Baade, Dr., 250n
Badische Anilin, 54
Balance of payments, *see* Payments
Baltic countries, eastern, 271
Bank for Industrial Obligations, 67n
Bank for International Settlements, 338–339, 341n, 365n
Banking business, 351, 421
Bankruptcies, 217, 224
Banks, 35, 42, 43, 44, 231, 239, 244; government control in, 244, 245, 245n; loans to, 193; private, 30n, 44, 69n, 199, 212, 384, 385
Basle Committee, *see* Wiggin Committee
Belgium, 9, 126, 271, 317, 321, 323, 325, 422, 423; foreign trade of, 89n, 101, 121, 298, 400, 419, 420; industrial status of, 87n, 101, 162n, 221, 367n, 395, 398, 405, 406, 409–410; and Reparations, 21, 22, 23, 61, 74
Bemberg, 167
Benzol, 101, 101n, 394
Berlin, 171; banks of, 212
Bills drawn, volume of, 220n
Birth rate, 13, 38
Bismarck, O. E. L. von, 241, 263
Blast furnaces, 107, 109–111, 109n, 113, 115, 118, 379, 397, 411
Blockade, Allied, 8
Bonds, 34, 206; yields on, 197, 202
See also Securities

See also Mineral reserves, *and under individual resources*

Navy, 8, 306, 307

Newfoundland, 105n

Nitrates, synthetic, 172–173, 172n, 174, 175, 298, 407

Occupation, armies of, 9n, 10, 64, 71n, 74, 329

Occupied territory, 8, 9, 9n, 390

Opel, 147

Paper industry, 53, 54, 139–140, 179, 298n

Paris Conference, 65, 65n, 75, 76, 195, 198, 200, 218, 259, 303, 304, 305, 317, 325, 332, 333, 341, 342, 343–344, 359

Payments, international, 136, 192, 289, 329, 350, 360, 361; balance of, 285, 291n, 292–293, 299–305, 347–348, 349, 358, 369, 370, 390–392, 421; borrowing to meet, 292, 295, 305, 348, 349, 350, 356

See also Reparations, transfer of

Peace Conference, 18

Pearse, Arno S., 162n

Pensions, 33, 38; Allied, 12; war, 307, 310

Petroleum, 54, 294

Plant and equipment, *see* Industry, plant and equipment of

Plum, G., 163n, 164n

Poincaré, Raymond, 21, 23

Poland, 9, 10, 20, 86, 87n, 89, 99, 144, 271, 404, 420

Police, 307n, 315

Political issues, influence of, on financial world, 18, 19, 20, 21, 22, 23–24, 28–29, 198–199, 200, 218, 259, 303, 304

Population, 13, 38n, 57, 254, 260–261, 262, 363, 380, 381; child,

37–38, 261; composition of, 254, 260, 261, 262; health of, 13, 37–38, 57; underfeeding of, 13, 37, 47

Posen, 9

Post office, 244, 245, 246

Potash, 10, 14n, 176, 379, 406–408

See also Potash industry

Potash industry, 6, 51, 54, 98, 139–140, 175–178, 178n, 227, 227n, 243, 247, 379, 406–408, 411

See also Cartels

Power, 99, 101n, 134–137, 152, 156, 171n, 175n, 179n, 220n, 245, 246, 247

Price, M. P., 38n

Prices, 28, 29, 30, 34, 36, 41, 45, 46, 49, 60, 61, 82, 132, 142, 180, 187, 216, 217, 218, 252–253, 296, 307, 312, 312n, 319, 320; comparative levels of, 41, 89–90, 108, 114, 117–118, 118, 119, 131, 142, 151, 158, 166, 179, 211, 218, 221–224, 289, 297, 346–347, 351–352, 352–353; control of, 50, 95, 96–98, 100, 123, 124, 125, 178, 223–224, 226–227, 283n; export, 124, 129, 186, 286, 286n, 289; and export capacity, 186, 253, 283–284, 289; indices of, 27, 90, 143n, 171, 172n, 221n, 255n, 381–383, 401, 402, 406; and wages, 95, 100, 129, 252, 255, 255n, 283; since 1929, 368, 371

See also under individual products and industries

Private enterprises, loans to, 191, 193, 204

Production, 211, 379; capacity for, 75, 183, 185, 187, 238; cost of, 35, 78, 183, 186, 253, 289, 411; export percentage